THE WORK OF PÈRE LAGRANGE

IMPRIMI POTEST:

J. E. MARR, O.P.
Provincial, Province of St. Albert the Great

NIHIL OBSTAT:

JOHN A. SCHULIEN, S.T.D.
Censor librorum

IMPRIMATUR:

✠ ROMAN R. ATKIELSKI
Vicar General
Archdiocese of Milwaukee
December 6, 1962

Library of Congress Catalog Card Number: 63–15632

© 1963 THE BRUCE PUBLISHING COMPANY
MADE IN THE UNITED STATES OF AMERICA

TO
BILL AND ED
AND
DOROTHY

PREFACE

"MY BEST wishes for a happy and a holy New Year, one that will prove useful to the cause we both serve, the Church," P. Lagrange ended his letter to me, then a young professor and librarian, at the beginning of 1911. Father Braun brings out clearly in this book how the life of our esteemed friend, the Master of Jerusalem, was dominated by his desire to be of service to the Church. That desire had led Albert Lagrange to the seminary of Saint-Sulpice in 1878, and prompted him to enter the Dominican novitiate the following year, in the hope of thus serving her even more efficiently. Because of his zeal he welcomed the tasks that were imposed upon him, and these ranged from theology to oriental languages, archaeology, and geography. All his reading, writing, and teaching was done in the service of the Church.

Trials of many kinds awaited this man as he pursued his dedicated course. Hardly had he pronounced his first vows when his community was driven into exile by governmental decree. He was to be torn from his beloved convent of S. Etienne in mid-career, and at the end of his life he was — and this was a great sacrifice for him — to die in a monastery in which he had been received into the Order and which was therefore dear to him, but far from those in whose midst he would have preferred to die and be laid at rest.

To be sure, there were times in his life as in the life of every man, when he knew what weariness was, but real discouragement was not in his makeup. When more than eighty years old he was deeply involved in vast undertakings, and wrote vigorously of that "incomprehensible miracle which keeps us going under frustrating circumstances, although our very bones are so weary that we long for rest." That "we" meant the *École de S. Étienne* and his Dominican brethren, whose ceaseless endeavors under his direction and leadership had by then (1937) produced forty-six volumes of the *Revue biblique* and twenty-eight in the collection known as the *Études bibliques,* besides many other special lectures and writings on matters geographical, ethnographical, and archaeological.

His greatness became apparent during the latter part of 1912, when, at the peak of his powers, there was serious question whether his studies were proving useful to the Church. Directed to leave Jerusalem on September 3, he instantly turned his back on twenty years of pioneer work. But filial confidence underlay the grief he felt as he wrote, "I have always put my trust in Mary. . . . She will watch over us." Shortly after his return to France he was informed that the *Revue biblique* was to halt publication, or at least to change its name, as it could no longer go on as a biblical magazine. "The *Revue* has had its life," he wrote, "and with his own hand the Holy Father has written of his pleasure with it." No word of complaint, but the depth of his sorrow was revealed a few weeks later: "I am to do nothing. This is a great cross for me, for I had imagined that the moment had come when I could put my life of study to good use."

His loving obedience to the wishes of the Holy See did not go unnoticed in Rome, and on learning that the scholar who had been represented to him as dangerous to the Church was in fact humbly submissive, Pius X did not hesitate to reverse his decision. P. Lagrange did not know, when writing to a friend on Pentecost Sunday, 1913, "I feel that my course has ended, and I am done with science," that the Sovereign Pontiff had already sanctioned his return to Jerusalem as a teacher of exegesis, and had authorized the continuance of the *Revue biblique* along the same lines as before. On July 4, then, before the year of absence was up, he once again set out for the Orient.

His trials were not over, of course. The next of these in point of time was an enforced absence lasting from December, 1914, to November, 1918. Not only was he much concerned over his country's future, but during those years the very existence of his *Revue biblique* was in jeopardy. Only his own prodigious efforts kept it from foundering. Other alarms sounded again in 1920 and 1924, but these were

also the years in which his great New Testament works appeared —
the commentaries and his studies on Jewish and pagan backgrounds
and textual criticism. He had long since and definitively given up the
exegesis of the Old Testament. His *Gospel of Jesus Christ*, dedicated
to the memory of Leo XIII, was accepted in the name of Pius XI
by him who was to become Pius XII. On reading this book, the crown
of P. Lagrange's studies and meditations, one feels almost grateful
for those attacks upon him which compelled him to turn to this field
of scholarly endeavor.

P. Lagrange loved the Church and had a special affection for the
Holy Father. When Pius XI's first encyclical appeared, he wrote: "The
Encyclical is excellent, high-minded, clear, and manifests the Holy
Father's paternal feeling toward all members of the Church." When
the Concordat of 1929 was signed he wrote: "I am quite content to
be a nobody, or I would send my congratulations also to the Pope on
his successful solution of the Roman question. It is a victory of the
spirit over the powers of the flesh. . . . Was not P. Lacordaire sharply
criticized for having observed that Italian unity [between Church and
State] was doomed? The papacy has done well to rid itself of the
'tunic of Nessus.' "[1] And because he sincerely believed that the Apostle
Peter lived on in his successors, P. Lagrange was able to say, on
hearing of a condemnation which touched his beloved Saint-Sulpice,[2]
"Nothing will change my submission."

Some may perhaps be disappointed in these few lines, having expected that the president of the Pontifical Biblical Commission would
praise P. Lagrange as a biblical scholar; his titles to glory on that score
are clearly established elsewhere in this book. I can still remember how
impressed I was, when a young priest-student at St. Stephen's, at the
sight of the half-empty kerosene lamp which P. Lagrange used to put
outside his door early each morning — a mute but eloquent witness
to his passionate dedication to study. For thirty years after that I
kept in touch with him by letter, shared with him his works, his

---

[1] Nessus was a mythical character whose blood-poisoned shirt caused the death of its
wearer, Hercules.
[2] *E.B*, 497–504.

trials, his hopes. It occurred to me that I might do my fellow priests a greater service if I were to help them understand a bit better something of his nobility of character. He was in truth a noble son of that Church which he fondly called his holy mother — *Sancta Mater Ecclesia.*

EUGENE CARDINAL TISSERANT

Rome, Holy Thursday
April 22, 1943

FOREWORD

GREAT men impart a lasting impetus to the direction taken by their foundations or sciences. Perhaps the best way to enter into their thought and familiarize oneself with their methods is to study their lives, their spiritual lives, of course, for all details are not of equal importance. A thousand intangible bonds link masterpieces to their creators, and to be appreciated, no great work should be considered apart from its maker.

This applies to the work of P. Lagrange. The School which he founded may continue to be, in the years ahead, an outstanding center of modern Catholic thought; time alone will tell. At present the name Lagrange is highly respected in all schools of theology, and it is almost impossible to take up any important question in the Old or New Testament without using principles which he formulated or considering the views he expressed in his books, articles, and book reviews. It is obviously of prime importance that we examine his work as objectively as possible.

Today this is not particularly difficult to do, for although his exegetical career began more than fifty years ago, P. Lagrange was only yesterday in our midst, answering our questions. Can you ever forget, P. Benoit, those wonderful hours we used to spend together at Abey, in Lebanon? It was there that P. Lagrange used to go for his summer vacation, certain always of a warm fraternal welcome at the convent of the good Capuchin Fathers. The bench on which he loved to sit facing the Phoenician sea was always in the same spot underneath the fig trees. Mornings we read *De Utilitate Credendi,* and at the close of the day came together for the recitation of Compline. Evenings we spent on the terrace admiring the stars which you sought out with your long telescope. During those hours of relaxation, how often did we not ply the Master with questions about his long life! And I still remember how calmly and good-naturedly he would answer us, and how carefully he would choose his words.

During World War I, while in Paris, he penned his account of the first twenty-five years of the *École biblique*.[1] At the time of writing, the very uncertainty of the future led him for the first time to indulge his feelings and to dip into his memories. Years later the appearance of Loisy's *Mémoires* would prompt him to clarify further certain details of the modernist crisis which his modesty had earlier led him to gloss over.[2] Other details can be gleaned from his volume on the restoration of the sanctuary of St. Stephen in Jerusalem, an account of the beginnings of his Practical School of Biblical Studies.[3] There are a few magazine articles dealing with his years in Spain,[4] or on Jerusalem during the war,[5] which provide us with the only other significant autobiographical material available. World War II made it impossible for us to consult the records of the convent of St. Stephen's. We were, however, fortunate in having P. Vincent's splendid notice on the death of P. Lagrange.[6] Here was testimony from an old disciple, co-laborer and friend from whom the Master had no secrets. Covering as it did a period of forty years of study and strife in which he had himself shared, P. Vincent's invaluable contribution provides much hitherto unpublished information about P. Lagrange's early years, and fills up the main gaps in our other sources.

A notable feature of this book is its inclusion of a complete bibliography of the writings of P. Lagrange. The "Life" which precedes the bibliography makes it crystal clear that the inspiration behind his voluminous output was spiritual in character. The bibliography, like Ariadne's thread, should serve a useful purpose, enabling readers of P. Lagrange to explore his principles and methods, to see his work as a whole in its relationship to its parts.

[1] "Après vingt-cinq ans," *RB* 24 (1915), pp. 248–261.

[2] *M. Loisy et le modernisme, à propos des "Mémoires" d'A. Loisy* (Paris: Editions du Cerf, 1932).

[3] *Saint Étienne et son sanctuaire à Jérusalem* (Paris: Picard, 1894).

[4] "Souvenirs de Salamanque," *La Vie dominicaine* (1937), pp. 179–183, 221–225, 244–248.

[5] "A Jérusalem pendant la guerre," *Le Correspondant* (1915), pp. 640–658; "La Palestine autrefoi et aujourd'hui," *ibid.* (1918), pp. 3–30.

[6] "Le Père Lagrange," *RB* 47 (1938), pp. 321–354.

Many willing hands helped in the production of this book, because there are many who venerate this "Master" whom God has been pleased to raise up in His Church in the 20th century.[7] We hope that their labors and ours will help spread the flame of P. Lagrange and at the same time make Scriptures better known, so that men may find it easier to open their hearts to Him who is the Author of the Scriptures.

F. M. BRAUN, O.P.

Fribourg, June 29, 1943

---

[7] A striking example of the respect in which P. Lagrange is held was the cooperative effort of several French scholars (among them Cardinal Liénard, Chaine, Bardy and others) which resulted in the production of *L'oeuvre exégètique et historique du R. P. Lagrange* (English translation: *Père Lagrange and the Scriptures* [*Bruce Publishing Company*, 1946]). In it, experts from the many fields which P. Lagrange explored testified to the soundness and value of his work. P. Braun's work covers much the same territory, but carries the story on to 1938, offering in addition an invaluable (and unique) bibliography of P. Lagrange which runs to an impressive 1786 entries.

CONTENTS

Preface vii

Foreword xi

PART I. INTRODUCTION TO THE WORK OF PÈRE LAGRANGE

I. FOUNDER AND MASTER 3

I. Dates, 3–4. — State of biblical studies *circa* 1880, 4–6. — Dominican vocation, 6–7. — Novitiate at Salamanca, 7–8. — Problems of training for the apostolate, 8–10. — P. Cormier and P. Colchen, 10–11.

II. S. Étienne in Jerusalem and P. Matthew Lecomte, 12–13. — First plans, 13. — Arrival at Jerusalem, 13. — First impressions, 14–15. — Opening of *The Practical School of Biblical Studies,* 15. — Spirit and program, 15–17.

III. The Master and his way of teaching: Research, 17–18. — Recourse to original texts, 18–19. — Textual Criticism, 19–20. — Study of the background, 20–21. — P. Lagrange and his students, 21–22.

IV. Growth of school and scientific equipment, 22–23. — The *Revue biblique:* its program, 23–24. — Objections to, 24–25. — First collaborators, 25–26. — P. Lagrange's responsibility, 26–27. — The *Études bibliques:* Project of *A Complete Commentary on Sacred Scripture,* 27–28. — The *Book of Judges,* 28–29. — *Études sur les religions sémitiques,* 28–31.

V. A threefold work, proudly French, 31–32. — Place of the *École* in relation to other works of French charity in Palestine, 32–33. — Illustrious predecessors, 33–34. — Solemnities and protocol, 34.

II. IN THE LIGHT OF FAITH   35

    I. Relation of technique to faith, 35–36. — P. Lagrange
as a theologian, 36.
    II. Inspiration and the Biblical Question, 36–37. — Various
systems in vogue, 37–39. — Inspiration in the *Revue biblique,*
39–40. — Broad lines for treating problems of inerrancy,
40–43.
    III. Church's authority in matters of exegesis, 43. —
Contrast with Reformers' attitude, 44. — Is the Church
qualified to fulfill her mission? 44–45. — Restrictions in
matters of exegesis, 46–47. — Respect for Church authority
the gauge of independence, 47–48.
    IV. Authority of the Fathers as witnesses to the Christian
faith, 48–49. — As private doctors, 49–50. — Senses of
Scripture, 50–51. — Antecedents of allegorical exegesis,
51–55. — Value of the spiritual sense, 55–56. — P. Lagrange's neglect of the Fathers, 57–60. — Literalism of
P. Lagrange, 60–61.
    V. Thomistic Theology and modern systems of exegesis,
61–62. — Evolution or development of dogma, 63–64. —
Other schools of exegesis, 65.

III. TRIALS AND STRUGGLES   66

    I. Impression of calm created by P. Lagrange: Gabriel
Hanotaux, 66–67. — Fears of conservatives, 67–68. — Atmosphere of suspicion during the Modernist crisis, 68–70.
    II. Problem of Pentateuchal sources: Congress at Fribourg
(1897), 70–71. — Proposed solution, 71–72. — Criticism in
Études, 73. — The *Méthode historique:* conferences at Toulouse, 73–74. — Reaction to the *Méthode,* 74–76. — Anti-
modernist declarations: articles on the *Providentissimus,*
77–78; on Loisy's *Évangile et l'Église,* 78–81. — On quarreling, 81–82. — *Éclaircissement sur la méthode historique,*
82. — Dedication to work, 82–83.
    III. The *Commentary on Genesis (pro manuscripto):*
how it differs from Wellhausen's views, 83. — Response
of the Biblical Commission, June 27, 1907, 84. — P.
Lagrange stops writing, 85. — The *Lamentabili sane
exitu:* commentary on, 85–86. — Lagrange's confidence,
86–87. — *Commentary on St. Mark,* 87–89. — Locking
horns with Loisy, 89–91.

IV. Decree of the Consistorial Congregation, June 29, 1912, 92. — Meaning of the document, 92–93. Submission of P. Lagrange, 93–94. — Letter to P. Cormier, 94–95. — Departure from Jerusalem, 95–96. — Work in Paris and return to Jerusalem, 96. — Beginning of World War I, dispersal of professorial staff, 96. — Turkish occupation of the *École*, 96. — P. Lagrange at Paris: *"Apres vingt-cinq ans,"* 97–99. — Publications during the War, 99. — Illness, 100.

IV. THE GREAT WORKS   101

I. The *École biblique* after the War, 101. — Designation as the *École archéologique française de Palestine*, 101–102. — Gospel *Commentaries* and *Synopses*, 102. — *The Gospel of Jesus Christ*, 102–103.

II. Ancient Crete, 103–104. — Toward the Logos of St. John, 104. — Hermetic and Mandean studies, 104–106. — Pagan mystery religions, 106–112. — *Judaisme avant Jésus-Christ*, 112.

III. *History of the Canon of the New Testament;* Standard of judgment: Apostolicity, 112–113. — Fluctuations of the tradition, 113–115. — Final triumph of the tradition, 115–116. — *Textual Criticism*: progress after publication of his St. Mark, 116. — The *Caesarean text* and the *Chester Beatty Papyri*, 116–117. — Rejection of classification by families, 117. — *Rational criticism*, and new application of the rules of Griesbach, 118–121.

IV. Farewell to Jerusalem, 121–122. — Life at St. Maximin, 122. — New project — a *Commentary on Genesis:* E and J attributed to Moses, 122–123. — Interruption of work by death, 123–124.

V. SECRET OF A FULL LIFE   125

The "sources of his energy," 125. — Love of God and desire to be of use to others, 126. — Constancy under fire, 127–128. — Religious life, 128–131. — Spirit of prayer, 131–133. — A day with P. Lagrange, 133. — Last visit, 133–134. — The faithful servant, 135.

VI. THE HARVEST 136

    I. Modern discoveries and their consequences, 136–137.
    — The *École biblique,* 137–143. — *Letter of Dain Cohenel*
    (= Fr. Ruotolo), 143–145. — The *Reply of the Biblical*
    Commission (August 16, 1941), 145–148. — The *Divino*
    Afflante Spiritu, 148–150. — The *New Psalter,* 150–152.
    — The *Suhard Letter,* 152–154. — The *Bible de Jérusalem,*
    154–157. — Catholic Scholars and the Church, 157–161. —
    The legacy of P. Lagrange, 161–162.

PART II. BIBLIOGRAPHY

  I. Key to the Bibliographical Tables 163

 II. Abbreviations 165

III. Chronological Bibliography 167

IV. Index of Authors Reviewed 255

 V. Analytical Index to the Bibliography . . . 265

APPENDIX:

    Analysis of the Consistorial Decree of June 29, 1912   303

PART I

INTRODUCTION
TO THE WORK OF
PÈRE LAGRANGE

CHAPTER I

FOUNDER AND MASTER

ALBERT LAGRANGE was born in France at Bourg-en-Bresse, on the feast of St. Thomas Aquinas, March 7, 1855. After attending school in this village, he entered the minor seminary at Autun, and there was given an excellent classical training.[1] This was followed by his entrance into the School of Law in Paris. He was elected secretary of the law club. In his leisure hours he devoted himself to a deepening of his cultural background; as he was especially enamored of the literature of Greece, he made an intensive study of that language under Professor Duruy at the Sorbonne.[2] On July 6, 1878, he obtained his Doctorate in Law, and in the following October entered the seminary of Saint-Sulpice at Issy-les-Moulineaux, where he at once struck up a friendship with the Abbés Batiffol and Hyvernat,

---

[1] At the Petit Seminaire of Autun he had been required to learn St. Luke by heart (*RB* 4 [1895], p. 63) and it was to his masters there that he affectionately dedicated, his volume on textual criticism:

> "Patribus in Deo et praeceptoribus optimis
> Quibus ut alumnos in minore seminario augustodunensi degentes
> Spiritu Christi per Virginem Matrem informarent
> Et humaniora docerent
> Indefessae curae erat
> Olim parum docilis nunc tanti beneficii memor
> Et semper discipulus
> Hoc opus qualecumque
> D.D.D.
> Auctor"

[2] For the childhood and youth of P. Lagrange, the best and most comprehensive source available to biographers is the article by L. H. Vincent, "Le Père Lagrange," *RB* 47 (1938), pp. 321–328. Other details may be found in P. Fernessole, *Témoins de la Pensée catholique en France sous la IIIᵉ République* (Paris, 1940), p. 342 ff.

3

similarly destined for critical studies.[3] On October 5, 1879, Albert Lagrange was clothed in the Dominican habit at the novitiate of the province of Toulouse, in the venerable convent of Saint Maximin, in Provence. There, on October 6, 1880, he made his simple profession just as the Dominicans, victims of a decree of expulsion, were about to take the road into exile.

Until his ordination to the priesthood in Zamora, Spain, on December 23, 1883, Lagrange studied theology in the Dominican *Studium Generale* and at the University of Salamanca. Here he also took courses in Hebrew. In 1884 the exile ended, and he returned to Toulouse, and, for the next four years, taught Church History and Philosophy, while fulfilling regular preaching assignments. He kept up his biblical studies under the capable direction of Abbé Thomas, who held the chair of Holy Scripture at the *Institut catholique*.[4]

In 1888, P. Colchen, then provincial of the province of Toulouse, sent the young Dominican to the University of Vienna for specialized oriental studies. By early October he was deep in the study of Assyrian under David H. Müller, of hieroglyphic and hieratic Egyptian under Reinisch, of Arabic under Müller at the university and under Wahrmund at the School of Commerce, and of Talmudic Hebrew under Müller.[5] From March 10, 1890, when he arrived in Jerusalem to establish a school of Palestinian biblical studies, until his death on March 10, 1938, his entire life was spent in teaching, personal research, and the writing of scientific books.

Throughout the apparently simple pattern of his life, in which one day seemed to be little more than the monotonous repetition of the day before, there runs, like a thread of gold, an ardent desire to serve the Church and the good of souls by a selfless defense of revealed truth.

To serve the Church! One day in 1878, not a particularly glorious year in the history of modern Catholic thought, Albert Lagrange and Pierre Batiffol were walking together at the seminary at Issy, engaged

---

[3] Cf M. J. Lagrange, M. *Loisy et le modernisme, à propos des "Memoires" d'A. Loisy* (Paris: Editions du Cerf, 1932), p. 68: "After entering the Seminary at Issy in the autumn of 1878, I struck up a close friendship, based upon our taste for biblical and philological studies, with the Abbés Batiffol and Hyvernat."

[4] Cf Lagrange, "Souvenirs de Salamanque," *La Vie dominicaine* (1930), p. 179 f.

[5] Cf Vincent, *art. cit.*, p. 330.

in animated conversation. No longer children, the two seminarians were aware of the profound mediocrity into which Catholic scriptural studies and positive theology had fallen. The *Institut catholique,* founded three years before under the direction of Msgr. d'Hulst, was still in its infancy. Church history was brilliantly represented there by Abbé Duchesne, but as much could not be said of Scripture; M. Paulinus Martin was a distinguished Syriac scholar, but so poorly prepared to occupy the chair of exegesis that he soon gave it up.[6] In provincial seminaries the situation was worse, and those which considered a scientific approach to the Bible were the exception. In most, Hebrew and Greek were neglected, the Latin Vulgate was everything, and courses in Scripture were oftener than not taught by retired veterans who had won their spurs in other fields.[7]

Saint-Sulpice stood out in sharp contrast to such seminaries by reason of the fame enjoyed by many of her professors. Ernest Renan, then a teacher at the *Collège de France,* surrounded by all the prestige of science, was of the opinion that M. Le Hir was the only representative scholar at Saint-Sulpice.[8] He was thinking, of course, of the philological training he had received there. It is not certain that literary criticism was as well taught there as philology, for on weighing Renan's words, one is aghast at the misunderstandings that preceded the apostasy of the future author of the *Vie de Jésus.*[9] Vigouroux was laboring valiantly to harmonize the Bible with modern discoveries, but while calling attention to the critical difficulties then being raised

---

[6] Lagrange, M. *Loisy et le modernisme,* p. 18: "M. Paulinus Martin, professor at the *Institut Catholique* and a distinguished Syriac scholar, held the most routine views, even in the question of the textual criticism of the NT, where the Vulgate is on the side of criticism."

[7] Cf Mgr. Legendre, "L'enseignement des sciences bibliques dans nos Instituts catholiques" (*La Vie catholique,* 1925), and F. M. Braun, O.P., *L'Évangile devant les temps presents* (Paris, 1938), p. 32.

[8] E. Renan, *Souvenirs d'enfance et de jeunesse* (Paris, 1883), p. 270 ff.; J. Pommier, *La jeunesse clericale d'Ernest Renan* (Paris, 1933), pp. 107–124, 489–521.

[9] Renan, *op. cit.,* pp. 277–303. On page 294 he states: "Orthodoxy demands that we believe the books of the Bible to be the works of those whose names they bear," thus manifesting his ignorance of the fact that the definitions of the Church concerning the canonicity of the Sacred Books do not involve the person of the inspired authors. There are other such "confusions" but this suffices to indicate how badly informed Renan was in matters of "orthodoxy," although he declared that he could never bring himself to be subject to authority for reasons "of an entirely philological and critical nature."

by the German rationalists, he was unfortunately not always able to supply conclusive answers to the problems.[10] Lagrange and Batiffol profited by and were grateful for the training given them,[11] but they were grimly aware of the enormity of the task that had to be done if attacks on the Christian faith were to be met successfully. After surveying the situation, the two young men resolved, as a start, on a joint reading of the Greek text of the New Testament, recently published in the critical edition of Tischendorf.[12]

The friendly collaboration of these two young kindred spirits was of brief duration. Circumstances had united them; others now separated them. On October 9, 1879, Batiffol wrote to a friend of a pilgrimage which he made with his two friends, Lagrange and Hyvernat, to the tomb of the Curé of Ars. "Our joy at seeing one another was mixed with sadness. One of them, the more popular of the two, did not return with us to Paris, but instead made his way to the Dominican novitiate in Provence. He already has his degree in law, and is a young man of outstanding merit. A great future lies ahead of him. And he has given us an example of splendid sacrifice."[13]

Was this step really a sacrifice? In following the inclination which he had felt from the time he was seventeen years of age, Albert Lagrange was simply fulfilling the great ambition of his youth, confident that his dream of apostolic labors would not be shattered but rather, marvelously realized in the Dominican way of life, for the Order of Friars Preachers had as its goal the salvation of souls by preaching and the teaching of revealed truth.[14] The tradition which

---

[10] Lagrange, op. cit., p. 14: "M. Vigouroux's erudition was prodigious, his citations always perfect; one is astounded at his critical assurance. Was it simplicity, as in the case of Fillion, or the imperturbable sangfroid of the defender of a good cause who has decided that he will not be defeated? Either way, one does not do justice to the dignity of the Bible if he is constantly defending it."

[11] Cf the Foreword to his Saint Matthieu (Paris: Gabalda, 1923), p. ii: "I respectfully dedicate this work, my last perhaps, to my old Sulpician teachers of the Seminary of Issy, and to Bishop Batiffol, for our now almost jubilarian friendship which began in that beloved house. These teachers, unassuming and pious though learned, were filled with love for the Sacred Scriptures and stopped at nothing to impart that taste to us. At Issy, without dwelling on Renan, M. Le Hir's pupil, we can go back to Père Lacordaire, to Fenelon, to Bossuet, and to the founder, M. Olier."

[12] Fernessole, op. cit., p. 192.

[13] From an unpublished letter loaned by M. l'Abbé Jean Batiffol to P. Braun.

[14] Constitutiones Fratrum S. Ordinis Praedicatorum (Rome, 1954), Book I, ch. 1,

he now proposed to follow would oblige him to use his intelligence in the Church's service. But this is to serve Christ the Lord. Realizing what the program entailed, P. Lagrange would have approved Gilson's statement:

> To imitate the Church ought to be our rule, if we desire to put our intelligence at the service of Christ the King. To serve Him is to unite our efforts to His, to make ourselves, as Saint Paul says, His cooperators, that is, to work with Him or to permit Him to work in and through us, for the salvation of the intelligence which has been blinded by sin. But to work thus we must follow the example He Himself gives us: to free that nature which the world hides from us, and to use our intelligence as God meant we should when He created it.[15]

How did P. Lagrange realize this praiseworthy ambition? To answer this question we must follow the young Dominican student to San Esteban, in Salamanca. His recollections of his novitiate,[16] which he wrote for a modest publication of the Order after a lapse of more than fifty years, reveal by their detail how deeply they had been graven upon the mind of the young religious. More than anything else they reveal an interior life from which his scientific activity was never divorced, for he alternated between study and prayer, and consistently gave religious values first place.

The convent of San Esteban is one of the most famous Dominican centers of theology. Francis Vittoria had lived there, as had Medina and Bañez. There also one can see the symbol of Dominic and Peter Soto, two hands gripping a torch. The chapel "was attached to the church by a cloister done in the flamboyant style popular at a time when the sun never set upon Spanish dominions." Almost without leaving the cloister, Bañez could enter the side chapel to hear St. Teresa's confession and to reassure her of the supernatural character of her revelations. In so privileged a place the French Dominicans, accompanied in exile by their prior and provincial, quickly felt themselves at home.

---

3 # 1: "Ordo autem noster specialiter ob praedicationem et animarum salutem ab initio noscitur institutus fuisse. Quapropter studium nostrum ad hoc debet principaliter intendere, ut proximorum animabus possimus utiles esse. Huic proprio fini intime cohaeret docere ac tueri veritatem fidei catholicae, tum verbo in scholis, tum scripto multiplici."

15 *Christianity and Philosophy* (New York: Sheed and Ward, 1939), p. 112 f.

16 "Souvenirs de Salamanque," *passim*.

The Studentate was an area completely set apart from the rest of the house. Its tiny cells were neither well lighted nor airy, but in them the student brothers were alone with God. A high-vaulted little church stood in the center, alongside an enclosed and uncultivated garden. From the first, midnight office and all the monastic observances were carried out exactly as they had been at St. Maximin.

> The choir of the religious was above the first arch at the rear of the church. With its carved wooden stalls and huge pulpit in the center, it was a spacious home of canonical prayer. In it the night office, carefully sheltered from the brightness which electricity inflicts upon us, preserved all its mystery. At the end of the railing, out into the darkness only slightly broken by the sanctuary lamp, our voices tumbled into space, and as if uncertain of their way, climbed the pillars, crept along the vaulted ceiling, and finally reached the invisible Lord of the tabernacle, to whom we were already united in spirit.

The solitude of the exiles was almost complete. "Only rarely was the railroad used for journeys into France, and there were no automobiles. No one was permitted to roam about Spain, visiting Madrid or Toledo or Seville or Granada, lilting names of vanquished capitals, cities of poetry and of dreams. No news came from France, and in the novitiate there were no newspapers. Prayer and study, alternating harmoniously, made up our life."

On this subject he could speak out freely, and P. Lagrange warmed to the subject. He began with questions. "So it was far from the world? Was this any way to prepare men for apostolic work? What influence would a man have upon men of his day if he was ignorant of what they were thinking, of their attitudes, or of the state of society, at least through the medium of literature?"

> These are old questions [he went on] to which the Order of St. Dominic has always returned the same answers, for they are after all overshadowed by another: "What do men expect of us?" The answer is clear. They come to us looking for the "science of the saints" . . . or at least, for that knowledge which makes men Christians, I mean the apostolic truth taught in the Church. Let this be clearly understood. Such a science will always be imperfect and capable of further growth, but it should be able to keep step with the considerable progress made by scientific methods. The popular sciences of our day are an indis-

pensable help for philosophy, and scholarship has extended the field of history in a prodigious manner. Inscriptions are revealing new languages, new institutions and unknown facts, opening up to us the milieu in which the doctrine of salvation has grown. One must therefore note what has helped or hindered the progress of Christianity. The horizon is immense, the way difficult, the roads different, but the aim is always the same. No one can master completely all the aspects of sacred science; that staggering task must be shared. Will men require of us that we be up on agriculture or business? Must a seminarian or young religious, out of sympathy for all that is human or social, as they say today, be *au courant* in regard to problems whose solutions still elude specialists in the field? Must a confessor read all novels in order to know if he may allow others to read them? Talk to a farmer about the good points of this or that machine, of his chances of selling his grain at a certain price, and his mocking smile will teach you a lesson of good sense. No! That is not what he wants to learn from us."

P. Lagrange was obviously defending the primacy of properly ecclesiastical studies pursued in an atmosphere of meditation and of prayer, and he excuses himself for being carried away.

I am perhaps so vehement [he wrote] because I one day overheard a couple of seminarians on their way homewards from some congress, discussing in a public vehicle the balance between rent and production. Do not ask them if they have read Augustine's *City of God,* or Origen's *Apologia against Celsus.* Please God they knew something about the New Testament, for it is about it that we men of the Church are asked by students in our higher schools. The God of the prophet Osee complains that his people perish for a lack of knowledge (Os 4:5 f.). . . . Where shall they find it if the priest himself has rejected it? In that case, says Osee,[17] God will reject him also from his priesthood. Such a man will look for sympathy, he will find only scorn. A businessman is athirst for the word of God, and you talk to him about his business and his furnaces! You may think that an author will be pleasantly surprised if you have read his latest. Not at all. He and many others will feel that you have let him down.

Then, as if justifying the Dominican method pursued at Salamanca, he spoke of his old companions, all of them now dead. "I don't think anyone regretted the years spent in training of mind and will in that

---

[17] Os 4:6.

austere retreat, or that application to inward reform which ordinarily disposes for the choice graces God confers in view of the apostolate." He then recalled, and in so doing revealed his own views in the matter of discipline, some of the characteristics of his old superiors. His first master was Father Albert Gebhardt.

Of him one could say that he had only one breath, but a breath that was from on high — *vivere di spirito,* an Italian would say. Very timid and reserved, he forced himself upon no one, and few felt his authority, it seemed so fragile. But one who was really looking for direction discovered to his surprise how astonishingly decisive he was. He was not much in favor of exterior mortifications, and ruthlessly suppressed sudden movements of self-will, but he had much compassion for human frailty. His instructions defied analysis; it was impossible to single out in them the various points, yet during this half hour there stole over one a fascination which bit by bit led the soul into regions of affective prayer. . . . His successor, P. Lambert, held the reins in a firmer hand. To be sure, the steed leaped up, his flank torn by the spur, but the soothing hand upon his neck and mane induced him to perhaps even greater efforts to win the prize of the race.

The two provincials who spanned that period were Fathers Cormier and Colchen, and they stand out above all the others.

Who in our Order is not familiar with the figure — in the full sense of that word — of Père Cormier, a truly grand man. One imagines St. Bernard to have been like him. Like that saint, he drew from an intense life of contemplation his tireless energy for the outward ministry. Not that we compare his activity with that of the last Father of the Church, but on a lower level we see in him the same harmonious blend of the mystical and active life, an ideal which P. Cormier pursued with full deliberation. One spoke freely to him, as if despite oneself. He inspired confidence, and one was sure that he would make the right decision, or express that encouragement which made his decisions acceptable and almost always agreeable.

On the other hand, Père Colchen, graver and almost cold in appearance, might have intimidated a novice and closed up his heart

had one not heard upon his lips, rising as from the bottom of his soul, an ardent call to perfection, even to holiness. This did not often happen, for he spoke but little. Yet what eloquent actions. Afflicted with an illness of the spine, he was never without his cane. He would make his way slowly into choir for the High Mass at half-past eight, and one knew that he was coming from the grimy railroad station of Medina del Campo. In his poverty he once asked Brother Elias de Poumeyrac to pull a tooth for him — he had already tied the string to it! Of course I want you to smile at this, but only if you pay tribute to his uncomplaining acceptance of almost constant pain. He preached with simplicity, and was not what you might call an *intellectual*, but no one was more firmly convinced of the imperative duty of a Dominican to give himself to study. He usually appealed only to supernatural motives based upon faith: the Order of St. Dominic has furnished the Church with Doctors and canonized Doctors. A Dominican must therefore combine in himself knowledge and prayer. His duty is clear, and every man must adhere to it.

And it was doubtless this principle of faith that led P. Colchen to cooperate effectively in the establishing of the *École biblique de Jérusalem*.

These remarks serve as a bridge between P. Lagrange's early training and the intense activity that was to follow. Both Fathers Colchen and Cormier played important roles in the unfolding of his scriptural career, the first directing him to oriental studies and sending him to Vienna and Jerusalem;[18] the second, as Master General of the Order, encouraging him to continue his work out of obedience, supporting him in that field without counting the cost, and displaying a confidence in him which was indicative of his own holiness.[19] Some may have doubted the sincerity of P. Lagrange, but P. Cormier never did; recognizing the spirit that drove him on, he spoke up quickly in defense of Lagrange whenever dark clouds of ill will or lack of understanding cast their menacing shadows over him.

In a providential way unsuspected at the time the exile at Salamanca eventually insured the success of the humble foundation which, as a consequence of the same edict of proscription, was at that very moment being attempted in the Holy Land.

*   *   *

When he arrived in Palestine charged with the task of establishing at Jerusalem a school of Sacred Scripture, P. Lagrange was just thirty-

---

[18] See above, p. 4, and below, p. 13.
[19] See below, p. 94 f.

five years old. How he was to proceed he still had hardly any idea, although for a year now there had been much talk of the venture. All he knew was that he was to make a start. The plans originally called for a kind of home for French priests who wished to spend some time in the Holy Land. The founder of this modest establishment, P. Matthew Lecomte, a member of the Lyons province, had died on June 19, 1887. While on the first pilgrimage of penance organized by the Assumptionist Fathers, the idea of installing his own Order in Jerusalem had first occurred to him, and he had without delay written to Father Larocca, the Master General at that time.

> Why does the Order not seize the present opportunity to take again its place in the Holy Land? We were here in the early days, in both suffering and honor; why not now? We could once boast of houses in Jerusalem, Bethlehem, Nazareth, Acon, Tripoli, Damascus, etc. Why not revive at least the first of these? The body of Blessed Jordan of Saxony, whose heroic sacrifice is always present in God's sight, still lies in Acon (= St. John of Acre). Why should a new light not shine forth from his tomb as it did before, to guide our steps? After six centuries is it not time to honor him there as he deserves? Is it not time that our charity refresh itself in those waters in which the last patriarch of Jerusalem, our Nicholas of Hanaple, died, a victim of his love for his people?[20]

With the help of P. de Ratisbonne, the convert of miraculous-medal fame, and for the astronomical sum of some $15,000, Father Lecomte, ably assisted by M. Langlais, then the French consul in Jerusalem, finally succeeded in acquiring a sanctuary recently discovered north of Jerusalem along the Naplus road, not far from the Damascus gate. Informed persons believed it to be the place where St. Stephen was martyred.[21] After P. Lecomte's death, three or four Dominicans took up residence there in a makeshift dwelling. A pilgrim returning from the Holy Land thus briefly described their situation: "They have nothing but a plot of land on which there stands a single tree, and a tiny chapel in which a handful of people gather on Sunday."[22] It was

---

[20] *Saint Étienne*, p. 90 ff.

[21] *Ibid.*, p. 91 f.

[22] P. Lagrange always lingered over this graphic description when he spoke of the early days of the School.

believed that the harsh climate rendered the place wholly unsuitable for serious work, but the idea of a biblical school had never been entirely dropped. The idea was in its first and vaguest form due to P. Lecomte, whom Leo XIII had urged to found a center of theological studies in the Holy Land.[23] Taken up and developed under the impulse of many men — Vigouroux, Le Camus (later bishop of La Rochelle), and Guillermin (professor at the *Institut catholique* of Toulouse), his idea was finally acted upon. Credit for this is due to the appeal for help directed by the local superior, P. Meunier, to the three Dominican provincials of France. P. Colchen, whose Hebrew blood disposed him favorably to the idea of studying the Bible in Palestine, responded in a practical manner, with unexpected generosity assigning to the project the very man he had been counting on to teach Scripture in his own studium at Toulouse.

When P. Lagrange returned to France at the end of the academic year of 1889 to learn further details of his future assignment, he met P. Meunier in Marseilles, and was dumbfounded on hearing of the utopian plan then under consideration: Bible reading, study of the Fathers and of good commentators, visits to those places in the Holy Land which would confirm the biblical accounts.[24] Except for P. Séjourné, a young priest who had just entered the novitiate and was already destined for Jerusalem, he would not be able to count on a single more or less trained assistant. The recruiting of students was a worry left to the future. There was intriguing talk of "gaslit caves in which one could study during the six months of intense heat." But nothing was ready, or even close to being ready. Until, then, future decisions were made, P. Lagrange returned to his oriental studies at the University of Vienna, and had just gotten well into his work when, in mid-February, he was ordered to betake himself, *recto tramite,* to Jerusalem, and to investigate at firsthand the feasibility of the plan. He disembarked at Jaffa in a rowboat during a violent storm, on March 9, 1890; on the following day he met the little community then living amid the ruins of that sanctuary which the Empress Eudocia

---

[23] *Saint Étienne,* p. 99.
[24] Vincent, *art. cit.,* p. 331.

had built centuries ago in honor of the protomartyr, St. Stephen.[25]

The prospect of establishing a house for biblical studies in so privileged a place, and of linking the highly respectable activity of the present with the glorious souvenirs of the past, would have tempted an even less enterprising man. But to do so without money, or books, or assistants, or the assurance of future students, meant that P. Lagrange was faced with what were — humanly speaking — insuperable difficulties. His vow of obedience bound him to the task. Would it be rash of him to count on the extraordinary intervention of Providence? Before admitting defeat, he prudently decided to see what could be seen. He was gratified to discover that the climate of Jerusalem, instead of hampering, was wonderfully conducive to intellectual work. A trip through Palestine and Transjordan convinced him that many unsuspected advantages awaited intellectual pursuits in the Holy Land. "Jerusalem is singular in this," he later wrote, "the considerable material it provides for theoretical study is constantly being bathed in floods of light which emanate from the very atmosphere of the place. One advantage to be gained by a biblical school located in the land of the Bible is that everything the student sees helps to explain what he is studying, and focuses all his energies on one goal."[26] He did not mean that one could not study such auxiliary sciences (languages, epigraphy, geography, and archaeology) outside of Palestine, from books, maps, photographs, and the rest, but — "Only here can one gain that overall view which is as it were the *mens divinior* of the historian." He was thinking of Bourget's phrase, "historical *feel*," and was inclined to speak of an "historical *ecstasy*." Maurice Holleaux once said that moments of contemplation and thought before a landscape are more fruitful than hours of abstract study, and P. Lagrange recalled St. Jerome's remarks:

> Once a man has seen Athens, he is in a better position to understand Greek history. When he has sailed from Troas past Leucadia and the Acroceraunian mountains, he can understand the Fifth Book of the Aeneid better. Just so, a man will be able to look the more clearly into Holy Scripture, by as it were a kind of *intuition*, if with his

---

[25] Lagrange, *op. cit.,* p. 332.
[26] *Ibid.,* p. 164.

own eyes he has gazed upon Judea and there discovered the remains of ancient cities, some still bearing their ancient names, others perhaps changed.[27]

So P. Lagrange decided to go boldly ahead. A new law practically assured him of students, for clerical candidates were declared exempt from military service if they were living outside of France before they reached the age of nineteen. Under the circumstances the French provincials would in all probability send some of these young men to Jerusalem, and there those of superior talent could be singled out and directed toward specialized biblical studies. On the feast of St. Albert the Great, then, the *École biblique,* a practical school of biblical studies, opened its doors. The date was November 15, 1890.

M. Ledoulx, French consul at Jerusalem, presided benignly over the opening session. The youthful director of the School, P. Lagrange, confessed in his inaugural address that the undertaking was beginning "humbly, and especially in poverty — our scholastic equipment consists of a single table, a blackboard, and a map. It also begins with the help of our Lady Mary, of our good Saint Stephen, and in the confident belief that God wants this School also."[28]

The original school building was, "a single room, longer than it was wide, and lighted only from the door." Actually it was the old slaughterhouse of Jerusalem; the rings to which the animals had been attached were still fixed in the walls. The library consisted of a "few books — even a country Curé had more of them! — left behind by some missionary priest."[29] The staff was made up of himself and an old Maronite priest, P. Doumeth, who, having recently become a Dominican, taught Arabic. There was also a secular priest from the Latin Patriarchate, M. Heidet, whom a long stay in the Holy Land had made familiar with the places and customs of the land. Later on P. Séjourné would join the group.

What made up for everything, however, was the clear vision behind the plan of studies. Like the soul in the body of an infant, the School was pervaded by a *spirit* — none other than P. Lagrange himself —

---

[27] *Ibid.,* p. 161 f.

[28] Vincent, *art. cit.,* p. 333.

[29] Lagrange, "Après vingt-cinq ans," *RB* 24 (1915), p. 248.

which directed all its future developments. The spirit which emanated from his strong personality manifested itself in his daily life. It was a spirit of service toward the Church, of devotion for the good of souls, of serene piety sustained by the monastic office, and of persistence in work. His spirit was one of keen understanding, sincerity, tolerance, and collaboration with others in a common endeavor. And especially, as his students were quick to notice, it was a spirit of great fraternity. They instinctively experienced the exaltation described by Saint-Exupéry in his *Terre des hommes,* "Then only do we breathe, when we are bound to our brothers in a common purpose which is extrinsic to ourselves. This experience shows us that to love does not mean simply to gaze at one another, but to look together in the same direction. They only are comrades who bind themselves together with ropes like mountain climbers, and advance upon the same summit, where they regroup again."[30]

As he had studied under famous professors at the Sorbonne and at the University of Vienna, P. Lagrange was fully aware of the importance of ancient languages, and devoted the greater portion of his program to Semitic philology. In the early days he himself taught Hebrew, Arabic, Assyrian, general introduction to the Bible, history of the Ancient East, and biblical archaeology.[31] Besides these there were courses in epigraphy, topography, Palestinian geography, and exegesis. The land and its inhabitants came in for firsthand study.

> Depending on what is being treated in class, we visit the various sites for verification. Living under the tents, we are able to savor the past itself. Nothing much from modern times intervenes to alter these impressions. It is almost contemplation, yet it is study also. Neither Egypt with its archaeological riches, nor Sinai with its deserts filled with the remembrance of God, nor Syria with its Christian basilicas, lie beyond our reach. This personal contact with people and things, plus our constant references to the texts of the Bible, gives a simple and practical stamp to our studies and excursions; beyond question this is one of our prize resources.[32]

One of P. Lagrange's earliest disciples, Père Felix M. Abel, remem-

[30] *Terre des hommes* (Paris: Gallimard, 1939), p. 202.
[31] Vincent, *ibid.,* p. 334.
[32] *Saint Étienne,* p. 164 ff.

bered: "The only roads were the old Roman roads or desert trails. We sought out inscriptions amid unexplored ruins, and visited Petra by speedy (?) camel. We made the journey to Sinai by camel also, and to Madaba on donkeys. Thanks to a kind Providence we once escaped the bullets of Bedouin who were actively engaged in a *razzia*."[33] In his great commentaries on the Gospels P. Lagrange occasionally refers to those days. Apropos of the text "Where the body is, the vultures gather together," he writes, and his words convey a sense of the uneasiness he then felt, "I once observed a Bedouin near Petra follow the flight of the vultures in order to discover the body of my companion, P. Vincent, whom we thought to be dead. Soon after, however, P. Vincent returned safe and sound."[34]

*   *   *

Having once established a scientific atmosphere for his School, P. Lagrange fought to maintain it.

His courses were often, as it turned out, preliminary drafts of new books, and in them he worked out his own views on basic questions. Once he took up a problem, he did his own thinking, taking nothing for granted in advance. His preoccupation with key problems kept him on the alert for contemporary works, which he devoured in his hunger for knowledge. He always respected the person and opinions of others, and insisted that his students do the same. Nor was he harsh in his judgments. I recall how on one occasion a visitor — a non-believer — questioned the good faith of a certain critic who had a reputation for his singular views. P. Lagrange reacted at once, he "had never judged a man like that." In his eyes, respect for the persons and motives of others who did not share his religious convictions was simply a putting into practice of the gospel dictum: *Nolite judicare.* He never felt, however, that another's ideas could not be subjected to a searching evaluation.

P. Lagrange went to great length in his efforts to grasp the thought of even the most liberal critics.

---

[33] *La vie catholique* (April 2, 1938). A *razzia* is an expedition conducted for the purpose of pillage.

[34] *The Gospel of Jesus Christ* (London: Burns, Oates & Washburn, 1938), II, 81, note 2.

When he was writing his life of Jesus, [L. Bertrand wrote in *Figaro*] P. Lagrange could not take a step without running headlong into some objection or denial. The four gospel accounts are not only a tiny book, but one crushed beneath libraries of controversy, by avalanches and mountains of print. The remarkable thing about this Catholic exegete who had to plow through even the worst of this literature is that it does not seem to have bothered him. He read everything, tried all the intellectual poisons on himself, and emerged unscathed from the ordeal. One is especially impressed by this on reading his *Gospel of Jesus Christ*.

Men who were fortunate enough to know P. Lagrange personally were also perhaps even more deeply impressed. They knew him as a scholar who, although he had spent almost fifty years in the driest kind of studies, had managed to keep an open mind and a wide vision. He took pride in knowing of the latest literary movements. Endowed with refined taste and sensibilities, he appreciated everything beautiful. There comes back to me in memory that magnificent night when, the stars hanging bright in that Eastern sky, I heard him recite Victor Hugo's *Booz endormi*. Flaubert himself could not have delivered those famous lines in a more lyrical tone. But even more than the poem, I remember how this Dominican, clothed in his white woolen robes, reminded me of Booz of Judea, the patriarch of an ancient day "garbed in sheer probity and white linen." I brought up Renan's objections, and he, like a good soldier, did not flinch but faced them squarely, emphasizing their strength before proposing his own solutions. I have always remembered them as being very wise answers.[35]

The example which P. Lagrange set us — of being alive to our own times — was not prompted by superficiality or apologetic opportunism; he simply wanted his work to be as progressive, constructive, and well informed as possible. He was neither insensible to objections raised by modern criticism nor disturbed by them, but weighed them for what they were worth. Sooner or later, the honest confrontation of objections led to an increase in the light; moreover, objections are always intellectually stimulating.

Of course one cannot formulate solutions without consulting the sources, which in this case means the biblical texts in their original language. To read them by way of the Latin Vulgate, correcting pas-

---

[35] *Le Figaro* (April 12, 1929).

sages which had been badly translated, will not do; to proceed thus would place the Vulgate in a false light, and the texts thus taken up would not be seen, as they have a right to be seen, "in their concrete reality, in the nuances of their vocabulary and special constructions, in the genius of their language and in the secret of their literary composition. It is in this form and no other that the Word of God was produced," he observed, "and if a man truly regards the Bible as the word of God, he cannot take too much care to understand it just as it is."[36]

From what has been said one might conclude that the original texts have been preserved in all their original purity. It is, however, not that simple. Neither the Massoretic Hebrew text of the Old Testament nor the Greek text of the New (Erasmus' *textus receptus*) can be accepted without reservations. The day is past when non-Catholic exegesis, basing itself exclusively upon these editions, made sense out of passages which were plainly defective. Kittel's critical edition of the Hebrew Old Testament and Nestle's of the Greek New Testament make it clear that, before any serious translating or explanations of the text can be undertaken, a direct examination of the manuscripts is called for. In other words, studies in literary criticism must rest upon bases solidly established by textual criticism.

So important is textual criticism, now greatly stimulated by recent discoveries, that it attracted the attention of the Master of Jerusalem, and in his later works gave it much prominence.[37] The principles he expounded had guided him in his work long before he came to their explicit formulation. Textual criticism, he felt, had first of all to be a *rational* criticism; the merits of the principal variants could not be judged by a majority vote of witnesses grouped into more or less closely knit family groups; such a solution, at once too simple and too mechanical, was too unlike true research to be safely used. Quality comes before quantity, and one good codex, or one good, honest, and sober manuscript meant more to him than many others which were perhaps older but less reliable. He left no stone unturned in his efforts

---

[36] *RB* 9 (1900), p. 415.

[37] *Introduction à l'étude du NT: Deuxième partie, Critique textuelle, II. La critique rationnelle* (Paris, 1935). See below, pp. 118–121.

to evaluate the quality of manuscripts, and was greatly taken by the discoveries of papyri.

Outweighing all else in his eyes, however, was the internal and as it were, psychological examination of the tendencies manifested by each manuscript.

At the end of his patient research along these lines, the ancient manuscripts came to life for him and became almost persons, each having its own particular temperament, good or bad, elegant or crude, terse or wordy. When he came to make his choice among the variant readings, he was like a chess player moving his pieces about on a chessboard. With a bit of imagination one could make out the king and queen (the uncials), more important than all the others, then the bishops and the knights (e.g., D or ⊕), and the pawns (the minuscules) reinforcing the various positions. He directed the operations of these peaceful little armies, until one reading, and that perhaps not the one best supported, was declared victorious because it stood out as the most worthy, when tested against the ordinary signs of reliability.

Once a text has been decided upon, it has to be interpreted. This involves a careful evaluation of the immediate and remote context, of the cultural milieu, of the literary genus, and of the patristic tradition. To look for the *Sitz im Leben,* that is, into the background or situation of a text in the life of the times, has become an accepted rule of exegesis. But it has often been supported by a bookish kind of science; and P. Lagrange once smilingly defined *Sitz im Leben* as "sitting it [out] in a library!" When he used it, however, it was anything but that. Behind each book of the Bible he perceived a country, a definite ethnic group, ancient customs, traditional methods of composition. Archaeology and history helped him fill out the vision suggested to him by the texts, and this in turn led him to the doctrines they contained. As he pushed on, his syntheses became increasingly comprehensive.

P. Lagrange's method was like a slow climb up a steep mountain; the climber does not advance until he has first made sure of solid footing for his next step. Had he been able to pursue his aims to the end, P. Lagrange would have written a biblical theology, but he left that project for others, content to prepare the way for them. It was to prove to be both a difficult and a dangerous way for him.

A man like P. Lagrange is not always easy to follow, for his mind was extremely subtle and sharp. There were at S. Étienne no soft cushions, no orderly notebooks left behind by previous students. He taught us how to look, think, and judge. He was the Master, and his teaching was of a piece with his own solid work, and his ability to inspire others was simply phenomenal. "Some great scholars look upon themselves strictly as *savants* and their students as *bêtes-noires*. How much better if, at the end of our days, we had fewer published notes or articles to our credit, even one or two books less, and had with the time saved helped young men find themselves, and walk with firmer step for the rest of their lives."[38] The mind of the Director of the *École biblique de Jérusalem* ran along such lines. Students were the chief reason for the School's being, and he lavished considerable time on their training and their little exercises, insisting that they learn to think correctly, and striving to inspire in them that initial self-confidence without which one can do nothing.

As material proof of his solicitude, I have kept some of my own feeble attempts at exegesis which he read and annotated, as he did those of many others. The margins abound with ironic "oh's," imperious "?'s," vehement disagreement: "You have no right . . ." appeals for accuracy, suggestions for deeper study. More rarely, an encouraging "Very good" which took the sting out of well-deserved criticisms. Sometimes there would be personal interviews in which, our little efforts crumbling miserably at his first question, everything would have to be built up piece by piece. First, establish the state of the question, disengage the real problem; then, distinguish good arguments from bad, use only materials of prime quality, measure the exact meaning of conclusions, and their relation to other problems. One got away with nothing. Yet each of these practical meetings brought about a deep and lasting *direction of the mind*. In those days a man was not obliged to cover the entire field of biblical knowledge in two or three years. "You must always study," he was fond of saying, suiting his actions to his words. Sharing in that studious life so scornful of easy success, his students came to understand that the

---

[38] L. Arnould, "Le professeur de Faculté," *Revue des Deux-Mondes* (1935), III, 626.

intellectual life called for constant effort and that, in order to live it at all, one has always to be sure of fundamental principles.

This master, in short, did not impose his views on others. His natural honesty, soon enriched by experience, would not permit him to consider as certain what was probable, or as probable, what was debatable. He would not allow problems to be passed by without a *personal* look. "Now *look*," he would say. "Don't say 'P. Lagrange said so!' You must see it for yourselves." The student who ventured to lift his eyes or to take notes while he was explaining the peculiarities of some difficult text was soon called to order. "Look at it, now. Don't take my word for it. This is a *practical* school of Biblical Studies!"[39] At times obscurities would remain or new difficulties crop up, and a meeting would be arranged for later that afternoon. Then, seated beneath the swaying branches of the Aleppo pines in the garden, there ensued conversations in which time and distance faded away, and the difficulties raised by the last lesson were examined anew.

It was thus, some unfriendly critics observed, that he cast his spell over younger men. What he did actually was to inculcate in them a taste for accuracy and for the difficult. By initiating them into his methods he helped them become aware of themselves while providing them with the magnificent example of his own perfect objectivity.

*   *   *

The first convent having become too small, it was replaced by another and larger one joined to the now magnificently restored Eudocian basilica. The library also, with first call on all available funds, had grown steadily. A special building leading off the atrium of the basilica was next made available for all non-Dominican students. France supplied most of these, but Belgians came next. P. Lagrange liked to say that it was in Belgium that he had his most loyal friends.[40]

---

[39] Mgr. de Solages, "Le Maitre," *Mémorial-Lagrange* (Paris, 1940), p. 351.

[40] "Apres vingt-cinq ans," p. 255: "It is my happy obligation to single out his Eminence, Cardinal Mercier, Archbishop of Malines, for special mention. No other Ordinary has entrusted to us so many young priests destined for higher biblical learning, no other encouraged us with so enlightened a benevolence. . . . The professors at Louvain share in his sentiments, and nowhere else outside of France have we had so many faithful friends. It seems that the Belgian scholars like our way of studying the documents at firsthand; this immediate contact with the text makes the sites so charming, when they are seen."

Cardinal Mercier always arranged that one of his young priests, destined for the teaching of Scripture, should be at the school in Jerusalem. A deep understanding existed between this Prince of the Church, who initiated the Thomistic revival and was the founder of the Higher Institute of Philosophy at Louvain, and the Master of Jerusalem. They understood each other, and both were giants afire with an apostolic zeal for truth. "Is it because of unjustified prejudice, or because the required diploma is thereby obtained with more difficulty, or because of finances, that his [Cardinal Mercier's] example has been so little followed?" asks P. Levie.[41] The student body at the *École biblique* has always been rather small, twenty, more or less. But what is thus lacking in numbers is made up for by the marvelous camaraderie that prevails in the classrooms, on the archaeological expeditions, or at the Sunday recreation where all gather together, even the Swiss lay Brothers from the Val d'Anniviers, who by attending to the School's material needs cooperate in all its work.

Thus the School and convent, in a modest way, came to be transformed. It was not enough, however, to expand, to build up the scientific equipment. No institute of higher studies can prosper without intellectual exchange with other even far-distant workers. To meet this need, and perhaps also to encourage a spirit of research among former students now become his collaborators, P. Lagrange decided to launch the *Revue biblique*. At first it was planned as nothing more than a sort of family notebook "in which one would tell of the School's excursions, plans for the courses, news about pilgrimages." Under that aspect the project had never awakened great enthusiasm in P. Lagrange.[42] And yet, with the limited means at his disposal, how was one to publish a serious scientific review which would be printed in Paris, but edited in Jerusalem? The difficulties were overcome thanks to P. Faucher, a close friend of P. Lecomte; through his contacts it was arranged that the publishing firm of Lethielleux should undertake the task. The first issue of the *Revue*

---

[41] "Le Père Lagrange," *NRTh* (65) (1938), p. 469. Cf the author's very informative and highly readable *The Bible, Word of God in Words of Men* (New York: Kenedy, 1962) for an excellent survey of the development of biblical studies.

[42] *M. Loisy et le modernisme*, p. 69.

appeared in January 1892, little more than a year after the opening of School.[43]

The *Revue* was to be something between spoken word and printed book. It aimed at making available to its readers the teachings and discoveries of scholars. It would provide Catholic specialists in biblical matters with an opportunity to learn of and to exchange different points of view. It would help readers see the Bible as it really was and, by a serious study of the problems of the day, would hold the line against the aggressive rationalism then attacking the Sacred Books. It would bring into priestly rectories solid explanations based on the literal sense of the Psalms, Gospels, and Epistles. Thus, P. Lagrange wrote, it will contain "everything that will help make the Bible known: controversy, Semitic philology, ancient history of oriental peoples, biblical geography, sacred archaeology, bibliography, scholastic theology, mystical theology of the Sacred Scripture, history of exegesis — everything that helps biblical studies will find a place in the *Revue*."[44]

Objections were raised against the project, and fault found with it. Was it respectful to present the Holy Bible to the public, as one would present problems concerning heating or electricity, in a magazine? Would not the frank exposition of enemy objections give them too much publicity? Biblical matters called for the greatest circumspection, and it would be dangerous to provide an outlet for snap judgments in such an area. P. Lagrange appreciated these misgivings and tried to allay them. Of course the Bible is a holy book, he wrote, but is it a secret book that has to be kept hidden? Our silence will not prevent the objections of nonbelievers from becoming known. "Draw the blinds as tightly as you like," he wrote, "what will you then do when an error which originated in Germany and England penetrates into France, where it finds advocates whose style is more attractive than that of our own teachers? If error spreads first in special works, and then in periodicals and newspapers, who can hope to keep it shut up behind curtains?" As for the danger of superficiality, "A magazine, of course, makes no claim to the maturity of a large volume, but does

---

[43] *Ibid.*, p. 70; "Après vingt-cinq ans," *op. cit.*, p. 259.
[44] *RB* 1 (1892), p. 10.

a big book have to be written in order to reply to an article? My weighty tome will not even be off the press before the blow lands a second time."[45] Nonetheless, it was up to the *Revue* to prove its worth.

P. Lagrange had little trouble finding worthy associates. The Sulpicians came forward with men like Vigouroux and his friend Le Camus; from the Jesuits there came Fathers Cornely, Corluy, Knabenbauer, Van Kasteren; from the Dominicans, Fathers Didon, Faucher, Lacome, Ollivier, Scheil; and from the ranks of the secular clergy, the Abbés Batiffol, Hyvernat, Thomas, and Jacquier.[46] Loisy, who had already a reputation for brilliance — at the time (1892) he was still teaching in Paris at the *Institut catholique* — was not one of these collaborators. P. Lagrange had already experienced misgivings about him, and had hoped, when passing through Paris, to have a frank talk with him. As this visit did not materialize, he put off until later proposing to Loisy what he had to say.[47] Moreover, the first issue of the *Revue* had hardly come from the press when Loisy's own magazine (*L'enseignement biblique*)[48] appeared; when it ceased publication, Loisy at Batiffol's invitation submitted two book reviews to the *Revue*,[49] along with an article on the *Synoptic Apocalypse*.[50]The article was published with a footnote appended by the editors,[51] and this so

[45] *Ibid.*, p. 3 ff.

[46] M. *Loisy et le modernisme*, p. 70 f.

[47] *Ibid.*, p. 71.

[48] A fortnightly publication (Paris, 1892). "This publication," Loisy wrote (*Mémoires* [Paris, 1930], I, 202), "dealt with my lectures and was primarily intended to help my students prepare for their examinations; it was secondarily intended for those benevolent subscribers whom it might interest, but the number of subscribers and auditors did not exceed 200." On the first page we read: "For many years learned apologists have cherished the hope of establishing a review for biblical matters. The project has finally been realized, and we hope that the *Revue biblique* will everywhere be welcomed as it deserves. . . . Had we aimed as high, we should have abandoned our project, seeing that others had already undertaken to carry it out much more effectively."

[49] They dealt with the "Rainbow-Bible" of P. Haupt (4 vols.): *Leviticus* by S. R. Driver and H. A. White; *Samuel* by R. Budde; *Joshua* by W. H. Bennett; *Jeremiah* by C. H. Cornill. Cf *RB* 4 (1895), p. 270, and *ibid.*, 5 (1896), p. 128 f.

[50] "L'apocalypse synoptique," *ibid.*, pp. 173–198, 335–359.

[51] *Ibid.*, p. 341: "The *Revue biblique* cannot allow its readers to be uninformed as to what is being written by Catholics or Protestants, but the Editors feel that they must here associate themselves with the reservations of the author of this article in regard to M. Schell's opinion" (Editors' note).

incensed Loisy that he broke off all relations with the *Revue*.[52]

Two of the redactors, Vigouroux and Le Camus, deserve special mention. They were among the first to approve the undertaking and used their influence in its favor in circles where P. Lagrange was still unknown. But none was so generously committed to the *Revue biblique* as Batiffol, who from 1895 on filled the exacting task of secretary, in Paris. When Bishop Batiffol died, P. Lagrange recalled his loyal services with deep emotion: "His sympathy, loyalty, and liberality extended far beyond forgetfulness of self, and have won for him the right to the undying gratitude of the editors and the readers of the *Revue*. I who have benefited most deeply from all this, and who did not ever expect to survive him, bequeath this memory to those who will carry on the work which owes him so much."[53] The two friends of Issy, clearly enough, had come together again, and after a separation which they accepted with holy resignation, had joined again in a common cause. Each had kept his word, and their projected plans were now to be realized in a way that far exceeded their most optimistic expectations.

But no matter how precious the help which flowed in upon him from all sides, the main responsibility for the venture rested upon P. Lagrange. His name was not to appear on the title page which read, simply, *"Revue biblique,* a quarterly published under the direction of the professors of biblical studies at the Dominican Convent of St. Stephen's in Jerusalem." His collaborators were always free to withdraw, but he was too deeply involved to do so. The soundness of his judgment was proved by his first article, in which, contrary to the prevailing view, he argued that the original Jerusalem or City of David must have been located on the eastern hill south of the present temple area.[54] No one at the time suspected that the excavations of Ophel would, some ten years later, provide striking confirmation of his hypothesis.[55] He concentrated upon the basic questions and, during

---

[52] Concerning these incidents, see Loisy, *Mémoires* (Paris, 1930), I, 400 f.; and M. J. Lagrange, *M. Loisy et le modernisme,* pp. 81–83.

[53] *RB* 38 (1929), p. 320.

[54] *Ibid.,* 1 (1892), pp. 17–18.

[55] Cf the report sent to the *Académie des Inscriptions et Belles-Lettres* (May 29, 1914) on the excavations conducted by M. Raymond Weill on the "City of David." Cf *RB* 24 (1915), p. 280.

those first years, wrote many articles on archaeology, topography, epigraphy, literary and textual criticism, exegesis of both the Old and New Testaments. Exegesis held a special attraction for him, and the following titles indicate how closely he centered his interest on the *Biblical Question*:[56] "Le panthéisme dans l'Histoire Sainte,"[57] "L'Hexaméron" (Gn 1-2:4),[58] "L'inspiration et les exigences de la critique,"[59] "L'innocence et péché,"[60] "Les sources du Pentateuque" (a paper read at the Catholic Scientific Congress in Fribourg),[61] "Le Code de Hammourabi,"[62] "Les prophéties messianiques de Daniel."[63]

"I prefer the mind which delights in big books," he wrote in the first article of the *Revue biblique*, "but I cannot reply to an article by writing a book."[64] One gathers from his words that his articles were preliminary drafts which in time might develop into books.

Always on the alert for further progress, in 1900 he issued a "Projet de commentaire complet de l'Ecriture Sainte."[65]

> What we need is a Catholic commentary based on a good translation of the original text, featuring a careful textual criticism and giving special attention to literary criticism, the chief preoccupation of non-Catholics and basic to almost all of the problems raised in our days. Strictly dogmatic theology may take little interest in this, but the history of theology and all history, generally, depend upon the comparison of parallel works, on the dates assigned to documents, on the identification of their literary forms, on the distinction of sources. . . . It may appear that what is principal is being sacrificed to what is secondary. . . . All very true, but as there are different tasks in God's house, and as a division of labor is of prime necessity if overwork and confusion are to be avoided, a man should be permitted to apply himself, when necessary, to the humblest of needs, and to delimit his efforts.

---

[56] Cf below, pp. . . . .
[57] *Ibid.*, 1 (1892), pp. 605–616.
[58] *Ibid.*, 4 (1895), pp. 381–407.
[59] *Ibid.*, pp. 496–518.
[60] *Ibid.*, 6 (1897), pp. 341–379.
[61] *Ibid.*, 7 (1898), pp. 10–32.
[62] *Ibid.*, 12 (1903), pp. 27–51.
[63] *Ibid.*, 13 (1904), pp. 494–520.
[64] *RB* 1 (1892), p. 4.
[65] *Ibid.*, 9 (1900), pp. 414–423.

In order to avoid "overwork and confusion," P. Lagrange outlined his program with care. He proposed to make use of the original texts, not just now and then and by way of the Vulgate, but directly, making as faithful a translation as possible. He resolved therefore, to make generous use of textual criticism, and thus present his readers with the best possible text, which in turn would serve as the basis for his commentary. Literary criticism would help him determine the nature of the texts, their sources if any, and their meaning; thus their contribution to doctrine and to history could be easily seen.

As was his wont, P. Lagrange suited his actions to his words, and the first volume of the *Études bibliques* to appear was his commentary on the Book of Judges. It was composed along the lines just mentioned,[66] its basic text being the original critical text translated into French. Philological, geographical, and historical comments were disposed under the text, and longer notes or excursuses were inserted after each chapter or group of chapters. The theory of the sources of the Pentateuch, as P. Lagrange then understood it, had not failed to influence him, but he rejected Wellhausen's view that in Judges, E and J designated the same independent sources as in the Pentateuch.[67] At most, he conceded the existence of a Yahwistic school, without asserting the identity of the author who used Yahwistic fragments of the Pentateuch; he also conceded that there was a spiritual relationship existing between the E of Judges and the E of the Pentateuch, in the spirit of the prophets which had been inaugurated by Moses.[68]

Judges appeared in 1903. The purpose of his *Études sur les religions sémitiques,* which appeared soon after,[69] was well defined. He did

---

[66] Paris: Lecoffre, 1903. This work was favorably reviewed in *The Expository Times* 14 (1903), pp. 206 f., by J. A. Selbie, who considered it "one of the most hopeful signs of the times," and "in every respect a model commentary." He went on to say that "if the subsequent members [of the *Études bibliques*] maintain the high level reached in the work before us, these commentaries are sure of a warm welcome outside of the Roman Catholic Church as well as within its pale."

[67] This hypothesis would make J and E posterior to Moses by some 400 to 500 years.

[68] Cf *RB* 47 (1938), p. 178 ff.

[69] Paris, 1903; 2nd edition, 1905. Dr. W. F. Albright, in a letter of December 14, 1961, writes: "I have enjoyed rereading Père Lagrange's volume [*Études sur les religions sémitiques*], which is remarkably up to date in view of the extraordinary range and importance of discoveries made since, especially the Ugaritic epics and ritual texts. I think that the outstanding feature of his work is its solid learning and its good sense and prudence throughout. Whether he speaks of totemism or of the back-

not propose to explain *everything* about the religion of the ancient peoples who lived between Egypt and the Persian Gulf — that is, about gods and goddesses, sacred persons and things, sacrifices, the cult of the dead, Babylonian and Phoenician myths; he sought rather to clarify the origins of the religious ideas held by Israel's ancestors. By the time a second edition appeared, his *Religions sémitiques* had, because of its rich contents, already become a classic in the field. Inevitably the theory of evolutionary animism as applied to the origins of Semitic religion, and the religions of other ancient peoples, came up for discussion. Wellhausen's school had already reached its conclusion: that out of a chaotic mass of animistic, polydemonistic and polytheistic beliefs to which the Babylonian tablets bear witness, there had slowly emerged a monolatric (or henotheistic) cult which centered about Yahweh, the God of the Israelite tribes. This cult was, so went the theory, transformed into monotheism through the initiative of the prophets, and their monotheism was by a literary fiction projected back to the beginnings of the patriarchal period. At one time this view was widely held.[70]

P. Lagrange's studies led him to a very different conclusion. Animism did indeed lie at the root of Babylonian mythology, but mythology and religion are two different things. Religion supposes a belief in higher powers, and a desire to establish contact with them. Behind mythology there lies a curiosity which seeks to satisfy the first scientific questions a man asks when he finds himself confronted by the mysteries of nature. Although animism played a major role in mythology, its role in true religion appeared to P. Lagrange to be quite secondary. In antiquity, as a matter of fact, religious ideas, initially incapable of being expressed within the concept of the unity of God, appeared, so P. Lagrange thought, to be "impregnated with

---

ground of Philo Biblius, what he writes is eminently rational . . . Incidentally, I found myself anticipated in several observations I have recently made on my own. If Lagrange's book had been translated into English, its impact would have been much greater. But in the first decade of our century the time was singularly unpropitious for such a translation." In an earlier letter (October 13) Dr. Albright had expressed his astonishment at "the excellence of [Lagrange's] judgments, even where modern discoveries have revolutionized special fields."

70 J. Coppens, *The Old Testament and the Critics*. Translated by E. A. Ryan, S.J., and E. W. Tribbe, S.J. (Paterson: St. Anthony Guild Press, 1942), pp. 18–37.

a profound awareness of the superiority proper to divinity." When ancient man attributed power or goodness to a spirit, he made him beneficiary of this vague awareness of the unity and transcendence of the divinity — an awareness which clearly stands out from duly attested facts.[71]

His study of the god *El,* "a common and primitive god, and very probably one peculiar to the Semites," provided a solid basis for his observations. To be at all plausible, primitive polydemonism, which everywhere discerned distinct forces more or less clearly apprehended as supernatural, had to be able to prove that the most ancient divine names referred to distinct divinities, or, if they were common names for god, that these occurred in the plural, like the word *Elohim.* Unfortunately for this theory, P. Lagrange could prove that *Elohim* was a secondary form, and that El, which appears in the most ancient stratum of Semitic languages, appears in the singular as a personal name; one cannot, however, assert with absolute finality that El stood for a single, clearly defined, personality.[72] P. Lagrange's conclusion thus attributed to the Semites religious concepts which were far superior to animism and polydemonism. The views of the historians of religion, who were unwilling to concede any religious transcendence at all to the ideas of ancient man, were widely accepted by Old Testament scholars, and this is in itself proof that P. Lagrange could and did manifest an unusual scientific independence of mind.

In the realm of archaeology, the excavations at Ophel (1910) were to confirm his daring views as to the primitive site of Jerusalem. In 1929 his views about the god El were confirmed by the discoveries at Ras Shamra.[73] These texts, which definitely antedate the Bible, show that in the fifteenth century before Christ, El was already venerated on the Phoenician coast as a personal and supreme god, the god-king.[74] Utilizing these discoveries in his article on the Mosaic origins of the Pentateuch (1938), P. Lagrange pointed out with satisfaction that he had always been of this opinion. After the lapse of forty-five years he could stand by what he had written earlier:

---

[71] *Religions sémitiques,* 1st ed., p. 26 ff.

[72] *Ibid.,* p. 78.

[73] R. de Vaux, "Les textes de Ras Shamra et l'AT," *RB* 46 (1937), pp. 526–555.

[74] *Ibid.,* p. 181.

Analyzing the data relative to the name of God, we have shown that certain extremely ancient religious ideas were the common inheritance of the ancient Semites. To what extent these ideas had disappeared when the Hebrews enter the picture we do not know, and we consequently see no reason why we should attribute to their ancestors either spiritism or the most degraded kind of fetishism. Our conclusion does not exceed the premises.[75]

It not only did not exceed the premises but it anticipated the revelations which the ancient Orient was to make later on. The religion of Israel was placed in a true light as something "both historical and divine," and its superiority was asserted by linking it up with the germ of progress which had been sown in the heart of mankind by primitive revelation.

*   *   *

École biblique, Revue biblique, and *Études bibliques* are three complementary parts of one great work. Apostolic-minded at heart, P. Lagrange wanted his work to be a work of France. His love for his country ran deep, and he had been willing to go to war for France in 1870, but was too young at the time to do so. He liked to recall the year he had later put in at Soissons as a volunteer, for there he had learned "the meaning of discipline, the need for order, and the advantages of energy."

His country's affairs were of constant interest to him. In establishing the *École biblique,* he made it clear that its Catholicity should not hide the fact that it was also a *French* venture. S. Étienne was occupied by the Turkish army in 1915, and he wrote, proudly,

No one seems to have explained to the government of the Young Turks that an institution of higher learning, which has held itself aloof from all the excitement and occupied itself with the present only so as to instruct the modern Orient concerning its ancient glories, should be spared. When asked to vindicate the international character of the School, we replied that although we have extended a warm welcome to all who were not French, we did so precisely because our heart was French. The Dominican Order is to be found wherever the Church is, yet at the request of the French ambassador to the Holy See, M. Lefebvre de Béhaine, our convent in Jerusalem was

[75] *Religions sémitiques,* p. 83.

erected as a French house by Father Larocca, the Master General of the Order, and maintained as such by his successors. The practical school of biblical studies, closed because it was French, will be born again, French.[76]

In the Orient, despite the ups and downs of local politics which inflicted grave wounds on her, France has always been looked upon as a great Christian power and has enjoyed considerable prestige.[77] Not that her private ventures in commercial and industrial matters can compare with those of her competitors in that field, but in religious activities French priests, Sisters, and religious, perpetuating their time-honored traditions, have been second to none. Although it would be petty to draw up a list of her scholastic prowess, or to bestow prizes for virtue, P. Lagrange thought it proper to mention those of his compatriots who had represented his country with distinction. Among the missionaries of the Latin Patriarchate there was Bishop Poyet, outstanding for his reserve (he was from Lyons!) and his love for study.[78] And Frère Evagrius, director of an establishment in which he taught a sound and wholesome morality to more than 40,000 children — Christians, Jews, and Moslems. Of these children he once said: "How can you help them if you don't love them?" He died after spending fifty-two years in the Orient. Mother Sion, superioress of the Sisters of St. Vincent de Paul and the guardian angel of both young and old, collected both with a goodness so maternal that when the Turkish hospital was erected the Turks found it the most natural thing in the world to assign to her the care of their sick. And Mother Germaine, superior of the Sisters of St. Joseph (they were first to appear on the scene), was foundress of an orphanage which, by dint of prodigies of economy, confidence in God, and wise administration, she managed along with the French hospital and the classes already confided to her. And how many were there not among the *Dames de Sion,* the Benedictines of Calvary, the Franciscans of Mary, and the

[76] *RB* 24 (1915), p. 261.

[77] Thus Bishop, and later Cardinal, Gasparri, in an interview to the *Osservatore Romano* (November 5, 1907). Cf Lagrange, "Les Francais et les Allemands en Palestine," *RA* 24 (1917), p. 403 f.

[78] He hoped to establish an annual remembrance of the soul of Godfrey de Bouillon — an unconscious bit of revenge, seeing that the Germans, who were confident of the confiscation of Belgium, were already referring to him as "our Godfrey." *Ibid.,* p. 397.

Reparatrices, as well as the Brothers of the Christian Doctrine, White Fathers, and Benedictines, the one dedicated to the training of Greek and Syrian clerics, the other to the education of youth.

The *École biblique* had its own appointed place in the network of good which was inspired by French zeal. P. Lagrange ambitioned for his school nothing less than *caritas veritatis,* the charity of truth. His charity, like that which manifested itself in caring for the sick and orphans, the instruction of children, and care for the poor, for lepers, and for all that ragged clientele which flocked to the dispensaries, was to be French.

Other illustrious Frenchmen had preceded him in archaeological and geographical research in the Holy Land. "Following the uncritical De Saulcy, the Marquis de Voguë had in 1853 taken command of a domain over which he retained the mastery until his death. His books, *The Temple of Solomon* and *Churches of the Holy Land,* are an *editio princeps* of Palestinian archaeology." "M. Guerin used to ride off all by himself on his little donkey, going through the various villages in search of monuments and sites, and taking note of the country folk and their customs. . . ." M. Rey took an especial interest in the massive remains of Crusader constructions, and M. Clermont-Ganneau became *the* authority on Palestinian antiquities. The researches in natural history which the Duc de Luynes began at the Dead Sea were extended to the whole country by M. Lortet.[79] A kind of mental finesse not always conspicuous in scholars gave a certain family touch to all these efforts. As Lagrange has remarked, it takes finesse to interpret ancient remains in such a way as to understand both the monument and its place in history. One does not do this by accumulating facts, nor by that methodical organization so essential to the making of an encyclopedia or dictionary.[80] He then added, somewhat mischievously, "One day, Müller put the card marked 'Sycamores' into the 'Tomb at Palmyra'!" P. Lagrange never adopted a filing-system himself, for methodical organization was not one of his strong points, but his keen mind stamped him as a kindred spirit to the distinguished savants who had preceded him under the aegis of the *Consulate de France.*

[79] *Ibid.,* pp. 397–401.
[80] *Ibid.,* p. 400.

Like them, he willingly accepted, sometimes at the risk of his life, scientific missions in the name of the *Institut des Inscriptions et Belles-Lettres*,[81] and to it he faithfully sent reports and accounts of the discoveries made by the *École*.

It was, moreover, the conviction that he was performing a French work for the glory of God and the good of souls which lay behind his respect for the French consular authorities. At the solemn opening of the school year and on conventual feast days, the French tricolor would flutter atop the tower and the Consul General of France would appear, decked out in his uniform and preceded by his *qawwas*, themselves as resplendent as the janissaries of the Sultan. The Consul would be solemnly met at the door of the basilica and there presented with holy water, incense, and the book of the Gospels. M. Ledoulx was consul when the School was opened, and presided over that ceremony. He must have had a weakness for all charitable institutions, for he never missed attending their functions. The patriarch, Bishop Piavi, often sent his auxiliary to take his place, but Ledoulx, the "bishop of the outside," as he once wittily styled himself, was always on hand. The consul did not make a big thing of the incense,[82] but P. Lagrange was on hand to see that everything was exactly observed, and with all the distinction of a courtly gentleman leading an important guest into the heart of his home, would personally lead France's representative to the center of the choir.

Mere details of protocol, perhaps, but there was a symbolic freshness about them. We at any rate understood them to be so many acts of homage tendered to the distant fatherland in whose name good was being done.

---

[81] In the *CrAcInscrBl* for November 19, 1897, one may read how "M. de Vogüé reports that P. Lagrange, at the request of the commission for the Corpus, has returned to Petra, and that he had the good fortune there to find a series of new and important Nabatean inscriptions. On his return he was fired upon by a band of Bedouin, and two of the men in his party were killed. He and his companion P. Vincent, thanks to the swiftness of their mounts, escaped with their lives, but their equipment, cameras, photographs, and squeezes, were all taken and destroyed. Only the inscriptions they had on their persons were saved. M. de Vogüé is confident that the Academy will address an expression of warm sympathy to the intrepid missionaries, congratulating them for having escaped the perils they endured in order to enrich science with new documents."

[82] Lagrange, *art. cit.*, p. 399.

CHAPTER II

IN THE LIGHT OF FAITH

IT WAS only proper that P. Lagrange should have set high standards for his school, for any truly scientific work abhors the "almost good" and anything that is done for God deserves to be done well. But, as Gilson has pointed out,[1] this alone is not enough.

> It is impossible to place the intelligence at the service of God without respecting integrally the rights of the intelligence, otherwise it would not be the intelligence that is put at His service. But still more it is impossible to do so without respecting the rights of God, otherwise it is no longer at His service that the intelligence is placed.[2]

Let us see how P. Lagrange fulfilled this second condition.

To begin, it is not enough to say that in all his work he was a believer. The harmony between science and the faith demands more than that.

> What we perceive deep down in ourselves is an ever present difficulty, our inability to make our reason let itself be guided by faith. For such collaboration, faith no longer suffices. What is lacking is theology, that sacred science which is the keystone of the edifice in which all other sciences must take their place. A zealous theologian animated by good intentions will, we have said, do as much harm as he does good, if he pretends to "utilize" the sciences without having mastered them. But the savant, the philosopher, and the artist who are animated by the most ardent piety, will run into the worst of misfortunes if they pretend to refer their science to God without having, if not mastered, at least practiced the science of divine things. . . . It is possible to be a savant, philosopher, and artist, without having studied theology. But it is impossible without theology to become a Christian savant, philos-

---

[1] See p. 7.
[2] E. Gilson, *Christianity and Philosophy* (New York: Sheed and Ward, 1939), p. 117.

opher, or artist. Without it we can be on the one hand Christians, and on the other, savants, philosophers, or artists, but without it our Christianity will never permeate our science, our philosophy, and our art, reforming and vivifying them from within.[3]

P. Lagrange felt very strongly on this score. A faithful disciple of St. Thomas Aquinas, he had while still quite young obtained the Doctorate and the Masterate in theology. He insisted that his School should be a theological school.

> Biblical studies should above all be theological [he wrote]. The Dominican Order has made this strikingly clear by attaching to the *École biblique* a studium of St. Thomas where ecclesiastical students can obtain theological degrees just as they can at the Minerva in Rome [the *Angelico* to which he here refers was later located on Via San Vitale, and in 1932 moved to its present location on the Salita del Grillo]. At S. Étienne there is in fact but one school, a theological school as that term was understood in the Middle Ages when scholasticism was at its peak and the Bible recognized in all universities as the *alpha* and the *omega,* the book for students and for masters.[4]

This original plan was followed for many years but later modified, and specifically theological courses were discontinued when circumstances allowed students to be sent to S. Étienne when they had finished their theological training at home. But even then the theology of St. Thomas enjoyed undisputed preeminence. Biblical studies here might tend to greater and greater specialization, but they would never be divorced from theology, and P. Lagrange owed the tranquil confidence with which he faced the most critical of problems to that very fact.

The first and most controversial problem to be taken up was that of biblical inspiration. There were also the arguments against the divine origin of the Bible, the theory of the sources of the Pentateuch as urged by Wellhausen and his school, the so-called legendary, even mythical character of the first accounts in Genesis, and the alleged fiction of prophecy, at the time considered a literary fraud. Catholic authors stoutly asserted that there neither was nor could be any error in Holy Scripture, but it was answered that the errors in the Bible were a fact

---

[3] *Ibid.,* p. 120 f.

[4] *Saint Étienne et son sanctuaire à Jérusalem* (Paris: Picard, 1894), p. 166.

against which all logical arguments were unavailing. Hence the mounting bitterness of the debate. Many thought that the Church could not afford to maintain her dogmatic attitude in the face of the latest findings of science.

Such a controversy was raging at the *Institut catholique* of Paris. In 1893, Msgr. d'Hulst, then acting rector, had published in *Le Correspondant* a sort of detailed report on the liberal, middle, and traditional schools of Catholic exegesis.[5] He spoke of the *liberal* school with a certain complacency without, however, committing himself; it held for the restriction of inspiration to matters of faith and morals; what touched upon the natural sciences and history was not matter for inspiration, and so needed no safeguarding from error. Here, some thought, was a key to the solution of difficulties raised against biblical inerrancy in the name of science and ancient history. The system was in part borrowed from Canon Didiot,[6] a theologian from Lille, and from François Lenormant,[7] but as it went against the traditional thought of the Church concerning the extent of inspiration, Msgr. d'Hulst was quick to disavow it.

The case of Abbé Loisy was something else again. In June of 1893, while still teaching at the *Institut catholique de Paris,* he had seized upon d'Hulst's article in *Le Correspondant* as an excuse, in his last lecture of the year, to voice his own views.[8] He made his position clear: the Bible was not only filled with error in matters of science and history, but in doctrinal matters as well. He concluded that the biblical question involved not merely theological discussion, but critical history. "Instead of asking if the Bible contains errors, one should determine how much of what the Bible contains is true."[9]

Loisy had avowed that his article "unmasked with moderation and discretion the basic absurdity of the traditional view of biblical inspiration, and brought out the impossibility of seriously maintaining it in

---

[5] "La question biblique," *Le Correspondant,* 170 (January 25, 1893), pp. 201–251.

[6] *Logique surnaturelle subjective* (Paris, 1891), p. 103.

[7] *Les origines de l'histoire d'après la Bible et les traditions des peuples orientaux* (Paris, 1880), pp. viii, xvi.

[8] *Mémoires* (Paris, 1930), I, 250–252. This lecture was published, with changes of form only, in *Enseignement biblique* (November 10, 1893).

[9] *Mémoires,* I, 260.

the face of evident reality."[10] While voicing these haughty criticisms, he made a show of remaining in the Church, but to that part of the story we shall return later.

These remarks of the young professor at the *Institut catholique* bore a strange resemblance to those by which Renan sought to justify his leaving the Church.

> Even in its most mitigated form [Renan had written] Catholic teaching on inspiration does not leave room for any "colored" truth in the sacred text, or of any contradiction even in matters which do not concern faith or morals. In the countless skirmishes fought between critics and orthodox apologists over details of the allegedly sacred texts, there are times when by mere accident and against all expectations the defenders win. But it is impossible that they be right every time in this conflict, and if wrong only once, the thesis of inspiration crumbles to the ground. Implying as it does a supernatural fact, inspiration cannot be maintained when confronted by ideas dictated by modern good sense. An inspired book is a miracle. It has thus to be considered under conditions which affect no other book.[11]

From Renan to Loisy the objection had obviously not lost its force, and the answer to it required a preliminary agreement concerning the notion of inspiration. On this point there were many conflicting theories. According to some, inspiration was a kind of mechanical dictation in which the sacred writers played a purely passive role not unlike that of a mere machine. Once held by Protestants, at a time when the Reformation had sparked great enthusiasm for the Bible, the theory of inspiration-dictation was replaced wherever the winds of modernist progress blew strongly, by the almost opposite notion of a kind of ecstasy similar to that experienced by mystics and poets in the composition of their works. Catholics for the most part followed a middle course traced out by Cardinal Franzelin, who drew a distinc-

---

[10] *Ibid.*, p. 265.

[11] *Souvenirs d'enfance* (Paris, 1883), p. 294. The citation may be completed by what precedes (p. 292 f.): "In a divine book everything is true, and as two contradictions cannot be true at the same time, there can be no contradiction in it. Yet my attentive study of the Bible, which revealed to me its historical and aesthetical treasures, also proved to me that this book was no more exempt from contradictions, slips, and errors, than any other book from ancient times."

tion between the ideas in the Sacred Books and the words which expressed them.[12]

None of these systems succeeded in harmonizing the many elements of the problem. It is of faith that the Bible has God for its author.[13] Inspiration must consequently be something more than a simple product of human ecstasy. That the Bible is man-made is evident from a comparison of the differences in the doctrinal and literary expressions found in each book. It follows equally that the inspired authors were more than machines mechanically moved by the principal author. To leave the choice of words to men is both too much and too little. *Too much* because if God is the author of Scripture in each part and in the precise manner tradition has always understood, can it be that God did not also intervene in the words which play so important a part in the composition of a book and in the expression of the ideas? From a psychological point of view, is it possible that God could have communicated his own ideas to the sacred authors without in some way expressing them? Moreover, to limit the sacred writers to the mere expression of divine ideas would be *too little*. Comparing only the Gospels according to Matthew and John, there are striking personal differences which transcend the choice of words and the ordering of sentences.

St. Thomas' statement of the traditional view: "The Holy Spirit is the principal author of the Scriptures, men were his instruments,"[14] was helpful to P. Lagrange when he took up the problem of inspiration in the pages of the *Revue biblique*.[15] The sacred writers were God's instruments, he wrote, but not as so many machines. God moves all things according to their natures, and in using human instruments to write the books of the Bible, he fully intended them to use their minds and hearts as well as their executive faculties (hands and senses). As a result, Scripture possesses an unshakable authority, for they are wholly written under the inspiration of the Holy Spirit. It follows no

---

[12] *Tractatus de divine Traditione et Scriptura³* (Rome, 1875).

[13] *Concilium Tridentinum,* sess. IV (April 8, 1546); cf. *EB* 42, 45.

[14] *Quodlibet* VII, art. 14: "Auctor principalis S. Scripturae est Spiritus Sanctus. . . . Homo fuit auctor instrumentalis S. Scripturae."

[15] "Une pensée de saint Thomas sur l'inspiration scripturaire," *RB* 4 (1895), pp. 563–571; "Inspiration des Livres Saints," *ibid.,* 5 (1896), pp. 199–220; "L'inspiration et les exigences de la critique," *ibid.,* pp. 496–518.

less logically that the Bible expresses human thought in a human manner which is subject to the same laws of interpretation as is any other ancient writing. To properly understand the Bible, he concluded, one must appeal to philology, weigh the literary forms, and study the background of each book.

Except for minor differences, theologians and exegetes were often practically agreed on these basic principles. P. Lagrange had for many years pondered this problem, and based his exegetical method on principles. He marked out the direction to take when seeking answers to the serious difficulties constantly being raised against the Old Testament by rationalistic biblical scholars who thus manifested their contempt for the Church.

Catholics and conservative Protestants hold that while the books of the Bible may not be "miracles," they are at least supernatural in origin. Having God as their principal author, they cannot contain error which is incompatible with the God of truth. We have already referred to this as "biblical inerrancy."[16]

The philosopher knows that truth and error, properly speaking, are found only in that mental operation which is called the *judgment,* in which one affirms the objective relation of *this* predicate to *that* subject. If I were to say that the sun rises each morning, or that the hare chews its cud, or that the seventy-two names Luke gives in his genealogy of Christ represent all generations extending from the creation of the first man to the coming of the Savior, I would be guilty of error — my judgment would not square with the facts. But if I affirm nothing, and limit myself to speaking as men commonly speak about the rising and setting of the sun, following the evidence

---

[16] This official teaching of the Church is set forth in Leo XIII's encyclical *Providentissimus Deus* (November 18, 1893). Cf *RB* 3 (1894), p. 24: "The fact that it was men whom the Holy Spirit took up as his instruments for writing does not mean that it was these inspired instruments — but not the primary author — who might have made an error. For by supernatural power He so moved and impelled them to write — He so assisted them when writing — that the things which He ordered, and those only, they first rightly understood, then willed faithfully to write down, and finally expressed in apt words and with infallible truth. . . . It follows that those who maintain that an error is possible in any genuine passage of the sacred writings either pervert the Catholic notion of inspiration, or make God the author of such error."

of their senses, and if I draw up a genealogy following conventional rules, omitting all intermediate generations, it is clear that, since I have no intention of committing myself in such matters, I cannot be said to be declaring a truth, or responsible for errors or mistakes in judgment.

Before admitting the existence of error in the Bible it is only common sense to follow P. Lagrange's advice: determine *what it is that has been affirmed,* and *what has not been made the object of affirmation or judgment.* It is precisely here that the study of literary forms assumes capital importance. Are formal pronouncements on the natural sciences to be sought in a historical book? We have to understand how the ancients wrote their histories,[17] for history has many faces and a chronicler uses different forms than the paleographer. A poem with a moral lesson, like that of Jonas and the whale (which is found, incidentally, only in the prophetical literature), will for good reason have to be interpreted differently than a sober historical account. When dealing with books that are definitely historical, is it not *de rigueur* to take into account redactional procedures generally practiced in those days and in the social milieux in which the ancient biblical writers worked? Wisdom and sound critical judgment will distinguish between those facts for which the ancient historians vouched, and the traditions which they merely recorded, explicitly or implicitly, in writing.[18]

Among the "errors" which Renan had considered to be incompatible with biblical inerrancy and divine inspiration of the Bible were "fables, contradictions, traces of human composition."[19] "Fable" and "legend" are not words to be used lightly. Might not certain fictitious tales, P. Lagrange asked, be like the gospel parables, which are only apparently historical? Why should the Bible not make use of those edifying novelties so suited to the genius of Israel, and so often encountered in Jewish midrashic literature? The word "contradiction" calls for very delicate handling. What one critic calls a contradiction may

---

[17] Cf Guidi, "L'historiographie chez les Sémites," *RB* 14 (1906), p. 509.

[18] A. Durand, "Inerrance biblique," *DA* II, 752–787; "Critique biblique," *ibid.,* I. 760–819, and, in more scholarly form and with all desirable precision, quotations, and corrections, J. Vosté, *De Divina Inspiratione et Veritate Sacrae Scripturae* (Rome, 1932).

[19] *Souvenirs d'enfance,* p. 293.

simply represent a difference in point of view; Heraclitus had declared long, long ago that "tacit consent is worth more than manifest agreement."[20] Partial contradictions which are incidental to the sacred writer's purpose may be attributed to literary redaction or to free quotations of sources; in neither case can the author be taxed with error.

Behind all this is Renan's astonishing ignorance of the most fundamental rules of exegesis, an ignorance which led him, as it has led many others, to magnify out of all proportion the difficulties found in the Bible. It is to be deplored that the basic notions had not been more clearly drilled into Renan. His teacher, M. Le Hir, was chiefly interested in Semitic philology, and in that field had covered himself with distinction,[21] but he knew little of a criticism which rested upon a sound notion of inspiration. Or let us rather say that Le Hir's lack of theology robbed his courses in exegesis of the solidarity which would have reassured young Renan, if indeed his reasons actually *were,* as he claims despite his youth, only "of a philological and critical nature" and in no way "metaphysical, political, and moral."[22]

P. Lagrange's superiority is not traceable to his greater mastery of philology (on which score he confessed, with surely too great a mod-

---

[20] Ἁρμονίη ἀφανὴς φανερῆς κρείττων, cited by P. Lagrange at the beginning of his *Gospel of Jesus Christ* (Paris, 1928).

[21] Jean Pommier, *La jeunesse clericale d'Ernest Renan,* I, p. iii: "La specialisation hébraique," pp. 393–555; in the same work, cf *Appendix B:* "Les oeuvres posthumes d' M. Le Hir," p. 657 ff.

[22] Despite his protestations, Renan's reasons for doubting were antecedent to his critical studies. "Long before he had begun exegesis, his faith had been destroyed by German philosophy. 'I assure you,' he wrote to a friend on January 24, 1842, before beginning his studies at Saint Sulpice, 'one whose faith is not firm has only to give himself to it in order to lose it entirely. I have never had so many difficulties, nor so many positive doubts.' And he declared that as he read the Bible, Pascal alone kept him on the slope whereon he felt himself slipping." Cf V. Giraud, "Catholicisme et positivisme," *Revue des Deux-Mondes* (1938), p. 369. J. Pommier in his *Renan d'après des documents inédits* (Paris, 1923), p. 35, is of the same mind: "It would be erroneous to think that at this time Renan had systematized his objections to the faith. He still believed, but how feebly! His faith had not been destroyed, it languished, like something deprived of food. It had then, quite naturally, been strongly shaken when it came into contact with philosophy." — It is true that the philosophy he had been taught at Issy was a kind of mitigated Cartesianism to which a dash of Scotch positivism had been added, and that his philosophical reading was completely disorganized. He himself confesses (*op. cit.,* p. 246) that German philosophy, which was just then coming into prominence, fascinated him strangely. — Cf *Souvenirs d'enfance,* p. 298.

esty, his incompetence),[23] but rather to the fact that with all his wide
culture and spirit of faith, he was guided by solid theological principles and by an exceptional kind of prudence. Although other scholars
like Zanecchia[24] and P. von Hummelauer,[25] and from the University
of Louvain, P. Ladeuze[26] and Van Hoonacker,[27] shared his views,
there is no question but that he was the first to bring them out into
the open in all their practical consequences. He thus paved the way
for a method of exegesis which is now almost universal among modern
Catholic exegetes.[28]

*   *   *

Once biblical inspiration was locked in with doctrine, there could
be no retreating from it. P. Lagrange had worked out the main lines
of a method which served him well, but he was far too intelligent to
be overconfident in his own judgment, which incidentally was very
good. He was too keen a theologian to overlook the fact that Holy
Scripture "is a deposit confided to the Church, which alone can decide
the extent of her control."[29]

---

[23] L. H. Vincent, *art. cit.,* p. 30.

[24] D. Zanecchia, *Divina inspiratio sacrarum Scripturarum ad mentem S. Thomae Aquinatis* (Rome, 1898).

[25] F. von Hummelauer, *Exegetisches zur Inspirationsfrage* (Freiburg i. Br., 1904); "Bibbia ed 'alta critica,'" *Civiltà cattolica,* 9 (1903), pp. 397–413.

[26] He later became bishop, and was rector of Louvain from 1909 to 1940.

[27] At the very height of the polemics touched off by *La méthode historique,* Van Hoonacker had prepared an important study of this problem; in the interests of peace, however, it was not published until 1941. Cf. *EphThLov,* 17 (1941), pp. 201–236. In it one perceives the harmony of thought between the professors of exegesis at Louvain and those of the School at Jerusalem. Cf J. Coppens, "L'enseignement de la théologie à l'Université de Louvain depuis sa restauration en 1834. L'Écriture Sainte," *Le V° centenaire de la Faculté de Théologie de l'Université de Louvain,* 1432–1932 (Bruges, 1932), pp. 21–47; *Le chanoine Alvin Van Hoonacker. Son enseignement, sa méthode et son oeuvre exégètiques* (Bruges-Paris, 1935); Paulin Ladeuze, *Orientalist en exegeet* 1870–1940 (Brussel, 1941).

[28] J. Chaine, "The Old Testament," *Père Lagrange and the Scriptures* (Milwaukee: The Bruce Publishing Co., 1947), p. 14: "Such sound Thomistic notions enabled P. Lagrange to establish a sound theological doctrine fitting admirably into the teaching of the Church. His considerable influence has given new life to the question; to be convinced of this one has only to leaf through a few treatises on inspiration."

[29] *RB* 1 (1892), p. 2. Returning some years later to the same idea, apropos of recent controversies concerning the Church's interpretation of the Holy Scripture, P. Lagrange wrote: "In the interpretation of Scripture, of course, the Church's right is not restricted to dogmas of the faith. It needs hardly to be said that her right cannot be less here than it is elsewhere; in the interpretation of Scripture, then, it extends to everything that is required for the preservation of the deposit of faith entrusted to her.

Catholic theology is here basically opposed to a fundamental Reformation principle voiced by Luther, that the Bible alone is the rule of Christian faith.[30] Such biblical exclusivism, expressed in principle at the Diet of Worms, satisfies neither the demands of Scripture, which teaches nothing of the sort, nor the practice of the leaders of the Christian community during the primitive period when oral teaching was most important.[31] In stressing apostolic *tradition,* the ancient Churches were stressing the *authority of the Apostles* and that of their successors. To acknowledge this historical fact is to admit implicitly that the teaching Church has the power to pronounce judgment on the meaning of Scripture as well as on the meaning of doctrines transmitted orally. All private interpretations, even those traceable to the charismatic Spirit, were and are subject to her.

All this is more than enough to prompt the charge that Catholic scholars are kept under wraps, so to speak, and are not free to take up any truly scientific work. P. Lagrange spoke of this on a number of occasions, notably in a lecture on "Exegesis and the Catholic Church," delivered in Paris in 1917 at the *Institut catholique.*[32] The

An exegete is consequently subject to her authority in all of his interpretations. If the Church makes a decision, she cannot possibly be mistaken as to the extent of her power." Cf *RB* 9 (1900), p. 138.

[30] Compare his words in the Foreword to the *Revue* (1 [1892], p. 5 f.): "Theologians were greatly astonished when Luther, summoned to the Diet of Worms by the Emperor Charles V, would not consider any argument that was not taken from the Bible. The Emperor agreed — a concession fraught with consequences. Thus restricted, Eck and his associates also appealed to the Bible, but Luther again refused to debate with them, as he would recognize only some of the books which they cited against him, as inspired. In one of those flights of mystical enthusiasm which have carried away so many Germans, he cried, "They must grant freedom to the 'Word.'" The Bible thus became, for Protestants, a unique rule of faith. So rapid was the movement that it took Catholic theologians some twenty years to react to the insistent alarms sounded by a host of Lutheran theologians, who with new interpretations always on their lips, were forever and on every occasion appealing to texts more or less well understood, whether taken from the originals or from versions. It was at this time that there began, not — as Protestants once asserted — the study of the Bible, but doubt concerning the Bible."

[31] D. Van den Eynde, *Les normes de l'enseignement chrétien dans la littérature patristique des trois premiers siècles* (Gembloux-Paris, 1933), pp. 51-76

[32] *Le sens du christianisme d'après l'exégèse allemande* (Paris, 1918), pp. 1-30. English translation: by W. S. Reilly, S.S.: *The Meaning of Christianity according to Luther and his Followers in Germany* (New York: Longmans, Green and Co., 1920), pp. 23-53.

problem is whether the Church, which claims authority over exegesis, is equipped to exercise her mission. That she was so prepared, he demonstrated both from the point of view of pure criticism and of faith.

Critical point of view: The Church has the proper mental attitude; her understanding of the texts is facilitated by a mental outlook which is the same as that of the men who wrote these texts. As for the supernatural, in which the New Testament was conceived, the Church not only has the same attitude as the first community but she *is* the same society and custodian of the same faith. In interpreting the New Testament she feels obliged to rely upon tradition and in fact history compels her to do so; it is perfectly obvious that the faith was first preached before anyone in the primitive Church thought of writing about it. The inspired writings therefore call for the complement of tradition. Finally, the exegesis of the Church has always been conspicuous for good sense and clarity in every instance where, in order to avoid the scriptural difficulties raised *against* her, she might easily have had recourse to subtle allegories or rabbinism.

From the point of view of the faith: The Church is helped by the Holy Spirit.

> For Catholic Christians, this is both *de fide* and logical. We believe that God has revealed himself to man, and that he assures him of the benefits of that revelation in the Church of Jesus Christ. He therefore saw to it that this revelation would be preserved intact. It is contained in the Sacred Books. It is then necessary that the Church be assisted in the faithful transmission of the meaning of God's word.[33]

The principal and only really decisive argument is the last, which presupposes that the theology of the Church rests upon the positive testimony of apostolic faith. The consideration of the Church in the New Testament crops up in his commentaries on the Gospels and on Paul's Epistles, and was a subject on which he liked to dwell. The period extending from the time of the Apostles to the postapostolic period was more or less Abbé Batiffol's domain; his studies in the *Revue biblique* led to a later work (*Église naissante et le catholicisme*)

---

[33] *Ibid.*, pp. 34–35.

in which he vindicated the Church's titles to be "a visible, universal society having for a framework her rule of faith and her hierarchy."[34]

Also to be taken into consideration, without either exaggeration or understatement, are the restrictions which the Church insists upon in matters of biblical interpretation.

The Church does not call upon her children to renounce rational methods; she respects the intelligence too much to do that, and she wishes to lead all sciences back to God who is their author — *Deus scientiarum Dominus*.[35] To P. Lagrange this made great sense. Pope Leo XIII had approved the idea of his School with its practical orientation and in his brief of September 17, 1892, had praised the usefulness of the enterprise, exhorting both the director and his fellow workers "to keep up their courage, and to rely upon his protection."[36] Their confidence was already high when Leo, two months later, issued his great biblical encyclical, the *Providentissimus Deus* (November 18, 1893),[37] containing a plan for biblical studies in the Church that was at once traditional and progressive. The program of the *École biblique* as sketched out in the Foreword of the *Revue* was already in step with it:

In demanding of Catholic biblical criticism that it be guided by her, the Church simply asks of exegesis what she asks of any science — namely, that it not overstep its own proper limits, and that it be content to remain a science or a method, not overestimating its conclusions nor making definitive syntheses out of what are after all only hypotheses. The Church, moreover, asks her exegetes to keep in mind those truths of Revelation which are contained in her doctrine, not so as to transform them into scientifically demonstrated truths,

---

34 Batiffol's work appeared in 1909 and was later completed in his *La Paix Constantinienne* (Paris, 1914); *Le catholicisme de S. Augustin* (Paris, 1920); *Le Siège Apostolique*, 359–451 (Paris, 1924).

35 Cf E. Gilson, *op. cit.*, p. 154 ff. Cf also *infra*, Chap. VI, p. 147 ff.

36 Cf the letter published in *RB* 2 (1893), p. 1: "This useful and important enterprise being at the same time so laborious, we command you and yours, beloved Son, to build up your confidence, trusting in our authority and approval."

37 *Ibid.*, 3 (1894), pp. 1–28. "The program sketched out in the Foreword of our *Revue* — to preserve the doctrine of biblical inerrancy and to seek solutions to difficulties in an exegesis at once traditional and progressive — seems to conform to the program which the Encyclical proposes with authority."

but because their scientific endeavors will thus be spared much wasted effort.[38]

Now, all this goes completely against the modernist view, according to which history and dogmatic tradition should, because so radically different, go their separate ways, each heedless of the other. But is complete independence the condition *sine qua non* of history? Not at all, observed P. Lagrange. Such a view is simply untenable.

> In all historical research the historian's autonomy is limited. Suppose I resolve to dig up the truth about Napoleon, and become convinced that he lost the battle of Jena. I shall not hesitate to say so in writing. But I would thus become a laughingstock. Some facts are so firmly established that no amount of individual research can budge them. One may indeed appeal to "History." But let me ask you this — is history the Truth which infallibly inspires its disciples? Point to your documents and monuments and, as often as you like, to your interpretations of both; none of these can alter a duly recognized historical fact. Some limits History imposes upon itself, others are extrinsic to it. For example, if all witnesses were agreed as to the date of an eclipse, no historian would maintain that it took place on another day than that computed by astronomers, whose calculations he might himself be in no position to check. Not that astronomy outweighs history, but it can keep an historian from making mistakes. Why should not something like this be allowed when it is a question of the testimony of the Church?[39]

For P. Lagrange, then, the authority of the Church was a pledge of his independence. It was charged that his exegetical conclusions were imposed upon him by dogma, that as a Catholic interpreter he could not be free or entirely objective. He admitted that such a danger might be real in a society which had only the Bible as its rule of faith, for in that case it would simply have to find all the truths it believed in Scripture. "Nothing like that happens in the Catholic Church. Why should she seek by subtle exegesis for what she can find in her tradition? Catholics can and must believe certain dogmas which may not appear in the Scripture, for example, the perpetual virginity of Mary. There is no need to do violence to the texts in order

---

38 On this, cf the decree *Lamentabili sane exitu* (July 3, 1907).
39 "Le decret 'Lamentabili sane exitu' et la critique historique," *RB* 16 (1907), p. 549.

to discover that belief; the texts themselves are not disturbed."[40]

However, it is a quite different matter when the dogma is already contained in the Bible. Particular dogmas, although hidden beneath the inspired letter, have later been given more explicit formulations in words unknown to the primitive Church. The temptation to exaggerate the clarity of teachings which are only implicitly expressed has brought many a biblical commentator to grief, in that he fails to do justice to the exact historical meaning of the words of the Bible. P. Lagrange successfully avoided this pitfall. The zealous interpreters who fail here resemble those who admit only those doctrines which are spelled out in Holy Scripture. His loyalty to the Church which is guided by the Holy Spirit allowed him to relax. But what if the divinity of Christ were not taught in the New Testament? Even then, he would answer, the Catholic exegete would not have to distort the texts; the living faith of the Church would assure him of the *fact*.[41]

It is clear, then, that both in his critical work and in theological matters, P. Lagrange's respect for the authority of the Church was his guiding light. He was not upset at the charge that he therefore lacked a scientific spirit. Time itself had shown the value of theories which some had hoped might lead him to reject the teaching of the Church. He was genuinely convinced that the Church's directives had saved him a great deal of time. The field still left open to his inquisitive mind was immense. Was it not a good thing to be enlightened from on high? He did not accept enlightenment blindly; such a clear-sighted theologian kept his eyes and his mind open. And the critic in him profited because he was able to see both the reasons for and the limits of the obligations imposed upon him.

*   *   *

Had it been only a matter of definitions expressly formulated by popes and councils, this discerning scholar would not have been beset by so many complicated problems.

The Church teaches that in matters of faith and morals one may

---

[40] Lagrange, *The Meaning of Christianity*, p. 39.
[41] *Ibid., p.* 40. Cf *infra*, Chap. VI, p. 157 ff.

not interpret Scripture in a manner that runs counter to tradition,[42] and that the unanimity of the Fathers, once established, constitutes an authority which must be treated with respect. P. Lagrange regarded such guidance a positive benefit, and one which in any other field would be cordially welcomed. To have the unanimity of the Fathers is to be in contact with Christian beginnings; why not use such testimony?[43]

> This method is one which recent and scientific exegesis, never satisfied with the sources or elements of its information, should be willing to honor. The only difference lies in the fact that the Church by preference inquires into the meaning of Christianity from those who, having first learned of it, embraced it. She clings tenaciously to the testimony of the ancients, especially to that of the Fathers who were the shepherds of small Christian communities, who were responsible for the doctrine, who kept in close touch with the other churches, and who were above all solicitous for the purity of that faith which is the pledge of eternal life.[44]

These lines show how clearly he understood the authority of the Fathers as witnesses to the faith, and also their limitations as authorities. To be binding, the Fathers must present not an absolute, but a morally unanimous front. With characteristic independence of mind, P. Lagrange observed that, aside from those cases in which the fundamentals of the faith were involved, "unanimous consent occurs much more rarely than one might expect if he listened to those who constantly appeal to the authority of all the Fathers."[45] The Fathers, then,

---

[42] Cf "Providentissimus Deus," *RB* 3 (1894), pp. 13 f. It is highly instructive to read, in this connexion, the *Divino Afflante*, § 7, which clarifies the relations between Catholic exegesis and ecclesiastical, patristic and other traditions.

[43] *Meaning of Christianity*, p. 42.

[44] *Loc. cit.*

[45] *La méthode historique, surtout à propos de l'AT* (Paris: Lecoffre, 1904); *Historical Criticism and the OT* (London: Catholic Truth Society, 1905), p. 128, translated by Edward Myers, M. A. (references henceforth will be to the English edition). "As you see, there is no question here of particular cases of exegesis, but of important points: *iis doctrinae capitibus*, not historical but doctrinal points, such as are considered everywhere and always as certain theological truths, which will rarely be the case in the interpretation of a text — so much so that Father Hummelauer has denied that there is any exegetical tradition at all for the whole book of Numbers, which is not one of the least important." Cf also Cornely, *Introductio*, I, 593: "We say that the Church has defined the sense of but very few texts, and even fewer of them are explained by the unanimous consent of the Fathers."

may speak as private doctors, and as such have first claim to consideration as private doctors after the Pope, even when he is not speaking
ex cathedra. As private doctors they no longer constitute a special theological *locus* for interpretation, but the principle holds and is of
prime importance.[46] It was obviously not to be applied in a hit-or-miss
fashion, or without a careful preliminary investigation, for otherwise
all standards would disappear and, equal normative value being given
to divergent opinions, chaos inevitably result.

We must now take a look at the exegetical methods of the Fathers,
if only to do justice to those who criticized P. Lagrange for departing
from traditional lines by his literal exegesis, so notably free of allegorical and mystical interpretation.[47] What is involved here is the matter
of the different senses (literal and spiritual) of the Bible. The LITERAL
sense is what is stated *directly* either in so many words (*prout littera
sonat*) or *figuratively* (by metaphor, for example). The MYSTICAL or
typical sense, usually called the SPIRITUAL sense, is to be found in the
persons or things directly described by the words. Thus the literal
sense of "Moses made a bronze serpent and set it on a pole; and if a
serpent bit any man, he would look at the bronze serpent and live"
(Nm 21:9) is clear from the words themselves. But when St. John
suggests (3:14 f.) that the serpent typified the Son of Man lifted up
on the cross, a spiritual or mystical sense, one not directly signified
by the text but by the type or thing described, is involved.[48]

Confusion become inevitable here if the SPIRITUAL sense is not kept
carefully distinguished from what is called the ACCOMMODATED (also
loosely referred to as "spiritual") sense. The accommodated sense is not

---

[46] Lagrange, *op. cit.*

[47] The August 20, 1941, reply of the Pontifical Biblical Commission to such criticisms
is a veritable defense of scientific exegesis. Cf *infra,* p. 145 ff.

[48] The distinction is set forth by St. Thomas. "God is the Author of Sacred Scripture.
It is in His power to signify His meaning, not by words only (man can do that),
but also by things [i.e., events] themselves. Hence, since in all sciences things are
signified by words, this science has the property that the things signified by the words
have themselves a meaning. That first meaning, by which the words signify things,
belongs to the historical or literal sense. That by which the things signified by words,
signify still other things, is said to be the spiritual sense; it is based upon and presupposes the literal sense." Cf *Sum. Theol.,* I, q. 1, a. 10, c.; cf also A. Fernandez,
"Hermeneutica," *Institutiones biblicae* (Rome: Pontifical Biblical Institute, 1929), I,
377–393.

really a sense of Scripture at all, but simply an expression of an author's personal views or imaginings; St. Thomas makes no mention of
it when treating of the genuine senses of Scripture. The distinction is
a necessary one, nevertheless, however much it was distasteful to a poet
like Claudel, who wrote, *"J'appelle un chat un chat, et un sein un sein"*
"I call a cat a cat, and a womb a womb. To make these words mean
anything else is to indulge in the figurative sense."[49] Yet along with
real types, the Bible contains many others based on mere verbal analogies. To reduce them all to one common denominator and to cram
them all into a single definition would make them appear to be little
more than afterthoughts. The Bible would gain nothing from this
but would lose much of its serious tone; it would moreover also lose
those genuine figures or types which were directly willed by God.

There are always devout men who long for a renewal of patristic
exegesis, and some of these have reproached the *École de Jérusalem*
for its lack of interest in the mysteries which lie hidden beneath the
inspired page. P. Lagrange may have meant to forestall objections
on this score when he discussed the allegorical procedures of the
ancients; his views here reveal his profound understanding of history.[50]

Although allegorical exegesis flourished at Alexandria it was not,
apparently, a specifically Christian creation. Long before the Apostles
began to preach the Gospel, the philosophers of old had discovered in
allegory an excellent way to bridge the gap between the fables of
paganism and the lofty concepts of philosophy.[51] Homer would have
been considered wicked had he not made use of allegories; thanks
to them, legends which would have cast discredit upon the gods and
contributed to the corruption of youth were given an acceptable meaning. Thus, Zeus became the artistic fire; Hera, the air; Poseidon, the
water. The struggles between the gods represented the eternal struggle

---

[49] Letter of Paul Claudel to P. Bernard, *RTh* 44 (1938), p. 788.

[50] See especially "L'interprétation de la Sainte Écriture par l'Église," *RB* 9 (1900),
pp. 135–142; *Historical Criticism, loc. cit.; Éclaircissement sur la Méthode historique,
à propos d'un livre du R. P. Delattre, S.J.,* Pro manuscripto (Paris: Lecoffre, 1905),
pp. 18–60; *Meaning of Christianity*, p. 37 ff.

[51] For the allegorical method employed by Greek philosophers, cf E. Zeller, *Die
Philosophie der Griechen,* III, 1, pp. 321–336; P. Heinisch, *Der Einfluss Philos auf die
älteste christliche Exegese* (Munster, 1908), p. 7 f.; J. B. Frey, "La Révelation d'après les
conceptions juives au temps de Jésus-Christ," *RB* 13 (1916), p. 504 f.

between virtue and vice, and their scandalous unions were only symbolic mixings of the elements. The philosophers thus met again in
Homer; they did not have to reject him — no one could have done
that — each one could interpret him in his own way.[52]

Alexandrian Jews, enamored of the charms of Hellenism, hastened
to use a method which might make the Bible more acceptable to those
who accused them of being a stubborn people, blindly attached to the
barbarous, improbable tales and superstitions found in their sacred
books. Allegory helped these Jews reconcile their beliefs with Greek
philosophy, and likewise afforded them arguments to prove that the
Bible was the font from which the great thinkers of Greece had im-
bibed their wisdom! Outstanding for this kind of exegesis was Philo.
His principles of interpretation allowed him to turn from the literal
meaning whenever he judged it to be unworthy of God.[53] Apparently
insoluble difficulties and in fact even ordinary truths were handled
similarly. Words could thus be given the freest of interpretations
without benefit of context. There was only one basic law — *look for
a deeper meaning.*[54]

Flourishing at Alexandria when Christianity began, allegorism is a
general "tendency to substitute metaphor or symbol for proper meanings, to impose arbitrary and far-fetched accommodations upon natural
meanings, or so-called spiritual meanings — authorized neither by tradition nor by the Scriptures — upon the literal sense."[55] That such a
course has its dangers is obvious. The man who thus dilutes the
historical content of the Bible differs little from one who bolsters up

---

[52] Lagrange, *Meaning of Christianity,* p. 26 f.; Frey, op. cit., p. 505 f.

[53] Cf S. Siegfried, *Philo von Alexandrien als Ausleger des AT* (Jena, 1875); Heinisch,
op. cit.; Frey, *op. cit.;* Lagrange, "Philon: méthode d'exégèse," *Judaisme avant Jésus-
Christ* (Paris: Gabalda, 1931), pp. 546–554.

[54] The following is Philo's interpretation of the story of the fall (Gn 2:25–3:7):
Adam represents the *nous* (mind or reason), Eve the *aisthesis* (bodily sense); both are
naked: the mind is not yet adorned with virtues, the senses are devoid of actual
perception. They know no shame because not exposed to the contrary influences of
the passions. The serpent is the symbol of lust, because, like the serpent, pleasure
insinuates itself by tortuous movements. Its opposite, the brazen serpent, represents
temperance. When the mind has been bitten by pleasure, the serpent of Eve, it should
then turn its gaze toward the serpent of Moses, and thus it will recover health and life.
Cf Philo, "Allegorical Interpretation of Genesis 2–3," *Loeb Classical Library,* I (New
York: G. P. Putnam's Sons, 1928), II, 53–81.

[55] F. Prat, *Origène* (collection *Pensée chrétienne,* Paris, 1907), p. 133.

human opinion by appealing to the authority of the inspired word.[56] But allegorical interpretation, connatural to the oriental mind with its penchant for symbol and figurative speech, made it possible to treat of the most profound mysteries in a concrete and imaginative way, and, as it dealt with religion under its most spiritual aspect, was marvelously suited to the soarings of those of a mystical frame of mind.

The welcome which the Alexandrian Christians accorded this manner of exposition is perfectly comprehensible, for, in one way or another, they were children of their times and of their land, and the method was both fitted to their mentality and familiar to them from usage. No one made a more extensive or freer use of the spiritual sense than Origen, the director of the famous *Didascalia*. He had established his school so as to provide converts in love with Hellenism with a catechetical instruction adapted to their intellectual needs. For him as for many others, there was one basic assumption, that truth should be not proposed in the same way to the *many* (or the "simple") as to the *enlightened* and the *perfect*.[57] Difficulties were resolved by

---

[56] It is sad but interesting to note that once he had lost the faith Loisy found in allegorical exegesis a way of reconciling his thought with the demands of his ministry (he was chaplain to the Dominican Sisters at Neuilly). Concerning a sermon he had preached at a First Communion, he wrote, "Four good Dominican Fathers heard my commentary on the story of Elias in the desert, receiving bread from the angel and marching in the strength of that bread *usque ad montem Dei*. These good Fathers might have been convinced that I am not averse to the spiritual senses of the Scripture, and in fact the Sisters must have told them that the seven conferences of the Retreat had been drawn from Exodus and the story of Samuel" (*Mémoires*, I, 492). Thus also, at the *Institut catholique* of Paris, Loisy had tried to reconcile his radical literal exegesis with what he called the "need for orthodoxy." "Out of a 'need for orthodoxy,'" we read in his *Mémoires* (I, 140), "for a prudently tolerant orthodoxy, I was teaching that Isaias 7 was messianic prophecy in a wide sense, in that it looked to a happy future for Juda and the Davidic monarchy, that it was rich, so to say, in providential applications, and that it admitted of a twofold accomplishment: one, literal in its immediate perspective, the other spiritual and more perfect, in its far-distant perspective, i.e., in its Christian interpretation. I baptized the first as historical, and called the second, as I have just said, spiritual and providential. Artificial and subtle? I would not disagree with you. Yet I did not alter the real meaning of the text, and considered the Christian application, basically, as mystical speculation."

Loisy's example shows the danger involved in confusing allegorical with traditional exegesis; it also indicates (the allegorists to the contrary notwithstanding) that literal exegesis based upon the rules mentioned above is more respectful of tradition. Some, of course, will go on thinking that literalism and radicalism go together, and for a long time to come allegorism will be confused with "the great tradition of the Fathers."

[57] Batiffol in his *L'Église naissante et le catholicisme*[18] (1927), p. 377, n. 2, points

an appeal to the spiritual sense, and one could thus reserve to some truths that were not disclosed to others for whom the primer of baptism was, presumably, sufficient. Origen held for the primacy of the spiritual over the literal sense, and shook free from the letter as quickly as he could, striking out for the heights.[58] He thus opened the door to all sorts of daring speculations. However, notwithstanding his undeniable genius and those remarkable critical works for which contemporary exegesis is still indebted to him, Origen was mistaken.[59] "In the end, Christianity could only with difficulty be recognized in his system, and then as a kind of compromise between *Gospel* and *Gnosis,* a theology wherein tradition was rather approached than incorporated, wherein even those elements which at first satisfied would, when singly considered, become disturbing the moment one took cognizance of them."[60] Despite his genius, therefore, the Church refused to follow Origen's lead, for she "holds it as indubitably true that Scripture always has a literal sense and that it is wrong to hold that the Bible contains only a spiritual sense."[61] The Church has been faithful to the norms of her belief — the literal sense and tradition. In her prudence, which modern scholars cannot but appreciate, P. Lagrange saw "decisive proof of her infallible tact in exegesis."[62] Her position presupposes a clear distinction between the two senses of Scripture, one which the early Fathers left more or less vague and did not all use to the same degree. SS. Gregory of Nyssa, Hilary of

---

out how exclusively Alexandrian and how little Christian is the theory that the knowledge obtained by allegory is more sublime than that which is given to simple believers. Cf also J. Lebreton, "Le désaccord de la foi populaire et de la théologie savante," *RHE* (1923), p. 506.

[58] Origen, *Peri Archon* (= *First Principles*), IV, 8–27.

[59] Lagrange, *Éclaircissement,* p. 25.

[60] L. Duchesne, *Histoire de l'Église* (Paris, 1907), I, 357.

[61] Lagrange, *op. cit.,* p. 26.

[62] *Meaning of Christianity,* p. 43: "If we had to give a decisive proof of the infallible tact of her exegesis, it would suffice to recall that she refused to have recourse to the too facile proceedings of allegory, which by a stroke of genius Origen hit upon as a means of extracting her from difficulties. . . . She saw in the Old Testament a prediction, almost a sketch of the kingdom of God founded by Jesus Christ. There were in the personages or the facts of that ancient history — as St. Paul clearly teaches — types or figures of the new covenant. There was offered an easy passage from these types to symbols emptied of reality, and how many difficulties at once disappeared! But in overcoming difficulties of detail, she would be exposed to a fatal danger. Criticism would not fail to heap scorn upon so convenient a subterfuge."

Poitiers, and Ambrose of Milan, for example, reflected the influence of Alexandria, while others like St. Basil preferred the literal school of Antioch, represented by St. John Chrysostom. Saints Jerome and Augustine merit separate consideration. They were not insensitive to the spiritual sense, but its charms were not alluring enough to win them away from the literal sense.

Beside their indulgence in allegory, the Fathers displayed a fondness for what we may call purely *accommodated senses*. This was due to the continuing influence of Alexandria and of those rabbinical schools which persisted into the Christian era. "The current process, called a *midrash* or investigation, was something more of an inquiry than an explanation or, to borrow a word from the Greeks, *exegesis*. We seek to understand the text; they asked of it what it did *not* mean, primarily, and then dug deeper than the letter, combining texts so as to interpret a word by the meaning which it had elsewhere; when these texts were not enough, they had recourse to allegory, which then became the meaning intended by God in the first place."[63]

The Church Fathers were the heirs of the Jewish schools, of a method which was, P. Lagrange observed, all the more attractive because it spelled freedom from the literalism of the Law.

> Christians considered the Law a dead letter, and it suffered by comparison with the Gospel. One could not become resigned to drawing so little fruit from a book inspired by God himself. To read the Law for edification's sake was a waste of time. And then, how was one to explain it to the faithful assembled in Church? If God had spoken, was it not for all ages? One therefore plunged recklessly into the quest for spiritual senses. The current teaching of the Church was held to be reflected in the Old Testament; more accurately, it shed light upon it and transfigured it. Filled with the Spirit of God, the Fathers again find that same Spirit, and perhaps also introduce it everywhere. They had a yearning for God, and communicated it to others. The Bible, with such a commentary, is as it were created anew, and filled with Christian sap.[64]

In itself, the fascination exercised upon the Fathers by the spiritual senses of the Old Testament — not to mention of the New, where

[63] *Historical Criticism*, p. 119.
[64] *Ibid.*, p. 120.

spiritual interpretation is rare — was legitimate. St. Paul assures us that certain persons and events of sacred history are types of the New Covenant.[65] Why become upset over accommodations, it can be argued, if they contribute to the edification of the faithful?

But — rules are rules and must be followed. The typical sense of *things* involves a hidden meaning which the mere examination of the letter will fail to discover, one that can only be gotten at by pious conjecture;[66] each case, therefore, will have to be resolved by those who speak in the name of the Holy Spirit. If we are not to confuse the Word of God with any purely human interpretation, it must be made clear that such creative or accommodational exegesis, as P. Lagrange styled it, is not advanced as being the real meaning of the text or substituted for the literal sense. And it is always imperative that the basic literal sense be established with exactitude.[67]

Did the early Fathers observe any such restrictions? P. Corluy, a cautious, prudent, and distinguished exegete, writes,

> The Fathers, prompted by the Holy Spirit, often used spiritual senses to help explain passages whose literal meaning seemed to be unworthy of God, arguing that the literal sense was divinely inspired in view of the spiritual sense attaching to it, and not for itself. . . . Their allegorical and spiritual explanations were frequently farfetched and rather improbable, but they clung to their method as the only way to safeguard the divine inspiration of certain unimportant passages of the Bible.[68]

Quite recently, P. Vaccari reproached both Origen and the Alexandrian School for their abusive use of allegory; although the School had great merit, it had a poor reputation among the ancients.[69]

The excesses just mentioned were due in large measure to the spirit

---

[65] 1 Cor 10:11; cf Gal 4:24.

[66] *Historical Criticism*, p. 122: "St. Thomas respects the right of the creating Spirit to teach us by *things* as well as by *words*. But if the mouthpiece of the Holy Spirit possess the secret of these lessons *taught by things,* and can thus give the true spiritual sense of certain passages, none other can penetrate it except by pious conjectures."

[67] *Sum. Theol.,* I, q. 1, a. 10, ad 1m: "In Sacred Scripture no confusion results, for all the senses are founded on the one, the literal, from which alone can any argument be drawn." Cf the letter from the Biblical Commission (August 20, 1941).

[68] *La Science catholique* (1893), p. 489, cited by P. Lagrange in *Éclaircissement,* p. 32 ff.

[69] *Institutiones Biblicae* (Rome, 1929), I, 327–349.

of the times and can be readily explained. The works in which these excesses occur are not notable for clear-cut distinctions between exegesis and edifying literature; the homilies are a good example of such a *genre*. Might not one say as much for other writings, in which biblical texts were used only as illustrations of other points? Obviously, for in theological discussions or in the definitions framed by the various Councils, strict argumentation became the order of the day, and the literal sense then automatically took first place.

These remarks show how much stock the early Fathers really put in allegory, and also provide an answer to the complaints made against the practical kind of exegesis given at the *École biblique de Jérusalem,* that the School had wandered far from "the great patristic tradition." In outlining his projected commentary on Sacred Scripture, P. Lagrange had clearly stated his purpose: to provide a literal explanation of a carefully established critical text and a good translation of the original text. A modest goal, to be sure, but one that happened to be most urgently needed.[70] He quotes P. Corluy, and goes on to ask, "Does anyone think that we can still use the means [allegorical explanations] which the Fathers thought to be the only way of safeguarding divine inspiration? Do we know which of the spiritual senses were willed by God? If we have recourse to the explanations — *at times farfetched and quite improbable* — given by the Fathers, what chance will we have of making our voice heard by the critics?"[71] He was thinking,

---

[70] "Projet d'un commentaire complet de l'Écriture Sainte," *RB* 9 (1900), p. 8 ff. The importance of the project did not escape Paul Claudel, as is evident from this passage from his *Introduction au Livre de Ruth* (Paris, 1938), p. 22 ff.: "Our Lord has himself been touched . . . has fingers put into his wounds. . . . The literal interpreter does no more than did the Apostles. From close up and from afar, and in a correct and complete perspective, he examines the entire history of our redemption. He uses his eyes, his fingers, heart, and mind. *This* is what has happened, *this* is the answer the texts make to a prudent interrogation, *this* is no story or imaginary speculation, *this* is that solid something the Christian ought first to learn to understand. Here is a holy and a magnificent task, and in these past years none more necessary or more urgent. To such a task P. Lagrange and his disciples have dedicated themselves, and their fruits are invaluable. . . . It is no exaggeration to say that Père Lagrange has been the Nehemias and the Eliasib in this . . . restoration of our exterior works. . . ."
Such remarks ought to be remembered when reading the reproaches Claudel directs against exegetes who draw from Scripture the thin milk which comes "from the dry breasts of the literal sense" (*ibid.,* p. 47).

[71] *Éclaircissement,* p. 33.

of course, of St. Thomas' principle that the only way a believer can argue with those who will not recognize the Church's authority or that of tradition, is from the literal meaning of the text.[72] P. Lagrange's theological position forced him to assume the burden of the defense. Spurning facile accommodations which cause only irritation, he resolved to adhere as closely as possible to the literal sense, and at the same time to determine more exactly than his predecessors ever had what the sacred writers had intended to affirm. In discharging this task he acknowledged his indebtedness to the teachings of the Fathers, but as the *accommodated* sense is not, properly speaking, a *scriptural* sense, the digressions of the Fathers along these lines are quite unimportant; what *is* important and valuable are the ancient teachers themselves. "The Fathers bear witness to ancient ideas and customs," he wrote. "Most of them lived in that Orient which we would so much like to know, and they lived there when it was much less changed than it is today. Their citations contain scraps of recensions or particular translations, precious flotsam of texts which have now vanished. Geography owes a great debt to Eusebius and St. Jerome. But what makes them really important is their dogmatic value."[73]

Was then P. Lagrange's type of exegesis, so avowedly dedicated to a search for the "humble literal sense," condemned to hobble along the ground and, in St. Jerome's words, doomed to "gnaw at the shell without tasting the kernel inside?"[74] So at least the proponents of an exaggerated allegorism maintained, and they would have been right *if* the inner fruit of Scripture were necessarily bound up with types and symbols. The passage in the *Providentissimus* in which Leo speaks of truths which, although contained somehow in the literal sense, surpass the powers and grasp of human reason, is sometimes understood in this way.[75] But the context does not justify so limited a meaning,

---

[72] *Sum. Theol., loc. cit.*

[73] "Projet d'un commentaire . . . ," *op. cit.,* p. 9.

[74] "Epist. 58 ad Paulinum, 9:1," *PL* 22:585. St. Gregory uses a like expression in his "Moralia," 20, 9, *PL* 77:149.

[75] "The language of the Bible is employed to express, under the inspiration of the Holy Spirit, many things which are beyond the power and scope of the reason of man — that is to say, divine mysteries and all that is related to them. There is sometimes in such passages a fullness and a hidden depth of meaning which the letter hardly expresses and the laws of interpretation hardly warrant. Moreover the literal sense

and the pontifical document appears to have had something more general in view, namely, those mysterious depths which are proper to the Word of God. The truths contained in this Word often surpass man's capacity to understand; they are ineffable, and they lead to consequences whose richness is not perceived at first glance. His dedication to the "humble literal meaning," with the help of God's grace and of the Church, drew P. Lagrange into these depths in a great spirit of faith.

"Once a man accepts the Scriptures as inspired," P. Lagrange wrote, "he must grant that they contain more than the obvious and purely literal sense"; for lack of a better term, he called this the *supraliteral* sense. "The author of all the Scriptures being the same, his thoughts can be explained, one by the other. Further, as the Revealer is also the Author of the Scriptures, the thought of the Scriptures can therefore be commented upon by the truths of Tradition. One does not reach this conclusion by taking a text in itself, but it appears to follow from being confronted with another truth which has been affirmed by the same Spirit of God."[76] This is to recognize the legitimacy of that theological reasoning which starts from the literal interpretation of the texts themselves. One might here object that however legitimate this method may be, it opens the door to caprice and the whims of private interpretation. Not at all, he replied: "the conclusion will be a certain one if the meaning extracted from the text in question is honestly drawn from the Scriptures or Tradition; but if it is *any* kind of meaning, we will indeed tumble into the endless and capricious hair-splitting of the rabbis,"[77]

In this careful exposition of his views P. Lagrange had suggested that literal exegesis does not wholly exhaust the substance of Scripture. He was himself always very exact in his interpretation; yet like a current through a high-tension wire, a sense of mystery, of something

---

itself frequently admits other senses, adapted to illustrate dogma or to confirm morality" (*EB* 93).

[76] *RB* 9 (1900), p. 141. Cf. Fr. Raymond E. Brown, S.S., "The History . . . of a *Sensus Plenior*," *CBQ* 15 (1953), 141–162, and "P. Lagrange and the *Sensus Plenior*," *ibid.*, 17 (1955), 451–455; P. Benoit, "La plénitude de sens des Livres sacrés," *RB* 67 (1960), 161–196.

[77] *RB* 9 (1900), p. 142.

lying beyond the letter, flows through his writings. Reread the introductions to his gospel commentaries, and note how he concludes the
Foreword to St. Luke:

> We are only too keenly aware of the fact that our readers will find
> this commentary more literary than theological. Always conscious of
> the sacred character of a book which has God for its author, we have
> to the best of our ability studied the style and humble grammatical
> meaning of sentences and even of words in an attempt to understand
> the *human* work which St. Luke set out to write. Nothing would
> please us more than that some theologian would take and use what
> we have done so as to penetrate more deeply into the meaning of the
> Word of God. *Non omnia possumus omnes.*[78]

There was little danger, then, that his literalist exegesis would be
infected by that dryness which characterized so many biblical works
of the past century and makes them now so difficult to read. What
his exegesis may have lost in originality and poetical verve, it made up
for by its greater erudition, its carefulness, its objectivity in the reconstruction of backgrounds, and its more *oriental* subtlety in explaining
the sacred writings.[79] This personal and literal approach, contrasting
sharply with many pious commentaries which appeared after the time
of St. Thomas, was like fresh air and light.[80] It was also a far cry
from that liberal exegesis which destroyed coherent systems only to
raise upon their ruins systems entirely new and fashioned to please
a rationalistic spirit. The *technique* employed by P. Lagrange did not
differ notably from that in vogue in such schools, but there was an
entirely different orientation to his research; under his hands the
sacred texts were rejuvenated on being brought into vital contact with

---

[78] *Évangile selon saint Luc* (Paris: Gabalda, 1921), p. ii. Cf. T. Worden, "The
Cinderella of Catholic Theology," *Scripture* 8 (1956), pp. 2–12.

[79] *Historical Criticism*, p. 125.

[80] *Ibid.*, p. 123: "The school of literal exegesis from the time of St. Thomas to the
beginning of the 19th century really stands isolated, a mere academic exercise. It
knows little history, and still less philology. And it has lost even that practical knowledge
of the ancient world and of the East which makes the writings of the Fathers such a
valuable mine of information even for the historical critic. No rationalist however
much aware he is of the importance of the recent enormous development of human
knowledge could, without losing face in the eyes of the learned world, decline to read
and reread St. Jerome. But he may quite safely leave in their dusty obscurity the innumerable folios written from the 14th to the 19th century. I name no names, lest I
hurt anyone's feelings."

their authors. The doctrine of inspiration, touched on briefly above, demanded nothing less than this: one must get at the thought of the sacred writers in order to enter into the thought of God Himself. Exegesis must consequently be, above all, a *true* interpretation, not a dissection of the texts but a faithful exposition of what the sacred writers wanted to say. This means that all passages in their books should be pondered, for they are organic parts of one and the same whole.[81]

*　　*　　*

While pursuing his plan to provide both in general and in detail the true meaning of the sacred texts, P. Lagrange had to face difficulties raised against inspiration and biblical inerrancy in general, and also against particular interpretations which involved points of dogmatic beliefs.

The laborious task of discussion will often necessitate studies which are disappointingly meager in result, but this is part of the theologian's task. Theology must see to it that the pearl beyond price, the treasure entrusted to the Church by Christ, pays dividends; at other times it must defend that treasure,[82] an arduous task (as Newman has shown so well), because of the particular situation in which revealed truth finds itself when confronted with error.[83] But this difficult undertaking is all the more urgent because the erroneous opinions

---

[81] *Meaning of Christianity.*

[82] *Sum. Theol.*, I, q. 1, a. 8: "Sacred doctrine, since it has no science above it, can dispute with one who denies its principles, arguing if the adversary admits some of those things which are obtained from divine revelation. Thus we can argue with heretics from texts in Holy Scripture, and against those who deny one article of faith, we can argue from another. If our opponent believes nothing of divine revelation, there is no longer any means of proving the articles of faith by reasoning, but only of answering his objections — if he has any — against the faith."

[83] "Personal Influence, the Means of Propagating the Truth" (January 22, 1832), *Oxford University Sermons* (New York: Longmans, Green & Co., 1918), pp. 88–91 *passim:* "First, every part of the Truth is novel to its opponent; and seen detached from the whole, becomes an objection . . . next, men who investigate in this merely intellectual way, without sufficient basis and guidance in their personal virtue, are bound by no fears or delicacy. . . . The warfare between Error and Truth is necessarily advantageous to the former from its very nature, as being conducted by set speech or treatise; and this, not only for a reason already designated — the deficiency of Truth in the power of eloquence and even of words — but moreover from the very neatness and definiteness of method required in a written or spoken argument. . . . The exhibitions of the Reason, being in their operation separable from the person furnishing them, possess little or no responsibility. . . ."

which scholars may advance in the name of criticism seem somehow always to leave the upper rooms of the wise and find their way into the marketplace, where they are sure to find willing ears.

The successful execution of this delicate task called for a keen mind and literary skill, and Père Lagrange, a good Thomist and no stranger to the *philosophia perennis,* was well fitted for it. He knew the value of analogy and how to penetrate to the "forms" of things.[84] He was forearmed against theories which demanded the arbitrary dissection of the text, or rested upon hasty generalizations based on accidental differences or similarities; nor was he to be taken in by the confusing and equivocal patronage of biblical criticism and the comparative history of religions. His solutions to biblical problems were quite satisfactory, but not rigid. In the field of New Testament study alone, for example, he gave an excellent explanation of the Synoptic Problem, establishing the literary dependence of the *Greek Matthew* and of *Luke,* or *Mark* and *Matthew Aramaic.* And he restated the argument for the Johannine authenticity of the Fourth Gospel, ably strengthening it by combining in his argument the testimony of the book and the voice of tradition. Reacting against the cavalier fashion in which Liberal Protestantism had rid itself of embarrassing texts only to create a Christianity after its own image, he insisted upon Jesus' supernatural claims. Against the eschatologists, always so eager to trace the institution of the Church and the most profound of Paul's ideas to an "illusion," he presented the Kingdom of God as something at once present and future, inward and yet externalized, according to its successive stages and its various aspects. His commentary on Galatians was a refutation of Baur's famous "antagonism" between the Christianity of the dispersion (supposedly represented by Paul), and that of the apostolic community of Jerusalem. Finally, for we cannot go into great detail here, he reacted against the theory of sources and redactional strata borrowed from the Old Testament criticism, and upheld the basic unity of the Gospel and the Christianity of the Apostles.[85]

---

[84] Cf M. B. Allo, "Le Père Lagrange théologien," *RTh* 44 (1938), p. 433 f.

[85] In *M. Loisy et le modernisme* (p. 179), he thus sums up his thought: "When a document presents itself as a unique work, it may be possible to detect its different authors if the different parts are conflicting, and are joined to others so as to form continuities which were cut up and redistributed in order to make up one single history. But if

Thomistic principles and training also served P. Lagrange well in handling the matter of development of doctrine within the Church. He took a definite stand against that popular theory of evolution which postulates a substantial transformation of revealed doctrine, implying, as Loisy would say, the relativity of both dogmatic formulas and of ecclesiastical authority. The first two conferences of *La Méthode historique,* of which we shall later have occasion to speak, take up this problem at some length. While maintaining that the New Testament revelation was definitive and absolute, P. Lagrange conceded that changes have, over the span of centuries, occurred in the Church's teaching. A persisting identity, however, does not exclude variety or progress, and, as he went on to show, such progress need not have involved either alteration in the apostolic teaching or the addition of doctrines which in the beginning were completely unknown. The progress which he discerned in the history of revealed doctrines brought two things into harmony: stable principles, without which the perpetuity of the faith was inconceivable, and a certain elasticity necessary to make them intelligible to every age by a more accurate presentation of the basic facts, and by a more profound penetration of their potential.[86]

As P. Lagrange saw it, there lies before the theologian the task of adapting the historical methods, so admirably developed in our times, to the service of the Bible, "just as the Middle Ages incorporated into theology the principles of faith and of philosophy."[87] He proves by several good examples that the use of these resources enable the theologian to know Revelation better, for the continuity of the Church's teaching appears more clearly when its dogmas, which today are pro-

---

the work itself is defective, it would be sophistic to identify the different sources according to an uncertain evolution. In such a hypothesis, historical criticism would be surrendering to philosophical prejudice. Let us hope for the sake of critical honor that the critics will not commit such an error of judgment. It is begging the question to distribute the sources according to a preconceived theory of the chronology of ideas, and then to establish the evolution according to these sources."

[86] He returned to this subject in connection with J. Guitton's *La philosophie de Newman. Essai sur l'idée de développement* (Paris, 1933), and quotes the author with satisfaction: "The truth of a doctrine arises from the fact that in it growth and variety, which are signs of life, are united to permanence in identity, which are characteristics of essences" (p. 197).

[87] *Historical Criticism,* p. 60.

posed to us in their full flowering, as also studied in their most primitive stages of germ or bud. "The historian," he said, "is like a painter. He likes to sketch in succession and with exactitude the acorn, the young oak, and the king of the forests."[88]

But he did not forget that comparison is not reason, and that in order to get to the bottom of things one has to make a preliminary and basic distinction between the Old and New Testaments. In the New Testament, dogma has reached its definitive stage in that, from the time of the Apostles on, no new revelation has come to add anything essential to the theme of Redemption. In the Old Testament, on the contrary, dogma evolved in some of its essential points. Although its basis was divine Revelation, the stable element of all later progress, the Old Testament was a record of the successive stages traversed by the Jews before they reached the transcendent monotheism of the time of Christ.[89] In thus strongly emphasizing the line dividing the two Testaments, P. Lagrange was not inclined to adopt Marcion's view that the Old Testament is of no value or interest to us. He instead made it abundantly clear that with the revelation of Jesus Christ mankind had entered upon an entirely new phase, not the natural flowering of Judaism but one that was brought about by the special intervention of God.[90]

This distinction duly established, the duties of the historian toward the Bible are easily spelled out. It is an indisputable principle of St. Thomas that the Old Testament is a light which increases; hence, even though certain settled attitudes may thereby be rudely jostled, it must be shown (for theology worthy of the name cannot refuse a respectful exegete the use of nuances) how that light grew. As for the New Testament, it is necessary to understand it well both in its fullness and in its details, as did the first readers of the Gospels and the Epistles. One must try to rediscover, in their first freshness, the sources of living water which Jesus' words caused to flow upon the world.

Having thus cleared the road, P. Lagrange was able to advance his

---

[88] *Ibid.*, p. 66.
[89] *Ibid.*, p. 67.
[90] *Ibid.*, p. 69 f.

reasons for believing. His studies had often led him to uncover faulty reasoning behind various critical systems, and there emerged from his explanations of these systems the elements of an almost complete demonstration. He refrained from "assembling what was best in them in an eclectic manner, as if to honor the Church for having always taught that best." "This might appear to be begging the question, for by hypothesis the best would already be what the Church taught."[91] Still he could and did point out that what had appealed to people in each of these systems was already contained in the ecclesiastical magisterium.[92] The antiquity of the Gospels, the moral perfection of Jesus, His messianic consciousness and claims to equality with God, the incomparable elevation of His teaching, the existence of witnesses to His life who were commissioned to succeed Him, the existence of the first apostolic communities and of the cult which they rendered to Christ as God — on all these fronts, once the occasions of acrid controversy, criticism had in the end been forced to yield ground. The points thus gained are enough to justify the claims which the Catholic faith makes — not because she wishes forcibly to impose herself as evidence that is directly verifiable, but in order that she might present herself as a supernatural light which anyone might with perfect reason welcome, or at least hope one day to find.

---

[91] M. Loisy et le modernisme, p. 243.
[92] Loc. cit.

CHAPTER III

TRIALS AND STRUGGLES

In P. Lagrange, a scholar and theologian of unusual talents, knowledge and faith, the two fonts of Christian learning, were marvelously balanced and blended. He was a student of outstanding value. Fully conversant with all biblical problems, he was also a master of the techniques of scientific investigation. He was, moreover, able to integrate his prodigious labors with his faith in God, not only by demonstrating that science does not contradict faith — in itself, this would not have sufficed — but by taking an active part in a modern effort aimed at the better understanding of both the Old and the New Testaments. A theologian of remarkable depth and a man of deep faith and ardent piety, he was docile as a child to the teachings of the Church which he had made his own during long hours of prayer. In all his critical work his theological training was put to good use.

This inward balance of knowledge and faith accounted for his great serenity. Those who knew him were impressed by his air of peace, and Pierre Loti, one of the many who made their way to the simple parlor at St. Étienne for a visit with him, made a point of mentioning it. More recently still, Gabriel Hanotaux:

> Several of the Fathers, P. Lagrange, my confrère at the Academy of *sciences coloniales* (*sic!*) among them, were on hand to extend us a warm welcome. This great scholar knows all there is to know about Christian beginnings. During my visit at the convent, beneath the high-vaulted ceiling of this Church of France, and in the library where for many years rare books have been gathered so that one might learn of God, it seemed as if some pleasant, peaceful light was being poured out about us. The leaded windows of white glass, the white beards,

the white robes, everything produced in us the relaxing, tranquil certainty of those whose lives are spent in the search for the truth and in the performance of good. What discordant doubt would dare raise its head in this splendid harmony? These men are heirs to centuries of witnesses, with St. Paul and St. Jerome standing at the head of the list; these men are the continuation of that list. They have received and hand on both what has been said and what cannot be uttered. A word of praise arose to my lips, but he broke in, "Work and prayer . . . what more can one ask of God?" And hardly had I begun to speak again when he said, clearly and distinctly: "To lead to heaven those whom one loves."[1]

White windows, white beards, white robes. . . . One might suppose that P. Lagrange had accomplished all that he did smoothly, without encountering the least difficulty.

It was not like that at all.

Besides the financial worries which plague all such foundations, he experienced a form of adversity which a conscientious Catholic scholar finds particularly difficult to endure.

The brilliance which sparkled in his teaching and was later to find expression in his writings ran counter to too many deep-seated habits, and disturbed too many in their peaceful slumber, not to provoke reactions. In launching the *Revue biblique* he had plainly stated his general position:

There are some [he wrote] who hang on grimly to traditional ideas, while others almost instinctively tend toward novelty. (It is to be understood that we are not speaking here of anything touching upon faith or morals.) If *conservative* refers to those who abandon an ancient opinion only when forced to do so by the evidence uncovered by discoveries made by others, one must hold these conservatives to lack moderation, inasmuch as they exclude from their own labors not only change, but also that progress in the light which the Church has always cherished. And those liberals who have an antecedent and marked preference for new opinions are likewise lacking in prudence, and in their turn detract just as much from the dignity of Christian exegesis. The proper mean is to search for the truth and after due reflection to choose the most probable opinion, taking the tradition of the ancient Church into consideration as something which is of great

[1] "Regards sur l'Égypte et la Palestine," *Revue des Deux-Mondes*, 4 (August 15, 1928), p. 870.

value. Here again I presuppose that no question is involved touching on the authority of the Church.[2]

Nothing could have been more soberly stated. But not everyone agreed that respect for tradition can be allied with progress, or that the defense of the faith can go hand in hand with freedom of scientific research. From here it was but a step to the arousing of fear on the one hand, and offense on the other.

We have pointed out how during Renan's time Catholic exegetes had in general adopted an attitude of passive defense. P. Lagrange resolved to take his place in the forefront of every research project that touched upon the Bible. But there were others who had also been reared in the Catholic fold and who also emphatically and repeatedly appealed to the progress made by historical criticism, under the veil of pseudonyms which gave the impression that they were many in number;[3] and they declared that if a modicum of Christian truth acceptable to a critical mind were to be saved, it was imperative that the ground be drastically cleared of the weeds which were choking it.

By "clearing the ground" Loisy meant nothing less than a rejection of the entire "past" of the Church, of Christ Himself, and even of the personal God of the Bible, by a painless transformation which while safeguarding appearances, would in the end transform all dogmas into pure symbols. He openly broke with the Church in 1908, but as early as 1883 he had let it be known that he wished to get rid of the ballast in order "to refloat the barque of Peter, now gashed fore and aft by philosophy, the sciences, and history."[4] The influence of Renan, who

---

[2] *RB* 1 (1892), p. 10 f.

[3] M. Turmel began his work of destruction under the names of Herzog and de Dupin; A. Loisy used the pseudonyms of A. Firmin, Molandre, F. Jacobé, Jacques Simon, Isidore Deprès, Étienne Sharp, Jean Lataix, and Jean de la Rochelle. He explains why in a letter (November 22, 1898): "As for the big task (apologetics), I shall cut it up as much as possible into small morsels, using a false name; since no one suspects that I am so occupied with theological matters, no one will guess whence it comes" (*Mémoires* [Paris, 1930], I, 501). — Cf *M. Loisy et le modernisme:* "La guerre masquée," pp. 87–101. P. L. Couchoud has faithfully followed the same method (cf. "Christianisme").

[4] The year 1883 marks the appearance of the "Dialogue entre l'Église et un jeune savant" (cf *Mémoires,* I, 120–126). Loisy concluded: "One will note that the author has already read a bit of Renan." The objections which the young scholar advances are those which plagued him at the beginning of his lectures at the *Institut catholique* of Paris. Here is a sample: "Jerusalem, Babylon, and Persia, Alexandria have furnished

had been his teacher from 1882 to 1885,[5] is seen in his appealing to criticism for the verdict. But his philosophy weighed heavily in his critical balance.[6] All his life Loisy looked upon progressive relativity as *the* basic truth. Everything changes, he argued. The Church has changed and so have dogmas, and they must change again in order to keep in step with the human mind, which is itself subject to the law of change.[7] Soon after leaving the seminary Renan left the Church, thinking reform to be impossible; Loisy chose to remain within the fold so as to be able to work from inside, to induce this Church (which he insisted on calling his mother)[8] to deny her supernatural origin,

---

you with your *Credo;* you have harmonized it with Aristotle's philosophy, and the result is a very imposing monument. But you should realize as we do that the edifice is very cold and dark, that in more than one place it is about to crumble; it is built upon sand. Kant, a German whose name you have doubtless heard, has destroyed metaphysics. Your creation and your deluge have been found upon the brick tablets of Niniveh. The Jews have borrowed the angels and demons from Persia, thus supplying you with something to put in your heaven and your hell. . . . Your gospel announces the appearance of the Kingdom of God upon earth. . . . Since you have seen nothing appear, you indefinitely delayed the time for its perfect establishment. Thus did you begin to take root here below. . . . Your origin would be divine, if only the account you have given us were true. But we have found that your story is a tissue of fables. . . . Our philosophy, our sciences, and our history have pierced the old barque of Peter through and through. In another minute you will sink, and your best friends will be unable to save you" (*ibid.,* p. 122).

[5] *Ibid.,* pp. 132–136.

[6] Cf Jean Guitton, *La pensée moderne et le catholicisme* (2nd collection, 1st series, 1935–1936, Aix-en-Provence, 1936), pp. 88–124. The author shows clearly (p. 89) that "From the outset of his intellectual career, Loisy hesitates over the capital question, whether God is distinct from nature, or mingled with it. He hesitates; more than that, he makes it more or less axiomatic that while faith distinguishes between God and nature, unaided reason tends to pantheism." — How imperceptibly he passes from a denial of God's transcendence to the cult of humanity; "a transposition by degradation and corruption of the Christian idea" is what next occupies him (see p. 101 ff.).

[7] "No doctrine is unchangeable. A doctrine that is contradicted either is destroyed by the contradiction, or is transformed in order to avoid it. Thus tomorrow's orthodoxy is not today's, but will be a hybrid result of this orthodoxy and today's heresy. Orthodoxy is one of the myths upon which traditional Christianity rests; one cannot say that the myth is productive of good. Theological illusion or prejudice affirm the immutability of a mutable thing, i.e., of one that has never stopped defining itself and which determines itself, i.e., which changes indefinitely, according to the temporal need and opportunity" (*Mémoires,* I, p. 35). These ideas had already been expressed by the "young savant" in 1883 (*ibid.,* p. 124 f.).

[8] Long after he had lost his faith in Jesus' divinity, Loisy continued to remain in the Church, which to him seemed to be the society best able to advance the moral progress of humanity. P. Lagrange put his finger on this inconsistency of Loisy's thought: "In a way his attachment to the Church was sincere, for the Church was

her mission to the world, and the truths which had been confided to her care.

The difference in positions is more clear-cut today than in the years 1900–1910, when the Modernist crisis was coming to a head. The critical methods which P. Lagrange was trying to restore to a place of honor in the Church's service had not yet proven their worth; indeed, to a superficial eye they were not unlike the ones patronized by rationalistic or rationalizing scholars.

*   *   *

The first flurry of excitement was connected with discussions about the oldest books of the Bible, the Pentateuch (or, if Josue is included, the Hexateuch). When the *Revue biblique* began, the theory about the formation of these books was about to receive, from Wellhausen,[9] what we might almost call its classical statement. Basic to it was the hypothesis of four principal sources: the Yahwist (J), the Elohist (E), the Deuteronomist (D), and the Priestly or Sacerdotal Code (P). J and E were assigned a date between the ninth and eighth centuries; P, one from the time of the Exile (586–538 B.C.). Between the two extremes was the Deuteronomist, given a date sometime before the reform of Josias (621 B.C.). As if by accident the most striking texts of the ancient religion of Israel fell into the evolutionary pattern in vogue at the time among the historians of comparative religion, who were then preoccupied in plotting the curve of man's religious development. Beginning, as we have seen, with animism and passing through polydemonism, polytheism, and henotheism, they reached a

---

still, in his eyes, humanity's best chance to raise or to maintain itself at a certain moral level. He thus satisfied his positive humanitarian instinct." In contrast to Luther, who based everything on the word of God, or to Harnack who maintained the autonomy of a religious conscience illumined by that of Jesus, "if Loisy had renounced the Church, he would have had nothing left. He therefore made it a point of honor not to leave the Church, but clung to it. The great picture he had in mind included a great society, and it was important that it appear to contain that Church whose past had been so glorious, and of which he had been a minister. If there were no Church, there would be no work for him to do, and his message pointless" (*M. Loisy et le modernisme,* p. 142).

[9] *Die Composition des Hexateuchs* (first in articles, 1876–1877, then in book form 1885, 1889–1899). Cf J. Coppens, *The Old Testament and the Critics,* translated by E. A. Ryan, S.J., and E. W. Tribbe, S.J. (Paterson: St. Anthony Guild Press, 1942), p. 25 ff.

transcendent monotheism. Based on "a philosophy of religion as sure of itself as that found in the *Discours sur l'histoire universelle,* the whole system appeared to be a declaration of war against revelation. Apologists who came to grips with it emphasized its dangerous aspects and, in the face of such peril, considered any concession to it to be compromise; they also felt that conclusions resulting from such an examination of the texts should be ignored."[10]

Oddly enough, the critics had been set on their path by Jean Astruc, a Catholic doctor who died in 1766 at Paris. His famous *Conjectures sur les mémoires dont il parait que Moïse s'est servi pour composer le livre de la Genèse,*[11] was supported by arguments too well known to need repeating here. Whole sections were characterized by their use of the divine names of *Yahweh* or *Elohim;* there were doublets and parallel accounts, each with its own style and tone; and, in particular, there were different laws in regard to the same matters. Did a defense of the traditional Mosaic authenticity of the Pentateuch require the rejection, *en bloc,* of all these facts?

Thus matters stood when the Fourth International Scientific Catholic Congress opened in Fribourg, Switzerland, in August, 1897.

The second half of the Congress, presided over by P. Lagrange, was devoted to biblical affairs. P. Semeria first read a long memoir on Baron von Hügel, setting forth the state of the problem.[12] P. Lagrange then left the president's chair and took his place at the lectern. Without going deeply into the intricacies of the problem, he took up certain preliminary questions which would have first to be answered before anything else could be done.[13] Briefly, he laid before the assembly this consideration, that in Moses we encounter two traditions of unequal value. According to the one, Moses was the first lawgiver of Israel, and Mosaism basic to the entire history of Gods' people. The second tradition, of a literary order, simply asked: "Did Moses draw up the

---

[10] Cf Dom Chamard's article in the *Univers* (April 28, 1887).

[11] Bruxelles, chez Fricx, Imprimeur de Sa Majesté, vis-à-vis l'Église de la Madelaine (*sic*), 1753.

[12] Cf *Compte rendu du quatrième congrès scientifique international des catholiques, tenu a Fribourg (Suisse)* from August 16–20, 1897. Second section: *Sciences exégètiques* (Fribourg, 1898), pp. 231–265.

[13] *Ibid.,* pp. 179–200, and *RB* 7 (1898), pp. 10–32.

Pentateuch as we now have it?" That Israel's history cannot be explained apart from his legislative work is a proven fact. "The Bible would no longer be the history of salvation if it falsified history here, and faith is endangered when the main facts concerning the Kingdom of God are called into question. But all the arguments of prudent historical criticism impel us to ascribe to Moses the historical role with which tradition has invested him." Does it follow that Moses personally, *propria manu*, wrote the entire Pentateuch? P. Lagrange thought not, pointing out how the ancient Semites wrote history, and citing certain current juridical fictions in the fields of legislation and jurisprudence. To have been the author of a set of laws it was not necessary, he thought, either that Moses had personally written everything or sanctioned it by his signature. Human legislation, because it does not deal with man as he is in himself, that is, in his metaphysical being, *must* evolve, for it deals with concrete historical man who lives in an environment that changes with the times. Successive redactions based on the same fundamental principles, along with additions and modifications in detail rendered necessary by new conditions, would not therefore have *altered* the primitive body of legislation.[14] As long as these developments were the natural extension of the primitive Mosaic legislation, their authority derived from that of the first lawgiver. The phrase "God said to Moses" means therefore that "this law emanated from the divine authority [since it is] according to the mind of the first lawgiver."

It therefore seemed reasonable to P. Lagrange to view the documentary theory with favor, provided that certain important reservations were made. (The apologetes viewed the theory with much suspicion). Assigning to E and J a date around the time of the Exodus, he thought that they comprised texts written by Moses, together with older sections dealing with the history of the patriarchs as well. Our Deuteronomy then represented the end of a long development, and the Priestly Code or Leviticus was a more or less idealized summary of the religious institutions of Israel. Moses was the author of Deuteronomy, which was a résumé of the Book of the Covenant also written by him. "In the same way the *Institutes of Justinian* (A.D. 534)

---

[14] *Ibid.*, p. 18 f.

might well be termed the *Institutes* of [the earlier] Gaius, were there not many more differences between them, due to the influence of Christian ideas."[15] Moses was also the author of P, for this was a résumé of J and E plus certain additions which did not change its historical meaning.[16] P. Lagrange thus allowed considerable room for later redactions. Since, however, these enhanced the value of the more ancient elements which were from the time of Moses, he felt that tradition had after all not done badly in ascribing the entire Pentateuch — primitive core and later developments both — to the pen of Moses.

This résumé of his views, here reduced to the barest of outlines, contained a number of interesting comments on such subjects as the redaction of the Sacred Books, the evolution of laws, biblical testimony, and tradition. All these points P. Lagrange intended to take up more exhaustively in his future commentary on Genesis. His remarks about the sources of the Pentateuch were favorably received by one of the largest audiences to assemble at the Fribourg meeting, but severe criticism greeted the appearance of his articles along these lines in the *Revue biblique* some months later. In a magazine called *Études*,[17] it was implied that P. Lagrange had not expressed his real mind on the matter, that he was bent on a work of sheer destruction, and had given no indication of how he proposed to replace what he was destroying.

The attack subsided for a time but erupted with fresh violence in 1902, the year of his conferences on the historical method at the *Institut catholique* of Toulouse. These conferences were published the following year in a slender volume of the *Études bibliques*.[18]

[15] *Historical Criticism and the Old Testament*, tr. by Edward Myers, M.A. (London: Catholic Truth Society, 1905), p. 173 f.

[16] *RB* 7 (1898), p. 29 ff.

[17] Cf the issues of October and November 5, 1898. P. Méchineau writes: "It is not without some surprise that we have seen some of our brethren in the faith going over to a camp which until now we have regarded as the camp of the enemy. Some console themselves by thinking rightly or wrongly that these deserters were not theologians, and consequently their adhesion to the documentary theory was no reason for consternation among Catholics. But this answer, if ever valid, no longer holds, for we cannot say that the eminent Director of the *Revue biblique* [Lagrange] does not wield with equal dexterity the weapons of theology and criticism. The defection of such valuable men to the camp of our opponents has disturbed some very excellent people." (Cf *M. Loisy et le modernisme*, p. 102 f.).

[18] *Historical Criticism*, cf. note 15.

For readers of the *Revue biblique* the ideas expressed in this book were not particularly novel. Now however they were presented in a simplified, synthetic form, each article closely articulated with the others, with all technical discussion put to one side. He treated of critical exegesis and the teachings of the Church, the evolution of revealed truths in the Old Testament, inspiration and the findings of biblical criticism, solutions of difficulties raised by science, the weaknesses of a defensive concordism,* the historical character of the civil legislation of the Hebrews, and its adaptation to diverse times and circumstances. Finally he took up the historical character of the prepatriarchal traditions. These latter subjects corresponded to those he had brought up at the Congress at Fribourg, while the others established the bases for a Catholic biblical criticism along the lines of the program traced out in the introduction of the *Revue biblique* and in the "projected commentary." Now for the first time, the Master set before the general public what were, on the whole, his personal views. He was possibly ill-advised in this. Merely to have excluded women from the audience at Toulouse — only ten of them were given special permission to attend[19] — was not precaution enough to forestall the misunderstandings which his seemingly daring applications were almost certain to arouse.

If the conferences at Toulouse created quite a stir, their appearance in print touched off a wave of public protest. [20]

Many who heard P. Lagrange on that day and others who later read his book were deeply grateful to him for having thus provided them with certain rational, theologically sound, carefully tested principles which could be used when dealing with problems dangerous to the faith. Some were the more grateful in that they were exposed to the contagion of schools steeped in sheer rationalism.[21] P. Lagrange

---

* Concordism is an attempt to prove that a strict harmony prevails between Scripture and the positive sciences, especially geology, biology, anthropology, as if the Bible were some sort of master blueprint of all science. All such attempts have foundered; the Bible is not a textbook of science, but a record of revelation and of salvation.

[19] *M. Loisy et le modernisme, loc. cit.*

[20] *Loc. cit.:* "Complaints were lodged with the Archbishop concerning the novelty of the doctrine. Bishop Germain attended the fifth conference, taking it upon himself to show his goodwill toward me, and to calm the discontented ones."

[21] After briefly describing the contents of the six conferences, Canon Maisonneuve

had had such people chiefly in mind when he said at Fribourg, "In times like ours one can no longer remain inactive without compromising the salvation of souls, and alienating from the Church the intellectual forces which remain faithful to her. By marching forward one can gain many others."[22] This statement speaks more perhaps for his optimism than for his prudence, and one's judgment of it will depend on whether he is, by temperament or habit, inclined toward time-honored solutions or toward progress. P. Lagrange was convinced that mental stagnation was more harmful to souls than progress in knowledge, but he was also mindful of the principle of authority with which the Church is divinely invested. A good scholar should be willing to correct what mature examination has shown to be inexact or even uncertain. His brief application to the historical books of the principle of "sensible appearances" — a helpful principle when treating of the so-called scientific errors in the Bible — was merely a minor point[23] which could be quickly rectified without necessitating

wrote: "One might wish there had been greater clarity on many points, one might raise doubts, point out difficulties, object to certain special applications. One can attempt and adopt *other* interpretations of this verse or that biblical fact than those which P. Lagrange has adopted. Some will perhaps have reservations on the score of the principles themselves. . . . Yet I feel that the historical method, in its broad lines, is necessary; it is very difficult and delicate to manage, and not everyone can handle it. Before all else it calls for a deep, rich erudition, a knowledge of the idioms, archaeology, and epigraphy of the Orient. On the other hand, an exegete cannot do without theology, which will help him direct and verify his theories. Lastly and above all, an exegete should be a man endowed with penetration, prudence, calm, and clarity. And if you add to all these qualities a sharp mind, a soberness of language enlivened now and then with an ironic aside, a clear style which courses after ideas and subject matter wherever they twist and turn, an elegant simplicity and strength of mind beneath the reserved expression, and finally, if above all else you add a deeply religious soul whose sole aim is to make the faith better informed, more profound and more docile — then you have a portrait of Père Lagrange. His audience followed him with sympathy and interest, and the Archbishop of Toulouse, wishing to extend to P. Lagrange and to his Order a delicate mark of his benevolence, attended the [fifth] lecture" (*Revue du Clergé français* [December 1, 1902]).

[22] *Compte rendu du congrès scientificque des catholiques,* p. 182.

[23] "We must remember first that the sacred writers, or to speak more accurately, the Holy Spirit 'who spoke by them, did not intend to teach men these things (that is to say, the essential nature of the things of the visible universe), things in no way profitable to salvation.' Hence they did not seek to penetrate the secrets of nature, but rather described and dealt with things in more or less figurative language, or in terms which were commonly used at the time, and which in many instances are daily used even today, by the most eminent men of science. Ordinary speech primarily and properly describes what comes under the senses; and somewhat in the same way the sacred

any basic change in his *Méthode historique,* that excellent introduction to Old Testament study.

Many Catholics, however, were surprised at the novelty of the positions taken by P. Lagrange, and alarmed when he began to apply to the Bible principles with which they were not familiar and did not understand. Intelligent discussion might have proved quite profitable; feelings were running too high for that. Matters were further complicated by the intemperate zeal of apologists who, under pretext of unmasking the modernist poison concealed behind a false front, so lowered the level of the controversy that abusive language replaced argument.[24]

It is only elementary justice that another man's opinions should not be viewed with suspicion without grave cause. The deplorable excesses which ensued should never have taken place, especially in view of

---

writers — as the Angelic Doctor also reminds us — 'went by what sensibly appeared' or put down what God speaking to men signified, in the way men could understand and were accustomed to" (*EB* 106). After repeating this passage of the encyclical, P. Lagrange observed that the Pope concluded, a few lines later, with the statement: "The principles here laid down will apply to cognate sciences, and especially to history." He thought he recognized here the thought of P. Cornely (*Historica et critica introductio in VT libros* [Paris, 1885], I, 518 ff.), and of P. von Hummelauer (*Exegetisches zur Inspirationsfrage* [Freiburg i. Br., 1904], 50 f.) concerning the theory of appearances. Cardinal Satolli, prefect of the Congregation of Studies, was of the same mind. "As for your interpretation of the thought of Leo XIII," he wrote on March 5, 1905, "it is, as far as I can judge, correct."

But P. Lagrange did not simply compare science and history, just like that. In his "A propos de l'Encyclique 'Providentissimus'" (January 1, 1895 [*RB* 4 (1895), p. 53]), he remarked apropos of an interpretation advanced in the *Gazette de France:* "I note once again, since the Encyclical (cf *EB* 108), a tendency to place biblical history on the same level as the sciences. It does not seem, however, that the Sovereign Pontiff intended to equate them completely when he says that his remarks concerning physics can be applied to the natural sciences, and especially to history, and so forth." The sentence in question had a very precise meaning; it was simply a transitional phrase "applicable less to a particular solution than to the whole manner of defense in answering objections." P. Lagrange had already made this clear (*RB* 28 [1919], p. 598) when the encyclical *Spiritus Paraclitus* of Benedict XV appeared (September 15, 1920), giving in an official way the meaning of the phrase: a recommendation to defend the historical value of the Bible, and not equating difficulties from history with those from the natural sciences.

[24] Cf, for example, S. Schiffini, *Divinitas Scripturarum adversus hodiernas novitates asserta et vindicata* (Torino, 1905). Concerning P. Lagrange he has this to say: "Id solum differt methodum historiae apparentiae et methodum rationalisticam, quod rationalistae se exhibent quales sunt, et aperte dicunt quod sentiunt, dum in altera methodo celatur verbis quod reapse sustinetur. Haec itaque methodus errori mendacium addit."

P. Lagrange's repeated and explicit professions of faith against modernism, the first of which appeared on the occasion of the publication, in 1893, of Leo XIII's *Providentissimus Deus.*

The central section of the *Providentissimus,* devoted to the doctrine of biblical inspiration and inerrancy, caused great resentment among the as yet undeclared modernists. Despite his filial letter of submission (reproduced in his *Mémoires*),[25] Loisy compared the encyclical to "a catapult, set up by Rome against criticism, but one which affects and bothers only children of the Church."[26] Apparently some Catholics felt the same way. A sensational article "The Encyclical and English and American Catholics," published anonymously in the *Contemporary Review* (April, 1894), stated that "since the publication of the papal encyclical, the Bible has become a kind of Prince Rupert's drop; one has only to break the tiniest bit from one end of it, and it breaks into a thousand pieces. For today's Catholic, the Bible, the Catholic Church, Christianity and Revelation, everything — depends on the accuracy of the Scriptural count of Esau's wives."[27] In other words, where the authority of the Sacred Books was involved, the tiniest error in historical matters would render all critical work impossible.

The *Providentissimus* appeared in French translation in the *Revue*[28] and was followed by a "not at all resigned, but joyful," acceptance.[29] The director spoke out against the extremist views which had been raised against the papal letter. "The encyclical is not an *ex cathedra*

---

[25] "I experience great consolation in coming today, in the simplicity of my soul, to assure the Vicar of Jesus Christ of my complete submission to the teachings he has promulgated in the Encyclical concerning the Study of Sacred Scripture" (*Mémoires,* I, 312 f.).

[26] *Ibid.,* p. 308.

[27] *RB* 4 (1895), p. 56.

[28] *Ibid.,* 3 (1894), pp. 1–28.

[29] *Éclaircissement sur la Méthode historique* (Paris: Lecoffre, 1905), p. 6: "The *École biblique de Jérusalem* and the *Revue* will endeavor to follow the direction marked out in the encyclical. Professors and members of the staff will not congratulate themselves the less for these lessons, reminders, and commands which are given to all Catholics, than for the encouragement which the Sovereign Pontiff deigned to address to them last year. To preserve the doctrine of biblical inerrancy and to look for solutions to difficulties, in an exegesis at once traditional and progressive — such was the program we sketched out in the Foreword to this *Revue;* it appears to be conformable to what the encyclical develops with authority. We therefore ask of those who hear the voice of the Common Father of the faithful, and especially of our collaborators, that they help us to pursue the work undertaken with his blessing."

document," he wrote, "but in addressing it to Catholics, the Sovereign Pontiff is exercising his office as universal shepherd, pointing out to the faithful the path they are to follow in these burning questions. It has therefore a right to respect and to obedience."[30] He did not feel that it hampered unduly the sincere efforts of critics; it was, rather, an urgent invitation to cultivate with greater determination the disciplines which would bring a healthy light to bear upon the Bible. He noted with joy the Pontiff's desire that biblical studies be stressed in seminaries, universities, and special schools; the Pope insisted on a knowledge of languages, especially the Semitic languages, awareness of modern discoveries, special training and exercise in literary criticism.[31] To be sure, the encyclical upheld the doctrine of inspiration and its corollary, inerrancy, but this was traditional teaching and prompted his recommendation to establish contact with the original texts. As for the difficulties raised by the natural sciences, the Pontiff gave a common-sense solution usable in particular cases that might arise in the future. He was less explicit in regard to historical difficulties, but the general principles cited in connection with inspiration allowed judicious consideration of the literary problems raised by the Biblical Question and by a careful, detailed examination of the text. He also insisted on the fundamental truth that God is the author of the Bible and of all its parts.

A more subtle position concerning the very meaning of Christianity according to modern thought had appeared in conjunction with Loisy's *L'Évangile et l'Église* (1902).[32] Presented as one of a series of widely circulated red volumes, the booklet set out to refute the conferences which Harnack had two years before given to students of the University of Berlin on the *Essence du christianisme*.[33] Stanchly maintaining belief in God, and with no less determination upholding the right of every man to believe in Christ after his own fashion, Harnack found the essence of Christianity to consist in the revelation of the

---

[30] M. J. Lagrange, "A propos de l'Encyclique 'Providentissimus,'" *RB* 4 (1895), p. 54.

[31] *Ibid.*, p. 62 f.

[32] Paris, 1902.

[33] *Das Wesen des Christenthums* (Berlin, 1900). Cf Lagrange's review, *RB* 10 (1901), pp. 110–123.

Student at the minor seminary
at Autun, 1868.

The young lawyer, Paris, 1878.

Père Lagrange, 1937.

fatherhood of God and in the lofty spiritual mission of Jesus. As the greatest religious genius mankind has produced, Jesus was more conscious of God as the Father than other men had ever been, and His was the privilege of establishing the invisible kingdom in the souls of men.

In his refutation of Harnack, Loisy had taken up the challenge to meet the Berlin critic on his own field, using his own weapons. He had shown that the system rested upon the shaky foundation of two texts which Harnack interpreted in a most debatable fashion. But Loisy's refutation masked his own unexpressed purpose, and his own ideas concerning primitive Christianity were insinuated rather than plainly stated. He held that Jesus had not announced an interior and moral, but a transcendent, eschatological kingdom. Convinced that it was His mission to establish this kingdom, Christ one day realized that He was the Messia, the Son of God. After His death the Apostles awaited the realization of His kingdom. When its coming was delayed the Church was set up in its place— realism's revenge on illusion. It followed, then, that Jesus was not really the Son of God. Nor was the Church, properly speaking, His work. As it had resulted from a decisive change in the evolution of primitive Christianity, it could in the course of time be transformed again; her institutions and beliefs were destined to evolve, not in any mere accidental way, but essentially and radically. It should be repeated that Loisy insinuated all this very skillfully, as he confesses in his *Mémoires*,[34] "I did not limit my criticisms to Harnack, but insinuated with discretion, truthfully enough however, a basic reform of traditional exegesis, of official theology, of ecclesiastical government in general."[35] "There was no need to arouse

---

[34] Loisy himself has shed light on this point. "Historically speaking, I did not admit that Christ had founded the Church or the Sacraments; I held that the dogmas had been gradually formed, and that they were not immutable; the same held for ecclesiastical authority, in whose name I was a teacher of men. I followed in the footsteps of Firmin in the *Revue du Clergé français,* which was not at all surprising, as I published the follow-up on his articles. Part of my book would have pleased all Catholics, but the other part, notwithstanding the cautious way I expressed myself, could, even though it was presented more or less under the shelter of the first, arouse some opposition. This was all the more inevitable as my precautions did not tend to hide my opinions, but to remove from them any note of aggressiveness" (*Mémoires,* II, 168).

[35] *Ibid.*

opposition." His words, in substance and in form, are a thumbnail sketch of all modernism.

P. Lagrange received his copy of the red book on February 1, 1903, just as he was leaving for Rome in answer to the summons of Leo XIII. He read the book during the five days his ship lay in quarantine in the harbor of Alexandria,[36] and his reaction was prompt, clear, and decisive.

> This time [he wrote] the mask had been cast aside. Loisy not only no longer believed, but he was cutting himself off from the Church. The attack he was launching against the Church was the more dangerous in that it was presented in her defense. I had therefore understood his previous moves badly. I promised to tell the public clearly where I stood. . . . I had delayed too long in pointing out the differences between the *Revue biblique* and Loisy because I was unwilling to stamp myself as orthodox at the expense of a writer whose destructive intentions were not clearly evident. All the more reason to act at once, when he was striking secretly but with set purpose at the very foundations of Christendom.[37]

P. Lagrange did not wait to return to Jerusalem before putting his plan into execution. The promised review, appearing in the April issue,[38] began with these words: "All Christianity is actually at stake and seriously compromised, however pure the author's intention." The review covered twenty-one pages in small type, and was a relentless, point-by-point criticism of Loisy's thesis, a fact which should have served to allay all suspicion of P. Lagrange in those who knew even a little of what was going on.

But nothing of the sort. By a coincidence which many looked upon as complicity, the *Méthode historique* came from the press almost simultaneously with Loisy's *L'Évangile et l'Église*. Passions reawakened by this circumstance were given full rein. In violent tones, reviews,[39]

---

[36] *M. Loisy et le modernisme*, p. 122.

[37] *Ibid.*, pp. 123–130.

[38] *RB* 12 (1903), pp. 292–313.

[39] In particular, cf the article by P. Cereseto: "Tre classi di dottori," *Scuola Cattolica*, 1902–1903). The first class of teachers, he wrote, is made up of "those whose doctrine derives directly from that of Christ and is substantially conformed to it" (p. 278). Among the second must be ranged the great heresiarchs, whose two distinctive characteristics "were and always will be, pride and hypocrisy" (p. 222). To the third belong

newspapers, and even pious magazines denounced the modernism of
P. Lagrange, the "wolf in sheep's clothing," and called upon him to
"stop wreaking havoc in the sheepfold of the Good Shepherd, adjured
him not to dishonor further the white wool of St. Dominic, not again
to ascend the altar which he daily profaned with his sacrilegious,
sophisticated, piety."[40]

Only one who lived close to this learned religious during such
a time could appreciate both his predicament and his sufferings. P.
Vincent, who did, has given us a faithful, detailed picture of the relentless attack directed against his master.[41] It would, perhaps, be indeli-
cate to dwell upon the fact that P. Lagrange continued to work while
under this cloud of suspicion and did not allow discouragement to
weaken his obedience or lessen his sense of responsibility, except that to
do so gives us the measure of his great heart and of his selflessness. It
is especially worthy of note that he never indulged in the luxury of discouragement. Instead of rushing to defend his good name, he preferred
to excuse his attackers, attributing their suspicions to a good faith
which was poorly informed in an area beset with difficult problems.
He would not hear of his followers indulging in fruitless controversy.
During these trying times, however, it did not go unnoticed that he
visited Calvary and Gethsemani more frequently than usual, and that
after each visit he invariably returned to the convent with renewed
calmness and energy.[42]

Indifferent to petty quarreling — small change, he called it — P.
Lagrange departed from this procedure only in reviews of books and
articles penned by his critics.[43] Once only did he vary his procedure.

"those moderate Catholic teachers who have publicity as their principal aim. To this
end they set out to learn ancient languages, archaeology, paleography, paleontology, etc.,
and then, armed with this scientific knowledge, they descend into the combat arena.
There, however, they are blinded by the splendid armor of their foes and begin to
praise them; next, like cowards, they disparage the worth of Catholics, and show themselves ready to make extreme concessions to the champions of heresy and of rationalism,
if only these will notice in their publications some of their own literary productions.
Among teachers of this category one finds, of course, P. Lagrange, along with Bishop
Mignot, Archbishop of Albi, P. Durand, S.J., and others." Cf *RB* 12 (1903), p. 632 f.

40 L. H. Vincent, O.P., "Le Père Lagrange," *ibid.,* 47 (1938), p. 344.

41 *Ibid.,* pp. 344–348.

42 *Ibid.,* p. 346.

43 "La questione biblica. Tradizione e progresso nell'esegesi e Bibbia ed Alta Critica,"

In a large volume of 380 pages, entitled *Autour de la question biblique — Une nouvelle école d'exégèse at les autorités qu'elle invoque*,[44] a well-known orientalist, P. Delattre, undertook to destroy the authority of P. Lagrange. The works of lesser lights P. Lagrange could ignore, but this author's opinion concerning difficulties raised against the Bible in the name of orientalism was much too important to be allowed to go unchallenged. P. Delattre had moreover centered the debate on the question of Christian tradition. He was not the only one to wonder whether the interpretation of the encyclical and of tradition, as expressed in the *Méthode historique*, was only clever or a mistake, and felt that the attempt to reconcile modern criticism with old principles was doomed inevitably to failure.

Although this argument may have pleased some of the more conservative element, it was likely to dishearten men of goodwill, and these had a right to an explanation. Unfortunately, as the tone adopted by P. Delattre was polemical, any defense ran the risk of appearing to be a personal *apologia*, something quite displeasing to the ordinary reader. Reluctantly, therefore, did P. Lagrange enter the fray. If only to parry the blows directed at himself, he felt that the more serious objections of his opponent had to be answered and he countered with his *Éclaircissement sur la méthode historique*.[45] In the interests of peace, his superiors thought it best not to allow even so small a book to be published, and only a few copies were printed *pro manuscripto*. P. Lagrange turned again to his work, confidently awaiting the end of the tempest. His silence was quickly interpreted by some of his bitterest enemies as an admission that he was unable to refute their arguments.

Notwithstanding the opposition, P. Lagrange continually widened the scope of his studies. The religion of the Persians and its relation-

---

Civiltà cattolica (July, 1902–January, 1903); cf *RB* 12 (1903), p. 473 ff.; A. Delattre, *Autour de la question biblique* (Liège, 1905) jj. 284–287; L. Fonck, *Der Kampf um die Wahrheit der Heiligen Schrift* (Innsbruck (1905); cf *RB* 15 (1906), pp. 148–160; A. Houtin, *La question biblique au XX° siecle* (Paris, 1905); cf *RB* 15 (1906), pp. 502–506; S. Schiffini, *op. cit.*; cf *RB ibid.*, p. 323 f.

[44] Liège, 1904.

[45] *Éclaircissement sur la méthode historique, à propos d'un livre du R. P. Delattre, S.J.*, pro manuscripto (Paris, 1906), pp. xii–106.

ship to Judaism intrigued him. He set himself to disengage various aspects of the messianism in Daniel, in the Psalms, and in the latter prophets, doing justice, in passing, to Pascal's remarks on the messianic prophecies. Accounts of excavations of Crete and on the island of Elephantine appeared under his name. He explored the great streams of Jewish tradition concerning the kingdom and the fatherhood of God, and book reviews and articles flowed in a steady stream from his pen.[46]

*   *   *

In the general bibliography for 1906 mention is made of a commentary on Genesis, *pro manuscripto*. This book, on which he had worked for almost ten years while pursuing his extensive studies on the Pentateuch and the most ancient accounts of the Bible, has never appeared on any publisher's list, a singular fact which calls for explanation.

Was it because the ideas of P. Lagrange, who represented the liberal wing, led to results so similar to those of Wellhausen that the Biblical Commission intervened, forbidding Catholic exegetes to proceed further along this road?[47]

Basic to what is called Wellhausen's theory is a Hegelian concept of history involving an evolutionary process from fetishism and animism to monotheism. P. Lagrange had always opposed any such assumption, explicitly declaring that as the literary conclusions of the Wellhausen school were contained in it, those conclusions could not withstand an attack upon the basic assumption.[48] Anything more radically opposed to the Wellhausen school from a literary point of view as well as from one concerning religious history can hardly be imagined. Yet certain insights of that school concerning the existence of sources in the first

---

[46] See the general bibliography for 1904–1907.

[47] A. Bea, "Der heutige Stand der Pentateuchfrage," *Biblica,* 16 (1935), p. 176.

[48] P. Lagrange had written: "Some, like M. Hommel, make two parts of modern criticism: accepting the generally admitted literary conclusions, they seek to avoid the historical theories of the Grafians; but because the literary conclusions of that school are frequently the result of a philosophy of history . . . it is impossible to reject the historical conclusions without altering the literary conclusions" (*RB* 7 [1898], p. 12). P. Bea had cited the French text correctly, but, as P. Lagrange observed, had misinterpreted it, as if he had made the literary conclusions the foundation, and vice versa (cf *RB* 47 [1938], p. 166, n. 3).

five books attributed to Moses were valid and deserving of adoption.

On June 27, 1906, the Biblical Commission took up the question of the Mosaic authenticity of Genesis. Using the customary form of a reply to carefully formulated questions, it asked:[49]

> Whether the arguments amassed by critics to impugn the Mosaic authenticity of the sacred books designated by the name Pentateuch, are of sufficient weight . . . to justify the statement that these books have not Moses for their author, but have been compiled from sources for the most part posterior to the time of Moses?

To this query the Commission returned a formal negative. It conceded, however, that Moses could have used earlier oral or written traditions, and could have reproduced them either as they were, or in digest, or expanded according to his plan. It also allowed for the possibility that he may have entrusted to others the task of writing the work he had conceived under the light of inspiration, on condition that he later saw and approved what they had done. Finally, while reserving to the Church her right to speak, it allowed for certain modifications in the primitive work, made in the course of its transmission, as, for example, additions, glosses, interpolations, editorial changes, and copyists' errors.

This decision then excluded the hypothesis that the Pentateuch was composed of sources which were "for the most part" posterior to Moses (*ex fontibus maxima ex parte aetate Mosaica posterioribus*). P. Lagrange had never explicitly maintained the contrary. The theory of the legislative evolution of the Mosaic Code as he had developed it at Fribourg and Toulouse quite naturally suggested the idea of a Mosaic redaction limited to a rather small section of it. In view of the abuses to which the documentary system exploited by the liberals had given rise, and of the confusion which ideas as yet not fully worked out might cause in the minds of the younger clergy and of the faithful, the Commission was apprehensive lest the discussions on the Pentateuch might take a direction contrary to the traditional teaching of Israel and of the Church. It therefore fixed in precise formulas what it judged to be established by that teaching. Let it be

---

[49] *EB* 174–177. See below, p. 152.

said again that it actually excluded *only* the view that the Pentateuch had been composed of sources which were *in the main* posterior to Moses. But this is not to rule out either the theory of many sources or of the partial adaptation of the primitive work to new social and historical circumstances. Obviously the Commission considered the problem of the composition of the Pentateuch to be far from settled, and left to the exegetes the task of clarifying the matter within the framework of traditional positions; this must mean more than that Moses merely initiated the legislation which stemmed from the Book of the Alliance. In other words, a new formulation of the principles expressed in the memoir concerning the sources of the Pentateuch would have to be sought. Valid in themselves, these principles should, when applied, profit from various other aspects deserving of notice.

I once heard it said that a high Vatican official had advised P. Lagrange not to publish his commentary on Genesis. In any case, it was filed away for more than thirty years, and he did not again bring it out until shortly before his death. He had by then made many changes in it, but with his strength now declining, time was to run out before he could finish the task he had in mind. His last article in the *Revue,* however, provides us with the general lines of his thought.[50]

* * *

P. Lagrange was at this point in his labors when, on July 3, 1907, the *Lamentabili sane exitu* appeared, condemning sixty-five propositions expressive of modernism and ambiguous both by reason of their anonymity and their complexity. In October of that year P. Lagrange's article, "Le decret 'Lamentabili sane exitu' et la critique historique" appeared,[51] and in it he expressed deep satisfaction at the way the problem had been handled; the errors advanced in the name of criticism and history had been repudiated without violence being done to the liberty which historical criticism demands. He used the occasion to set forth in general the problem between criticism and faith. History and the dogmatic tradition are two quite distinct things, and yet are

---

[50] See below, p. 122 ff.
[51] *RB* 16 (1907), pp. 543–554.

perfectly reconcilable once their limited autonomy is recognized. He also argued that in the special area which involves the history of primitive Christianity and Christian dogmas, that limit is precisely indicated by the testimony of the Church. This open avowal, which provided the Director of the *Revue* with an opportunity to repeat what he had always maintained, had no more effect than had his other statements, and the controversy stirred up by the *Méthode historique* raged on unabated. Opposition broke out into the open and the very character of the Master and his beloved work, the *École biblique*, were impugned. The school was described as being in an "unhealthy" state, and earnest recommendations were made that it "be purged from the land,"[52]

P. Lagrange continued his labors as usual, unperturbed by the charges which crackled about him. He remained calm because he was reasonably certain that his published works had not shaken the Holy See's confidence in him. He was prudent enough, however, not to put this into words during the debate, revealing his *reasons* only when in 1932 Loisy's *Mémoires*[53] forced him to lift the veil on certain facts which until then had been kept secret.[54]

The Biblical Commission had been instituted by the apostolic letter, *Vigilantiae* (October 30, 1902), and P. Lagrange had been named one of its consultors. Several days later he was called to Rome by his Holiness, Pope Leo XIII, to discuss how the *Revue biblique* could be made into the official publication for that Commission.[55] The Holy Father was also considering assigning him to the Pontifical Biblical

---

[52] Vincent, *art. cit.*, p. 347.

[53] He does, however, allude to them when referring to "Venticinque anni dopo l'enciclica 'Providentissimus,' " *Civiltà cattolica* (February 15 and March 1, 1919). Cf *RB* 28 (1919), p. 599.

[54] *M. Loisy et le modernisme*, pp. 122–135.

[55] A kind of official act was drawn up to this effect on March 28, 1903, under the title of *Basi generali*, and approved by Leo XIII. It stated that "The writers of the *Revue* shall enjoy full liberty in their scientific work so long as they remain within the limits of Catholic teaching as exposed in the *Providentissimus* and in the Apostolic Letter *Vigilantiae*. . . . The direction of the *Revue* will remain as at present. . . . It will only be the official organ of the Commission for acts expressly published in its name. For the rest, the *Revue* will preserve its purely scientific character, and the Commission will be in no way responsible for it." The wishes of the Sovereign Pontiff led to the inauguration of the *Nouvelle série*, in which, from 1904 on, the acts of the Commission were published. *Ibid.*, p. 129.

Institute which he had decided to establish in Rome.[56]

These marks of pontifical favor, bestowed upon him when Loisy's *L'Évangile et l'Église* had already been condemned by the Cardinal of Paris and been delated to the Holy Office, proved clearly that P. Lagrange's enemies had not succeeded in undermining the Holy Father's opinion of him. His nomination as a consultor to the Biblical Commission had to be sure not gone unchallenged it had apparently precipitated a small war. Considering the denunciations made against him, the fact that he was approved at all meant "more than a simple dismissal of charges, and was rightfully construed as a victory for moderate, progressive exegesis."[57] The favor shown the *Revue biblique* did not mean positive approval of everything it contained, but it "at least [meant] that its method could be usefully employed."[58] Moreover, there had been no reproachful raking up of the past. In response to the Holy Father's wish, then, the *Nouvelle série* of the *Revue biblique* began in January, 1904, by which time the *Méthode historique* had received much noisy publicity and must have been known in high Roman circles.

The commentary on St. Mark appeared in 1911 as a contribution to the *Études bibliques,* the first fruits of the new direction taken by P. Lagrange in his studies. He had chosen St. Mark because this was the Gospel that most occupied the critics.[59] It was widely held that Mark was the source chiefly used by Matthew and Luke, both of whom also had access to a collection known as the *Logia,* or words of the Savior. The facts of Jesus' history, it was thought, rested in the last analysis upon the testimony of the second evangelist. Mark thus became *the* source for anyone who would write a life of Christ, or peer into the mystery of His person. Although one might be obliged to explain away in one way or another or to eliminate as secondary all supernatural features in Mark, by emphasizing the human character of

---

[56] Vincent, *art. cit.,* p. 343.

[57] Lagrange, *op. cit.,* p. 125.

[58] *Ibid.,* p. 126.

[59] *L'Évangile selon saint Marc* (Paris: Lecoffre, 1911). Cf Introduction: "La composition du second Évangile et la critique récente" (pp. xxxiii–1), and "Le temoignage historique du second Évangile: l'opinion de la critique liberale protestante" (pp. cxi–cxiii).

Jesus as presented in Mark, Jesus could be made into a man almost like other men, and into one who was belatedly canonized by His believing disciples. Harnack's conferences on the *Essence of Christianity* had widely publicized these ideas, and they were accepted in varying degrees in all liberal schools. An answer to them was urgently needed. There were, however, other and more personal reasons which decided P. Lagrange to take up the study of that evangelist whom antiquity had rather neglected. In the foreword of his first edition, he wrote "Does it not sometimes happen that a man is carried away by an almost instinctive sympathy?"[60] He had always found Mark's charm quite to his liking. There was such a genuineness about his Gospel and it gave such a moving impression of Jesus, that P. Lagrange began to entertain the hope of one day doing some work on this composition of the disciple of St. Peter.[61]

The commentary of St. Mark retained the same format used in the Old Testament studies which had appeared in the *Études bibliques*. It was the first volume of a series which would one day comprise all four Gospels. Loisy took up the three Synoptics simultaneously, but P. Lagrange preferred the older system, treating each evangelist separately. Actually there is no better way to acquire a thorough understanding of the texts, to grasp each author's line of thought, or to familiarize oneself with the characteristics peculiar to each of the Gospels. "An exegetical diatessaron or diatrion is hardly any better an idea than was the diatessaron of the gospels," he wrote.[62] It seemed to him that the comparative examination required by the Synoptic problem first called for an examination of each Gospel and its particular features. By failing to see the Gospels as each animated by its own proper spirit one ran the risk of reducing them to some vague form which had little correspondence with historical reality.

P. Lagrange proceeded to study St. Mark verse by verse, plunging deeply into the text. As difficulties arose he handled them either in the commentary or in special excursus. More general problems were

---

[60] *Ibid.*, p. ii.

[61] *Ibid.*

[62] *Ibid.* The allusion here, with a slight variation, is, of course, to Tatian's work, in which all four gospel accounts were fused into one.

discussed in the lengthy introduction. Here too was a section dealing with Mark's theology, especially his Christology.

The commentator's task was complicated by the fact that he had constantly to weigh the exegetical theories then being advocated by the liberal school and, especially in France, by Loisy. More than once the Master's progress was halted by discussions of Loisy's views. A road without so many detours would of course have been preferable, and these detours mark the commentary somewhat too much as being a work of its time. But he could not have done otherwise. In 1911 Loisy was the most brilliant exponent of modern criticism in France, and in his two huge volumes[63] he had by ingenious and subtle combinations of texts succeeded in casting discredit upon the Gospels. Loisy had in fact composed an entirely new gospel history, one in which he alone decided what should be retained. A Catholic scholar might have overlooked Loisy's critical theories only on the pretext that the Gospels contained the word of God and *he* was writing on the theology of the Bible. But P. Lagrange proposed to proceed as a critic, and before he could accept Mark's testimony as a principle of historical certitude he had first to test him to see if he was a reliable witness. He was consequently obliged to take up the cudgels each time Loisy arbitrarily refused to recognize Mark as such a witness. These discussions now seem to us to be *passé,* but they were absolutely unavoidable when P. Lagrange began his gospel studies. The debate could not have been declined.

The commentary on St. Mark marks an epoch in the history of Catholic New Testament exegesis. Before it, no truly scientific commentaries on the Gospels existed in the French language.[64] The very title of Abbé Fillion's *La Sainte Bible commentée d'après la Vulgate,* indicated that it was not to be compared with the philological works appearing in Germany. This need, then, along with the author's reputation, made of P. Lagrange's latest work something of an event.

His St. Mark was greeted with joy by some, for it provided them

---

[63] *Les évangiles synoptiques* (Ceffonds, 1907–1908).

[64] Special mention should, however, be made of the commentaries by Knabenbauer, *Evangelium secundum S. Marcum* (Paris, 1894), and of J. Schanz, *Kommentar über das Evangelium des heiligen Markus* (Freiburg i. Br., 1881).

with solutions to the basic problems of gospel history; others found in it ammunition for the guns which they were quick to train upon certain details. P. Lagrange did not hesitate to reshape these "targets" in the second edition of this commentary.[65]

Inasmuch as he had deliberately taken up his position on enemy ground, he did not at first suspect that his treatment of opposing theories and use of formulae accepted in other schools of thought would be so badly misunderstood. One section of his Introduction, entitled *Saint Marc et le recueil de discours* (*Q*), was more than enough to ignite the charge that, contrary to tradition, which was firm on the point, he held for the absolute precedence of the Second Gospel over that of Matthew. A more careful reading of what he said would have dispelled this suspicion and shown that he was using the term *Logia* or Q as did the critics whose theories he was evaluating, because he felt that the only way to combat them was to tackle them on their own grounds.[66] In the matter of date he preferred to follow Irenaeus[67] rather than Clement of Alexandria,[68] and suggested that the Gospel of St. Mark had been written after the death of the Apostles Peter and Paul, that is, after A.D. 67.[69] Irenaeus' testimony, which is better preserved than that of Clement and in slightly different form, seems to imply that Peter was in Rome in 42 — a view not easily squared with the Acts.[70] But as it seems certain that Luke used Mark,

[65] See the "Note pour la seconde édition" (Paris, 1920), pp. i*–iii*, and the Foreword to the fourth edition (1929), pp. i–iii.

[66] *Ibid.*, 2nd ed., p. ii* and in the 4th ed. (1929), pp. cxv–cxxi. It should have been remembered that P. Lagrange had already opposed, and in the clearest of terms, the existence of a "recueil" which contained only the words of the Savior, which the First Gospel used, and to which it added certain facts. "I refuse," he had written, "to recognize this primitive Matthew which has left no traces in tradition, and whom internal examination does not authorize the critic to create" (*RB* 5 [1896], p. 27).

[67] *Contra haer.* III, i, 1: "After their death — of Peter and Paul — Mark, Peter's disciple and interpreter, transmitted to us also, in writing, what had been preached by Peter."

[68] Eusebius, *Hist. eccles.*, VI, xv, 5–7: "When Peter had publicly preached in Rome, proclaiming the gospel by the Spirit which animated him, those present who were many, exhorted Mark, as one who had followed Peter for a long time and had remembered what had been spoken, to write down what had been said. Mark did so, then, and turned the gospel over to those who had asked for it. When Peter learned of this he did not strongly forbid it, nor did he urge it forward."

[69] *Saint Marc,* 1st ed. (1911), pp. xxviii–xxxi.

[70] *Ibid.*, p. xxix.

the date assigned to Mark depends upon the date which a comparison of Luke and Acts indicates for Luke; in other words, Mark had to be written before 64.[71] Irenaeus spoke of the second Gospel and of Peter's preaching in the same breath, and this did not rule out the possibility that the Gospel may have been written either during the Apostle's lifetime, or composed from notes taken from that preaching by one whom tradition unanimously considers to have been his disciple and interpreter.[72]

Concerning the famous and difficult "final" of Mark, the last twelve verses of his Gospel (16:9–20), P. Lagrange had cautiously proposed, not as a proven thesis but as the most probable opinion, that they were not the work of the same hand that had done the rest of the Gospel.[73] When the Biblical Commission ruled (June 26, 1921) that the arguments against the authenticity of these verses were not conclusive,[74] P. Lagrange suggested that the "final" supplementary verses may have been added to the unfinished Gospel at a later date by the evangelist himself as well as by another. "In such cases," he added, "it is always wise to avoid statements which are too absolute; one may hold the theory that it was Mark himself who touched up or finished off his work."[75]

It would be unjust to exaggerate the *corrigenda* and to overlook the many judicious, penetrating, and often decisive remarks made by P. Lagrange. With unerring instinct and a sure hand he answered most of the problems raised by rationalistic critics of the Gospel concerning the Kingdom of God, the messianism and divinity of Christ, the institution of the Twelve, the foundation of the Church, the mean-

[71] *Ibid.*, 2nd ed. (1920), p. i*: "There is nothing in the second Gospel to prevent us from accepting the text of St. Irenaeus who places its composition after the death of the Apostles Peter and Paul. But as I have already granted Luke's independence in the commentary — it seems to be more and more solidly established — the date assigned to Mark should take into account the one assigned to Luke's Gospel, and this, for reasons given in the commentary on the third Gospel, appears to be before A.D. 64."

[72] *Ibid.*, 4th ed. (1929), pp. xxxi–xxxii.

[73] *Ibid.*, 1st ed. (1911), p. 435 f.

[74] EB 409: "Whether the reasons by which some critics endeavor to prove that the last twelve verses of the Gospel of Mark (16:9–20) were not written by Mark himself but added by another hand, are of a kind to justify the statement that these verses are not to be received as inspired and canonical, or at least prove that Mark is not the author of said verses? Answer: In the negative to both parts.

[75] *Op. cit.*, 2nd ed. (1920), p. ii*.

ing of parables, and the eschatological discourse (Mt 24). The conclusions reached by him on these points were supported by a diligent study of the pertinent texts, and opened the way for a sound Catholic criticism understood in the sense described above. Those who have trodden this path recognize their debt to P. Lagrange all the more willingly because, in following his lead, they have never been asked to abdicate their own personal views. They particularly owe to him something much greater than the formal solutions of certain special problems, namely, how to adjust their minds to the text, so as to detect in them their nuances of meaning, how not to impose preconceived ideas upon them, and how to establish a direct and honest contact with them.

*   *   *

Just as the commentary on St. Mark was being hailed as a success, the support of the Holy Father, the head of the Church, upon which P. Lagrange counted so heavily, was suddenly withdrawn.

For some time there had been rumors to the effect that P. Lagrange's exegetical studies and the *Méthode historique,* in particular, were to be placed on the Index of Forbidden Books.[76] Although not without some foundation, the rumor was inexact. The Sacred Consistorial Congregation on June 29, 1912, issued a decree declaring the work of the German Dr. Holzhey (*Kurzgefasstes Lehrbuch der speziellen Einleitung in das Alte Testament*) "tainted by the modernist theories of rationalism and hypercriticism . . . [and] its introduction into seminaries even as a reference work was forbidden." Then, in a short phrase appended to the body of the decree, the same prohibition was extended to "other Commentaries of a like spirit, such as many writings of P. Lagrange" (*ceu scripta plura P. Lagrange*),[77] without further specification.

Had P. Lagrange then been "put on the Index"? Hardly that. No book of his, neither his *Méthode historique* nor any other, has ever been the object of ecclesiastical censure. This step had been taken with the training of seminarians in mind.[78] The confusion of ideas

---

[76] Loisy, *Mémoires,* I, 488–539.

[77] *Acta Apostolicae Sedis,* IV (1912), p. 530 f. For the decree and an analysis of it, cf Appendix, p. 303 f.

[78] The decree was principally directed against Dr. Holzhey.

engendered by controversies about biblical matters was such that it was judged necessary to put students of theology on their guard against the hypercritical tendencies to which certain works might give rise, in that they failed to do justice to patristic tradition and to the decisions of the ecclesiastical magisterium.

The Church realizes that it takes time for ideas to mature, and for minds to be readied to receive them with the desired moderation; she takes into account such things as diversity of times and of circumstances. In itself the method of P. Lagrange appeared conformable to what had been set forth in the *Providentissimus*. But the encyclical dealt with matters on the plane of principles, and left it to the specialists to work out particular applications. P. Lagrange was one of these pioneers. Having seen the havoc wrought by rationalistic criticism in the minds of men of his own times, reasons based on personal tranquillity did not keep him from becoming involved in the burning questions of the day, or from searching for solutions to urgent and dangerous problems. In the heat of the fray he now and then, naturally, made sweeping statements or hasty applications which he had to modify later. But *not often*.

Since youth is often prone to generalize and to leap at hasty, literal applications [of principles], the Congregation responsible for the direction of seminaries felt that special vigilance was called for in the matter of the training being given future priests. P. Lagrange had deliberately set himself the task of finding solutions for critical problems, leaving theological developments for others. His professional dedication to these difficult questions did not perhaps bring out in him those pedagogically desirable qualities of simplicity and clarity which are so helpful to beginners. P. Lagrange realized that his emphasis on criticism might prove harmful to young minds, that the *ceu scripta plura P. Lagrange* was actually a kind of parenthesis, that none of his writings had been mentioned by name, and that the paragraph which concerned him had been formulated in such a way as to imply that the matter was open to further inquiry — *salvo ampliori iudicio*.

All things considered, then, the steps taken had been benign. But it was also true that the reasoning behind this move was serious, and P. Lagrange, always fearful lest he might not be perfectly attuned to the mind of the Church for which he would willingly have given his life, was shaken. Even the idea that an authoritative tribunal of the Church seemed to feel that he had been proceeding in a wrong direction made him resolve to destroy with one decisive blow that work to which he had consecrated the strength of his youth and his more mature years.

Before doing anything else, however, he resolved upon an act of filial submission, and drew up the following declaration.

> Most Holy Father, prostrate at the feet of Your Holiness, I declare my sorrow for having saddened you and [wish to] renew my obedience. My first thought has been and my last shall always be, to submit myself in mind and heart, without reserve, to the commands of the Vicar of Jesus Christ. But precisely because I am at heart a most submissive son, I wish to assure a Father, the most august of Fathers yet still a Father, of my sorrow for whatever may have led to the reprobation of many of my works (no one of which was identified) as being tainted with rationalism. That my works contain mistakes I am ready to acknowledge, but that they were written in disobedience to ecclesiastical tradition, or to the decisions of the Pontifical Biblical Commission, permit me, Most Holy Father, to declare to you that nothing was further from my mind. Kneeling before Your Holiness, I beg your blessing.[79]

As he wrote, P. Lagrange made up his mind, insofar as the decision rested with him, to quit Jerusalem. He thought of transforming the School into a "center of Palestinian and oriental studies" and of making the *Revue biblique* over along these lines.[80] He submitted his views to the Most Rev. Father Cormier, the General of the Order, in a letter dated August 6, 1912.

> Most Reverend Father. Yesterday evening I received your letter of July 27th, and I am most grateful for your paternal good wishes in my regard. As yet I have not received the decree of the Consistorial [Congregation]. I know that you have never doubted my complete submission. You will be so kind as to guide me, to point out what steps I must take in this matter so that everything shall be done cor-

---

[79] L. H. Vincent, *art. cit.*, p. 348.

[80] *Ibid.*, p. 349. Cf also P. Fernessole, *op. cit.*, p. 364, for some impressive lines from Buzy.

rectly. You ask me about S. Étienne. This of course requires some thought. As for me personally, it is clear that I must no longer occupy myself with Holy Scripture. To submit and to begin again would be to imitate Loisy. Take up something different? What? No one would believe me to be in earnest. So, 1) I am giving up my Scripture courses for the coming year; 2) I will drop all further work on my commentary on St. Luke; and 3) I will not write at all, not even reviews on this subject. I say this, not from discouragement, but to show that I am docile to the direction of the Holy See which so clearly concerns me. I cannot continue on as director of the *Revue biblique*. I do not think anyone here would be willing to take it over. The only practical thing to do, I think, is what I proposed in the report I sent to you in Rome, namely, to change it into a *Revue des études palesti-niennes et orientales*. This change cannot be interpreted as anything but an act of deference toward the Holy See. I shall write to Gabalda about this. If you approve, I shall arrange with him and we can go ahead with it. Far from arousing others against authority, I ask that they continue their work, though the general opinion seems to me that it would be to our advantage, as Cardinal Rampolla has often advised, to restrict ourselves to oriental and archaeological matters. Had we but followed this advice in 1905, as I asked! Our subprior returns this Friday, or Monday next; we have an election ahead of us, and you will be informed of the results. My person should not be taken into consideration as I have repeatedly told you. If you feel it best to replace me, so much the better; I would not object to a year's vacation. The School might very well be considered a school for Palestinian and Oriental studies. It seems to me that you might very well represent this move as an act of deference to the wishes of the Holy Father. Here, we are already prepared for it. As for recrimina-tions, I must say that such is not in my character. Please grant me, Most Reverend Father, your blessing and prayers, and deign to accept this expression of my profound respect.

The measures proposed in this letter were not carried out. The School was to continue on as it had in the past, but P. Lagrange was recalled to France. As he left the Holy Land, on September 1, he spoke these few but moving words to his grieving disciples:

No bitterness, now, and absolutely no giving up! No soldier worthy of the name discusses the orders which throw him into the fray; still less can he flinch or desert. My prayers and my heart are yours. Do not however count on my help in the future; you know that I cannot, even indirectly and without appearing to do so, give it to you without being dishonest. If God wants this work to continue, he will keep it alive as he has in the past. But you will not be worthy of his help if you do not keep up your courage and enthusiasm, above all as true religious and children submissive in mind and heart to the Order and to the Church.[81]

In conformity with this policy, P. Lagrange divided his time in Paris between works of the ministry and research into oriental history and archaeology. He prepared his *Life of St. Justin, Philosopher and Martyr,* for the series entitled *Les Saints.* Lent found him preaching at S. Severin's on the great vocation of the Christian. In one of his sermons on devotion to the Pope, he spoke from the heart: "We who are descendants of the Celts know the meaning of reckless devotion, and we count not our steps. If the Pope curbs our efforts, commands us not to advance where our generosity would lead us, that is our trial. ... If he were to say to his soldiers: 'You are not fit to fight, go watch over the baggage,' we would do so with joy."[82]

This period of separation over which suspicion cast its pall was, by the grace of God, of short duration. Upon receiving P. Lagrange's protestation of loyalty, Pope [St.] Pius X expressed to P. Cormier his "great and complete satisfaction."[83] Knowing that he was acting according to the Holy Father's intentions, the Master General shortly thereafter directed P. Lagrange to return to Jerusalem, where he really belonged. Before the end of June, 1913, then, P. Lagrange was once again at S. Étienne, under orders to resume his courses in exegesis.[84] The *Revue* and the School had emerged from the test refined, more alive than before. The common endeavor was taken up again with renewed vigor; his speedy return was a cause for joy and for profound confidence in Divine Providence.[85]

In 1914 there was a lull before the storm of World War I broke. The professors were soon recalled to military service, and not long after that the *École biblique* was occupied by the Turks.

---

81 Vincent, *art. cit,* p. 349.
82 Fernessole, *op. cit.,* p. 364.
83 Vincent, *art. cit.,* p. 349.
84 *Ibid.*
85 *Ibid.,* p. 350.

Torn from his beloved convent at the beginning of December, P. Lagrange was shipped off, together with other religious of the enemy nations, to Orfo, in Upper Mesopotamia, two days distant by caravan from the end of the railroad! Thanks to the intervention of Pope Benedict XV, these religious were released before they reached their destination. P. Lagrange obtained passage aboard a ship at Beyrouth, and eventually reached Paris,[86] where he saw to the publication of the *Revue biblique*. Only the October number came out late.

> We ask our subscribers to excuse this delay [he wrote]. Early in August the professors of the *École biblique* were called from Jerusalem to serve their country, and the Director, left alone, was unable to keep in touch with Europe. Although the *École* was finally officially closed by the Ottoman authorities, that step, happily, does not affect the *Revue biblique;* it will continue to appear. Subscriptions for it will therefore be accepted as in the past. The first number of 1915 will appear in May.[87]

From time to time, news reached France from Jerusalem, where the Swiss lay Brothers were keeping a close eye on things. "The walls were still standing, as were the sanctuary and library, but the cloister once reserved for study had become a place of bustle and anarchy for which the governmental palace in Turkey served as the model."[88] From the changes made it seems that an occupational force was installed there. Some of the books had been carried off to unknown destinations.[89] Unhappy magazines, unhappy books, unhappy library!

Separated for the second time from his co-laborers and from the School, P. Lagrange, all by himself, celebrated, deep in his heart, on November 15, 1915, the twenty-fifth anniversary of the School's foundation. In a long article, entitled *Viae Sion lugent,* vivid and cherished memories flooded into his mind and brought tears to his eyes.[90]

First he mentioned the circumstances of the foundation, undertaken in defiance of all calculations of human wisdom. The ambitious pro-

[86] For details, cf M. J. Lagrange, "À Jérusalem pendant la guerre," *Le Correspondant,* 258 (1915), pp. 651–655.

[87] *RB* 23 (1914), p. 626.

[88] *Ibid.,* 24 (1915), p. 248.

[89] Later returned, they were all adorned with the magnificent stamp of the Ottoman library.

[90] "Apres vingt-cinq ans," *RB* 24 (1915), pp. 248–261.

gram of the beginning, contrary to the rules of human prudence, had
been made possible of realization by the religious life. With only place
names and the skimpy indications of the map of Madaba to guide
them, the first field expeditions had been crowned with success, and
in a short time had made possible an inventory of biblical sites. A
number of famous cities lying beneath shapeless ruins had been
identified. There were many trips to Sinai and to Petra, and no corner
of the Holy Land went unvisited. The unforgettable cruise around
the Dead Sea yielded a rich harvest of photographs, notes, never
fading memories. As time went on, the best students at the School
had become its distinguished specialists. P. Vincent and P. Abel were
busy reconstructing the history of the architecture and toponymy of
ancient Jerusalem, while Fathers Jaussen and Savignac risked their
lives collecting geographical and epigraphical materials in North
Arabia, at Medina-Saleh and even far-off Teima, hitherto adjudged
inaccessible. One of the youngest members of the group, P. Dhorme,
was already a master in Assyriology, and P. Carrière showed promise
as a future excavator. The many digs conducted by the English, Aus-
trian, German, and French archaeologists were regularly visited. Was
there any place these professors and students did not visit? They went
through the tunnel of Siloam beneath ancient Ophel, and explored
the mysterious substructures of Solomon's Temple (now popularly
known as Solomon's Stables). At the School many silent hours had
been spent poring over texts, deciphering "squeezes."* Many contributions were made to the twenty-three volumes of the *Revue
biblique*. But best of all, those marvelous recreation periods spent with
kindred souls! P. Lagrange was pleased that M. Bertrand had so
accurately understood and spoken of them, and quoted him as follows:

> Against the framework of a clear, clear light, and the most im-
> pressive and grandiose of histories, there unfolded before my eyes
> the calm beauty of the monastic life. A peaceful existence, a life divided
> between work, prayer, and the chanting of the divine office; it is the
> dreamed-of Paradise. . . . Yet I have nowhere else ever found a more

---

* Originally a wet, mushy paper which was smeared thinly over an inscription, allowed to dry, and then peeled off. One could thus study the inscription at one's leisure
from the impression on the "squeeze," or paper. Plastic foam is now used for this purpose
by the archaeologists.

modern atmosphere, one more vibrant with enthusiasm or more interested in science and open discussion. As I entered the library I could see myself and my fellow students again entering the old Normal School. The scapular and tunic of white wool deprives these young Dominicans of none of their gaiety, spontaneity, or sprightliness of step as they seek out references in the library, pore over books, or scan the papers and magazines just in from Europe.[91]

But no more. . . . The *École biblique* was already just a memory. *Pendent opera interrupta. Inter arma silent musae.*

These moving reminiscences of the quarter century just past are understandable, but it would have been quite unlike P. Lagrange to indulge in melancholy reminiscence had he not derived from it the strength to carry on courageously, as indeed he had to. The evocation of the past filled him with determination to hold together by his letters the disciples who were now in the armed forces, and to see that their common cause was kept alive. From 1914 to 1918, the soul of the *École biblique* seemed concentrated in his person.[92] He also contributed at this time to *Le Correspondant* and the *Revue pratique d'apologétique,* saw to the regular appearance of the *Revue biblique,* and wrote articles for it on a wide variety of subjects: "La justification d'après saint Paul," "L'homicide d'après le code de Hammourabi et d'après la Bible," "La mosaique de Chellal en Palestine."[93] He finished his commentaries on *Romans*[94] and on *Galatians*[95] for the *Études bibliques.* He also gave a lecture series at the *Institut catholique* of Paris on *Le sens du christianisme d'après l'exégèse allemande,*[96] and published a volume containing articles on archaeology and religious history.[97]

For all this extraordinary activity, he did not neglect his preaching office. A time arrived, however, when he found himself unable to

---

[91] *Ibid.,* p. 258.

[92] Vincent, *art. cit.,* p. 350.

[93] See general bibliography for the years 1915–1918.

[94] Paris: Gabalda, 1915.

[95] Paris: Gabalda, 1918.

[96] *Le sens du christianisme d'après l'exégèse allemande* (Paris, 1918), or: *The Meaning of Christianity According to Luther and His Followers in Germany,* translated by W. S. Reilly, S.S., (New York: Longmans, Green and Co., 1920).

[97] *Mélanges d'histoire religieuse* (Paris, 1915).

continue, his health having become so precarious as to necessitate surgery.[98] The physical pain that hospitalized him for many months did not dampen his remarkable energy any more than had his other trials. When the war ended in victory for the Allies, he was ready to take up again with the same courage the work which had been temporarily endangered. The choicest fruits of that work were still to come.

---

[98] Vincent, *art. cit.*, p. 350.

CHAPTER IV

THE GREAT WORKS

At the end of the article entitled "After Twenty-Five Years," P. Lagrange had expressed a confidence in the future which time was to prove well founded.[1] On the day following the Armistice he was on board a ship heading eastward toward Jerusalem. His collaborators and friends, none of whom had been injured during the war, regrouped around him as they were demobilized. Thus was inaugurated a new and final period which was to last for some twenty years, and to be marked by an intense literary activity. It got off to a good start.

In 1921, the *École biblique* was recognized by governmental decree as the *École archéologique française de Jérusalem,* after the pattern of similar famous schools in Rome and Athens.[2] To P. Lagrange was confided the honor of seeing to it that, in the study of Palestinian antiquities conducted in scientific cooperation with the English and American schools, France should have her rightful place. Such an unusual distinction and mark of confidence testify to the respect which his works had won for him in the scholarly world. It is especially note-worthy that both the distinction and the confidence were extended not only to a priest and a religious, but to one who was also a learned theologian, to one who had never disguised his intention of using his science in the understanding and defense of the Christian faith.[3] The

---

[1] *RB* 24 (1915), p. 261.

[2] *CrAcInscrBl* (1938), p. 145.

[3] M. B. Allo, "Le Père Lagrange théologien," *RTh* 44 (1938), p. 426. Writing of P. Lagrange's work on the first three gospels, C. K. Barrett (*Expository Times* 65 [1954] 143–46) declares: "Philologically these are among the most useful books on the Synoptic Gospels; critical orthodoxy in the Roman sense is not obtruded, and the whole work is balanced and fair." Cf. *ibid.*, 109–11.

homage went beyond the person of this Master and touched upon his
most intimate convictions, even upon his methods, always so open
and above board.

The work begun in 1911 with the publication of the commentary of
St. Mark now blossomed, at short intervals of time (1921, 1923, 1925),
with the appearance of his commentaries on the three remaining
Gospels. P. Lagrange was continuing his courses in exegesis while
working on the commentary on John, when, once again, his age suddenly weighing heavily upon his broad shoulders, his strength threatened to fail him. One day, during a class at the beginning of 1923 — I
distinctly remember that it had to do with Jesus' conversation at the
well with the Samaritan woman — he broke off abruptly, saying that
he could no longer *see!* A warning, yes, and it kept him from his
arduous task for *only a few hours.*

The generosity of a Catalan Maecenas was responsible for the publication, in Barcelona (1926), of a magnificent edition of his *Synopsis
Evangelica Graece,*[4] arranged along the lines of the exegetical positions
he had adopted in his commentaries.[5]

In 1928 it was the turn of *The Gospel of Jesus Christ,* a popular
explanation of the *Synopsis* stripped of all critical apparatus and of
all Greek and Hebrew words. This was the only "life of Jesus" P.
Lagrange thought it possible to write. It did not, however, as one
famous Protestant liberal thought, represent an extreme concession to
the critics he was combating,[6] for his profound study of the Gospels
had convinced him that "in the presence of their inspired words, one
despairs of any other attempt to reproduce the life of Christ."[7] Of all
his works none was written with more tenderness. *The Gospel of
Jesus Christ* gained for him a laudatory and much appreciated letter
from Cardinal Pacelli, then Secretary of State, who congratulated him
in the name of His Holiness Pius XI "for having added to the series
[*Études bibliques*] these new soundings in the fathomless sea of the

---

[4] M. J. Lagrange and C. Lavergne, *Synopsis evangelica* (Barcelona: Alpha, 1926).

[5] After collaborating with P. Lagrange on this painstaking work, P. Lavergne prepared a popular French adaptation of it (Paris: Gabalda, 1927), which has since been
translated into many languages.

[6] M. Goguel, *RHPR* 9 (1929), p. 498.

[7] *The Gospel of Jesus Christ* (London: Burns, Oates & Washbourne, 1938), p. xi.

divine word."[8] The dean of the Faculty of Protestant Theology in Paris declared: "The fact that in this book P. Lagrange not only sets forth the results of his critical works, but still more the fruit of his meditations, calls for appreciation and respect from those who share neither his faith nor his theology."[9]

The last chapter of *The Gospel of Jesus Christ* finds P. Lagrange at his best, for here more than anywhere else his deep religious convictions are revealed. Unlike Harnack and Loisy, he perceived in the growing light that Jesus had affirmed His divinity, and that the Apostles had accepted His teaching and confided it to the Church for the salvation of souls. In other words, he perceived "the implanting of divinity in humanity, grace making human nature a sharer in the divine nature," as essential to the Gospel. "Such a prodigality of gifts and such lofty demands seem to crush rather than attract our very limited reason." Faced with this stupendous fact so conformable to the pious beliefs of his youth and which forty years of relentless research had only confirmed, he wrote the following moving lines:

> We feel tempted to say that it is all too wonderful to be true. But what is there apart from this that is of any value to us, that bears the stamp of the infinite? If we turn away from this, we are confronted with nothingness. Whither should we go, O Lord? Shall we shut ourselves up in a state of supercilious or despairing doubt, or shall we rather gather around Peter, who says still: "Thou hast the words of eternal life," and surrender ourselves to the embrace of God in Jesus Christ?[10]

The Gospel of Jesus Christ was like the apex of a pyramid, built slowly, block by block, upon the broad foundations of Hellenistic and Jewish studies. It is the crown of his gospel commentaries.

His interest in Hellenistic studies dated from 1907. Sir Arthur Evans had from 1900–1905 been excavating the ruins of the palace of Minos at Knossos on the island of Crete, while English and Italian missions were exploring Zakro, Praesos, Palaicastro, and especially the great palace of Phaistos and Hagia Triada, bringing to light remarkably

---

[8] Letter of March 25, 1930, # 89211.

[9] Goguel, *ibid.*, p. 499.

[10] Lagrange, *op. cit.*, p. 340 f.

well-preserved remains of the Minoan civilization dating back to 2000–3000 B.C. Intrigued, P. Lagrange seized the opportunity to visit these sites for himself while returning from France. The Isle of Crete, he pointed out, was ancient Caphtor, whence came the Philistines. His archaeological visit resulted in a series of articles[11] which were later published in a small edition together with his remarks on ancient Crete and its relations with Greece, Egypt, and the Bible.[12]

When I arrived at S. Etienne this part of the story was already ancient if not almost prehistoric history. The interruption of World War I had been so long that by 1922 the period before 1914 belonged to an older generation. By the 1920's P. Lagrange had turned his attention to the main themes of St. John's Gospel, and was also following the trail of the Logos amid the fragments of Heraclitus the Obscure,[13] in the Stoics, and in Philo.[14] As usual, a number of trips helped clarify his understanding of that ancient Greece which, by the way it had posed the problem of life and sought to answer it, had helped in the moral formation of the peoples to whom Christianity was proposed, both before and even after their conversion.

This project completed, the question of the alleged borrowings of St. John led him to sift carefully through the *Corpus Hermeticum* (Hermetic books gathered under the name of Hermes Trismegistus), and the *Mandean* writings attributed to a baptist sect of that name. Scott[15] and Lidzbarski[16] had already made these strange writings available to the public, and suggested that John's thought may have been powerfully influenced by them. If true, this hypothesis would with one stroke deprive St. John of all originality and strip the fourth Gospel of the dignity which the Church accords it as one of her inspired writings; it would also reduce it to the level of a mediocre

---

11 "La Crète ancienne," *RB* 16 (1907), pp. 163–206, 325–348, 489–514.

12 *Ibid.*, reprinted from the *RB* with an additional chapter (Paris: Gabalda, 1908).

13 "Le Logos d'Héraclite," *RB* 23 (1922), pp. 96–107.

14 "Vers le Logos de saint Jean," *ibid.*, pp. 161–184, 321–371.

15 W. Scott, *Hermetica, the Ancient Greek and Latin Writings which Contain Religious or Philosophic Teachings Ascribed to Hermes Trismegistus,* edited with English translations and notes (Oxford, 1924).

16 M. Lidzbarski, *Das Johannesbuch der Mandäer* (Giessen, 1915); *Mandäische Liturgien mitgeteilt, übersetzt,* etc. (Göttingen, 1920); *Der Geniza übersetzt und erklärt* (Göttingen, 1925).

syncretist gnosis compounded of Christian ideas and the false mysticism of oriental paganism. The authority of the inspired text of John being thus at stake, P. Lagrange felt obliged to look into the matter personally. It was no easy task. The question of these sources is clearer today than it was when Reitzenstein's pan-iranism had considerably complicated the issue. It was a formidable undertaking to read these writings attentively, to establish their chronology, and then place them in their proper settings, to determine their exact meaning and to compare them with more or less similar passages in St. John. Adding to the difficulty was the way lofty passages alternated with absurd speculation. P. Lagrange tackled the problem, if not with the pleasure which contact with the great minds of antiquity always gave him, at least energetically, his passion for accuracy driving him to verify each step from the sources themselves. In the end, his studies yielded ten articles bristling with detail. As Lietzmann's studies[17] and Mrs. Drower's careful observations of the Mandean ritual[18] appeared later, certain minor points in these articles may now have to be restated and expanded, but the main lines of his painstaking research have proved sound.

Two different worlds of ideas emerge from the teachings of the Hermetic books and Mandean writings, and from the fourth Gospel. Hermeticism was concerned with knowledge, even revealed knowledge, but John's Christianity involves an object of faith, and the opposition between the two is radical.[19] In Mandeism the three unmistakable marks of oriental gnosis (emanation from a first principle, a creation which was not the work of the supreme God, and the fall of the soul into the lower world) make their appearance.[20] Nothing could be more divergent from John's theology concerning the creation of all things by one God. The Mandeans felt no need for a redeemer,

---

[17] H. Lietzmann, *Ein Beitrag zur Mandäerfrage*. Offprint from the Sb. Ak. Preuss (1930). Lietzmann in this study proves that the personage of the Baptist appears only in the last redactional layers, and that the whole baptismal liturgy simply plagiarizes the Syrian Nestorian rites.

[18] E. S. Drower (E. S. Stevens), *The Mandaeans of Iraq and Iran, their Cults, Customs, Magic, Legends, and Folklore* (Oxford, 1927). Cf also J. Thomas, *Le Mouvement baptiste en Palestine et Syrie* (150 a.C.–300) (Gembloux, 1935); F. Rosenthal, *Die Aramaistische Forschung seit Th. Noldeke's Veröffentlichungen* (Leiden, 1939).

[19] *RB* 35 (1926), p. 263.

[20] *Ibid.*, 37 (1928), p. 17.

and held that living water sufficed for the remission of sins.[21] As for
the literary contacts which certain verbal analogies had suggested, P.
Lagrange concluded that if any such relation existed (and this is
extremely doubtful for the Hermetic books), it was not St. John who
was dependent on the Hermetic books or the Mandean writings, both
of which were later than he [John] in point of time, but rather the
other way around. He noted that much ado had been made about
nothing and that, putting aside all question of dependence, the alleged similarities had little foundation in fact. He had, in other words,
gone to "much trouble, only to reach an unimpressive conclusion. But
it is always worthwhile to liberate the Gospel from compromising
comparisons."[22]

The debates concerning the sources of St. John which followed the
publication of the Hermetic and Mandean texts pertain to the comparative history of religions. Christianity was declared to be not essentially different from other religions, and its supernatural transcendence
was treated as an illusion; it is best conceived (it was said) as the
result of tendencies, ideas, and rites which at the time of Christ were
widespread throughout the length and breadth of the Greco-oriental
world.

Long before the awakening of interest in Hermetism or Mandeism,
a number of authors had felt that the New Testament fitted some such
theory. Reitzenstein in his *Die hellenistischen Mysterienreligionen*,[23]
and Bousset in his *Kyrios Christos*[24] had started a trend, and their
success in French circles was due in large part to Loisy's *Les mystères
païens et le Mystère chrétien* (1913).[25] Loisy concluded that the
Gospel of Jesus was not a religion. Jesus had come merely to fulfill the
eschatological hopes of Israel in the establishment of the Kingdom
of God; yet, less than thirty years after his death, before the first
Christian generation had died away, a religion independent of the

21 *Le Judaisme avant Jésus-Christ* (Paris: Gabalda, 1931), p. 426.

22 *RB* 35 (1926), p. 264.

23 R. Reitzenstein, *Die hellenistischen Mysterienreligionen — ihre Gründgedanken und
Wirkungen* (Leipzig, 1910; 3rd ed., 1917).

24 W. Bousset, *Kyrios Christos. Geschichte des Christusglauben von den Anfängen
des Christentums bis Irenaus* (Göttingen, 1913; 2nd ed., 1921).

25 Along the lines of articles published by him (1913–1914) in the *Revue d'histoire et
de littérature religieuses* (2nd ed., with corrections, 1930). Cf. *Mémoires*, III, 231.

Gospel had emerged. As reflected in Paul's Epistles and John's Gospel, its chief characteristic was its *mystique,* the cult rendered to the person of Jesus and a sharing in the power of His death and resurrection. The new religion was explained as being due to the influence of the Greek mysteries, from which it was supposed to have borrowed heavily. The mystery religions later disappeared because the Christian Mystery taught a better doctrine concerning God and immortality, because its divine Savior was more alive than were the shadowy deities of Hellenism, and because it could boast of a greater unity of belief and social organization.[26] The *Mémoires* reveal that by 1911 Reitzenstein's views, so compatible to Loisy's own philosophical and religious relativism, had won Loisy over. He at once set about applying the principles.[27]

Long before 1913 P. Lagrange, abstracting from the arrogance manifested by the science of comparative religions toward both Judaism and Christianity, had examined that system carefully. His famous *Études sur les religions sémitiques* appeared in 1903, and an article on "La religion des Perses et la reforme de Zoroastre" in 1904; he also wrote a number of book reviews on the subject. He was convinced that only if the comparative method remained within the limits fixed by historical criticism, it might help clarify certain aspects of Christianity. Once it deviates from rigorous method, however, as always happens when rash conclusions are drawn from superficial similarities, it becomes dangerous and leads to deplorable confusion.[28]

Cumont's book, *Les religions orientales dans le paganisme romain,* prompted a long study in 1910.[29] In that same year P. Lagrange

---

[26] *Mémoires,* III, 232.

[27] *Ibid.,* 231: "As Mr. Jack had asked me to give him something for the October number of the Hibbert Journal, I sent him a long article on the Christian mystery, in which I took up the subject treated by Reitzenstein in his last work [see above, note 23] and attempted to sharpen the conclusion" (*Letter of July 16, 1911*).

[28] Cf his reviews: of H. Gunkel's *Zum religionsgeschichtlichen Verständnis des NT,* RB 13 (1904), p. 271; of S. Reinach's *Orpheus* (Paris, 1909), *ibid.,* 19 (1910), p. 138 f.; of C. Clemen's *Religionsgeschichtliche Erklärung des NT* (Giessen, 1909), *ibid.,* p. 281; of A. Deissmann's *Licht von Osten* (Tübingen, 1908), pp. 627–628; of G. de Baudissin's *Adonis et Eschmoun, ibid.,* 21 (1922, p. 126 f.; of A. Loisy, *Les mystères païens et le Mystère chrétien* Paris, 1919), *ibid.,* 29 (1920), pp. 420–446.

[29] "Les religions orientales et les origines du christianisme, à propos de livres récents," *Le Correspondant* (1910). This study was reproduced in his *Mélanges d'histoire religieuse* (Paris: Gabalda, 1915), pp. 69–129.

also composed a detailed refutation of Reinach's *Orpheus*,[30] and systematically studied the mystery religions of Demeter and Kore,[31] Cybele and Attis,[32] Isis and Osiris.[33] The religion of Dionysos-Zagreus, which first engaged his attention in 1920,[34] was important enough to warrant his writing a large book, *Orphism*,[35] on the subject. It was his last contribution to the *Études bibliques,* and appeared in 1937.

But it was Loisy, principally, who had driven him into active research. When later writing of that time, Father Lagrange summarized his main conclusions.[36] Briefly, the explaining of Christianity by mystery religions represented a different approach from that of the liberal Protestantism of Harnack, and from the eschatological school (the influence of this last on Loisy's *Évangile et l'Église* was clear). "By her refusal to accept the solution proposed in [Loisy's] little red book, the Church had, in 1903, neatly escaped;[37] [had she accepted it] everything would have had to begin all over again."

P. Lagrange felt that the explanations based upon the mystery religions were both *unconvincing* and *unnecessary*.[38]

Unconvincing, first of all. Bousset's theory, accepted by Loisy with reservations, posed two alternatives. First, Christianity rests, not on this or that particular mystery, but upon some general idea distilled by judicious analysis and refined in the beaker of criticism. But in that case it was something of which paganism was never conscious.[39] The

---

[30] *Quelques remarques sur "l'Orpheus" de M. S. Reinach* (Paris: Gabalda, 1910).
[31] "Les mystères d'Eleusis et le christianisme," *RB* 28 (1919), pp. 157–217.
[32] "Attis et le Christianisme," *ibid.*, pp. 419–480.
[33] Review of Loisy's *Les mystères paiens et le Mystère chrétien, ibid.*, 29 (1920), 435–441.
[34] *Ibid.*, pp. 424–435.
[35] *Introduction a l'étude du NT: III. Critique historique — Les Mystères: L'Orphisme* (Paris, 1937). Cf "Orpheus and the New Testament," *CBQ* 8 (1946), pp. 36–51.
[36] "L'influence des mystères paiens," *M. Loisy et le modernisme* (Juvisy: Editions du Cerf, 1932), pp. 200–217.
[37] *Ibid.*, p. 201.
[38] On this matter, cf. E. Magnin, "The Comparative History of Religions and the Revealed Religion," *Père Lagrange and the Scriptures* (Milwaukee: The Bruce Publishing Co., 1946), pp. 126–169.
[39] Lagrange, *op. cit.,* p. 203. Cf also p. 214: "It is said that, abstracting from the abominations of the mysteries as they were practiced, St. Paul could have been attracted by the sublime idea of a god suffering in expiation for the sins of mankind. But to repeat: such an abstraction is unreal. No one has the right to compare the Christian mystery with the pagan mystery, because the pagans did not have any; all they had

second possibility is that St. Paul (for it was he, or the *mystique* of his epistles, which is chiefly responsible for the Christian cult) was inspired by the mysteries in their concrete reality. Yet in the concrete the mysteries must have aroused only feelings of disgust.[40] Much is made of the profound similarities, e.g., that the dead and risen gods exercised a saving power for men of all times. . . . But this is not really decisive, for no text earlier than the fourth century[41] attributed a saving power to the deaths of the gods. Nor is the notion of substitution or of "vicarious satisfaction" a credible one, for none of the mystery religions represented the death of the god as a means of salvation for believers. No pagan would ever have suspected that Osiris, surprised and slain by Tryphon, was dying for him, or that Attis had, in order to save him, sacrificed his manhood to the mother goddess.

Taking up the *certain* facts, P. Lagrange sought to give them their proper meaning. The mysteries were salvation religions which, by establishing the initiates in a relationship with deities who had powers in the life beyond the tomb, promised them salvation in the next life. Initially true only for Osiris and Kore-Persephone and her mother Demeter, this was true only in a derived fashion for Attis and Dionysos. But then how was one to explain the union? The similarities with Christianity are clearest in the cult of Dionysos, but the union there was completely symbolical: the initiate became a "Bacchus" in an orgiastic rite which transposed into eternity the idea of a perpetual feast.[42] Imagine comparing this idea with Paul's concept of union with Christ, realized by an inward renewal which is a supernatural rebirth and a destruction of sin, and which leads (the believer) to imitate ever more faithfully the virtues of Christ.

If hope in a future salvation and the rites practiced with it in view are the reasons why Christianity is linked with the mysteries, then the

---

were the mysteries and their gods, and these gods were not saviors. One could not even propose the gods to the initiates for imitation unless it was, as in the case of the adepts of Attis, that they were fanatically about to make a sacrifice of their virility."

[40] *Ibid.*, p. 203.

[41] *Ibid.*, p. 209.

[42] *Ibid.*, p. 213. Cf F. Cumont, *Les religions orientales dans le paganisme romain*[4] (1929), p. 201 ff.

hypothesis is, to say the least, *unnecessary*. Jesus' preaching was an exhortation "to be saved." His demand was categorical — everything was to be sacrificed for salvation, and an energetic effort made to embrace it as quickly as possible. There was, then, no need to change the Gospel into a salvation-mystery; it has never been anything else.[43] The rites of primitive Christianity were never a borrowing from the pagan mysteries. Paul expressly declared that he had received them from the Christian Church which he had joined after his conversion.[44] Where resemblances are found they are entirely verbal. The salvation to which the mystery initiates aspired was a projection into eternity of an earthly ideal of happiness, conceived of as an unending feast similar to those which delighted earthly believers;[45] Paul, however, conceived the looked-for immortality as of a heavenly order, projecting its first rays here below, inwardly transforming and purifying and engaging the believer, here and now, in the works of a holy life. Even to compare the Eucharist, which is truly the eating of God, with the ancient Dionysiac rite of a bull slain and eaten raw (when the victim was not a child), would be, in Paul's words, to confuse the flesh with the spirit. Here too the dependence is between the belief and the rites on either side, but not between the two rites.[46] St. Paul formally declared that faith in the saving death of the Savior had been made known to him by revelation, that he had taken the trouble to check whether this was the faith of the Apostolic Church and whether the historical foundations for it were transmitted to him by Christian tradition in a way conformable to Scripture, i.e., by way of the Jewish religion.

What role then can be attributed to the mysteries in the formation of the faith at the beginning of Christianity? That the mysteries gave rise to superstitious practices among the people can be admitted. It was impossible that the faithful who lived in a world accustomed to religious feeling having its origin, partially, in the better instincts of the human soul, should have been able to shake themselves completely

---

[43] Lagrange, *op. cit.*, p. 210 f.
[44] *Ibid.*, p. 211 f.
[45] Cumont, *op. cit.*, p. 203.
[46] Lagrange, *op. cit.*, p. 212.

L'école biblique de Jérusalem.

Courtyard of
the Basilica of
St. Stephen.

La Vierge d'Autun

Père Lagrange's memorial card.

free from the [influence of the] mysteries;[47] these also played a part
in predisposing pagans the more readily to welcome the religion of
divine intimacy and hope which was preached by Christ. "Nothing
holds Christianity so much in check as an absolute, forbidding concept of God's transcendence. When it comes to this, Jews and Moslems
are as a rule inflexible. The poor people who searched so passionately for contact and intimacy with the gods were better prepared
to receive the good news of the Incarnation."[48] However, this accidental
and secondary role was not what Loisy had in mind for the mystery
religions. Interestingly enough, the comparative approach, having
attempted to fall back on the Mandean gnosis,[49] was already on the
wane. Before reaching this conclusion, P. Lagrange had once again
taken great pains in his research. He had the satisfaction of showing
that the Christian faith has nothing to fear from comparisons with
the other religious beliefs of mankind, and that such comparisons,
far from discrediting it, served rather to bring out the profound
originality and unquestionable superiority of Christianity.

The questions raised by the comparative history of religions apropos
of Hellenism were not the only ones which had to be clarified so that
the New Testament might be seen in its true light. The New Testament writings are all deeply rooted in the very land of Israel, a factor
which became more and more important when the School of Forms
initiated its study of the backgrounds. SS. Paul and John, once looked
upon as the most strenuous proponents of Hellenism in early Christianity, now took their place in the stream of Israelite thought!

P. Lagrange began his New Testament studies with his *Messianisme
chez les Juifs* (1909), and here carefully examined the period extending from 150 B.C. to A.D. 200. In 1931 he enlarged the scope of this
work so as to include problems concerning the history, institutions,

---

[47] *Ibid.*, p. 206.

[48] *RB* 29 (1920), p. 446.

[49] It is thus that "a philologist and critic like Reitzenstein, who had admitted the
influence of Hermeticism on the Christian religion and especially on the fourth Gospel
(cf. above, p. 105), according to the writings of the third century, seriously proposes
Mandean influence in the redaction of the Synoptics" (*M. Loisy et le modernisme*,
p. 216 f.). For the sake of the record, it should be noted that A. Loisy definitely
rejected all Mandean influence on primitive Christian thought (cf *Le Mandéism et les
origines chrétiennes* [Paris, 1934]), thus avoiding this absurd view.

and teachings of *Judaism* before Jesus Christ.[50] Not so methodical as the classic study by Schürer,[51] which he had no intention of replacing, his *Judaisme* dealt with the relations existing between nascent Christianity and declining Judaism, and utilized only the basic sources. The work gives evidence of P. Lagrange's remarkable gift of synthesis, and clarifies the main points of the Jewish apocalyptic via the history of the Maccabees. Various other chapters, especially the excellent treatments of the great themes of Judean Judaism before the time of Christ, of foreign influences, and of the attempts made at hellenization, manifested deep insight in such matters.

Judaisme avant Jésus-Christ marked P. Lagrange's seventh important book. Mention should also be made here of an abridged edition of his commentary on St. Mark,[52] of a highly critical study of Renan's *Vie de Jésus*,[53] and of a controversial volume against M. Bayet's *Les morales de l'Évangile*.[54] He contributed some fifty articles to various periodicals, and reviewed many books for the *Revue biblique*.[55] It can be said without exaggeration that his scientific output during these ten years alone would have done credit to the lifetime output of many a scholar.

At an age when most men would have been content to retire gracefully, P. Lagrange turned to "unfinished business," and, as he entered his seventy-eighth year, set to work on an *Introduction à l'étude du Nouveau Testament*. This project was to be of at least four parts, several of which would require two or more volumes to complete.

The first of these to appear (1931) was his study of the formation of the New Testament canon.[56] The Church receives the twenty-seven books of the New Testament as divinely inspired and on a par with

---

[50] Paris: Gabalda, 1931.

[51] *Geschichte des jüdischen Volkes*[4] (Leipzig, 1901–1909).

[52] Paris: Gabalda, 1922.

[53] *La vie de Jésus d'après Renan* (Paris: Gabalda, 1923) was translated into English by Maisie Ward: *Christ and Renan, a Commentary on Ernest Renan's "Life of Jesus"* (New York: Benziger Brothers, 1928).

[54] Subtitled: *Réflexions sur Les morales de l'Évangile de M. A. Bayet* (Paris: Grasset, 1931).

[55] Cf the general bibliography.

[56] *Introduction a l'étude du NT: I. Histoire ancienne du canon du NT* (Paris: Gabalda, 1933).

those of the Old Testament.[57] How the Church came to draw up this very limited collection of books is a matter of dispute between Catholics and conservative Protestants, the latter reproaching Catholics for taking too liberal a position and for accepting what is an artificial creation. How was the sacred character of these twenty-seven books manifested at the outset of her tradition, that is, what was the chief criterion of canonicity? It was, for P. Lagrange, the apostolic origin of the writings. No decisive proof can be advanced in matters which revolve around hints and conjectures, but his theory rested upon *this* fact, that a Gospel or Epistle (whether doctrinal or not) was virtually recognized as sacred once it was perceived to be the work of an Apostle, or, as in the case of *Mark* and *Luke,* when represented as guaranteed by an Apostle.[58] Actually there are only two solutions to the problem. Either the Church has received a special revelation (of which there is now no trace) concerning the sacred character of each book,[59] or, knowing in general that the writings of the Apostles were inspired (for they possessed the fullness of the Holy Spirit including the charism of inspiration granted to the prophets of old), she simply inquired into the apostolic origin of the books submitted to her judgment, establishing this point by inquiries made of the ancient communities in which these books were accepted.[60]

The main objection to this explanation is that tradition has wavered in regard to some books; some of them entered the canon at a late date, others were later excluded from it. But the objection does not hold. Once a truth has been revealed, it does not follow that the Church at once possesses a *distinct* knowledge of it. Gropings, hesitation, and even partial steps backward were always possible before she formally made up her mind.

In any case, this history must be considered period by period. There

---

[57] *Ibid.,* p. 171.

[58] *Ibid.,* pp. 12–14, 171–175.

[59] *Ibid.,* pp. 171–175.

[60] P. Lagrange returned to this point in *RB* 44 (1935), p. 216: "This then is the theological question: is the inspiration of a particular book certain only through an explicit revelation? Would it not be enough to say that it was contained in the apostolic authority, when an Apostle wrote to fulfill his ministry, or when it was widely known that the writing of a disciple had been received and proposed as sacred by an Apostle, as Clement of Alexandria relates that Mark was approved by Peter?"

were three periods in all. During the first (from A.D. 45–150), the Church received as a rule of Christian faith and morals (and implicitly held as inspired) those books which were presented to her as having an apostolic guarantee.[61] In what way was an Apostle inferior to a prophet? "He preaches an even loftier truth. If he writes, he will have as much or even more authority than a prophet, sharing as he does that Spirit which, in view of the relationship between Alliances, must now be regarded as more abundantly given."[62] Books recognized as apostolic were always read in the churches. This is a fact. Such reading did not, of course, confer upon them a single iota of added authority, but was merely a sign that they possessed such authority from the beginning. Doubts, however, soon arose, and with them began the second period (A.D. 150-350). Among the books read in public there were some whose apostolic origin was uncertain, such as the *Epistle to the Hebrews,* the two small *Letters of John* (the name of the Apostle does not appear in these at the beginning), *2 Peter,* and *Jude.* The author of the *Epistle of St. James* was recognized as a brother of the Lord, but was he one of the two James mentioned in the apostolic "lists"? The *Apocalypse* (= Revelation) had come under suspicion because of the use made of it by the Millenarists. A further cause for doubt was the anti-Jewish trend initiated by Marcion,

---

[61] *Histoire ancienne du canon,* pp. 33–43.

[62] *Ibid.,* p. 10. Cf also *RB* 44 (1935), p. 217 f.: "We have been courteously but firmly rebuked for having gratuitously imagined this inspiration of the Apostles. True enough, we did not draw up a complete list of the most significant witnesses — although one should not overestimate their precision — in order to prove that inspiration, a thing distinct in itself, was a privilege of the apostolate. Indeed, we attached less importance to these texts than to the great fact of the diffusion of the Holy Spirit, which so clearly distinguishes the New Alliance. If Moses and the prophets, the chief personages of the Old Testament, were inspired by the Holy Spirit, as is believed, is it not [also] necessary to be inspired by that Spirit to speak in the very name of God, to abrogate the Old Law, and to portray in Jesus Christ the divine climax of prophecy? There was the danger of exaggerating the use of charisms: no one can doubt that the Apostles exercised them fully, especially in teaching, the most important act of their ministry, by means of a writing whose permanence rendered it superior to books which were in part abrogated or in any case subordinate to the last and final Revelation. It is this that allows us to draw an argument from the two texts in 2 Peter: Paul's letters are Scripture (3:16), and, on the other hand, the prophets, men of God, were borne along by the Holy Spirit (1:21). Were not the letters of Paul inspired? He was instructed by Jesus Christ and in close communion with the Holy Spirit. It is indeed the authority of the Holy Spirit which Paul claims for himself (1 Cor 2:13; 7:40)."

and aimed at eliminating from the New Testament anything that appeared to be infected with Judaism or closely bound up with the Old Law. Other ancient works such as the *Gospel according to the Hebrews,* the *Letters of Clement of Rome* and *of Barnabas,* the *Shepherd of Hermas* were not at first listed among the sacred books, but occasionally found a place there. For two centuries, these hesitations continued.[63] During the third and final period (A.D. 350 on), the canon was gradually fixed, and lingering doubts vanished; the collection of twenty-seven books appears to have been closed before official approval was given to it by the definitions of the Councils.[64]

The principle of apostolicity admitted everywhere by the close of the second century was of recognized importance, and the Church invariably referred to it when, in sorting out the books submitted to her for judgment, she consulted tradition and took her cue from the practice of the Churches. P. Lagrange concluded that it was this principle, applied in the light of tradition, which in the end overcame all hesitation and led to that state of tranquil possession which was ratified by the Councils of Trent and Vatican I.

This explanation of the formation of the canon quite naturally met with opposition. Some (Ogara)[65] thought the solution too daring, others (Cerfaux)[66] too conservative. In taking up a problem in which both faith and history had something to say, P. Lagrange had worked out a solution which was at once theological and historical; hence the differences of views. The Church has defined it as a matter of faith that the twenty-seven books of the New Testament constitute a collection of sacred and inspired books. "As children of the Church we must believe this with a divine faith. If the Church imposes it upon us, it is because she has the right to do so, and it is only by her authority that we can be sure of this point."[67] But as the Church, the guardian of revealed truth, carries out her mission *in a human manner,* we may therefore ask ourselves what precisely were the principles upon which she actually based her judgment. The solution which seems to be

---

[63] *Histoire ancienne du canon,* pp. 44–133.
[64] *Ibid.,* pp. 134–163.
[65] *Gregorianum* 15 (1934), pp. 451–466.
[66] *Ephemerides Theol. Lov.,* 11 (1934), pp. 635–637.
[67] *Histoire ancienne du canon,* p. 171.

supplied by history takes into account the different aspects of the problem in a profound and elastic way. The solution is frankly conservative inasmuch as it begins with the definitions of the Church; at the same time it is somewhat daring in that it rejects the hypothesis usually shared by theologians, namely, that a special revelation was made concerning the inspiration of each single book. Here we have a good example of the harmony, mentioned above, which can exist between faith and critical research, for this solution brings the insights of the believer and of the scholar to bear upon the same point.

The Master of Jerusalem, once he had finished his history of the canon, set about preparing an introduction to textual criticism. Readers of the *Revue biblique* were informed of his interest in this project.[68] To ascertain how much progress he made in this field before his introduction was published, one need go back no further than 1911, which saw the publication of his commentary on St. Mark. At that time P. Lagrange still held to the principles formulated by Westcott and Hort,[69] ascribing a capital importance to Vaticanus and Sinaiticus, which the two Englishmen considered the best witnesses of what they called the *neutral text*. He was not very impressed by the so-called *Western* text, represented by the Codex Bezae and the Old Latin and Syriac versions. The *Syrian recension*, represented by Alexandrinus (A) and most of the manuscripts of the *Koiné*, was chiefly used by the Byzantines but had not inspired him much either, despite the esteem it had enjoyed among the humanists of the Renaissance.

In the intervening years, the discovery of many new manuscripts and numerous biblical papyri called for a fresh evaluation of positions. Besides the neutral, Western, and Syrian groups of Westcott and Hort (referred to by Von Soden as Hesychius, Pamphilus, and Lucian), there now appeared a new text, called *Caesarean* because Origen seems to have used it while at Caesarea in Palestine. Widely used from the Caucasus to Gibraltar, it is represented by Codex Θ (= *Koridethi*, first edited in 1913), by two families of minuscules

---

[68] Cf especially the announcement of the project of a textual criticism of the NT, *RB* 42 (1933), pp. 481–498.

[69] *The New Testament in the Original Greek* (London, 1881).

(1 and 13) and by the Georgian and Armenian versions; it was distinguished from the three known groups, but manifested certain resemblances to the first two. The gospel papyri acquired by Chester Beatty in 1930 held yet another surprise in store. Originating probably at Fayum in Egypt, these bore witness to a codex earlier by over a century than all known manuscripts. When these papyri were published in the splendid edition of Sir Frederick Kenyon (1933), P. Lagrange put everything else aside and, although his eyes protested, sought to wrest from the texts their precious secrets. Three lengthy studies appearing in the *Revue biblique* of that year were the result. His conclusion was that the papyri pointed toward the existence of an extremely ancient manuscript tradition, noteworthy as being a blend of the neutral and occidental texts.

Here then was more than enough to challenge the classifications which had been worked out by the princes of textual criticism. A careful study of the groups already established led to similar results. The so-called *neutrality* of Vaticanus and Sinaiticus had been exaggerated; although to a lesser degree, they too, like the other texts, were the result of a revision which, however moderate it may have been, was more than just a simple transcription free of intentional corrections. Westcott and Hort had held that Sinaiticus and Vaticanus were in most cases enough to settle disputed cases, but these very ancient codices now lost something of their supremacy as it became increasingly evident that the *Western* text was not a homogeneous whole, but clearly preserved a number of good readings not occurring elsewhere. The chief foundations of the classical positions, briefly, had all been shaken, and the immense amount of material classified by the scholars would have to be revised along new lines. Inflexible reconstructions were now useless, as was the groupings of texts into families properly so called; mechanical rules of judgment had to be abandoned, sweeping judgments avoided. As the sources of information multiplied and were better understood, textual criticism was to learn modestly to aim first at the study of particular cases, and not at blanket theories which in our present state of knowledge are likely to lead to error.

P. Lagrange's *Introduction to Textual Criticism*[70] was published in 1935, the jubilarian fruit of twenty-five years of study in that field. A large quarto volume of 686 pages, it was intended as a manual for students.[71] Logically it should have been preceded by a treatment of paleography, descriptions of manuscripts, enumeration and evaluation of those parts extrinsic to the text, prefaces, summaries, and pericopes. Pleading his incompetence in these fields, P. Lagrange entrusted the task to his distinguished friend in the Vatican Library, M. Devresse. For what touched upon the history of the Armenian and Georgian versions, much in debate in view of the problem of the *Caesarean* text, he again disqualified himself and enlisted the help of P. Lyonnet, S.J. Since he had not himself "spent his whole life — hardly long enough a time at that — deciphering manuscripts and cataloging the variant readings," he hoped only, "without pretending to be complete, to provide students with a few principles which he had himself found to be of value." When we said above that textual criticism had been forced to learn modesty, we had in mind the wonderful example given by a great master in this Foreword, wherein he professes ignorance of what he has not himself studied at firsthand by direct contact with the original sources.[72]

Nevertheless, while setting forth the "few principles" he had tested out in his many years of biblical study, P. Lagrange had written a huge book. The subtitle, *La critique rationelle,* indicates clearly his conviction that the work of textual criticism demanded much careful reflection. Not every exegete was to undertake the impossible task of himself establishing his own text, "as if he were the first to take up the subject, oblivious of the work of specialists." To be that individualistic is not good.[73] Certain general rules based on proven results are necessary, provided that they are more than mere material formulas.[74] This rule is particularly relevant in the classification of textual authorities (i.e., the manuscripts). P. Lagrange felt that these

---

[70] *Introduction à l'étude du NT. Deuxième partie: Critique textuelle II: La critique rationnelle* (Paris: Gabalda, 1935).

[71] *Ibid.,* p. vii.

[72] *Ibid.,* pp. vii–ix.

[73] *Ibid.,* p. 17 ff.

[74] *Ibid.,* pp. 17–40.

should be sorted according to a much surer indication of their inner relationship, namely by their general tendencies than by other principles of similarity.

The results of his inquiry are as follows. The theory of a neutral text being set to one side, the manuscripts at the disposal of the New Testament critics fall into four recensions. The first of these, designated by the letter B, is headed by *Vaticanus* and *Sinaiticus,* and corresponds to the so-called *neutral* text of Westcott and Hort. This recension is held to be the best because it is most reliable in reproducing the texts, and does not attempt to tone down striking statements or attenuate difficulties by explanations or arbitrary harmonizations. P. Lagrange realized that these codices contained *lapses* which defy explanation, as well as deliberate corrections, but these are rare and generally relatively unimportant. He thought highly of these manuscripts.[75]

Then, at the opposite extreme, there is type D, a recension represented by manuscripts of the ancient *Western* group (Codex *Bezae,* or D, and certain Old Latin and Syriac versions). Very different but also very ancient, this text displayed a taste for harmony and for additions designed to eliminate obscurities, difficulties, and even apparent contradictions.[76]

Between the first two types, both of which are of Egyptian provenience, are the representatives of the so-called *Caesarean* text; less sober than those of the type B, they are more restrained than those of the D type.[77]

The fourth and last group, designated by the letter A, is dominated by *Alexandrinus* (= A). An ecclesiastical text from Constantinople, it is preserved in the greatest number of uncial and minuscule manuscripts and is the prototype of the *textus receptus* (*non recipiendus!*) published by Erasmus and widely propagated in the later editions of Robert Estienne (1534) and the Elzevier brothers (1624).

The principles upon which P. Lagrange's synthesis was based were not original with him but corresponded to the rules laid down by Griesbach (d. 1812): (1) The revisors, when they failed to understand

---

[75] *Ibid.,* pp. 32, 42–82.
[76] *Ibid.,* pp. 32, 42–82.
[77] *Ibid.,* pp. 144–168.

certain subtle phrases, would use the more common terms, gray colors. (2) Accustomed to expressions in current use when citing the Gospel, they did not always preserve the original flavor of each author. (3) They toned down crudities of style or grammar so as to render texts of an indirectly Semitic origin more intelligible to Greek readers. (4) In order to have the heart of the gospel message in a single Gospel, they tried to make the Gospels as much alike as possible, and made use of approximations, a harmonizing procedure which St. Jerome deplored as the chief reason for the confusion existing in the Latin manuscripts. (5) In certain definite but very rare instances, measures were taken against foreseeable theological difficulties. (6) Even more rarely the revisors reflected the language of the land, especially where that language was Latin. (7) On rare occasions the authority of one of the Fathers influenced the constitution of the text; that of Origen, for example, was considered to be the best.[78]

What was *new* was the use to which P. Lagrange put these rules. Ordinarily they were applied to the matter of variant readings; he used them to classify manuscripts and versions.[79] New too was his seeing in deliberate corrections, indications of the origin and value of the different recensions.[80] New also his breaking away from divisions of manuscripts into families according to the material reproduction of manuscripts.[81]

His refusal to treat the various authoritative groups according to

---

[78] "Projet de critique textuelle . . ." *RB* 42 (1933), p. 496; cf also *op. cit.,* pp. 33–40.

[79] *Ibid.,* p. 27: "The point of departure must always be the hypothesis of three or four recensions. But before asking them to give their testimony, their existence and the value of this testimony must be solidly established. . . . To be sure, one must consult the manuscripts in order to distinguish the recensions, and if one recension is considered to be better than another, it is because of the manuscripts which are best representative of it. For us, then, as for Tischendorf, the oldest manuscripts are the best guarantee. But instead of judging in each case which variant is preferable according to rational standards, we would prefer to use these criteria to help determine which recension or manuscript type is best."

[80] *Ibid.,* pp. 19–24.

[81] *Ibid.,* p. 25 f.: "What keeps us from attributing, with Dom Quentin, so much authority to this sectioning-off of families, is that it presupposes — aside from purely involuntary *lapsus,* a mechanical reproduction of the manuscripts. We concur with M. Havet (*Manuel de critique verbale* [Paris, 1911], p. 418) when he writes 'The genealogy of the manuscripts is subject to so prodigious a complexity that this apparent algebra sins by its simplicity (so unexpected), and by its deceptive rigor.' "

the majority rule, as if they were so many voters each having a ballot of equal worth, was also new.[82] Similarly new was his defining the limits of the most daring liberties taken by the revisors, and his stand, "contrary to the theories of radical literal criticism, that despite certain unimportant changes, the texts of the New Testament have come down to us in a remarkably complete form, being substantially what they were when they left the hands of their authors."[83]

Obviously not all the mysteries touching upon the origin and mutual relations existing between ancient texts were *ipso facto* equally clarified, for, in the present state of our knowledge, such a thing is simply not possible. However, by provisionally synthesizing the results of fifty years of research, P. Lagrange was able to mark out the progress achieved, fix a starting point for the further study of problems, and to sketch out a rational method to be employed in their solution. One may therefore agree with qualified scholars in this field who say that his contribution was an extraordinary one, and that his book "will most probably remain for a good many years the best and most reliable guide a beginner can find, a treasure-house of information for the more advanced student."[84]

*   *   *

This truly magisterial opus, which P. Lagrange wished to make the foundation of his New Testament work, was very nearly not finished, as his strength often threatened to desert him again. The doctors insisted that he leave Palestine as soon as possible, and urged him for the sake of his health to take a complete rest in a temperate climate. But it went against his grain to abandon what he considered his battle position, and like St. Paul he was resolved to pursue his course unto the end. Leave Jerusalem? Out of the question; he would die there. It required the paternal insistence of the Most Rev. Martin S. Gillet, then Master General of the Order, to overcome his resistance. On hearing the call to obedience—the rule of his entire religious life

---

[82] *Op cit.*, p. 27: "They are not voters coming to vote, casting ballots which are valid in themselves. They are documents having a validity which is the validity of the sources and of the methods which gave them their final form."

[83] *Ibid.*, p. 31.

[84] Kirsopp and Silva Lake, "De Westcott et Hort au Père Lagrange et au delà," *RB* 48 (1939), p. 497.

—he set out for St. Maximin in Provence, where he had spent the days of his novitiate.

No one who knew P. Lagrange expected him, once he had returned to France, to follow the quiet regime prescribed for him by the physicians. At Jerusalem his absence was keenly felt, and all the more painfully at this time because it appeared to be so final. The brethren at St. Maximin, fully aware of their good fortune in having such a master in their midst, moved to profit by it, and it was soon arranged that P. Lagrange would give a course in exegesis to the students, one hour each week on Genesis, another on St. John. Just as in medieval times listeners crowded about the feet of famous masters, so now the whole community flocked to his lectures. For two years, despite an increasing feebleness, P. Lagrange continued to teach, his mind clear and his memory keen. He also worked steadily on his *Introduction au Nouveau Testament,* and in 1937 added to it the volume dealing with the pagan mysteries (*Orphisme*). His interest in the *Revue biblique* was as keen as ever, and he offered to correct the galleys for each issue. In addition he conducted a series of conferences for university teachers and student groups in many university towns of the *Midi.* Finally, and here is added proof of the remarkable continuity of his thought, he began the revision of the commentary, set aside some thirty years before, on Genesis.[85]

As at the Fribourg Congress in 1898, P. Lagrange favored the hypothesis of Elohist and Yahwist documents, and of the Priestly Code (to this latter he assigned a rather recent date). What was new was his attribution of both E and J to Moses. He felt that the distinction between these two documents corresponded to a change which had taken place in Israel's religious history after the revelation of the Exodus. From that moment on the Eternal One, who until then had been adored as Elohim, assumed the name of Yahweh, thus emphasizing the intimacy and close alliance which he would now maintain with the patriarchal people charged with its universal mission. With the conquest of Canaan about to begin, Moses stirred up the people, demanding of it the sacrifice of certain present goods in view of future hopes. At such a time he would surely have recalled to them the

---

[85] Vincent, "Le Père Lagrange," *RB* 47 (1930), 352–354.

great deeds of the past enshrined in the traditions preserved in Egypt — this was the *Elohist,* filled with souvenirs of the patriarchs, and in which God was invariably designated by his old name. The *Yahwist,* on the other hand, had been composed under the direction and at the instigation of the great lawgiver of Israel, and came into being after God had said to him: "I am who I am. It is thus that you shall answer the children of Israel: He who is, sent me to you. . . . You shall speak thus to the children of Israel: 'Yahweh, the God of your fathers, the God of Abraham and the God of Jacob, sends me to you.' This is my name forever, and thus am I to be remembered throughout the ages (Ex 3:14 ff.)." Once this revelation had been made, nothing could have been more natural than that Jewish history should have been rewritten from a new point of view. The Yahwist did precisely that. In style so different from E, different in the handling of facts, a more familiar manner of describing the relationship between Israel and its God, all this resulted in a harmony not unlike that of the four Gospels, faithful witnesses of one and the same Jesus, but from different points of view.

It is difficult to explain how two works as different as E and J could have been written by one man, but there is a simple solution at hand, namely, that Moses was the author of both inasmuch as he was the instigator, the inspiration, and the approver of a work written by another. This much granted, Moses becomes the author of all of Genesis, of which the *Priestly Code* (=P, a résumé), contains additions that do not change the meaning of that incomparable work. With E and J in existence, Moses could readily have fused them into a single work in order to change the nation's use of the name Elohim into that of Yahweh. And this he did, not because he wanted to abolish the name of Elohim, but so as to bring out in a more tangible way the unity existing between the nation's past, and the present which was now opening wide to messianic hopes.[86]

On rereading these brief remarks and looking at what P. Lagrange says in his posthumous article, written after forty years of thought on the matter, one finds himself thinking of Moses who, after having

---

[86] Lagrange, "L'authenticité mosaïque de la Génèse et la théorie des documents," *ibid.,* pp. 163–183.

crossed the desert, was to die at the threshold of the Promised Land into which he could do no more than to direct his gaze.

The busy pen fell from P. Lagrange's hand as he was correcting the proofs for his last article, on the Pentateuch. On a Friday, March 4, 1938, he had given his regular lecture on the Passion, but the following day failed to appear at his customary hour for Mass in the cell of P. Lacordaire, having during the night been suddenly stricken with the flu. A dangerous congestion of the lungs set in, and on the following Wednesday he was anointed in the presence of his brethren. On Thursday morning, with a last smile at the name of Mary, he raised his arms heavenward and murmured his last word — "Jerusalem!" A few moments later he surrendered his soul to the Master he had served so well, and entered into the heavenly Jerusalem on March 10, 1938, the anniversary to the day when, about to begin his life's work, he had first set foot upon the streets of the earthly Jerusalem.

CHAPTER V

SECRET OF A FULL LIFE

"If you would judge a man correctly," Montaigne once wrote,[1] "you must long observe him, following his path to see whether his constancy rests on a firm foundation and whether 'the way of his life is thoroughly considered and thought out.' If the variety of events causes him to alter his pace (I mean his *path,* for the pace may be faster or slower), let him go, for such a man is one who runs before the wind. . . ."

We have patiently followed P. Lagrange from the moment he entered religious life down to his dying day, and have noted that, despite the obstacles which beset it, his path was remarkably straight and consistent with the ambitions of his youth. Montaigne also believed it wrong to try to judge a man from external actions only. One has to enter into a man's soul in order to discover the sources of his energy, an undertaking so noble and so fraught with peril that, according to the author of the famous *Essays,* few should ever make the attempt.

This alone might give us pause, were it not that the driving force in P. Lagrange's life is so consistently revealed in everything that he did. Ryckmans with fine insight says that it is only the "love for God and for the Church, a passion for the truth and for scientific research combined with absolute detachment, which make it possible for a man to pursue, in isolation, a strenuous, unending task."[2] P. Lagrange always sought to do what he could for the good of souls.

His desire to be of service and his preoccupation with the salvation

---

[1] *Essays,* II, 1: "On the Inconstancy of our Actions."

[2] G. Ryckmans, "Le Père Lagrange," *La Revue catholique des idées et des faits* (December 22, 1933), p. 6.

of souls had directed him to the Order of St. Dominic and dominated his entire career. Whether he was faced with many heavy burdens or confronted with difficulties which would ordinarily have halted many men, he made his decisions with calm and consistent courage.

There are few pages where he so clearly stated his purpose as in the Foreword to the *Revue biblique.*

> I venture to liken Holy Scripture, a holy thing ordained by God for the salvation of souls, to the Sacraments. Catholics cannot do too much to show their love and veneration for the Sacrament of the Altar, recognizing that all their ceremonial pomp and all the splendor of their art fail to do It justice. Yet the priest exposes It to profanation when he gives It to one who, unknown to him, receives it sacrilegiously. The good of souls requires this. I love to hear the Gospel chanted by the deacon as he stands at the lectern surrounded by clouds of incense; the words sink more profoundly into my soul then than when I find them fought over in magazines. This "holy thing" is *a light for souls,* and I must make it shine in them, even if this means that it must go forth from the sanctuary.[3]

His proposal to start a *Revue* in which the theories of liberal exegetes would be examined had been opposed, and he had argued for the spiritual value of such a *Revue*. "The truth cannot disappear, but it can be obscured in men's minds, and this can bring about spiritual ruin. And what can be most fatal for souls is not so much material error, into which any theologian may inadvertently fall, as the suspicion that the theologians say nothing either because they are in doubt of the truth, or do not know it is being attacked."[4] "Where *the good of souls* is at stake," he added, "a mistake traceable to haste will be less harmful than inaction."[5]

When P. Lagrange was writing his famous lecture on the "Sources of the Pentateuch," and shortly afterward when he was about to inaugurate the collection known as the *Études bibliques,* prudent friends urged him to confine his efforts to purely oriental studies, and thus forestall almost certain criticism.[6] But his *desire to do good* with-

---

[3] *RB* 1 (1892), p. 2.
[4] *Ibid.,* p. 3.
[5] *Ibid.,* p. 4.
[6] L. H. Vincent, "Le Père Lagrange," *RB* 47 (1938), p. 342.

out counting the cost drove him forward, as it had driven St. Francis de Sales. He knew what this would demand of him in long-term efforts, exhausting labor, and unpleasantness, but such considerations did not deter him. He heartily endorsed P. de Grandmaison's remark that it "doesn't really matter much if my reputation is strewn in pieces along the road that is traversed by truth."[7] At various times he expressed his willingness to give up Scripture studies because he thought his silence might be more useful to the Church than his continued speaking out. If at times he somewhat hastily sponsored views not sufficiently thought out, or went back over this or that conclusion to sharpen or even to correct it, he was only doing what every pioneer has to do. Looking back over the road he traveled for more than fifty years, one is amazed to perceive how sound his thought, how accurate and balanced his solutions, and how constant his motives for acting. In this regard nothing is more significant or more impressive than the spiritual *testament* which was found in his desk after his death.

> I declare before God that it is my intention to die in the Holy Catholic Church to which I have always belonged with my whole heart and soul since the day of my baptism, and to die there faithful to my vows of poverty, chastity, and obedience, in the Order of St. Dominic. To that end I commend myself to my good Savior Jesus, and to the prayers of his most holy Mother who has always been so good to me.
>
> I declare also most expressly that I submit to the judgment of the Apostolic See all that I have written. I believe that I can add that I have always had the intention, in all my studies, of contributing to the good, and by that I mean: to the reign of Jesus Christ, to the honor of the Church, to the good of souls.

Such strength of will and unflinching honesty would be inexplicable without a driving passion behind them. The work conceived by P. Lagrange "in the joyous rashness of youth and inexperience" defied all calculations of human prudence. In one way or another, he would try "to create a complete method of study and teaching, one which would combine teaching with the scientific exploration of the land. . . ." "This was perhaps a mistake," he wrote, "and certainly hampered the

---

[7] Cited by P. Jean Levie, "Le Père Lagrange," *NRTh* 65 (1938), p. 467.

professors in their own researches. The American school changes directors annually; it is a mission in Palestine which begins over again each year. The German school has kept the same director, but he is the only permanent element there, and speculative teaching there is reduced to practically nothing. The *Görresgesellschaft* provides scholarships for young Catholic priests who have time to travel about the land. The professors at S. Étienne bit off too much when they undertook both oriental studies *and* the exploration of the land." But on the whole he did not regret his policy; the religious life helped him carry out the plan. "The ideal of sacrifice which the religious life demands of a man makes it possible to count on his living for a long period far from the joys of home and fatherland; its ideal of fraternity creates in the land where Jesus walked a veritable family workshop where all knowledge is shared in common."[8]

For one like P. Lagrange, Dominican religious life was not just talk. A Dominican religious is obliged to tend toward perfection, toward that greater love of God which also awakens the love for one's neighbor. This law, so basic to his profession, imposes upon a Dominican the rigorous obligations of his state in life, as well as unselfishness and dedication to the good of souls.

His vow of obedience served to stimulate his enterprising spirit, especially as he felt that a man who was entrusted with a task in the Church should do his level best to make it succeed. The founding of a *practical* school of biblical studies had at first sight seemed so certainly doomed to failure before it began that, had it not been imposed upon him by obedience, it is unlikely that he would have interrupted his university studies even to make the attempt. And when later the modernist crisis was at its height and he found himself under attack from all sides, unable to open his mouth without arousing serious suspicions, he would have given it all up, had not the General of the Order commanded him to continue. He therefore remained at his battle post; good soldiers do not question the orders of their commanding officers.[9] Yes, obedience served him well. A superficial viewer might suppose that by paralyzing his freedom of movement, it must

---

[8] *RB* 24 (1915), p. 249.
[9] Cf above, p. 96.

have hindered him from giving his best. The story of his life proves that such was not the case.

His labors, pursued for half a century without notable interruption, were productive, sound, and of an amazing variety. If the voice of obedience had not periodically spoken to him, his application of principles might possibly have carried him into the dense and tangled thickets of the Old Testament, and he might never have produced his remarkable commentaries on the Gospels. Who can say which was the greater good? Biblical criticism has given us a host of freethinkers who left powerful systems behind them. But what they all lacked — and the reason why their systems were replaced by others quite opposite, within a short span of years — was precisely a lack of discipline, of that control which could have rescued them from being fascinated by their own opinions, or from making sweeping conclusions from their otherwise quite correct observations. It is no recommendation for the methods of F. C. Strauss, of Renan, and, closer to our own day, of Loisy, that their "undisciplined" works tended to the complete destruction of religion and substituted for it a cult of progress or of humanity. In contrast, consider the clear-cut lines which, in the absence of any planned organization, guided the many-sided work of Lagrange, the Master of Jerusalem, toward the summits of faith which had drawn the Apostles themselves.

The monastic observance called for by the Constitutions of the Friars Preachers furnished an appropriate framework for the work of the Master. Each time he returned to the convent after an absence, he experienced a new thrill of joy. "It is good to visit famous cities like Petra and Palmyra (both swallowed up now by the desert), or the famous labyrinth of Minos, to spend hours in the museums of Cairo, Athens, or Candia. How swiftly the time passes then! But most pleasant of all, by far, are those moments when we find ourselves back once again at our beloved S. Étienne, where brethren can count upon the support of their own."[10]

P. Lagrange was first of all a good religious, and then a great scholar. The ideal of his Dominican profession came before everything else,

---

[10] *RB* 24 (1925), p. 258.

and explains why he lived, worked, suffered, and risked his life as he did. Those who lived with him will vouch for the fact, and will recall those little mannerisms, which, without his ever being aware of them, revealed the warmth of his religious life.[11] I have no intention of writing an edifying history of P. Lagrange, because it would be imprudent of me to do so, and would have been distasteful to him. I will therefore simply mention briefly his punctilious respect for the Constitutions of his Order, even in minor matters. He was regular at Conventual Office. He used objects placed at his disposition carefully, and was consistent in his submission to the decisions of his superiors. Austere but not harsh, his unfailing thoughtfulness for his fellow religious was one of the most potent factors in his influence over others. Newman has put it well:

> The silent conduct of a conscientious man secures for him from beholders a feeling different in kind from any which is created by the mere versatile and garrulous Reason. . . . Men naturally prize what is novel and scarce; and considering the low views of the multitude on points of social and religious duty, their ignorance of those precepts of generosity, self-denial, and high-minded patience which religion enforces, nay their skepticism (whether known to themselves or not) of the example in the world of severe holiness and truth, no wonder they are amazed when accident gives them a sight of these excellences in another, as though they beheld a miracle; and they watch it with a mixture of curiosity and awe.
>
> Besides, the conduct of a religious man is quite above them. They cannot imitate him, if they try. It may be easy for the educated among them to make speeches, or to write books; but high moral excellence is the attribute of a school to which they are almost strangers, having scarcely learned, and that painfully, the first elements of the heavenly science. One little deed, done against the natural inclination for God's sake, though in itself of a conceding or passive character, to brook an insult, to face danger, or to resign an advantage, has in it a power outbalancing all the dust and chaff of mere profession; the profession whether of enlightened benevolence and candor, or, on the other hand, of high religious faith and of fervent zeal.[12]

---

11 J. Chaine, "Journée et menus propos du Père Lagrange," *Mémorial Lagrange* (Paris: Gabalda, 1940), pp. 355–360.

12 "Personal Influence, the Means of Propagating the Truth," *Oxford University Sermons* (New York: Longmans, Green & Co., 1918), p. 92 f.

When the venerable old man, grown gray-haired as he pored over his texts, came to take up his residence at St. Maximin, the younger members of the community were not surprised at his enthusiasm for things Dominican; his attachment to the rules of his Order had become a necessary part of him. They could also see that fame had not altered his almost childlike simplicity; it never had. They found themselves remembering Jesus' words, "Unless you become like little children, you shall not enter the kingdom of heaven."[13]

An exquisite simplicity, the mark of all great souls, lay behind the piety everywhere present in his work. From the beginning of his novitiate he nourished his devotion by reading the Bible,[14] and his critical studies, far from drying up that devotion, served to intensify it. The jealous way in which he guarded it lay behind his care to make of S. Étienne a genuinely Dominican convent, one which radiated from the church in which the brethren could daily assemble for the celebration of the Holy Sacrifice of the Mass and for the solemn chanting of the Divine Office.

Before rebuilding the ancient basilica of Eudocia on the spot hallowed by the blood of the protomartyr Stephen, P. Lagrange's devotion toward Mary led him to confide these holy precincts to her care.

> It was in her honor that the cloister wall was built [he wrote], and the niches in that wall recall the mysteries of the Rosary. Already those processions so dear to the Orient wend their way along the circular road of this fortress. It is wonderful thus to relive with Mary, in close proximity to Bethlehem and Calvary, these moments in the life of her Son Jesus.[15] . . . But Mary prepares the way for Jesus. Every third Sunday of the month, the Blessed Sacrament makes its way with modest pomp along the same route, recalling the days of His hidden life when the people of Jerusalem witnessed His kindness and meekness.[16]

Jesus and Mary, brought together or, rather, ever united, were the

---

[13] Mt 18:2.

[14] We were told this by P. Lagrange himself. Being strongly attracted by Scripture, he obtained permission from his director to use the Bible exclusively for his spiritual reading. His biblical vocation, so obviously motivated by religious reasons, dates from this contact with the Sacred Books.

[15] *Saint Étienne et son sanctuaire à Jérusalem* (Paris: Picard, 1894), p. 172.

[16] *Ibid.*, p. 173.

two poles of his devotion. He turned effortlessly from the one to the other with a tender intimacy inspired by a great spirit of faith. It was during his morning Mass and afternoon visit to the Blessed Sacrament that he put himself most actually in the Lord's presence and renewed his desire to serve Him, unstintingly dedicating his life *usque ad mortem* for the good of souls.

Mary, however, was his queen. He invoked her help on every occasion, and took pleasure in dedicating his works to her. He announced the inception of the *Études bibliques* and the commentary on St. Matthew on March 25, the feast of the Annunciation. The commentaries on SS. Mark and Luke were dated December 8 and 7, the feast and vigil of the Immaculate Conception. His preoccupation with her rises to the surface in his introduction to the commentary on St. John: "John's Gospel is the choicest of all. No one can acquire its spirit unless he has reposed upon the bosom of Jesus, and received Mary from Jesus as his own mother. The name of Mary revives our confidence. It is through her that we ask the supernatural light needed for understanding a book so charged with divine meanings."[17]

He saluted Mary in passing on many occasions. Writing on the Infancy Gospel, he declared:

If it be not presumptuous to go so far in the analysis of the development of His human character, we may say that there was in Him, as there is in many others, something of His Mother's influence. Where do we find the grace, the exquisite delicacy, the kindly tenderness that we find in Him? And these are precisely the characteristics of such as have had their hearts softened by the tenderness of a mother's love, their minds refined by communication with a beloved and revered mother who has taken delight in teaching them how to appreciate the more delicate refinements of human life.[18]

On the crucifixion, he wrote:

Our piety towards Mary discerns, in her attitude at the foot of the Cross, an indication of her place in our redemption. She suffered in the suffering of her Son, she suffered with Him for our sins. In suffering with her Son she adds nothing to His infinite merits, but joins

---

[17] *Évangile selon saint Jean* (Paris: Gabalda, 1925), p. 1.
[18] *The Gospel of Jesus Christ* (London: Burns, Oates & Washbourne, 1938), I, 55.

her own to His. Associating herself with the work of Him whom she had given to the world for its salvation, she participated in His dying work no less than she did at His birth.[19]

From his living in the presence of Jesus and Mary, there came to P. Lagrange both strength and light, and a great supernatural peace which immunized him to vainglory or childish fear, and helped him to endure willingly whatever situations arose. His will *to serve* dominated all his days. Ryckmans, one of his outstanding students, has described that life for us.

By seven o'clock each morning, his Mass and thanksgiving finished, P. Lagrange retired to his cell. Until midday he was cut off from among the living; unseen, unapproachable almost, and one hardly ever caught sight of him. But now and then his tall, bulky figure, bent now with age, would be seen hurrying toward the library, where a reference had to be verified or a book consulted. His tired eyes gave him an abstracted air, but beneath his brimless hat, the face behind the grizzled beard, at which he tugged so impatiently, was alive. He wrote countless pages in a small but regular script. He kept his morning hours sacrosanct, reserved them for intense concentration and thought, only slackening his pace when it was time for midday Office. Then, exemplary religious that he was, he regularly took his place in choir. He relaxed during the recreation which followed lunch, and in it manifested an exquisite simplicity and openness of soul. He would shake with silent laughter at the wit displayed at those times, and his own sallies were worth remembering. He spoke with deliberation, with a courtesy inherited from an old bourgeois line of France. For me, he was one of the last of the humanists. The Greek and Latin classics were his companions during the heavier hours of the day, and he spent the afternoons reading proof, or leafing through the piles of books brought in each day by mail.[20]

It was thus that he lived until he died.

I can see him now in my mind's eye less than a week before his death. Taking advantage of a trip to Marseilles, I journied to S. Maximin one fine afternoon in March. The prior told me that he had not informed P. Lagrange of my coming visit, lest the news excite him. And then, through the open door, I saw him at his worktable, a batch

---

[19] *Saint Jean,* p. 494 f.
[20] Ryckmans, *loc. cit.*

of proofs in one hand, his absent gaze turned inquiringly toward the visitor who was arriving unannounced during his busy hours. But soon we were engaged in one of those cordial, intimate conversations the Master loved to hold with his old pupils. He was now eighty-two years of age, I was told, and his eyes protesting fiercely at his continued demands. What was he working on? Ah, that Pentateuch *redivivus!* A long article on it was ready for the next issue of the *Revue biblique.* The commentary on Genesis was "on the way," already half finished. "La Genèse, c'est un os que l'on me donne à ronger jusqu'à la mort!" he smiled. "Really," he said, after a pause, "I should be preparing for death, but the Master General insists that I continue to work; I shall do so, with God's help."

At the end of his career, this great religious could again, as he had once before in his "Après vingt-cinq ans," cast a reflective eye back over the route he had traveled. The *École biblique et archéologique française de Jérusalem,* his doing, had been officially recognized by the government of France, and had also served as a model for other similar institutions. Its professors were respected authorities in various fields touching on the Bible, and his pupils occupied chairs of theology in famous universities and far-off seminaries. One of them, Tisserant, wore the cardinalitial purple and presided over the Biblical Commission. Another, P. Vosté, was secretary of that Commission. The *Revue biblique* now comprised many volumes, and *Études bibliques* had become indispensable tools of scholarly research. P. Lagrange had shown those who were uneasy at the negative results of rationalistic criticism that the faith had nothing to fear from a calm search for the truth.[21] He had provided apologists wrestling with concordism with solutions to the principal difficulties raised against Scripture. Theological schools could thank him for sound principles of interpretation, for a method that was critical yet traditional, and for the commentaries which served as a basis for scriptural teaching. He had also placed the Gospel in a new light for those believers who wished to contemplate the true figure of Jesus Christ. He had, moreover, restored

---

[21] It is to this that J. Guitton has borne such eloquent witness in his "Influence of P. Lagrange," *Père Lagrange and the Scriptures* (Milwaukee: The Bruce Publishing Co., 1946), pp. 170–178.

to Catholic exegesis an awareness of its own dignity, and given it confidence that it possessed those scientific titles which gave it a right to be heard in the most critical circles.

Like the good servant in the parable, then, he had served well in the house of his Master, courageously putting his talents to fruitful use and sparing neither his time nor strength. Riches he had never sought.[22] He had kept faith with the call of his youth.

We who have lived by his spirit and have counted upon his affection find ourselves terribly alone after his departure. But we rejoice at the thought that he has entered into the joys of his Master. There, more than ever, we can count on him.

---

[22] The colophon on the title pages of the *Revue biblique,* 1892–1894, bore the significant legend: *Doctrinam magis quam aurum* ("Doctrine rather than riches").

CHAPTER VI

THE HARVEST*

OF THE making of books there is no end, writes the author of the *Imitation,* and his words are especially true in the field of Scripture. The surprising amount of activity lately observable in biblical matters may be traced in large part to an almost uninterrupted series of discoveries during the first half of the twentieth century. In less than fifty years the dust of the past has yielded the Code of Hammurabi (1901), the Elephantine Papyri (1903), the proto-Sinaitic inscriptions (1904), the Hittite archives of Boghazkoi (1907), the Nuzi Tablets (1925), the Khorsabad King List (1932), the Mari Tablets (1935), and then, surpassing expectation, the Dead Sea Scrolls (1947 on).[1]

Faced thus with a sudden embarrassment of riches, biblical scholars have turned with a will to the decipherment and evaluation of the new finds, and busied themselves with the task of assimilating the new material. The resultant gain has been a greater understanding of ancient customs and of religious and political backgrounds; chronologies have been readjusted, and progress marked on many fronts.

No sensible author ever turns his manuscript over to a printer without the somewhat melancholy thought that his work, inescapably a product of its time, will soon be out of date, its achievements surpassed by later authors who build upon his foundations or who may have new materials to work upon.[2] So rapid has been the forward

---

* This chapter has been added by the translator.

[1] Archaeology has contributed mightily to the advance of scriptural studies. Earlier discoveries of interest and value to Scripture students are the Rosetta Stone (1798), the Behistun inscription (1835), the Stele of Mesha (1868), the Siloam Inscription (1880), and the Tell el-Amarna Letters (1887).

[2] Fr. Braun's work on P. Lagrange came out in 1943, and antedated the *DAS.* The effect which the Second Vatican Council will have on Scriptural studies will doubtless be considerable.

march of biblical science, and so bewildering the multiplication of terms of reference, that few studies remain for long the last word on any subject.[3]

If an author's contribution to knowledge turns out to be not completely useless, P. Lagrange wrote many years ago,[4] it does not particularly matter what happens to his articles or books. The biblical scholar who is motivated by his faith and a desire to do good to others can be reasonably confident that his efforts will not prove to be entirely fruitless. *Habent sua fata, libelli.* If his sudden inspirations or insights — wrongfully called by some intuitions[5] — do not find an immediate audience, all is not lost; the spoken word swiftly vanishes, but the written record remains, and if that record contains something of value, it will one day be recognized. *Magna est veritas et praevalebit.* Time will reveal the fatal weaknesses of certain theories but brings out the inner strengths of others, accumulating proof for the brilliant conclusions arrived at by the workings of first-class minds.

One ought not be scandalized unduly at the time lag between the insights of scholars, who are, as we are wont to say, "born before their time," and their popular acceptance. Time, absolutely indispensable for the scholarly work of synthesis, works for the common good or, shall we say, for the harvest.

It is time now to gather in the fruits of the work of P. Lagrange.

THE ÉCOLE BIBLIQUE

P. Lagrange was a prolific scholar, producing in his lifetime eighteen books, scores of articles, and hundreds of book reviews. Most of his work appeared in the *Revue biblique* or in the *Études bibliques.* More important than any of his books, however, is the *École biblique et archéologique française de Jérusalem* with which his name shall forever

---

[3] Written only a short time ago, P. de Vaux's articles on the *Hebrew Patriarchs* (cf *RB* 53 [1946] and 55 [1948]) and his remarkable study on *Israel* (cf *Dict. de la Bible, Supplément,* IV [1947], cols. 729–777) must already be reworked in order to incorporate into them the new material that has since come to light.

[4] Cf *RB* 9 (1900), p. 442 f., where P. Lagrange shows a healthy realism.

[5] It should not be forgotten that the sudden insights of scholars are seldom lucky guesses, but conclusions reached after intensive preliminary work.

be associated. Founded in 1890, the School now has a history, and its present flourishing conditions indicates that a long future lies ahead of it.

At times the *École biblique* has teetered precariously on the brink of ruin. One has but to recall how frequently it was subjected to attack and how often it was viewed with suspicion by well-meaning critics to appreciate how far the School has come, and to savor properly the high praise lavished on it by Pope Pius XII in the *Divino Afflante Spiritu.* In a way quite unprecedented in an official papal document, Pius takes up and repeats the honorable mention given on another occasion to the *École biblique.* Summarizing the positive steps taken by his predecessors for the advancement of biblical studies, he writes:

> Wherefore the same Pontiff [Leo XIII], as he had already praised and approved the school for biblical studies founded at St. Stephen's, Jerusalem, by the Master General of the Sacred Order of Preachers — from which, to use his own words, "biblical science itself had received no small advantage, while giving promise of more" — so in the last year of his life he provided yet another way by which these same studies . . . "might daily make greater progress and be pursued with the greatest possible security."[6]

The reminder of Leo XIII's eulogy of the *École biblique,* along with Pius XII's words of praise, bear eloquent testimony to the esteem with which the School has come to be regarded, and are "highly significant of Pius XII's desire to approve the achievements and tendencies of the school founded and for long presided over by Father Lagrange."[7]

Deprived of the presence of its founder early in the 1930's, and of his active cooperation by his death in 1938, the *École biblique* continued the work for which it was founded, notwithstanding the hazards attendant upon life in the Near East, where the descendants of Ismael and Isaac carry on their unending fratricidal feud. The restrictions imposed upon foreigners living in Jerusalem have at times been galling

---

[6] *Enchiridion biblicum,* 4 (Roma: Arnodo, 1961), #541. Cf *RSS (Rome and the Study of Scripture* [St. Meinrad: Grail Publications, 1958], p. 83).

[7] J. Levie, S.J., *The Bible, Word of God in Words of Men* (New York: P. J. Kenedy & Sons, 1962), p. 146.

and heavy, especially during and immediately after the War of 1947–1948. But despite such handicaps, the School has remained open, continuing its archaeological expeditions whenever possible, often under conditions which would cause one less inured to an atmosphere of crisis and tension to blanch.

The school year at S. Étienne begins in October. The schedule is adapted to study: two hours of class each morning, one in the afternoon. Before the coming of the early rains in late October, a ten-day trip to some part of Palestine or Syria is arranged; during the Easter vacation another and longer voyage takes place. One thus sees a considerable portion of Bible lands in the course of a year at St. Stephen's: Lebanon and Syria, Egypt and the pyramids to Karnak and Luxor, across the Suez Canal to Mt. Sinai, then on to Eziongeber, to Petra, a fabled rose-red city half lost in time. The route of the Exodus, traced out by automobile, ends with a swing around the eastern edge of the Dead Sea, en route to Jericho and Jerusalem.

Trips such as these are a feature of the life at the *École biblique* and engrave themselves unforgettably upon the memory; one never quite recovers from such experiences. Dozens of pictures, taken with varying success, later serve to supplement lectures on Old and New Testament passages.[8]

In addition to the annual voyages, there are also weekly archaeological promenades to some site or other in Jerusalem. These are anything but the typical tourist visits, for they are made with chapter and verse in mind, theory and practice thus mutually complementing each other. Those who have studied at St. Stephen's will remember thus visiting the ruins of Ophel, sloshing through the tunnel of Siloe,[9] passing the *sinnor*[10] on the way to the spring Gihon; they will also remember inspecting the foundations of the Church of the Resurrection, locating the various pools in and around the city, walking in the

---

[8] How profitable these trips can be to Bible readers everywhere is shown by the appearance, in Dutch, French, and English, of Fr. L. H. Grollenberg's *Atlas of the Bible* (London: Nelson, 1956).

[9] For a discreet account of the extraordinary Parker Expedition, cf *RB* 20 (1911), pp. 566–591; *ibid.,* 21 (1912), pp. 86–111, 424–453, 544–574.

[10] It was probably through this well shaft dug by the Jebusites that "Joab went up" (1 Chron 11:4–6), thus delivering the hitherto impregnable city into David's hands.

Temple area, visiting Haceldama, Gethsemani, the Mount of Olives, Bethany, and so on.

And then there are the monthly archaeological trips, begun usually by car and continued on foot. In the course of a year the visitor can hardly fail to acquire a rather good knowledge of the Holy Land by personal visits to many important sites mentioned in the Bible: Anathoth, Hebron, Samaria, Nazareth, the Sea of Galilee, Jericho and the Dead Sea, Amaan (ancient Philadelphia), Jerash, and many other places pass vividly before the inner eye as often as the liturgy brings pertinent sections of the biblical narrative to mind.

The student body of the *École biblique* has never been large, judging by our standards. In the charming convent of St. Stephen's there are twenty-seven rooms for the Brethren; the *École,* a separate building, can house fifteen guests; nonresident students and auditors augment that number. As the lectures are given in French, the majority of students quite naturally come from France and Belgium, but many come from many other countries also; in 1962 there were at the *École biblique* representatives from all five continents.

The infant school has grown and become father to a family of scholars scattered throughout the Christian world. Some of the alumni of the School have attained important positions in the Church. Most of the students at St. Stephen's became seminary professors or teachers in famous universities: among these, Fathers Colunga, Chaine, Spicq, Ryckmans, Festugière, might be singled out for special mention.

It is indicative of P. Lagrange's foresight and detachment that with his retirement and death the momentum of the School did not slacken. He had early manifested a genius for detecting and selecting talented younger men for tasks particularly suited to them, and as a result had many strong hands to assist him and to take up the burden when failing health obliged him to leave Jerusalem. His successors have never been carbon copies of himself. He had once said: "If everybody walks along the same path, it becomes a rut. I would like to be *one* furrow in a field — a well-plowed field!"[11]

---

[11] For this item I am endebted to Fr. André Legault, C.S.C. Cf. "Anointings in Galilee and Bethany," *CBQ* 16 (1954), p. 138. For the story of the detection of P.

At any rate P. Lagrange's wish has been amply fulfilled. Twenty-five years after his death the *Revue biblique* ran to seventy volumes, each several hundred pages in length. This "supreme Catholic review devoted to the Bible"[12] is issued under the direction of P. Pierre Benoit, O.P. Born in 1905, P. Benoit is professor of New Testament exegesis at St. Stephen's. Many of his articles have been translated and given in digest in other languages; the more important of them have recently been published in two volumes (*Exégèse et Théologie*); selections • from this work are presently being translated into English.[13] His revision of P. Synave's commentary on St. Thomas' tract on prophecy[14] is available in English translation under the title of *Prophecy and Inspiration,*[15] and contains searching studies on inspiration, biblical inerrancy, and literary forms. He has pursued his analysis of inspiration in the second edition of Robert-Tricot's *Initiation biblique,* our English *Guide to the Bible.*[16] Besides contributing to the *Jerusalem Bible* (*Matthew* and the *Pastoral* Epistles), he has exercised a tremendous influence on young biblical scholars on both sides of the Atlantic.[17]

The *École biblique* is at present under the guidance of the gifted P. Roland de Vaux, O.P., who has spent thirty years of his life (he was born in 1903) in Palestine, first as a student, then as a staff

---

Vincent's abilities, cf *CBQ* 17 (1955), pp. 233–247. Independence of mind has indeed characterized the men who compose the staff at the *École biblique.* Always respectful of another's right to his own views, they make up their own minds. Thus it was noticed by friendly observers, with a smile, how P. Lagrange and P. Abel used to say the Stations. They began from opposite ends of the Holy City, P. Lagrange from the Antonia, and P. Abel from the Citadel. There was little danger at S. Étienne, then, of the path becoming a rut!

[12] Levie, *op. cit.,* p. 128, writes, "The magisterial series of the *Études bibliques* and the sustained excellence of the *Revue biblique* has long commended the School to the learned world, though the public has known little of it."

[13] Paris: Editions du Cerf, 1961, 2 vols., 461 pages. Fr. Zerwick, S.J., in reviewing this work, speaks of P. Benoit as "unus ex maxime fecundis in re exegetica scriptoribus nostris" (*Verbum Domini,* 40 [1962], p. 49).

[14] *Somme Théologique, La Prophétie,* 2–2, qq. 171–178 (Paris: Desclée et Cie., 1947).

[15] New York: Desclée, 1961. In this publication the text of the Angelic Doctor is omitted. The notes have, however, been revised and expanded.

[16] New York: Desclée, 1961. P. Benoit's contribution covers pp. 9–54.

[17] Cf *RB* 68 (1961), pp. 161–196, for his very intelligent presentation of the "fuller sense."

member at the School. A rare pedagogue and a scholar endowed with exceptional judgment, he is professor of the Old Testament and is widely known for his work at Khirbet Qumran.[18] Readers of the *Revue biblique* have enjoyed his delightful account of the "oriental" way in which he elicited from the Bedouin the exact location of the caves from which the Dead Sea Scrolls were being taken.[19] Thanks to him and to Mr. G. Lankester Harding, director of the Jordan Department of Antiquities, the work of recovery has been organized on a scientific basis.

As president of the Board of Trustees of the Rockefeller Museum of Jerusalem, P. de Vaux was, along with Msgr. Patrick Skehan of the Catholic University of America, Fr. Milik, and Frank M. Cross (now of Harvard University), one of the few men allowed instant access to the newly discovered scrolls. Because of the part P. de Vaux played in their discovery, he was in 1959 invited to give the Schweich Lectures at the British Academy in London.[20] Before this he had been elected president of the Second Congress of the International Organization of Old Testament Scholars, and had delivered the presidential address at the international Congress held at Strasbourg from October 27 to November 1, 1956.[21]

Besides taking a personal part in the recovery of the fragments of the scrolls and the exact documentation, mapping, and reconstruction of the excavations at Qumran and Murabba'at, P. de Vaux has directed the nine campaigns of excavation undertaken by the *École biblique* at Tell Far'ah near Naplus. His detailed reports on this remarkable tell indicate that it was the site of an important city in the fourth millennium B.C., and at a later date the site of Tirzah (1 Kgs 14:17), where King Omri lived before moving the capital of the northern kingdom to Samaria.[22]

---

[18] The *Revue* has followed this fascinating development very closely, the first article appearing in Volume 56 (1949), p. 234 ff.

[19] *RB* 60 (1953), p. 245 f.

[20] The title of these lectures was "L'Archéologie et Qumran." They were published as *L'Archéologie et les Manuscripts de la Mer Morte* (London: Oxford University Press, 1961), pp. xv–107, 42 plates.

[21] Cf *ZAW* 68 (1956), pp. 225–227, "A propos de la Théologie Biblique."

[22] Cf *RB* 54 (1947), pp. 394–433, to 68 (1961), pp. 557–592. *The Biblical Archaeologist* (1949), p. 66 ff., has followed these excavations with interest.

Some idea of the tremendous vitality and drive of the Director of the *École biblique* may be gleaned from the fact that between 1938 and 1963 he has written not less than thirty-five articles for the *Revue biblique*, has contributed *Genesis, Samuel* and *Kings* to the *Jerusalem Bible*, and has published his *Institutions de l'Ancien Testament.* This study of the social framework of the Old Testament has been translated into English under the title *Ancient Israel*,[23] and is hailed by no less an authority than Dr. William Albright as being "without a peer in the field."

With the death of P. Lagrange (1938), and then, at intervals, by those of P. Abel (1953), and P. Vincent (1950), the *Revue* lost three of its most reliable and valuable contributors. Others, however, have caught up the slack. P. Couroyer has produced eighteen articles dealing with Egypt and the Bible, while over the same period Pères Benoit, Boismard, and Tournay have each written seventeen and P. Spicq, fourteen.

"A MOST GRAVE DANGER..."

It was not only in the secular fields of archaeology and epigraphy that activity was observable during the first half of the twentieth century. From 1900 onward, the Church gave ample proof of her traditional concern for everything that touched directly or indirectly upon the Bible. Reacting in a realistic fashion to the biblical skirmishes of the times, she issued, at intervals, a number of biblical directives which it will be the burden of this chapter to examine. We shall thus be enabled to see how well P. Lagrange and his work have withstood the test of time.

Three years after P. Lagrange's death, a letter, forty-eight pages long, was sent to all archbishops and bishops of Italy, including the Holy Father himself. The letter was signed by a Dain Cohenel, the pseudonym chosen by its author, an Italian priest named Dolindo Ruotolo. Entitled *A Most Grave Danger for the Church and for Souls: the Critical-Scientific System of Studying and Interpreting Holy Scripture, Its Evil Misconceptions and Aberrations,* it was a virulent attack on

---

23 New York: McGraw-Hill Book Co., 1962, pp. xxiii–592.

the modern scientific approach to the Bible.[24] According to the author, the modern approach was, behind its mask of research and pretended literal exactitude, a deplorable manifestation of pride, presumption, and superficiality. He proceeded to mount his attack on four different fronts.

1. The Literal Sense

While conceding in principle that the literal sense is the basis of all biblical interpretation, Fr. Ruotolo clearly favored a purely subjective and allegorical kind of exegesis. He berated scholars for their narrow preoccupation with the literal sense alone; thus obsessed, they compounded the evil by understanding the Sacred Text in an exclusively *material* fashion.

2. The Use of the Vulgate

The Tridentine Decree concerning the Vulgate is well known. Fr. Ruotolo declared that Trent had recognized the superiority of the Vulgate and declared it preferable to the Greek or Hebrew or Aramaic text of the Bible. Reproving modern exegetes for attempting to interpret the Vulgate with the help of other ancient versions and with the aid of the original texts, he was convinced that the decree of Trent had given such certitude to the Sacred Text that there was no further need for the Church to prolong her search for the authentic Word of God. Not only were matters of faith and morals definitely assured by the Vulgate, but also all questions of a literary, geographical, or chronological import.

3. Textual Criticism

Fr. Ruotolo felt that textual criticism was an evil, for it treated the Word of God as if it were a mere human production. To practice textual criticism on the Bible was, in the ultimate analysis, to mutilate Scripture and to impugn the authority of the Church. He considered the original texts, under such circumstances, to be of little or no value.

---

[24] Cf *EB* 522–533 and *RSS* 136–145. It may be noted at once that all of Fr. Ruotolo's writings have been placed on the Index.

4. *Original Languages and the Auxiliary Sciences*

The study of oriental languages and of the auxiliary sciences of philology, archaeology, and history was, in Fr. Ruotolo's eyes, the occasion for a manifestation of pride and vainglory. Orientalism was a fetish; and modern oriental science, nothing but rationalism, naturalism, modernism, scepticism, and atheism in disguise.

REPLY OF THE BIBLICAL COMMISSION

That such a letter could have been written at all in the twentieth century is little short of astonishing and indeed not a little appalling. But however ill-advised and intemperate the attack, the Pontifical Biblical Commission drew up a courteous rebuttal of it (August 16, 1941)[25] in the interests of those who might be troubled by the author's insinuations and charges, and who might thus be diverted from studying Scripture.

The Commission's reply is a model of common sense and sober scholarship. The validity and primacy of the literal sense is firmly established in principle and in fact, and it is pointed out that scholars who have contributed most to the Church and to the faith were those who consistently preferred the literal to the allegorical sense. Appeal is made to St. Thomas ("All the senses are founded on one — the literal — from which alone can any argument be drawn"[26]) and quotations from St. Jerome and from the encyclicals of Leo XIII and Benedict XV are marshaled to show how unswervingly the Church has always clung to the literal sense of Scripture.

As for the Vulgate text, which the Council of Trent recommended as authentic, such authenticity was intended in a juridical sense, and in no way implied the superiority of the Vulgate over the original texts. Moreover, the decree of Trent had force only in the West, and did not minimize the authority of the ancient versions used in the Eastern Church, but merely conferred on the Vulgate a place of honor denied to other *Latin versions*. All this is abundantly clear from the

[25] *EB* and *RSS loc. cit.*
[26] *Sum. Theol.,* I, q. 1, a. 10, ad 1um.

minutes of the Council of Trent and from any good work on biblical introduction.

The Commission next pointed out that from the time of Origen and St. Jerome down to our own day, the Church has sought to establish the best possible form of the original texts and versions. Textual criticism is an exacting but rewarding science, encompassed by many difficulties and dangers; by entering into this field Catholic commentators give evidence of their veneration for the Sacred Text. The words of the Commission concerning textual criticism were to be taken up and expanded in the *Divino Afflante Spiritu,* where it is called an "art" and recognized as productive of great and praiseworthy results in the editions of profane writings. It can therefore be "also quite rightly employed in the case of the Sacred Books because of that very reverence which is due to the Divine Oracles."[27]

Finally, Fr. Ruotolo's rejection of the ancillary sciences and oriental languages runs counter to the tradition of the Church from St. Jerome's time to our own, and overlooks the fact that Leo XIII had recommended such studies on several occasions, and that Pius X had in turn made the study of Greek and Hebrew obligatory in all theological institutions of the Church.

We have gone into detail concerning this letter for several reasons, one of which is that the letter might plausibly be construed as an attack upon P. Lagrange and his principles. It was precisely these four points which he had strenuously advocated by word and deed since the beginning of the *École biblique.* However, as there is no allusion made to his name, it is perhaps more defensible to say that the writer of the letter was not attacking any one particular exegete so much as modern exegesis as a whole.

The impassioned appeal made for the "meditative" or personal interpretation of Scripture was an unexpected throwback, so to speak, to the early days of Christianity, and illustrates once again the fascination which the spiritual sense has always exercised upon believers. It is as if the Alexandrian School had once more come to life in the twentieth century. At any rate, the literal sense had once again to fight for its right to existence.

---

[27] *DAS* 17; *RSS* 90.

The letter is, however, important in that it expresses the great anxiety felt by many at the disturbing direction taken by modern exegesis. The fear that the new approach, with its insistence on the human side of God's inspired words to men, will somehow strip Scripture of its divine quality and in the end reduce the Bible to the level of an ordinary human book is quick to awaken. Nor can it be denied that a too ready application of the techniques perfected in the positive sciences can, if imprudently used concerning matters of revelation and inspiration, wreak havoc in the fold of Christ; the list of those lost to the Church via this route is unfortunately not a short one. One can then appreciate the anxiety and acknowledge the zeal that prompted this letter.[28]

On the other hand, the letter brings into sharp relief the dilemma constantly facing the Catholic scholar. Shall he choose to flee from methods which in the past have had unfortunate results for the faith, or should he courageously peer into them to see if they necessarily lead to such lamentable results? The second choice demands a stout heart and a hide of leather, as scholars like St. Jerome, Cajetan, P. Lagrange, and others can testify.

The record has shown that P. Lagrange was providentially inspired to make the second choice. There is no question but that a real scholar should stay abreast of his times and should continue to grow in intellectual stature. Like St. Justin, who "frequented the most celebrated schools of learning among the Greeks that he might try what they were"[29] — P. Lagrange sat at the feet of famous German professors to learn what they were saying and to observe their methods. He wanted to modernize the old principles. Gilson's statement,[30] "the first rule of our action should be that piety never dispenses with technique," brings out the futility of trying to fight against machine guns with crossbows.[31] "Let us get some of the machine guns on our side," P. Lagrange had, in effect, concluded, and it is because he followed up his words

28 T. Worden, "Is Scripture to Remain the Cinderella of Catholic Theology?" *Scripture*, 8 (1956), pp. 2–12.

29 Leo XIII thus compares Saint Justin and Saint Thomas in his *Aeterni Patris*.

30 E. Gilson, *Christianity and Philosophy* (New York: Sheed and Ward, 1939), p. 115.

31 The remark is that of Eugène Chevreul (d. 1889), and appears in P. Vincent's article on P. Lagrange, *RB* 47 (1938), p. 338.

with decisive action that the name Lagrange, today, more than any other, is associated with our biblical revival. "His scholarship and influence, sometimes acknowledged and sometimes not, lie behind innumerable biblical works addressed to the learned or to the general public."[32]

THE "DIVINO AFFLANTE SPIRITU"

The careful and conservative position adopted by the Church in matters concerning the Bible is seldom to the liking of those who are considered liberal and progressive. In the main, however, the Church's stand has been justified by the passage of time, although it is also true that the conservative attitude of the Holy See, coupled with its vigorous stand against modernism, has had the effect of discouraging exegetical studies of any particular depth on a large scale. One unfortunate consequence of such a stand has been that the initiative in biblical studies was left in the hands of those who were either uninterested in or little concerned with tradition or the exigencies of Catholic doctrine. In short, it has amounted to what one might almost call an isolationist position in a world not meant for isolation.

It is now recognized that World War I had the effect of radically shaking up certain cherished rationalistic positions. At any rate, a change of tone in biblical studies can be observed from about 1920 on. Taking a realistic measure of the situation, doubtless prompted in part by the publication of the letter discussed above, Pope Pius XII issued, on September 30, 1943, the third great biblical encyclical to appear within fifty years, the *Divino Afflante Spiritu*.[33]

A thoroughly positive and constructive tone characterizes this encyclical. It breathes forth a more liberal attitude. It has kind things to say about textual criticism, and optimistically strikes a progressive note, encouraging Catholic scholars to take up the tasks of Catholic exegesis. At the same time the Pontiff enjoins upon those who keep a watchful eye upon the biblical scholars to practice charity toward them, abhorring that intemperate zeal which imagines that whatever is new should for that very reason be opposed or suspected.[34]

---

[32] Alexander Jones, "Water and Spirit," *Life of the Spirit*, 11 (1956–1957), p. 13.
[33] *EB* 538–569; *RSS* 80–107.
[34] *RSS* 102.

Outlined in this encyclical is a practical program for the promotion of biblical studies. There is an insistence upon the critical approach, and the importance of oriental languages is stressed; the original texts must not be neglected. The literal sense calls for thorough investigation. Besides this, the wholly distinctive genius of the oriental mind must be taken into account, along with the literary forms and the manner in which the sacred writers thought and wrote. Archaeology, history, and the ancient literatures are to receive close study in the hope of gleaning from them information which will help in the exposition of the proper meaning of Scripture.

The *Divino Afflante,* universally hailed as a wise and far-seeing document, has been called the *Magna Charta* of biblical studies, and is compared to the *Providentissimus Deus* as the *Quadragesimo Anno* is to the *Rerum Novarum.* These comparisons and plaudits are well justified. But particularly significant is the fact that the *Divino Afflante* can be considered as giving an official stamp of approval to the efforts of Catholic scholars of the caliber of P. Lagrange during the fifty years which preceded the encyclical itself.

In Spain the publication of the *Divino Afflante* was also looked upon as a personal triumph for Father Albert Colunga, O.P.,[35] whose contributions to *La Ciencia tomista* and to *Semanas biblicas,* "à la Lagrange," helped prepare the ground for the encyclical. It was hailed as a triumph for Father Ubach, O.S.B., another alumnus of the *École biblique,* who pioneered along the same paths as did Fr. Colunga. But most of all, the *Divino Afflante* is looked upon as a vindication of P. Lagrange, to whom most of the credit for the change in attitude in Catholic biblical studies must be given. By his heroic labors he gave respectability to Catholic biblical scholarship, and he did more than any other to lift the level of Catholic scriptural studies out of mediocrity.

The *Divino Afflante* is a faithful echo of P. Lagrange, and indeed in the critical area of literary forms. Thus we read:

"By this knowledge and exact appreciation of the modes of speaking and writing in use among the ancients can be solved many difficulties

---

[35] A former student of P. Lagrange, Fr. Colunga died, in his eighties, in May, 1962.

which are raised against the veracity and historical value of the Divine Scriptures. . . .[36]

Forty years before these lines were written, P. Lagrange had said:

It [the theory of literary forms] still seems to me to be the most fitting for the resolution of the difficulties raised against the veracity of the Bible. . . .[37]

Again, in speaking of the importance of understanding the *mode* of writing used by the ancients, Pius XII declared:

No one who has a correct idea of biblical inspiration will be surprised to find, even in the Sacred Writers as in other ancient authors, certain fixed ways of expounding and narrating, certain definite idioms, especially of a kind peculiar to Semitic tongues, so-called *approximations*. . . .

What is so significant here is that the encyclical adopts the very word — *approximations* — suggested by P. Lagrange to characterize certain forms of historical narrative encountered in Hebrew antiquity.[38]

THE NEW PSALTER

The *Divino Afflante* was soon to bear fruit. The very first indication of this was a discreet clarification[39] of an earlier response of the Commission[40] concerning the reading in church of translations made from the original texts. Next, on March 24, 1945, in an Apostolic Letter entitled *In Cotidianibus Precibus*[41] Pius XII spoke of a widespread hope, entertained for many years by many priests, of having a Latin psalter which would "bring out more clearly the meaning the Holy Spirit had inspired, [and] give truer expression to the devout sentiments of the Psalmist's soul by reflecting his style and words more exactly."[42]

Taking cognizance of this legitimate longing for a psalter which would reflect some of the progress made in biblical circles in the

---

[36] *RSS* 99.
[37] *Historical Criticism and the O.T.* (London: Catholic Truth Society, 1905), p. 103.
[38] *Ibid.*, pp. 11, 183; *RSS* 98.
[39] *EB* 535–537; *RSS* 146–147.
[40] *EB* 520.
[41] *EB* 571–575; *RSS* 108–111.
[42] *RSS* 109.

1500 years that had elapsed since St. Jerome's translations of the beloved "prayer book of the Old Testament," the Pontiff had entrusted to the professors of the Pontifical Biblical Institute the task of making a new Latin translation of the Psalms which would, insofar as possible, take into account both the venerable Vulgate version of so ancient a dignity, as well as the other ancient versions, making use of sound critical norms whenever they differed.

On the whole, the new Psalter is much clearer than the Old Vulgate version, and certainly contributes to a much better understanding of the Psalms which play so important a part in the daily life of the Church, and of the priests and Sisters who must recite the Psalms. It is no reflection on the translators to say that their work is not wholly satisfactory, for there are places where, "even after every help that textual criticism and a knowledge of languages can offer has been exhausted, the meaning . . . is still not perfectly clear. . . ."[43] A certain amount of unhappiness has also been expressed over the Latinity of the new Psalter; while it is grammatically correct, it seems to have lost that splendor of accustomed sound which accompanies the old Vulgate text. The new Psalter can be used for the private recitation of the Office, but it has proven rather difficult to recite chorally, a fact which may be due to the novel terms introduced into a familiar pattern of monastic prayer. The liturgical books except for breviaries have not as yet been changed to match the new Psalter.

P. Lagrange did not write much on the Psalms as such, but the idea of a new psalter would have pleased him.[44] In his article on two contrasting commentaries on the Psalms, he pleads for an up-to-the-minute look at the text of the Bible, in words which are reminiscent of his famous "Projet d'un commentaire complet. . . ."[45]

> On the terrain of the Bible, things go more slowly because of the sacred character of the inspired books, and also because of the mistrust which certain rash scholars inspire. Still, one can practice a genuine criticism without harm to dogma. One should show his respect for

[43] *Ibid.*, 110.

[44] *RB* 13 (1904), pp. 251–259, comparing Calmet and Fillion; and "Messianisme dans les Psaumes," *ibid.*, 14 (1905), pp. 39–57, 188–202.

[45] *Ibid.*, 9 (1900), pp. 414–423.

Sacred Scripture both by learning from it in a spirit of faith and by using all the resources of reason and of human knowledge in order to understand it.[46]

And again,

Far better to take part in the progress of criticism than to record its backward steps. . . . Yet one must go forward. . . . It is important that priests realize that Catholic tradition does not impose upon them the mentality of a two-year old. . . .[47]

THE SUHARD LETTER

Five years after the *Divino Afflante* there appeared the now famous response to a query submitted to the Pontifical Biblical Commission by Cardinal Suhard of Paris. The response was issued on January 16, 1948, over the signature of Fr. James M. Vosté O.P., secretary of the Commission, and dealt with two problems: (1) the sources of the Pentateuch, and (2) the literary form of Genesis 1-11.[48] In both cases, the progressive tone so noticeable in the *Divino Afflante* is sustained, and it can with justice be said that this letter is one of the first concrete applications of the principles set forth in the encyclical.

The problems raised in the Letter of Cardinal Suhard are extremely complicated, and the reply was clearly not intended as a final solution to them, but was rather meant to dissipate some of the fears and suspicions that have for so long paralyzed Catholic exegesis of the Pentateuch. The Secretary of the Biblical Commission, after expressing his pleasure at the filial confidence which prompted the Cardinal to institute the official inquiry, assures him of the Commission's desire to promote biblical studies while safeguarding for them the greatest freedom within the limits of the traditional teaching of the Church. Catholic scholars are warmly encouraged to peer into the many as yet unsolved problems found in the Bible, and are urged to try to find solutions for them which will be satisfactory to the indubitable conclusions of profane sciences while maintaining the age-old doctrine

---

[46] *Ibid.,* 13 (1904), p. 251.

[47] *Ibid.,* pp. 258–259.

[48] *EB* 45–48; *RSS* 148–151. This *Letter* was praised as explicitly expressing the "attitude of the best OT scholarship towards the problems of the early chapters of Genesis," in *PEQ* 81 (1949), p. 10.

of biblical inerrancy. Fr. Vosté also quotes Pope Pius XII's timely injunction that the labors of the exegetes be viewed with patience and charity, fairness, and justice. "Let all abhor that intemperate zeal which imagines that whatever is new should for that reason be opposed or suspected."[49]

Concerning the Cardinal's first inquiry, the Commission judges that the answers given by it in 1905, 1906, and 1909 "are in no way opposed to further and truly scientific examination of these problems ... [and] that there is no need, at least for the moment, to promulgate any new decrees regarding them."[50] It is noted that the theories concerning the origin of the Pentateuch, theories which have been in vogue until now, have been set aside by many independent scholars "who look for the elucidation of certain redactional peculiarities of the Pentateuch ... in the special psychology, the peculiar processes of thought and expression, better known today, of the early Oriental peoples, or in the different literary style demanded by the diversity of subject-matter."[51] Catholic scholars are invited to study these problems with an open mind, and are assured that, in the light of sound criticism and use of subsidiary sciences, they will doubtless find how great the part and influence Moses exercised in the composition of the Pentateuch.

The second section of the Cardinal's query deals with the question of the literary forms of Genesis 1-11. "Complex problems demand complex answers," P. Lagrange once remarked, and here surely is a case in point. "The literary forms of Genesis 1-11 correspond to none of our classical categories, and cannot be judged in the light of Greco-Latin or modern literary styles. To declare, however, that these narratives do not contain history in our modern sense of the term could easily convey the idea that they do not contain history at all. Actually, they relate in a simple and figurative language, adapted to the understanding of a less developed people, truths which are basic to the economy of salvation, along with a popular account of the origin of the human race and of the Chosen People."[52]

---

[49] *RSS* 149.
[50] *Loc. cit.*
[51] *Ibid.*, p. 150.
[52] *Loc. cit.*

When one turns from a reading of the reply to Cardinal Suhard to P. Lagrange's *Méthode historique,* written almost fifty years earlier, one is simply astonished to find how modern that little book proves to be. The *Letter* of 1948 is full of resonances from the last of its six chapters, entitled "On Primitive History"[53] wherein the role of the sacred writer and his purpose in writing is so reasonably and logically presented. Two sections in his *L'Éclaircissement sur la Méthode historique* take up the question of Primitive History in Genesis, and Apparent History.[54] One cannot but marvel at the soundness of P. Lagrange's views in such matters, and at the way in which the *Divino Afflante* and the *Letter to Cardinal Suhard* have approved them, indirectly at least. And it is to be noted here too how the judicious P. Lagrange never said *is* when he should have said *may be,* nor did he hesitate to say *is* when that was the word to say.[55]

As for the truly ambitious program marked out for Catholic exegetes in the *Letter to Cardinal Suhard,* involving a study of all literary, scientific, historical, cultural, and religious problems connected with Genesis 1–11, and a close study of the literary processes of the early oriental peoples, their psychology, their way of expressing themselves, and their very notion of historical truth,[56] and so on, one is in a much better position today in this regard than he was before the publication of Pritchard's *Ancient Near Eastern Texts.*[57] The source material which is now available to all, was, fifty years ago, practically unknown.

THE BIBLE DE JERUSALEM

When Charles Peguy lamented his ignorance of Hebrew, he was voicing his regret at not being able to understand the Bible as a Hebrew could. To read the Bible in Hebrew or Greek and to

---

[53] *Historical Criticism . . .,* pp. 180–214.

[54] Pp. 60–76, 76–89. It will be recalled that the *Éclaircissement* was never published because of the violence of the debate at that time (1905).

[55] Fr. James M. Connolly in his *Voices of France* (New York: Macmillan, 1961), p. 34, looks upon P. Lagrange as "one of the principal influences in the contemporary biblical revival in France," and on p. 40 says of him that he "brought to the study of Scripture and to the biblical movement as a whole a valuable sense of balance."

[56] *RSS* 150.

[57] University of Princeton Press, 1955.

understand the allusions with which it is filled, to penetrate its mentality so different from our own, is in fact a special privilege not given to many. But the Christian is comforted by the knowledge that if he himself cannot so act, he has, across time and space, many friends who can: an Ignatius of Antioch, a Jerome, an Augustine, a Thomas Aquinas, and, closer to our own times, a P. Lagrange, along with his numerous disciples and imitators. Modern readers of Scripture can also draw on the Fathers of the Church, on saints, theologians, and scholars, each functioning according to his particular gifts in his own niche in that venerable Church which, like Mary who "kept all these things in her heart," watches over the precious deposit of Revelation.

In a word, in the Church where all good things are possessed in common and where each man is at the service of every other, one senses, as he reads the Bible, a whole host of believers of every age and clime peering over his shoulders saying the words with him.

Three years after the end of World War II the first fascicule of the *Bible de Jérusalem* (the *Jerusalem Bible*) was quietly presented to the public. In the next seven years forty-two other volumes followed, and by 1955 a new Catholic Bible was an accomplished fact.

The *Jerusalem Bible,* representing the fruit of the collaboration of some forty scholars, is a fresh, new translation made directly from the Hebrew and Greek texts. Some of the scholars involved in it were biblical scholars, others were *littérateurs* whose task it was to render the translation intelligible to modern readers, while others worked to make the presentation palatable to the reading public. The project was launched in 1946 under the immediate direction of P. de Vaux and P. Benoit. Among the collaborators were twelve Dominicans, seven Sulpicians, five Jesuits, four secular priests, and two Benedictines; one Marist, one Franciscan, one Oratorian; one Basilian also took part. Only one of the five laymen, Étienne Gilson, is well known to Americans, but the others enjoy a considerable reputation in France.

The end product of this cooperative work simply defies flattery and has, since its appearance, exhausted the superlatives of its reviewers.[58]

---

[58] Cf Alexander Jones, *art. cit.,* p. 18. Fr. Jones is currently working on an English translation of the *Jerusalem Bible,* which he considers, "in all sobriety, the best Bible in the world."

One of the first things to strike the eye is the attractive disposition of the text. Instead of the solid page of unrelieved print, there is now a well-aerated arrangement of paragraphs in double columns, each logical unit being preceded by an explanatory (or descriptive) heading. The eye is charmed by the discovery of poetry printed as poetry.

The footnotes in this excellent Bible call for special praise. One notes with relief that there is nothing in them of the defensive; they reveal, instead, the wholesome respect the editors have both for honest difficulties presented by the text, and for the intelligence of readers who earnestly desire to know more about that text. There runs throughout the notes a clear, positive, theological point of view; the editors are obviously of the opinion that exegesis and theology should not be separated. Technical terms of frequent occurrence are explained more fully in "key notes" which contain a highly condensed and up-to-the-minute summary of the point in question, and also, very often, a brief digest of the development of important themes across the various books of the Old or New Testaments.

An ingenious system of marginal cross-references enables the reader to turn quickly to the place where the principal explanation of a word or phrase is to be found. Thus, to give but one example, "Son of Man," in Daniel 7:13 is crossreferenced to Matthew 8:20 ff, which indicates that the term "Son of Man" will be fully explained there.[59]

Each great section of the Old and New Testaments is preceded by an excellent introduction, sixteen of them in all, and each characterized by modernity and prudence. There runs throughout an awareness of and appreciation for the dynamic and developing nature of God's revelation of Himself to man.

The *Jerusalem Bible,* the fruit of sixty years of tireless cultivation of the field of biblical studies, makes full use of modern resources, information, and technique, and is a fitting monument to the *École biblique* and to its founder, P. Lagrange.[60] The word "monument"

---

[59] The important themes of the Bible (e.g., *Alliance, Body, Church, Kerygma, Spirit,* and so on) are alphabetically listed in a special table of contents. A chronological table provides a synchronized view of sacred and profane history, along with some excellent maps of Palestine, Jerusalem, and the Near East.

[60] Cf Fr. Charles Davis, *Liturgy and Doctrine* (New York: Sheed and Ward, 1961),

is perhaps equivocal, suggesting the attainment of a static condition. In biblical studies such a condition is never reached for long. The *Bible de Jérusalem* makes no claim to have uttered the last word on all questions, and is best described as a "work in progress." The warm welcome which awaited it has spurred its contributors on to redoubled efforts, and the original fascicles have been constantly reworked, the notes in particular being further expanded and clarified. That the public appreciates the worth of this Bible may be judged from the fact that within five years the new translation had gone through six editions. By 1961, more than half a million copies of the New Testament had been purchased.[61]

The driving force behind this magnificent venture and *animateur* of the whole project is P. Thomas Chifflot, O.P. Had he not encouraged, harried, cajoled, and prodded the various participants, as editors must, the work might well have ground to a halt. As it is, the finished product stands as a tribute to his patience and perseverance. Fr. Dell' Aqua, of the Vatican Secretariate of State, sent him the following message:

> In the spirit of the *Divino Afflante Spiritu,* the *Bible de Jérusalem,*
> using the latest knowledge won in this field, comes as a timely answer
> to the legitimate critical needs of our times. His Holiness is therefore
> pleased to congratulate you, and P. de Vaux, the Director of the *École
> biblique de Jérusalem.*[62]

Such words of praise for a work issuing from the *École biblique* and in the spirit of the Founder of that School would have been sweet indeed to the ears of P. Lagrange.

CATHOLIC SCHOLARS AND THE CHURCH

The most frequent complaint leveled against Catholic scholars,

---

p. 20 f., who speaks of this Bible as "a landmark, both in restoring the Bible as a living element in the thought and piety of the faithful, and in presenting a Catholic understanding that is both critical and theological."

[61] Cf Conleth Kearns, O.P., "The Success of the *Bible de Jérusalem," Ang* 37 (1960), pp. 201–211. In the judgment of H. H. Rowley this Bible is "throughout sound in scholarship and graceful in style." *Figaro* calls it simply "un veritable chef-d'oeuvre."

[62] *Analecta S.O.P.,* 33 (1956), p. 421.

and one which Father Braun has several times touched on in his life of P. Lagrange, is that they lack freedom to do any genuine scientific work. Inasmuch as Catholics are not permitted to challenge even the basic doctrines of their Church, they are assumed to be wearing intellectual blinders, and to be deprived of the spirit of free inquiry.[63] The insinuation is perfectly plain — that objectivity of study is unknown in the Church.

It is apparently not commonly known that the Church has *very rarely* imposed her views upon scriptural scholars, a fact which, considering the size of the Bible, is astonishing. Out of seventy-two books, fewer than twenty texts have been given a dogmatic explanation; most of these deal with the Sacraments, that is, with the New Testament; the field of inquiry left open to Catholic scholars is, then, simply immense.[64] And this is true even if the Church has erected warning fences around certain areas through the action of the Pontifical Biblical Commission.

The precise function of the Biblical Commission needs an honest and sympathetic understanding. It was established in 1902 by Pope Leo XIII,[65] in a particularly difficult period in the Church's life. Since the French Revolution and throughout the whole of the nineteenth century, the Church had been attacked from without as a citadel of medievalism and superstition, and beset also from within by those of her children who had been captivated by the alluring claims of modernism.

It must be candidly admitted that Catholic biblical scholarship was at this time at a very low ebb and woefully unprepared to face the vigorous challenges of the age. One can understand, however much he may regret the necessity, that under conditions of siege a beleaguered city will adopt measures which would normally not

---

[63] In his presidential address at the International Congress held in Strasbourg, P. de Vaux branded as a sophism or paradox the attitude that only the absence of any religious convictions can guarantee genuine research (cf *ZAW* 68 [1956], p. 225).

[64] Pius XII writes (*RSS* 102): "There are but few texts whose sense has been defined by the authority of the Church, nor are those more numerous about which the teaching of the Holy Fathers is unanimous. There remain therefore many things, and of the greatest importance, in the discussion and exposition of which the skill and genius of Catholic commentators may and ought to be freely exercised. . . ."

[65] *EB* 137–148.

even be considered. And so it was that under Pius X many directives were issued to guide biblical scholars, restraining them from following up the fascinating new theories then so much in vogue.[66]

It is precisely these restrictions which are so annoying to Protestant scholars. First of all, however, it should be noted that the directives of the Biblical Commission are not, strictly speaking, decrees, but rather responses to questions. Very carefully worded, they are chiefly normative in character and in principle rescindible. The 1905 response on the sources of the Pentateuch, for example, left the door wide open for further critical work; that of 1906 on the Mosaic authenticity of the Pentateuch and of 1909 on the historical character of Genesis 1-3 have proved to be so sound that, as P. Vosté pointed out in his letter to Cardinal Suhard, there is no need at present to say anything more; none of these directives are in any way opposed to truly scientific examination of these problems.[67] The same can be said of other responses of the Commission on a dozen or more crucial issues.

Nevertheless, so long as these restrictions remained on the books, they exercised a restraining influence on Catholic scholars. But especially after the appearance of the *Divino Afflante*, responsible authorities became increasingly anxious to find some way of safeguarding and encouraging the forward progress which had been made since 1905.

First, then, came the reply to Cardinal Suhard (1948), stating that the responses of the Biblical Commission were in no way opposed to a scientific examination of these problems in the light of the results acquired during the past forty years of scholarly research.[68] This was in truth a very promising beginning.

The *Enchiridion Biblicum*, a handy manual containing papal enactments down through the centuries concerning the study of Scripture, was first published in 1927. No second edition appeared until 1954, but almost simultaneously with that edition two highly significant reviews of it appeared. The first was done by the then secretary

---

[66] No less than twenty-seven pronouncements of Pius X are listed in the *EB*.
[67] *EB* 578; *RSS* 149.
[68] *Loc. cit.*

of the Pontifical Biblical Commission, Fr. Athanasius Miller, O.S.B.;[69] the second, by the undersecretary of that Commission, Fr. Arduin Kleinhans, O.F.M.[70] What makes the two reports so interesting is their extraordinary similarity of thought and even of expression, where they speak of the earlier responses handed down by the Biblical Commission. Here is a cross section of the reviews:

Insofar as matters are treated in these decrees, concerned neither directly nor indirectly with the truths of faith or morals, the research worker can *obviously* continue his investigations with complete freedom and make use of his conclusions, although always and in everything without prejudice to the teaching authority of the Church (Miller).	Inasmuch . . . as there are opinions in these decrees concerned neither directly nor indirectly with the truths of faith and morals, the interpreter of Sacred Scripture may carry on his scientific investigation in complete freedom and benefit from them, but always without prejudice to the teaching authority of the Church (Kleinhans).

When one considers the high positions held by these two men, it seems clear that Catholic biblical scholars were thus unobtrusively being given to understand that they are perfectly free to interpret the responses of an earlier day more liberally (*in aller Freiheit, plena libertate* . . .).[71]

Thus a much more relaxed attitude is evident in the magisterial pronouncements of the Church. The true scholar will at once sense this attitude of confidence and be encouraged by it. To be sure, the new "attitude" cannot be construed as a renunciation of authority, and every serious scholar will recognize the fact that in proportion as a directive of the Biblical Commission touches upon faith and morals, his liberty must be accordingly the more cautiously exercised. Apart from these areas, however, the interpreter can *obviously* (the word is Fr. Miller's) continue his investigations with complete freedom.

P. Lagrange was himself a member of the Pontifical Biblical Commission, and the following words from the *Divino Afflante*

---

[69] *Benedictinische Monatschrift,* 31 (1955), p. 49 ff.

[70] *Antonianum,* 30 (1955), p. 64 f.

[71] Cf also Dom J. Dupont, O.S.B., "A propos du nouvel *Enchiridion Biblicum,*" *RB* 62 (1955), pp. 414–419; J. Levie, S.J., *op. cit.,* pp. 186–190.

seem especially pertinent both to him and to the new attitude expressed in the reviews of Fathers Miller and Kleinhans:

> This true liberty of the children of God which adheres faithfully to the teaching of the Church and accepts and uses gratefully the contributions of profane science, this liberty, upheld and sustained in every way by the confidence of all, is the condition and source of all lasting fruit and of all solid progress in Catholic doctrine. . . .[72]

It is well to keep in mind that our present enthusiastic scriptural revival was not forced upon us by ecclesiastical authority but rather arose from the initiative of men like Père Lagrange.[73]

Like St. Thomas Aquinas before him, P. Lagrange died with his work unfinished. He too had been involved in all the major intellectual biblical disputes of his times, and Pope's derisive lines concerning

> Exegetes who major issues shun
> And hold their farthing candles to the sun

could not be applied to him. He knew what the problems were, for one thing, and faced them with all the considerable resources he could command. Supple and elastic of thought, impatient of closed systems as his master St. Thomas had been, P. Lagrange is a model of an open mind, ever searching for that precious "something more" which is the mark of a true scholar. A particularly impressive trait shared by the saint and by the scholar was the skillful way in which they succeeded in safeguarding the rights of both faith and reason, without sacrificing the one or the other. They were alike also in their respect for the tradition which brought them into living contact with the Apostles and with Christ. And both men were passionately interested in what was new, and in anything that could serve the new Chosen People as it marches on toward God.

The great legacy of P. Lagrange is, however, not so much his writings as his spirit. There have been other scholars with a great capacity for work, intelligent men hungering for knowledge, willing and eager to recognize and foster ability in others. He gives us an

---

[72] EB 565.

[73] Cf Carroll Stuhlmueller, C.P., "Catholic Biblical Scholarship and College Theology," *The Thomist*, 23 (1963), pp. 533–563.

example of a believer who guides his life by the twin beacons of faith and reason. He shows that restraint need not be destructive of freedom (any more than sun, wind, and rain destroy the seed rooted in good ground), that it is possible to be cheerful under undeserved criticism, to be strong enough to do the good that needs doing. Instead of striking back in anger at his critics, instead of allowing himself to be atomized and distracted and destroyed by futile attempts to answer every critic, every objection, or to plug up each threat to the dike of truth, he chose with full deliberation *to present the truth objectively,* in all its glorious vitality and freshness. Like the good steward in the Gospel, he brought forth from the treasure chest of Scripture things both old and new. In his free pursuit of truth he never forgot, as a loyal son of the Church, that he was handling a treasure— God's own Word.

Père Braun has compared P. Lagrange to Moses, an apt comparison, and amply justified. But might he not also be well-compared to the great Abraham who, in obedience to a divine call which led him to go forth from the land of his birth, was ever ready, if God so willed it, to sacrifice all that was most dear to him. Abraham became the father of all believers, and his posteriority as numerous as the stars in the heavens. The children of P. Lagrange may not be so numerous, but that matters little, if, like their believing father, they too will shine for God's honor and glory.

PART II

BIBLIOGRAPHY

Key to the Bibliographical Tables

I. The following bibliography contains three items which have been arranged in chronological order: books, articles, book reviews.

1. **Books.** Books (and their list numbers) are set in **boldface** type. Various translations or later editions of some of them are listed under the date of the first publication. Tables of contents are provided only when the title alone does not adequately describe the contents.

2. **Articles.** These are articles which appeared in the *RB* and many other periodicals (see *Abbreviations*). The titles of the articles (and their list numbers) are set in a *lighter* **boldface** type.

3. **Book reviews.** All book reviews are listed in ordinary Roman type, but their list number has been *italicized*. The symbol o which appears after certain references indicates an unsigned review which, for internal reasons, has been credited to P. Lagrange. In making these decisions we were fortunately able to consult with P. Vincent, who approved our choices with but two minor exceptions of no great consequence.

II. The AUTHOR and ANALYTICAL Indices refer to numbers in the principal (chronological) Index, the three different types of number instantly identifying either book, article, or review.

ABBREVIATIONS

AmArch	=	American Journal of Archaeology
Ang	=	Angelicum
Bi	=	Biblica
BibZ	=	Biblische Zeitschrift
BLitE	=	Bulletin de Littérature Ecclésiastique
ByzZ	=	Byzantinische Zeitschrift
BzAss	=	Beiträge zur Assyriologie
CBQ	=	The Catholic Biblical Quarterly
CivCatt	=	Civiltà Cattolica
Cor	=	Le Correspondant
CrAcInscrBl	=	Comptes rendus de l'Académie des Inscriptions et Belles-Lettres
CSS	=	Cursus Sacrae Scripturae
DA	=	Dictionnaire d'Apologétique de la Foi Catholique
DAS	=	Divino Afflante Spiritu
DB(S)	=	Dictionnaire de la Bible (Supplément)
EB	=	Enchiridion Biblicum
ÉB	=	Études Bibliques
EphThLov	=	Ephemerides Theologicae Lovanienses
ÉPO	=	Études Palestiniennes et Orientales
Ét	=	Études
ÉtEccl	=	Études ecclésiastiques
Exp	=	The Expositor
ExpTim	=	The Expository Times
GSC	=	Die griechischen Schriftsteller der drei Jahrhunderte, herausgegeben von der Kirchenväter-Kommission der königlichen preußischen Akademie der Wissenschaften, Leipzig, 1897 und folg.
Herm	=	Hermes
JAmOrSoc	=	Journal of the American Oriental Society
JAs	=	Journal Asiatique
JBibLit	=	Journal of Biblical Literature
JHellSt	=	Journal of Hellenic Studies
JSemLL	=	Journal of Semitic Language and Literatures
JThSt	=	The Journal of Theological Studies
Kath	=	Der Katholik
MB	=	Musée Belge.
MelUnSJos	=	Mélanges de l'Université St-Joseph, à Beyrouth
Mus	=	Museon
NRTh	=	Nouvelle Revue Théologique
OLZ	=	Orientalische Literaturzeitung

PEQ	= Palestine Exploration Quarterly
PO	= Patrologie Orientale
RApo	= Revue Apologétique
RArch	= Revue Archéologique
RArchOr	= Recherches d'Archéologie Orientale
RAss	= Revue d'Assyriologie et d'Archéologie Orientale
RB	= Revue Biblique
RBen	= Revue Bénédictine
RClFr	= Revue du Clergé français
RCr	= Revue Critique
RÉtA	= Revue des Études Anciennes
RÉtJuiv	= Revue des Études Juives
RHE	= Revue d'Histoire Ecclésiastique
RHLR	= Revue d'Histoire et de Littérature religieuses
RHPR	= Revue d'Histoire et de Philosophie religieuses
RHR	= Revue d'Histoire des Religions
RömQ	= Römische Quartalschrift
RScPhilTh	= Revue des Sciences Philosophiques et Théologiques
RScRel	= Revue des Sciences Religieuses
RSem	= Revue Sémitique d'Épigraphie et d'Histoire ancienne
RSS	= Rome and the Study of Scripture
RTh	= Revue Thomiste
RThPh	= Revue de Théologie et de Philosophie
SbAkPreuss	= Sitzungsberichte der preuß. Akademie der Wissenschaften, phil.-hist.-Kl.
ScuolCatt	= Scuola Cattolica
StRel	= Studi Religiosi
ThLZg	= Theologische Literaturzeitung
ThQ	= Theologische Quartalschrift
ThT	= Theologisch Tijdschrift
TS	= Texts and Studies
TU	= Texte und Untersuchungen
VDom	= La Vie Dominicaine
Vit	= La Vie Intellectuelle
VS	= La Vie Spirituelle
VSS	= La Vie Spirituelle : Supplément
ZAss	= Zeitschrift für Assyriologie
ZAW	= Zeitschrift für die Alttestamentliche Wissenschaft
ZDMG	= Zeitschrift der Deutschen Morgenländischen Gesellschaft
ZDPV	= Zeitschrift d. Deutschen Palästina-Vereins
ZKTh	= Zeitschrift für Katholische Theologie
ZNW	= Zeitschrift für die Neutestamentliche Wissenschaft

CHRONOLOGICAL BIBLIOGRAPHY

1878

1 **Du principe de l'Origine et de ses applications, en Droit romain. — De la règle : En fait de meubles la possession vaut titre, en Droit français.** Thèse pour le doctorat en Droit. In-8º de 203 pp. Paris, A. Derenne.

1888

2 Un évêque du Vᵉ siècle, Rabulas, évêque d'Édesse † 435. (*La Science catholique, 15 sept. 1888*). [nº 1108, pp. 185–226.]

1890

3 Une inscription nabatéenne. *ZAss* V 289–292.

1892

4 Avant-propos. *RB* I 1–16.
5 Topographie de Jérusalem. *RB* I 17–38.
6 La nouvelle histoire d'Israël et le prophète Osée. *RB* I 203–238.
7 Une inscription phénicienne. *RB* I 275–281.
8 Une inscription palmyrénienne. *RB* I 433–438.
9 Lettre de Jérusalem (excursion au Jourdain). *RB* I 439–456.
10 La Vierge et Emmanuel. *RB* I 481–497.
11 Le panthéisme dans l'histoire sainte. *RB* I 605–616.

BOOK REVIEWS

12 Arintero (J. G.), El diluvio universal demostrado por la geologia. 1892.— *RB* I 469–470. o
13 Bliss (F. J.), Fouilles de Tell-el-Hesy (*Palestine exploration fund. Quarterly Statement*, april 1892). *RB* 1 472–474. o
14 Bloch, Phœnicisches Glossar. Berlin 1891.— *RB* I 472. o
15 Congrès scientifique international des catholiques. Paris 1891. *RB* I 465–466. o
16 Euringer (S.), Der Masorah Text des Kohelet, kritisch untersucht. Leipzig 1890.— *RB* I 471. o
17 Euting (J.), Sinaïtische Inschriften. Berlin.— *RB* I 471–472. o

18 Lesêtre (H.), Notre-Seigneur Jésus-Christ dans son saint Évangile. — *RB* I 466. o
19 S. (A.), La tendance naturaliste dans l'exégèse (*NRTh* 1892). — *RB* 1 475. o
20 Vernes (M.), Du prétendu polythéisme des Hébreux. Paris 1891. — *RB* I 470–471. o
21 Viçwa-Mitra, Les Chamites. Paris 1892. — *RB* I 470. o

1893

22 Comment s'est formée l'enceinte du Temple de Jérusalem. *RB* II 90–113.
23 Inscription samaritaine d'Amwâs. *RB* II 114–116.
24 Bustes palmyréniens. *RB* II 117–118.
25 La Révélation du nom divin « Tétragrammaton ». *RB* II 329–350 (signé du pseudonyme : Henry Barns).
26 Congrès des orientalistes à Londres. *RB* II 146–147.
27 Épigraphie sémitique. *RB* II 1893, 220–222.
28 Lettre de Jérusalem (lampe euch., inscr. gr. au Sinaï). *RB* II 631–634.

BOOK REVIEWS

29 Baedeker (K.), Palestine et Syrie. Leipzig 1893, 2ᵉ éd. — *RB* II 635–636.
30 Driver (S. R.), Notes on the Hebrew text of the Books of Samuel. Oxford 1890. — *RB* II 154–155.
31 Fillion (L. Cl.), La Sainte Bible commentée. Vol. IV. Paris 1893. — *RB* II 645–646.
32 Gebhardt (O. von), Das Evangelium und die Apocalypse des Petrus. Leipzig 1893. — *RB* II 636–637.
33 Hahn (L.), Das Evangelium des Lucas. Breslau 1892. — *RB* II 640–642.
34 Halévy (J.), Interprétation d'Ézéchiel (16–18), (*RÉtJuiv* 1892). — *RB* II 283–286.
35 Hatch (E.) and Redpath (H. A.), A concordance to the Septuagint and the other Greek versions of the Old Test. Part I. Oxford 1892. — *RB* II 154.
36 James (M. R.) : cfr Ryle (H. E.).
37 Loisy (A.), Le discours d'Elihu dans le Livre de Job (*Enseignement biblique*). — *RB* II 159–160. o
38 Mader (E.), Itinerarium curiense in Terram sanctam. Curiae Raetorum 1893. — *RB* II 642–643.
39 Portmans (M.), Exercitia spiritualia. Liége. — *RB* II 645.
40 Pörtner (B.), Die Autorität der deuterocanonischen Bücher des A. T. Münster 1893. — *RB* II 643–645.
41 Redpath (H. A.) : cfr Hatch (E.).

42 RYLE (H. E.) and JAMES (M. R.), Psalms of the Pharisees, commonly called the psalms of Solomon. Cambridge 1891. — *RB* II 155.

43 SCHEIL (V.), Deux traités de Philon, réédités d'après un papyrus du sixième siècle environ (*Mémoires publiés par les membres de la mission archéologique française au Caire*. Vol. IX). Paris 1893. — *RB* II 455–456.

44 SWETE (H. B.), The Old Testament in Greek, according to the Septuagint. Vol. II. Chronicles-Tobit. Cambridge 1891. — *RB* II 153–154.

45 VERNES (M.), Le cantique de Débora (*RÉtJuiv*). — *RB* II 284–286.

46 VIGIL (B. M.), La Creacion, la Redencion y la Iglesia ante la cienca, la critica y el racionalismo. Madrid 1892. — *RB* II 638–640.

46a VIGOUROUX (F.), *DB* fasc. 3. — *RB* II 155–156.

1894

47 S. Étienne et son sanctuaire à Jérusalem. In-8° de xvi–190 pp. très illustré. Paris, Picard.

48 Lettre de Jérusalem (Milliaire arabe, Mizzeh, notes topographiques). *RB* III 136–141.

49 L'apocalypse d'Isaïe (xxiv–xxvii). *RB* III 200–231.

50 Excursion à Sebbé (Maṣada). *RB* III 263–276.

51 Lettre de Jérusalem (lettre de M. Vigouroux, conférences de Saint Étienne, fouilles anglaises à T. el-Hésy). *RB* III 439–451.

52 Une tradition biblique à Jérusalem : Saint Étienne. *RB* III 452–481.

53 Néhémie et Esdras. *RB* III 561–585.

54 Le X⁰ congrès des orientalistes à Genève. *RB* III 629–631.

BOOK REVIEWS

55 CARA (R. P. de), Degli Hittim o Hethei e delle loro migrazioni (*CivCatt* 1893). — *RB* III 153.

56 HALÉVY (J.), Revue sémitique d'épigraphie et d'histoire ancienne. Paris 1893 et 1894. — *RB* III 302–306.

57 HOONACKER (A. VAN), Le vœu de Jephté (*Mus* 1893). — *RB* III 151–153.

58 KEPPLER (P. W.), Gethsemane (*ThQ* 1893). — *RB* III 155.

59 MERX (A.), Ein samaritanisches Fragment über den Ta'eb oder Messias. Leyde 1893. — *RB* III 482–484.

60 ROHART (Abbé), De oneribus biblicis contra gentes. Lille. — *RB* III 151.

61 SCHIFFERS (M.), Die Emmaüs Frage und der Context des hl. Lucas (*Kath* 1893). — *RB* III 154–155.

1895

62 Les sources du troisième Évangile. *RB* IV 5–22.
63 A propos de l'encyclique « Providentissimus ». *RB* IV 48–64.
64 Chronique de Jérusalem (fouilles de M. Bliss à Jérusalem, église au Mont des Oliviers, etc.). *RB* IV 88–96.
65 Le récit de l'enfance de Jésus dans saint Luc. *RB* IV 160–185.
66 La question de Néhémie et Esdras. *RB* IV 193–202.
67 Le palimpseste syriaque du Sinaï. *RB* IV 287–288.
68 Le nouveau manuscrit syriaque du Sinaï. *RB* IV 401–411.
69 Origène, la critique textuelle et la tradition topographique. *RB* IV 501–524.
70 Une pensée de saint Thomas sur l'inspiration scripturaire. *RB* IV 563–571.
71 Chronique de Jérusalem (fouilles de M. Bliss, voyage de Bliss au pays de Moab, nouvelles de Bethléem). *RB* IV 622–626.
72 L'authenticité et les erreurs de la Vulgate (à propos d'un art. de *RClFr*, 1er mars 1895). *RB* IV 645–650.

BOOK REVIEWS

73 ANONYME, Palästina und Syrien von Anfang der Geschichte bis zum Siege des Islams [Un petit lexique de géographie palestinienne]. Berlin. — *RB* IV 303–304.
74 AZIBERT (J.), Concordance des évangiles (*EtEccl* 1894). — *RB* IV 644–645.
75 BURKITT (F. C.), [Édition de Tyconius.] (TS.), Cambridge 1894. — *RB* IV 305–306.
76 CHABOT (J. B.), Recension du « Lexicon syriacum de Brockelmann » (*RCr* 1894). — *RB* IV 125–127.
77 CHEYNE (T. K.), Isaiah (*Exp* 1895). — *RB* IV 462–463.
78 CONYBEARE (F. C.), Philo about the contemplative life. Oxford 1895. — *RB* IV 457–458.
79 DAUSCH (P.), Der neutestamentliche Schriftcanon und Clemens von Alexandrien. Freiburg i. Br. 1894. — *RB* IV 630–633.
80 ERMANN (A.), Aegyptische Grammatik. Berlin 1894. — *RB* IV 278–279.
81 FIOROVICH (R. P.), Sanctuaire de saint Étienne (*Saint François et la Terre Sainte* 1895). — *RB* IV 456–457.
82 HATCH (E.), and REDPATH (H. A.), A concordance to the Septuagint and the other greek versions of the Old Test. Part IV. Oxford 1895. — *RB* IV 458–459.
83 HOONACKER (A. VAN), Le lieu du culte dans la législation rituelle des Hébreux (*Mus* 1894). — *RB* IV 297–299.

84 JÜNGST (J.), Die Quellen der Apostelgeschichte. Gotha 1895. — *RB* IV 629–630.

85 MADAN (F.), A summary catalogue of western manuscripts in the Bodleian which have not hitherto been catalogued in the 4° series. Vol. III. Oxford 1895. — *RB* IV 458.

86 MUSS-ARNOLT (W.), A concise dictionary of the Assyrian language. Berlin 1894. — *RB* IV 461.

87 OLLIVIER (M. J.), Les amitiés de Jésus. Paris 1895. — *RB* IV 450–452.

88 REDPATH (H. A.) : cfr HATCH (E.).

89 SCHICK (C.), Histoire des constructions de la ville de Jérusalem. (*ZDPV* 1894). — *RB* IV 1895 301–302.

90 STEINDORFF (G.), Koptische Grammatik. Berlin 1894. — *RB* IV 279.

91 VITEAU (J.), Étude sur le grec du Nouveau Testament. Paris. — *RB* IV 457.

92 WINER (B.), Grammatik des N. T. Sprachidioms. Göttingen 1894. — *RB* IV 457.

1896

93 **Milliaire arabe trouvé au Couvent grec de Koušiva.** *CrAc-InscrBl* 306.

94 **Les sources du troisième Évangile.** *RB* V 5–38.

95 **Origène, la critique textuelle et la tradition topographique (fin).** *RB* V 87–92.

96 **L'inspiration des Livres Saints.** *RB* V 199–220.

97 **Hexaméron** (traduction, commentaire, origine du récit de la création). *RB* V 381–407.

98 **'Aïn Kedeis.** *RB* V 440–451.

99 **L'inspiration et les exigences de la critique.** *RB* V 496–518.

100 **De Suez à Jérusalem par le Sinaï.** *RB* V 618–643.

BOOK REVIEWS

101 AMÉLINEAU (E.), Notice des manuscrits coptes de la bibliothèque nationale renfermant des textes bilingues du Nouveau Testament. Paris 1895. — *RB* V 130–131.

102 ANONYME, Réflexions pratiques sur les petits prophètes. — *RB* V 653.

103 BELSER (J. E.), Apologie de saint Paul dans l'épître aux Galates. — *RB* V 649–650.

104 BUHL (Fr.) : cfr GESENIUS (W.).

105 CHABOT (J. B.), Grammaire hébraïque, 4ᵉ édit. — *RB* V 145–146.

106 CONYBEARE (F. C.), A propos de la finale de Marc (*Exp.* 1895). — *RB* V 311.

107   Corpus inscriptionum semiticarum. — *RB* V 294–295.
108   DRIVER (S. R.), A critical and exegetical commentary on Deuter-
         onomy. Edinburgh 1895. — *RB* V 644–645.
109   EUTING (J.), Sinaïtische Inschriften. Berlin 1891. — *RB* V
         293–294.
110   GAUTIER (L.), Au delà du Jourdain. Genève 1896. — *RB* V 474.
111   — — Au pays des Philistins (*Revue chrétienne* 1896). — *RB*
         V 474.
112   GESENIUS (W.), Hebräisches und aramäisches Handwörterbuch
         (bearbeitet von FR. BUHL), 12ᵗᵉ Aufl. Leipzig 1895. *RB* V
         131–134.
113   GIBSON (Mrs D.), Studia sinaitica. Vol. V. Cambridge 1896.
         — *RB* V 479.
114   GORE (C.), Dissertations on subjects connected with the Incar-
         nation. London 1895. — *RB* V 452–454.
115   HARRIS (J. R.), [A propos du comm. de S. Ephrem sur le
         Diatessaron de Tatien.] — *RB* V 480.
116   HAUPT (E.), Die eschatologischen Aussagen Jesu. Berlin 1895.
         — *RB* V 474–476.
117   HOMMEL (F.), Aufsätze und Abhandlungen arabisch-semitolo-
         gischen Inhalts. München 1892. — *RB* V 289.
118   — — Süd-arabische Chrestomathie. München 1893. — *RB* V
         289–291.
119   — — Sümerische Lesestücke. München 1894. — *RB* V 291–292.
120   HOONACKER (A. Van), Nouvelles études sur la restauration
         juive après l'exil de Babylone. Paris et Louvain 1896. — *RB*
         V 645–647.
121   JAMES (M. R.), IV Ezra (*TS*). Cambridge. — *RB* V 310.
122   KEPPLER (P. W.), Wanderfahrten und Wallfahrten im Orient.
         Freiburg i. Br. 1895. — *RB* V 303.
123   KIRWAN (de), Concordisme et idéalisme dans l'Héxaméron
         (*Cosmos* 1895). — *RB* V 141.
124   LEWIS (Mrs A. Smith), [Manuscrit syriaque du Sinaï.] Cam-
         bridge. — *RB* V 479–480.
125   MARTI (K.), Kurzgefaste Grammatik der Biblisch-Aramäischen
         Sprache. Berlin 1896. — *RB* V 478.
126   MANDELKERN (S.), [Concordance de l'Ancien Testament.] —
         RB V 478.
127   MAZOYER (P.), La question biblique. Paris. — *RB* V 149–150.
128   MEYER (A.), Jesu Muttersprache. Freiburg i. Br. 1896. — *RB*
         V 649.
129   MÜLLER (D. H.), Die Propheten in ihrer ursprünglichen Form.
         Wien 1896. — *RB* V 454–456.
130   MUSS-ARNOLT (W.), A concise dictionary of the Assyrian
         language. Part III. Berlin. — *RB* V 305.
131   NESTLE (E.), Philologica sacra. Berlin 1896. — *RB* V 649.

132 RAABE (R.), Petrus der Iberer. Leipzig 1895. — *RB* V 457–460.

133 RESCH (A.), Aussercanonische Paralleltexte zu den Evangelien (*TU*). Leipzig 1895. — *RB* V 281–282.

134 ROBINSON (M. A.), Euthaliana (*TS*). Cambridge. — *RB* V 310–311.

135 ROBINSON (M. F.), [Fragments d'évangiles apocryphes coptes]. Cambridge (*TS*) — *RB* V 653.

136 SCHANZ (P.), Das Alter des Menschengeschlechts. Freiburg i. Br. — *RB* V 478.

137 SIEGFRIED (C.) und STADE (B.), Hebräisches Wörterbuch zum Alten Testamente. Leipzig 1893. — *RB* V 131–134.

138 SOULLIER (Chan.), Le mont Sion et la cité de David. Tulle 1895. — *RB* V 143–144.

139 STADE (B.) : cfr SIEGFRIED (C.).

140 TOSTIVINT (Abbé), La captivité des Juifs (*Analecta juris pontificii*). — *RB* V 144.

1897

141 Mosaïque et inscriptions de Mâdabâ. *CrAcInscrBl* 490–493.

142 Exposé des documents rapportés de Pétra en 1897. *CrAcInscrBl* 699–700.

143 Épigraphie sémitique (Milliaires arabes; inscr. samar. d'Amwâs). *RB* VI 104–106.

144 Le Sinaï. *RB* VI 107–130.

145 La mosaïque géographique de Mâdabâ. *RB* VI 165–184.

146 Notre exploration de Pétra. *RB* VI 208–230.

147 L'innocence et le péché. *RB* VI 341–379.

148 Jérusalem d'après la mosaïque de Mâdabâ. *RB* VI 450–458.

149 Du Sinaï à Jérusalem. *RB* VI 605–625.

150 L'inscription coufique de l'église du Saint-Sépulcre. *RB* VI 643–647.

BOOK REVIEWS

151 American Oriental Society. April meeting 1897 [Titres de quelques ouvrages présentés.] — *RB* VI 495–497. o

152 ANONYME, Un mouvement rétrograde du rationalisme biblique. [Revue non citée, à la date du 1ᵉʳ avril 1897]. — *RB* VI 487–489. o

153 ARINTERO (J. G.), [Controverse avec Valbuena à propos du déluge.] (*Ciudad de Dios*). — *RB* VI 491 o

154 BALL (C. J.), The Book of Genesis. Leipzig 1896. — *RB* VI 1897 310–311.

155 BATIFFOL (P.), Anciennes littératures chrétiennes. Paris 1897. — *RB* VI 633–634.

156 BONUS (A.), Collatio codicis Lewisiani rescripti evangeliorum

sacrorum syriacorum cum codice Curetoniano. Oxonii 1896. —
RB VI 493–494. o

157 BROGLIE (de), Questions bibliques. Paris 1897. — *RB* VI 1897
487. o

158 BROSSE (E.), L'aurore indienne de la Genèse. Paris 1896. — *RB*
VI 322–324. o

159 CARUCCI (Y.), Le lezioni del breviario Salernitano intorno a S.
Matteo. Salerno 1897. — *RB* VI 491–492. o

160 Congrès scientifique international des catholiques. Fribourg.
1897. — *RB* VI 635–638. o

161 Congrès international des orientalistes. Paris 1897 (section
sémitique). — *RB* VI 638–641. o

162 CORSSEN (P.), Monarchianische Prologe zu den vied Evangelien
(d'après la *RCr* 1897). — *RB* VI 498–499. o

163 GRIMME (H.), Grundzüge der hebräischen Akzent und Vo-
callehre. Fribourg en Suisse 1896. — *RB* VI 497. o

164 HACKSPILL (L.), Die Aethiopische Evangelienübersetzung (*ZAss*
1896). — *RB* VI 159. o

165 HALÉVY (J.), [Recension de l'histoire d'Israël de Wellhausen.]
(*RSem* 1896). — *RB* VI 322. o

166 HATCH (E.) and REDPATH (H. A.), A concordance to the
Septuagint and the other Greek versions of the Old Test. Part
VI. Oxford 1897. — *RB* VI 627–628.

167 HETZENAUER (M.), Édition critique du texte grec du Nouveau
Testament. Innsbruck 1896. — *RB* VI 158. o

168 HOLTZMANN (H. J.), Lehrbuch der neutestamentlichen Theologie. Freiburg i. Br. 1897. — *RB* VI 1897 468–474.

169 HOMMEL (F.), Die altisraelitische Überlieferung. München 1897.
— *RB* VI 628–630.

170 KÖNIG (E.), Sur la forme יְחוּת (*ZAW* 1897). — *RB* VI 497. o

171 MENUGE (Abbé), Histoire sainte à l'usage des cours supérieurs
d'instruction religieuse. — *RB* VI 489–490. o

172 MORIN (G.), Mémoire de la Soc. des Antiq. de France. Vol.
LVI. S. Lazare, s. Maximin. — *RB* VI 1897 486. o

173 POELS (H. A.), Examen critique de l'histoire de l'Arche. Vol.
I. Louvain et Leyde 1897. — *RB* VI 630–632.

174 REDPATH (H. A.) : cfr HATCH (E.).

175 SCHÖPFER (Dr), Bibel und Wissenschaft. Brixen 1896. — *RB*
VI 158–159. o

176 TIMES, 29 mai 1897, Découverte des Logia de Behnessa. — *RB*
VI 494–495. o

1898

177 Les sources du Pentateuque. *RB* VII 10–32.
178 Phounon (Num. XXXIII, 42.). *RB* VII 112–115.

179 Recherches épigraphiques à Pétra : lettre à M. le Marquis de Vogüé. *RB* VII 165-182.
180 La cosmogonie de Bérose. *RB* VII 395-402.
181 La Prophétie de Jacob. *RB* VII 525-540.
182 Saint Jérôme et la tradition juive dans la Genèse. *RB* VII 563-566.
183 Les Nabatéens. *RB* VII 567-588 (signé du pseudonyme H. L. Vincent).

BOOK REVIEWS

184 ABBOT (T. K.), Commentary on the Epistles to the Ephesians and to the Colossians. Edinburgh 1897. — *RB* VII 319-320.
185 AZIBERT (J.), Synopsis Evangeliorum historica, seu vitae Domini nostri Jesu Christi quadruplex et una narratio. — *RB* VII 471-473. o
186 BAETHGEN, Die Psalmen. Göttingen 1897. — *RB* VII 156-157. o
187 BOUR (R. S.), L'inscription de Quirinius et le recensement de saint Luc. Rome 1897. — *RB* VII 313. o
188 BUDDE (K.), Das Buch der Richter. Freiburg i. Br. 1897. — *RB* VII 635-637. o
189 CHARLES (R. H.), The Assumption of Moses. London 1897. — *RB* VII 158. o
190 DEISSMANN (A.), Neue Bibelstudien. Marburg 1897. —*RB* VII 480-481. o
191 GIGOT (F. E.), Outlines of Jewish history from Abraham to Our Lord. New York 1897. — *RB* VII 152-154. o
192 HAUCK (A.), Herzog's Realencyclopädie für protestantische Theologie und Kirche. Bd III. Leipzig. — *RB* VII 157. o
193 HOLZINGER (H.), Genesis. Freiburg i. Br. 1898. — *RB* VII 479-480. o
194 HÜGEL (B^on von), La méthode historique et les documents de l'Hexateuque (*The Catholic University Bulletin*. Washington 1897). — *RB* VII 475-477. o
195 HUMMELAUER (F. de), Nochmals der biblische Schöpfungsbericht. Freiburg i. Br. — *RB* VII 478-479. o
196 — — Commentarius in Exodum et Leviticum. Paris 1897. — *RB* VII 136-138.
197 JAMES (M. R.), Acta Johannis (*TS*). *RB* VII 160-161. o
198 KNABENBAUER (J.), Commentarius in Evangelium secundum Joannem. Paris 1898. — *RB* VII 640-641. o
199 LEWIS (Mrs. A. Smith), A Palestinian Syriac Lectionary (*Studia Sinaitica* VI). — *RB* VII 161-162. o
200 MARGIVAL (Abbé), État des études bibliques (*La Quinzaine*, mars 1898). — *RB* VII 465-466. o
201 NOURRY, Méthode exégétique de dom Calmet (*Annal. de phil. chr.*, 1897). — *RB* VII 316-317. o

202 REINACH (Th.), Le texte de Josèphe relatif à Jésus (*RÉtJuiv* 1897). — *RB* VII 150–152. o

203 RESCH (A.), Das Kindheits Evangelium nach Lucas und Matthaeus. Leipzig 1897. — *RB* VII 634–635. o

204 RÉVILLE (A.), Jésus de Nazareth. Paris 1897. — *RB* VII 466–469. o

205 RUCKERT, Die Lage des Berges Sion. Freiburg i. Br. 1897. — *RB* VII 322–323. o

206 SABATIER (A.), L'apôtre Paul; esquisse d'une histoire de sa pensée. Paris 1896. — *RB* VII 469–470. o

207 SALMON (G.), Some thought on the textual criticism of the New Testament. London 1897. — *RB* VII 318. o

208 SANDAY (W.), [Sur la méthode historique en théologie; rapport présenté au congrès anglican de Nottingham, sept. 1897]. — *RB* VII 317–318. o

209 TRENKLE (F. S.), Einleitung in das Neue Testament. Freiburg i. Br. 1897. — *RB* VII 155–156. o

210 VINCENT (M.), A critical and exegetical commentary on the Epistles to the Philippians and to Philemon. Edinburgh 1897. — *RB* VII. 320–321. o

1899

211 Lettre à M. Clermont-Ganneau sur l'emplacement de la ville biblique de Gézer. *CrAcInscrBl* 247–251.

212 Étienne. *DB* Vol. II 2033–2035.

213 Les Khabiri. *RB* VIII 127–132.

214 Le Sinaï biblique. *RB* VIII 369–392.

215 Gezer. *RB* VIII 422–427.

216 Deux chants de guerre. *RB* VIII 532–552.

217 La Dormition de la Sainte Vierge et la maison de Jean Marc. *RB* VIII 589–600.

218 Revue des controverses sur l'histoire d'Israël au temps de Moïse. *RB* VIII 623–632.

219 Saint Jérôme et saint Augustin, à propos des origines de la Vulgate (*BLitE* 1899). [= n° 1108, pp. 167–184].

BOOK REVIEWS

220 BLASS (Fr.), Evangelium secundum Lucam, secundum formam quae videtur romanam. Leipzig. — *RB* VIII 168–170. o

221 DALMAN (G.), Die Wörte Jesu. Leipzig 1898. — *RB* VIII 329–330. o

222 DESPRÉS (J.), La question du Pentateuque (*RClFr* 1899). — *RB* VIII 325. o

223 DUHM (B.), Die Psalmen. Freiburg i. Br. 1899. — *RB* VIII 636–637. o

224 DYNELEY PRINCE (J.), A critical commentary of the Book of Daniel. Leipzig 1899. — *RB* VIII 642. o

225 ECK (Abbé) : cfr HUMMELAUER (F. de).

226 FRANKENBERG, Die Datierung der Psalmen Salomos (*ZAW* : Beihefte 1896). — *RB* VIII 331. o

227 GALL (A. von), Altisraelitische Kultstätten (*ZAW* : Beihefte 1898). — *RB* VIII 331. o

228 HEINEKE (R.), Synopse. Gießen 1898. — *RB* VIII 330. o

229 HOONACKER (A. Van), Le sacerdoce lévitique dans la loi et dans l'histoire des Hébreux. London 1899. — *RB* VIII 471–474.

230 HUMMELAUER (F. de), Le récit de la création (trad. fr. de M. l'abbé Eck). Paris. — *RB* VIII 322–324.

231 —— Das vormosaische Priesterthum in Israel. Freiburg i. Br. 1899. — *RB* VIII 470–471.

232 —— Commentarius in Numeros. Paris 1899. — *RB* VIII 609–613.

233 JASTROW (M.), The religion of Babylonia and Assyria. Boston. — *RB* VIII 474–476.

234 LÖHR (M.), Die Bücher Samuelis. — *RB* VIII 166–168. o

235 LOISY (A.), Nature et développement de l'espérance messianique en Israël (*RHLR* 1899). — *RB* VIII 163–164. o

236 —— Sur Osée IX 10–13 (*RHLR* 1898). — *RB* VIII 324. o

237 —— Sur Jo. II 1–12 (*RHLR* 1899). — *RB* VIII 324. o

238 MANDELKERN (S.), [A propos de sa concordance de l'A. T.] — *RB* VIII 331–332. o

239 MASPERO (G.), Histoire ancienne des peuples de l'Orient classique. Paris. Vol. I et II. — *RB* VIII 307–310.

240 MÉCHINEAU (R. P.), La thèse de l'origine mosaïque du Pentateuque (*Et* 1898). — RB VIII 159–160. o

241 MÜLLER (D. H.), Strophenbau and Responsion. Wien 1898. — *RB* VIII 170–172. o

242 PLUMMER (A.), S. Luc². Edinburgh. — *RB* VIII 334–335. o

243 RAHMER (M.), Die hebräischen Traditionen in den Werken des Hieronymus. — *RB* VIII 327–329. o

244 ROTHSTEIN (G.), Die Dynastie der Laḥmiden in al-Ḥirâ. Berlin 1899. — *RB* VIII 330–331. o

245 SCHÜRER (E.), Geschichte des jüdischen Volkes im Zeitalter Jesu Christi³. Leipzig 1898. — *RB* VIII 310–313.

246 SELLIN (E.), Serubbabel. Ein Beitrag zur Geschichte der messianischen Erwartung und der Entstehung des Judenthums. Leipzig 1898. — *RB* VIII 637–638. o

247 SINGER (W.), Das Buch der Jubiläen. Bd I. Stuhlweißenburg (Ungarn) 1898. — *RB* VIII 155–158.

248 TAYLOR (C.), The Oxyrhyncus Logia and the apocryphal gospels. Oxford 1899. — *RB* VIII 641–642. o

249 Torrey (C. C.), The composition and historical value of Ezra-Nehemiah (*ZAW* : Beihefte 1896). — *RB* VIII 331. o

250 — — Die Datierung d. Psalm. Salomos (*ZAW* : Beihefte 1897). — *RB* VIII 331.

250a Vigoroux (F.), *DB* V. II. — *RB* VIII 160–163. o

251 Weiss (B.), Textkritik der vier Evangelien. Leipzig 1899. — *RB* VIII 634–636. o

252 Zanecchia (D.), Divina inspiration sacrarum scripturarum ad mentem S. Thomae Aquinatis. Romae. — *RB* VIII 335. o

1900

253 L'itinéraire des Israélites du pays de Gessen aux bords du Jourdain. *RB* IX 63–86; 273–287; 443–449.

254 L'interprétation de la Sainte Écriture par l'Église. *RB* IX 135–142.

255 Le lieu de la lapidation de Saint Étienne. *RB* IX 142–143.

256 Débora (Juges : récit en prose ch. IV, cantique ch. V). *RB* IX 200–225.

257 Projet d'un commentaire complet de l'Écriture Sainte. *RB* IV 414–423.

258 Les fouilles anglaises (Dʳ Bliss à Tell Djedeideh, près de Beit Djebrin). *RB* IX 607–609.

BOOK REVIEWS

259 Batiffol (P.), Tractatus Origenis de libris SS. Scripturarum. Paris 1900. — *RB* IX 293–295.

260 Benson (E. W.), The Apocalypse. London 1900. — *RB* IX 640–641.

261 Bertholet (A.), Deuteronomium. Freiburg i. Br. 1899. — *RB* IX 151–152. o

262 Breen (A. E.), A harmonized exposition of the four Gospels Rochester. — *RB* IX 161–162. o

263 Briggs (E. G.), [Sur le mot Sélah-Diapsalma.] — *RB* IX 160. o

264 Budde (K.), Die sogenannten Ebed Jahwé-Lieder. Gießen 1900. — *RB* IX 311–313. o

265 Cheyne (T. K.), Encyclopædia biblica. London 1899. — *RB* IX 319–321. o

266 — — Introduction to the Book of Isaiah. London 1895. — *RB* IX 295–298.

267 — — The Book of the Prophet Isaiah (a new English translation). Stuttgart 1898. — *RB* IX 295–298.

268 — — The Book of the Prophet Isaiah (critical edition of the Hebrew text arranged in chronological order). Leipzig 1899. — *RB* IX 295–298.

269 CLERMONT-GANNEAU (Ch.), La lettre de Jésus au roi Abgar, la Koutbi juive. . . et la mezoûzah. (*RArchOr* 216 ss.). — *RB* IX 644.

270 CORNELY (R.), Synopses omnium librorum sacrorum utriusque Testamenti quas ex sua « Introductione speciali in Vet. et Nov. Testamentum » excerpsit, retractavit, complevit Rudolphus Cornély S. J. Paris 1900. — *RB* IX 642–643.

271 DESSAILLY (Abbé), Question biblique (*La Science catholique* 1900). — *RB* IX 472. o

272 DITTMAR (W.), Vetus Testamentum in Novo. Göttingen 1899. — *RB* IX 149. o

273 FAULHABER (M.), Hesychii Hierosolymitani interpretatio Isaïae prophetae. Freiburg Br. 1900. — *RB* IX 477–479. o

274 FÉRET (P.), La Faculté de théologie de Paris et ses docteurs. Vol. I : XVIe siècle. Paris 1900. — *RB* IX 311. o

275 FONCK (L.), Streifzüge durch die biblische Flora. Herder 1900. — *RB* IX 476–477. o

276 GUTHE (H.), Geschichte des Volkes Israel. Freiburg i. Br. 1899. — *RB* IX 645–647.

277 HARRIS (J. R.), The Gospel of the twelve Apostles together with the apocalypses of each of them. Cambridge 1900. — *RB* IX 642.

278 HASTINGS (J.), A dictionary of the Bible. Vol. II. Edinburgh 1899. — *RB* IX 155–158. o

279 HAULER (E.), Didascaliae Apostolorum fragmenta veronensia latina. Leipzig 1900. — *RB* IX 647.

280 HAUPT (P.), Die Regenbogen-Bibel. Leipzig. — *RB* IX 158–160. o

281 HOLTZMANN (H. J.) und KRÜGER (G.), Theologischer Jahresbericht. Berlin 1899. — *RB* IX 644–645.

282 HÜHN (E.), Die messianischen Weissagungen des israelitisch-jüdischen Volkes. Freiburg i. Br. 1899. — *RB* IX 473–474. o

283 — — Die alttestamentlichen Citate und Reminiscenzen im Neuen Testament. Tübingen 1900. — *RB* IX 643–644.

284 KAUTZSCH (K.), Die Apocryphen und Pseudepigraphen des Alten Testaments. Freiburg i. Br. 1898–1900. — *RB* IX 313–314; 474–475. o

285 KITTEL (R.), Die Bücher der Könige. Göttingen 1900. — *RB* IX 459–460.

286 KRÜGER (G.) : cfr HOLTZMANN (H.).

287 LIDZBARSKI (M.), Ephemeris für Semitische Epigraphik. Gießen 1900. — *RB* IX 643.

288 MASPERO (G.), Histoire ancienne des peuples de l'Orient classique. Vol. III. Paris 1890. — *RB* IX 309–311. o

289 NESTLE (E.), Einführung in das griechische N. T. Göttingen 1899. — *RB* IX 149–150. o

290 NISIUS (J. B.), [Articles divers sur l'interprétation de la Sainte Écriture par l'Église]. — *RB* IX 135–142.

291 PARISOT (J.), [Sur le mot Sélah-Diapsalma]. — *RB* IX 160–161. o

292 PIEPENBRING (C.), Histoire du peuple d'Israël. Paris et Strasbourg. — *RB* IX 472–473. o

293 ROBERT (U.), Heptateuchi partis posterioris versio latina antiquissima. Lyon 1900. — *RB* IX 648–649.

294 SMITH (H. P.), A critical and exegetical commentary on the Books of Samuel. Edinburgh 1899. — *RB* IX 457–459.

295 STEUERNAGEL (C.), Das Deuteronomium. Göttingen. — *RB* IX 151. o

296 TOY (C. H.), Proverbs. Edinburg 1899. — *RB* IX 1900 641–642.

297 VALBUENA (R. F.), Egipto y Asiria resucitados. Toledo 1898. — *RB* IX 480. o

298 —— Cubrió el diluvio toda la tierra? Toledo 1897. — *RB* IX 479–480. o

299 WIEDEMANN (A.), Die Toten und ihre Reiche im Glauben der alten Ägypter. Leipzig 1900 (*Der Alte Orient*, Bd II). — *RB* IX 647–648.

300 WHITE (H. J.) : cfr WORDSWORTH (J.).

301 WINCKLER (H.), Die politische Entwicklung Babyloniens und Assyriens. Leipzig 1900 (*Der Alte Orient*, Bd II). — *RB* IX 647–648.

302 WORDSWORTH (J.) and WHITE (H. J.), Novum Testamentum D. N. J. C. latine, secundum editionem sancti Hieronymi. Pars I, 5. Oxonii 1898. — *RB* IX 153–155. o

303 WRIGHT (A.), The Gospel according to S. Luke. London 1900. — *RB* IX 637–639.

304 ZAHN (Th.), Forschungen zur Geschichte des neutestamentlichen Kanons und der altkirchlichen Literatur. Bd VI. Leipzig 1900. — *RB* IX 616–620.

1901

305 Mosaïque découverte prés de Jérusalem et représentant Orphée charmant les animaux. *CrAcInscrBl* 223–225; 252.

306 Compte rendu d'une mission à Mâdabâ et du dernier déblaiement de la mosaïque d'Orphée à Jérusalem. *CrAcInscrBl* 571–574.

307 Études sur les religions sémitiques : I. Les Sémites; II. Les déesses Achéra et Astarté. *RB* X 27–54; 546–566. [= n° 446, pp. 41–69; 119–139.]

308 **Choses d'Élam**, d'après la publication des textes de Suse par le P. Scheil. *RB* X 66–72.

309 **Dernières nouvelles de Jérusalem** (aqueduc romain du temps de Septime-Sévère). *RB* X 106–109.

310 **Les prêtres babyloniens d'après une publication récente :** H. Zimmern, Beitrage zur Kenntnis der babylonischen Religion. Leipzig 1901. *RB* X 392–413.

311 **L'inscription de Mésa.** *RB* X 522–545.

BOOK REVIEWS

312 ARINTERO (J. G.), La crisi scientifico-religiosa. Valladolid 1901. — *RB* X 634–637. o

313 BACHER (W.), Die älteste Terminologie der Jüdischen Schriftauslegung. Leipzig 1899. — *RB* X 142–143. o

314 BENZINGER (J.), Die Bücher der Chronik. Tübingen 1901. — *RB* X 643. o

315 BÉRARD (V.), Les Phéniciens et l'Odyssée (*RArch* 1901). — *RB* X 138. o

316 BERTHOLET (A.), Leviticus. Tübingen 1901. — *RB* X 642. o

317 BRANDSCHEID (F.), Novum Testamentum graece et latine. Freiburg i. Br. 1901. — *RB* X 640–641. o

318 CHEYNE (T. K.), Encyclopaedia biblica. Vol. II : (E.-K.). London 1901. — *RB* X 477–479. o

319 Congrès des savants catholiques à Munich. — *RB* X 480–481. o

320 CORNILL (H.), Die metrischen Stücke des Buches Jeremia. Leipzig 1901. — *RB* X 644–645. o

321 Corpus Inscriptionum Semiticarum. — *RB* X 139. o

322 DAUBNEY (Rev.), The use of the Apocrypha in the Christian Church. Cambridge 1900. — *RB* X 148–149. o

323 DESJARDINS (G.), Authenticité et date des livres du Nouveau Testament. Paris 1900. — *RB* X 315. o

324 DUHM (B.), Das Buch Jeremia. Tübingen 1901. — *RB* X 643–644. o

325 DUSSAUD (R.), Histoire et religion des Noṣairîs. Paris 1900. — *RB* X 138. o

326 FEINE (P.), Das gesetzesfreie Evangelium des Paulus nach seinem Werdegang dargestellt. Leipzig 1899. — *RB* X 145–146. o

327 FÉROTIN (M.), Apringius de Béja : son commentaire de l'Apocalypse. Paris 1900. — *RB* X 632–633. o

328 FONTAINE (R. P.), [A propos de l'inspiration.] — *RB* X 311–312. o

329 FOSSEY : cfr SCHEIL (V.).

330 GARDNER (P.), Exploratio evangelica. London 1899. — *RB* X 1901, 125–126.

331 GAUTIER (L.), Autour de la Mer Morte. Genève 1900. — *RB* X
       158–159. o
332 GIESEBRECHT (F.), Die Geschichtlichkeit des Sinaibundes. —
       RB X 143–144. o
333 GIGOT (F. E.), General introduction to the study of the Holy
       Scriptures. New York 1900. — *RB* X 150. o
334 GREGORY (C. R.), Textkritik des Neuen Testaments. Bd I.
       Leipzig 1900. — *RB* X 319. o
335 GUNKEL (H.), Genesis übersetzt und erklärt. Berlin 1901. —
       RB X 616–619.
336 HARNACK (A.), Das Wesen des Christenthums. Leipzig 1900.
       — *RB* X 110–123.
337 HETZENAUER (M.), Wesen und Principien der Bibelkritik. Inns-
       bruck 1900. — *RB* X 144–145. o
338 HOLZINGER (H.), Exodus. Tübingen 1900. — *RB* X 147. o
339 HUMMELAUER (F. de), Commentarius in Deuteronomium. Paris
       1901. — *RB* X 609–616.
340 JÉQUIER (G.) : cfr MORGAN (J. de).
341 KENYON (F. G.), Facsimiles of biblical manuscripts in the
       British Museum. London 1900. — *RB* X 646–647. o
342 LAMPRE (G.) : cfr MORGAN (J. de).
343 LOISY (A.), A propos de l'attribution du Magnificat à Élisabeth
       (*RHLR* 1901). — *RB* X 631–632. o
344 MARTI (K.), Das Buch Daniel. Tübingen 1901. — *RB* X 641–
       642. o
345 MARTIN (F.), Textes religieux assyriens et babyloniens. Paris
       1900. — *RB* X 312–314. o
346 MERCATI (G.), Note di letteratura biblica e cristiana antica.
       Roma 1901. — *RB* X 637–639.
347 MIGNOT (Mgr), Lettre sur l'apologétique et la critique biblique.
       — *RB* X 467–471.
348 MOORE (G. F.), The Book of Judges. Leipzig 1900. — *RB* X
       149–150. o
349 MORGAN (J. de), JÉQUIER (G.), LAMPRE (G.), Fouilles à Suse
       en 1897, 1898 et 1898–1899. Paris 1900. — *RB* X 471–476.
350 MÜLLER (D. H.), Südarabische Altertümer im Kunsthistorischen
       Hofmuseum. Wien 1899. — *RB* X 639–640. o
351 MÜLLER (M.), Listes royales égyptiennes. (Recueil de travaux.
       Vol. XXII). — *RB* X 140. o
352 — — Le papyrus Golénischeff. — *RB* X 318–319. o
353 PATERSON (J. A.), The Book of Numbers. Leipzig 1900. — *RB*
       X 645–646. o
354 PRAT (F.), Les historiens inspirés et leurs sources (*Et* 1901).
       — *RB* X 311–312. o
355 PREUSCHEN (E.), Antilegomena. Die Reste der außerkanon-

ischen Evangelien und urchristlichen Überlieferungen. Gießen 1901. — *RB* X 641. o

356 REDPATH (H. A.), A concordance to the proper names in the Septuagint. Oxford 1900. — *RB* X 324. o

357 REINACH (S.), Interdictions alimentaires et la loi mosaïque (*RÉtJuiv* 1900). — *RB* X 141. o

358 REINACH (S.), Mémoire sur le totémisme chez les anciens Celtes (*CrAcInscrBl* 1900). — *RB* X 140–142. o

359 SCHIEL (V.), Recueil de travaux. Vol. XXII. — *RB* X 139–140. o

360 —— Textes élamites-sémitiques, première partie accompagnée de 24 planches en héliogravure (*Mémoires Morgan,* vol. I). Paris 1900. — *RB* X 1901 66–72.

361 —— Recueil de travaux relatifs à la Philologie et à l'Archéologie égyptiennes et assyriennes. Leipzig 1892. — *RB* X 633. o

362 —— et FOSSEY, Grammaire assyrienne. — *RB* X 633. o

363 SCHULTEN (A.), Die Mosaikkarte von Mâdabâ und ihr Vehältnis zu den ältesten Karten und Beschreibungen des heiligen Landes. Berlin 1900. — *RB* X 152–153. o

364 SWETE (H. B.), An introduction to the Old Testament in Greek. Cambridge 1900. — *RB* X 321–323. o

365 WEBER (V.), Die Abfassung des Galaterbriefs vor dem Apostelkonzil. Ravensburg 1900. — *RB* X 319–320. o

366 WINCKLER (H.), Geschichte Israëls in Einzeldarstellungen. Teil II : die Legende. Leipzig 1900. — *RB* X 299–305.

367 ZAPLETAL (V.), Der Totemismus und die Religion Israels. Fribourg en Suisse 1901. — *RB* X 482–484; 649–651. o

368 ZIMMERN (H.), Der alte Orient. Vol. II, 3. Leipzig 1901. — *RB* X 1901 320. o

1902

369 Inscriptions phéniciennes du temple d'Esmoun à Saïda. *CrAcInscrBl* 496.

370 Deux hypogées macédo-sidoniens à Beit-Djebrîn (Palestine). *CrAcInscrBl* 496–505.

371 Introduction au livre des Juges. *RB* XI 5–30. [= n° 445.]

372 Notes d'épigraphie sémitique (Inscriptions palmyréniennes et hébraïques). *RB* XI 94–99.

373 Études sur les religions sémitiques : Les morts. *RB* XI 212–239. [= n° 446, pp. 269–296.]

374 La controverse minéo-sabéo-biblique. *RB* XI 256–272.

375 Note sur les inscriptions trouvées par Macridy-Bey à Bostanech-Cheikh. *RB* XI 515–526.

BOOK REVIEWS

376 BAUDISSIN (W. W.), Einleitung in die Bücher des Alten Testaments. Leipzig 1901. — *RB* XI 285–287. o
377 BURKITT (F. C.), S. Ephraim's quotations from the Gospel. Cambridge 1901. — *RB* XI 147–149.
378 CHEYNE (T. K.), Encyclopaedia biblica. Vol. III (L-P). — *RB* XI 630–631.
379 CLERMONT-GANNEAU (Ch.), L'année sabbatique des Nabatéens. (*RArchOr* 1901). — *RB* XI, 137–138.
380 —— Le droit des pauvres et le cycle pentaétérique chez les Nabatéens (*RArchOr* 1901). — *RB* XI 137–138.
381 Corpus Inscriptionum semiticarum. — Paris 1901. — *RB* XI 138.
382 CUMONT (F.), Le Dieu Orotalt d'Hérodote (*RArchOr* 1902). — *RB* XI 625–626.
383 DELITZSCH (F.), Babel und Bibel. *Leipzig* 1902. — *RB* XI 456.
384 DOBSCHÜTZ (E. von), Die urchristlichen Gemeinden. Leipzig 1902. — *RB* XI 475–476. o
385 DORNSTETTER (P.), Abraham. Die Anfänge des hebraïschen Volkes. Freiburg i. Br. 1902. — *RB* XI 480–481. o
386 ENGELKEMPER (W.), Die Paradiesesflüsse. Münster 1901. — *RB* XI 256–272.
387 GAYRAUD (Abbé), La crise de la foi. — *RB* XI 135–136.
388 GEBHARDT (O. von), Die lateinischen Übersetzungen der Acta Pauli et Theclae (*TU*). Leipzig 1902. — *RB* XI 630.
389 GREGORY (C. R.) Textkritik des Neuen Testamentes. Leipzig 1902. — *RB* XI 629–630.
390 GRIMME (H.), Psalmenprobleme. Fribourg en Suisse 1902. — *RB* XI 478–479. o
391 HACKSPILL (L.), La Vocation de Jérémine (*BLitE* 1902). — *RB* XI 627.
392 HJELT (A.), Die altsyrische Evangelienübersetzung und Tatians Diatessaron. Leipzig 1901. — *RB* XI 317–318. o
393 HOGAN, Les études du clergé. Paris 1901. — *RB* XI 469. o
394 HOMMEL (F.), Vier neue arabische Landschaftsnamen im Alten Testament nebst einem Nachtrag : die vier Paradiesesflüsse in altbabylonischer und altarabischer Überlieferung. München 1901. — *RB* XI 256–272.
395 HÖPEL (H.), Die höhere Bibelkritik. Paderborn 1902. — *RB* XI 602–604.
396 HOUTIN (A.), La question biblique chez les catholiques de France au XIXᵉ siècle. Paris 1902. — *RB* XI 626.
397 JENSEN (P.), Assyrisch-babylonische Mythen und Epen. — *RB* XI 312. o

398 Julius (C.), Die Griechischen Danielzusätze und ihre kanonische Geltung. Freiburg i. Br. 1901. — *RB* XI 143–144.
399 Kautzsch (E.), Die bleibende Bedeutung des Alten Testaments. Tübingen 1902. — *RB* XI 605–606.
400 Knabenbauer (J.), Commentarius in Ecclesiasticum. (*CSS*). Paris 1902. — *RB* XI 608–609.
401 Knudtzon (J. A.), Weitere Studien zu den El-Amarna Tafeln. (*BzAss* 1901). — *RB* XI 146. o
402 Köberle (J.), Die Motive des Glaubens an die Gebetserhörung im Alten Testament. Erlangen 1901. — *RB* XI 146–147.
403 König (E.), Fünf neue arabische Landschaftsnamen im Alten Testament beleuchtet mit einem Exkurs über die Paradiesesfrage. Berlin 1902. — *RB* XI 256–272.
404 — — Stilistik, Rhetorik, Poetik in Bezug auf die biblische Literatur komparativisch dargestellt. Leipzig 1900. — *RB* XI 476–477. o
405 — — Hebräisch und semitisch Prolegomena und Grundlinien einer Geschichte der semitischen Sprachen. Berlin 1901. — *RB* XI 477–478. o
406 — — Neueste Prinzipien der alttestamentlichen Kritik. Berlin 1902. — *RB* XI 628–629.
407 Lammens (H.) et Martimprey, Notes épigraphiques et topographiques sur l'Emésène (extrait du *MB* 1902). — *RB* XI 625.
408 Lévi (J.), L'Ecclésiastique ou la Sagesse de Jésus, fils de Sira. Paris 1901. — *RB* XI 606–608.
409 Lindl (E.), Die Datenliste der ersten Dynastie von Babylon (*BzAss* 1901). — *RB* XI 146.
410 Loisy (A.), Les mythes babyloniens et les premiers chapitres de la Genèse. Paris 1901. — *RB* XI 119–124.
411 Luther (B.), Die israelitischen Stämme (*ZAW* 1901). — *RB* XI 124–130.
412 Magnier, Encore la critique et la Bible (*Revue canonique* 1901). — *RB* XI 135.
413 Martimprey : cfr Lammens (H.).
414 Meissner (B.), Falkenjagden bei den Babyloniern und Assyrern (*BzAss* 1901). — *RB* XI 146.
415 Meissner (B.), Ein altbabylonisches Fragment des Gilgamosepos. Berlin 1902. — *RB* XI 629.
416 Monceaux (P.), La Bible latine et Afrique (*RÉtJuiv* 1901). — *RB* XI 136–137.
417 Muss-Arnolt (W.), Theolog. and Semit. Literature for. . . 1900. Chicago 1901. — *RB* XI 147.
418 Nestle (E.), [Note sur les Semicinctia de saint Paul] (*ExpTim.* 1902). — *RB* XI 465–466. o
419 Norgate : cfr Williams.

420 OMONT (H.), Notice sur un manuscrit grec de l'Évangile de saint Matthieu. Paris 1900. — RB XI 136.

421 PELT (J. B.), Histoire de l'Ancien Testament³. Paris 1902. — RB XI 300. o

422 PETERS (J. P.), The Old Testament and the new scholarship. London 1901. — RB XI 604–605.

423 REINACH (S.), Les déesses nues dans l'art oriental et dans l'art grec (Chroniques d'Orient, 2ᵉ série). — RB XI 139–140.

424 — — La mévente des vins sous le haut-empire romain (RArch 1901). — RB XI 297–298. o

425 ROLFFS, Harnack's Wesen des Christentums und die religiösen Strömungen der Gegenwart. Leipzig 1902. — RB XI 473–475. o

426 RONZEVALLE (S.), Interprétation d'un bas-relief de Homs (document publié par le P. Lammens dans MB du 15 oct. 1901, 273, n° 28), RA 1902 386–391. — RB XI 625.

427 ROUVIER (Dʳ), Étude sur la numismatique des villes de la Phénicie (Journal international d'archéologie numismatique). — RB XI 138–139.

428 ROYER (J.), Die Eschatologie des Buches Job unter Berücksichtigung der vorexilischen Prophetie. Freiburg i. Br. 1901. — RB XI 144–145.

429 SCHEIL (V.), Textes élamites-anzanites. (Mémoires Morgan. Vol. III). — RB XI 298–299. o

430 — — Une saison de fouilles à Sippar. Le Caire 1902. — RB XI 624–625.

431 SCHLÖGL (N.), Canticum canticorum. Vindobonae 1902. — RB XI 479–480. o

432 SCHOLZ (A. von), Kommentar über den Prediger. Leipzig 1901. — RB XI 142–143.

433 SCHRADER (E.), Die Keilinschriften und das Alte Testament. Bd I, 3 (neu bearbeitet von Dr. H. Winckler). Berlin 1902. — RB XI 451–456.

434 SENSE (P. C.), A critical and historical enquiry into the origin of the third Gospel. London 1901. — RB XI 632–633.

435 SÖDERBLOM (N.), La vie future d'après le mazdéisme. Paris 1901. — RB XI 315–316. o

436 STEUERNAGEL (C.), Die Einwanderung der israelitischen Stämme in Kanaan. Berlin 1901. — RB XI 124–130.

437 Studia biblica et ecclesiastica. Vol. V [Vie de sainte Nino. Description du codex Ψ et collation du codex 1071]. Oxford 1900 et 1902. — RB XI 632.

438 SUCONA Y VALLÉS (T.), Los Salms de David. Tarragona 1901. — RB XI 314–315. o

439 TORGE (P.), Aschera und Astarte. Ein Beitrag zur semitischen Religionsgeschichte. Leipzig 1902. — RB XI 476. o

440 VALBUENA (R. F.), Egipto y Asiria resucitados. Vol. III. Toledo 1901. — *RB* XI 314. o

441 VIGOUROUX (F.), *DB* Fasc. XXI. Paris 1902. — *RB* XI 626.

442 WEBER (O.), Studien zur südarabischen Altertumskunde : Das Alter des minäischen Reiches. Berlin 1901. — *RB* XI 256–272.

443 WINCKLER (H.) : cfr SCHRADER.

1903

444 **Le méthode historique, surtout à propos de l'Ancien Testament** (*ÉB*) : In-16 de VIII–221 pp. Paris, Lecoffre.
  I. L'exégèse critique et le dogme ecclésiastique
  II. L'évolution du dogme, surtout dans l'A. T.
  III. La notion de l'Inspiration d'après les faits bibliques
  IV. La méthode historique, même en matière scientifique
  V. Caractère historique de la législation civile des Hébreux
  VI. L'histoire primitive
 — 2ᵉ édition augmentée de XX–261 pp. Paris, Lecoffre 1904.
 — English translation. : Historical criticism of the Old Testament by E. Myers. [2ᵉ éd. selon la 2ᵉ édition originale]. London 1906.

445 **Le livre des Juges** (*ÉB*). In-8º de XLVIII–338 pp. Paris, Lecoffre.

446 **Études sur les religions sémitiques** (*ÉB*). In-8º de XII–420 pp. Paris, Lecoffre.
 — 2ᵉ éd. augum. de XVI–527 pp. Paris, Lecoffre 1905. (Ouvrage couronné par l'Académie des Inscriptions et Belles Lettres.)

447 **Le Code de Hammourabi.** *RB* XII 27–51.

448 **L'Ange de Jahvé.** *RB* XII 212–225.

449 **El et Jahvé.** *RB* XII 362–386.

450 **Nouvelle note sur les inscriptions du temple d'Echmoun.** *RB* XII 410–419.

BOOK REVIEWS

451 ABBOT (L.), Ethical principles (*Biblical World*, March 1901). *RB* XII 144.

452 AMELLI (A.), Un trattato di S. Girolamo scoperto nei codici di Monte Cassino (*StRel* 1901). — *RB* XII 478. o

453 BARNABÉ d'Alsace (R. P.), Questions de topographie palestinienne. Jérusalem 1903. — *RB* XII 458–467.

454 — — Deux questions d'archéologie palestinienne : I. L'église d'Amwâs; II. L'église de Qoubaibeh, l'Emmaüs de S. Luc. Jérusalem 1902. — *RB* XII 457–467.

455 — — Le Prétoire de Pilate et la forteresse Antonia. Paris 1902. — *RB* XII 457–467.

456 BARNES (E.), Étude sur Is. IX 1–6 (*JThSt* 1902). — *RB* XII 144.

457 BÖHMER (J.), Der alttestamentliche Unterbau des Reiches Gottes. Leipzig 1902. — *RB* XII 322–324. o

458 BONACCORSI (G.), La Volgata al Concilio di Trento (*ScuolCat* 1902). — *RB* XII 633–635. o

459 BOUSSET (W.), Die Religion des Judentums im neutestament- lichen Zeitalter. Berlin 1903. — *RB* XII 620–625.

460 BUDDE (K.), Die Bücher Samuel. Tübingen 1902. — *RB* XII 149–150. o

461 BURNEY (C. F.), Notes on the Hebrew text of the Books of the Kings. Oxford 1903. — *RB* XII 473. o

462 CARLETON (G.), The part of Rheims in the making of the English Bible. Oxford 1902. — *RB* XII 470. o

463 CARPENTER (B.), Introduction to the study of the Scriptures. — *RB* XII 471. o

464 CARR (A.), S. Matthew : the Revised Version. Cambridge. — *RB* XII 469–470. o

465 CERESETO, Tre classi di dottori (*ScuolCat* 1903). — *RB* XII 632–633. o

466 CHAMARD (Fr.), Le linceul du Christ. Paris 1902. — *RB* XI 318. o

467 CHARLES (R. H.), The Book of Jubilees or the little Genesis. London 1902. — *RB* XII 649. o

468 CHEVALIER (U.), Autour des origines du Suaire de Lirey avec documents inédits. Paris 1903. — *RB* XII 481.

469 CHEYNE (T. K.), Critica biblica : [I. Isaiah and Jeremiah; II. Ezechiel and the Minor prophets; III. 1–2 Samuel]. London 1903. — *RB* XII 647. o

470 CIVILTÀ CATTOLICA 1902–1903. La questione biblica. Tradizione e progresso nell'esegesi e Bibbia ed « Alta Critica ». — *RB* XII 473–477. o

471 DÖLLER (J.), Bibel und Babel oder Babel und Bibel. Paderborn 1903. — *RB* XII 486. o

472 ECKER (J.), Porta Sion. Trier 1903. — *RB* XII 638–639. o

473 FOSSEY (C.), La magie assyrienne. Paris 1902. — *RB* XII 481. o

474 FRACASSINI (Abbé), La critica de' vangeli nel sec. XIX, Firenze. 1902. — *RB* XII 477–478. o

475 GRANELLI (E.), De inspiratione verbali S. Script. 1902. — *RB* XII 635. o

476 GRIMM (K. J.), Euphemistic liturgical appendixes in the Old Testament. Leipzig 1901. — *RB* XII 468–469. o

477 GRIMME (H.), Das Gesetz Chammurabis und Moses. Köln. — *RB* XII 487. o

478 GUILLAUME II. [Lettre à l'amiral Hollmann sur la Révélation] (*Das Vaterland*, 21. Febr. 1903). — *RB* XII 334–336. o

479 GUNKEL (H.), Israel und Babylonien. Göttingen 1903. — *RB* XII 488–489. o

480 HETZENAUER (M.), Epitome exegeticae biblicae catholicae. Innsbruck 1903. — *RB* XII 639–640. o

481 HILPRECHT (H. V.), Die Ausgrabungen im Bêl-Tempel zu Nippur. Leipzig 1903. — *RB* XII 486–487. o

482 HOBERG (G.), Die älteste lateinische Übersetzung des Buches Baruch. Freiburg i. Br. 1902. — *RB* XII 331–332. o

483 HOLBORN, The Pentateuch in the light of today. Edinburgh 1902. — *RB* XII 470–471. o

484 HUMMELAUER (F. de), Josue (*CSS*). Paris 1903. — *RB* XII 618–620.

485 JEREMIAS (A.), Im Kampfe um Babel und Bibel. Leipzig 1903. — *RB* XII 486. o

486 JONES, The oldest code of law in the world. — *RB* XII 487. o

487 LAGRANGE (M. J.), Études sur les religions sémitiques. Paris 1903. — *RB* XII 630–631.

488 LEWIS (Mrs A. Smith), Apocrypha syriaca : the protoevangelium Jacobi and transitus Mariae. — London 1902. *RB* 651–652. o

489 LIDZBARSKI (M.), Balsamen (*Ephemeris für sem. Epigr.* 1900–1902). Gießen 1902. — *RB* XII 330–331.

490 LOISY (A.), L'Évangile et l'Église. Paris 1902. — *RB* XII 292–313.

491 MAC FADYEN, I Reg. XVII 17–24 (*ExpTim* 1902). — *RB* XII 143–144.

492 MARTIN (F.), Textes religieux assyriens et babyloniens. Paris 1903. — *RB* XII 481–482. o

493 MINOCCHI (S.), La questione del divorzio nella Bibbia (*StRel* 1902). — *RB* XII 478–479. o

494 — — Storia dei Salmi (*StRel* 1902). — *RB* XII 479–480. o

495 — — Origini e vita storica della lingua ebraica (*StRel* 1902). — *RB* XII 479–480. o

496 MÜLLER (M.), Traité de Ramsès II avec les Hétéens (*Mitteilungen der vorderasiatischen Gesellschaft* 1902). — *RB* XII 328–329. o

497 — — Les fils de Misraïm (*Gen.* X 13–14). — *RB* XII 329–330. o

498 NAGEL (G.), Der Zug des Sanherib gegen Jerusalem. Leipzig 1902. — *RB* XII 327–328. o

499 NESTLE (E.), [Note sur l'autel ἀγνώστῳ θεῷ des Actes XVII 23.] (*ExpTim* 1903). — *RB* XII 471–472. o

500 PALMER, De cruce deferenda. [Note phil. sur le mot σταυρός.] (*ExpTim* 1903). — *RB* XII 472–473. o

501 PEISER, Der Prophet Habakuk. 1903. — *RB* XII 645. o

502 PERLES (F.), Bousset's Religion des Judentums im neutestamentlichen Zeitalter. Berlin 1903. — *RB* XII 620–625.
503 PETAVEL-OLLIFF (E.), Le plan de Dieu dans l'évolution.
Lausanne 1902. — *RB* XII 321. o
504 PETERS (N.), Der jüngst wiederaufgefundene Text des Buches
Ecclesiasticus untersucht. Freiburg i. Br. 1902. — *RB* XII
326–327. o
505 PROCKSCH (O.), Geschichtsbetrachtung und geschichtliche
Überlieferung bei den vorexilischen Propheten. Leipzig 1902.
— *RB* XII 325–326. o
506 RIEDEL (W.), Alttestamentliche Untersuchungen. Leipzig 1902.
— *RB* XII 324–325. o
507 SANDERS (L.), Études sur S. Jérôme. Bruxelles 1903. — *RB* XII
636–637. o
508 SCHRADER (E.), Die Keilinschriften und das Alte Testament.
Vol. II³ (neu bearbeitet von Dr. H. Zimmern). Berlin 1903. —
RB XII 628–631.
509 SMITH (D.), Our Lord's use of common proverbs (*Exp* 1902).
— *RB* XII 142–143.
510 STUDI RELIGIOSI 1902. La veracità storica dell'Esateuco —
RB XII 477–480. o
511 SWETE (H. B.), St. Matthew XXVIII. 16–20 (*Exp* 1902). —
RB XII 141–142.
512 WEATHERALL, The Books of the Old Testament. London 1902.
— *RB* XII 471. o
513 WINCKLER (H.), Die babylonische Kultur in ihren Beziehungen
zur unserigen. Leipzig 1902. — *RB* XII 486. o
514 — — Die Gesetze Hammurabis (*Der alte Orient*, 4. Jahr). —
RB XII 487. o
515 — — Keilinschriftliches Textbuch. Leipzig 1903. — *RB* XII
645–646. o
516 WREDE (W.), Das Messiasgeheimnis in den Evangelien. Göttingen 1901. — *RB* XII 625–628.
517 ZAHN (Th.), [Le pays des Gadaréniens, Géraséniens ou Gergé-
séniens] (*Neue Kirchl. Zeitschrift* XIII). — *RB* XII 646. o
518 ZAPLETAL (V.), Der Schöpfungsbericht der Genesis (I, 1–II, 3).
Fribourg en Suisse 1902. — *RB* XII 144–146.
519 ZIMMERNN (H.) : cfr SCHRADER (E.).

1904

520 Inscriptions grecques recueillies à Bersabée. *CrAcInscrBl*
54–55.
521 Rapport sur une exploration archéologique au Negeb.
CrAcInscrBl 279–305.

522 La religion des Perses : la réforme de Zoroastre et le Judaïsme. *RB* XIII 27–55; 188–212.

523 Deux commentaires des Psaumes (Calmet, 1734; Fillion, 1893). *RB* XIII 251–259.

524 Les prophéties messianiques de Daniel. *RB* XIII 494–520.

BOOK REVIEWS

525 Abbott (E. A.), From letter to spirit. London 1903. — *RB* XIII 137–139. o

526 Baillet (J.), Introduction à l'étude des idées morales dans l'Égypte antique. Paris 1912. — *RB* XXIII 153–154. o

527 —— Le régime pharaonique dans ses rapports avec l'évolution de la morale en Égypte. Paris 1913. — *RB* XXIII 153–154. o

528 Baldensperger (G.), Die messianisch-apokalyptischen Hoffnungen des Judenthums³. Strasburg 1903. — *RB* XIII 600–604.

529 Bardenhewer (O.), Geschichte der altkirchlichen Literatur, Bd II. Freiburg i. Br. — *RB* XIII 459.

530 Barnabé d'Alsace (R. P.), A propos du lieu du martyre de S. Étienne. — *RB* XIII 465–474.

531 Bauer (W.), Der Apostolos der Syrer in der Zeit von der Mitte des IV. Jahrh. bis zur Spaltung der syrischen Kirche. Gießen 1903. — *RB* XIII 617–619. o

532 Bérard (V.), Les Phéniciens et l'Odyssée. Vol. II. Paris. — *RB* XIII 461–464.

533 Bonaccorsi (G.), I tre primi Vangeli e la critica letteraria. Monza 1904. — *RB* XIII 458–459.

534 Bousset (D. W.), Die jüdische Apokalyptik. Berlin 1903. — *RB* XIII 600–604.

535 Bruders (H.), Die Verfassung der Kirche von den ersten Jahrzehnten der apostolischen Wirksamkeit an bis zum Jahre 175 n. Chr. Mainz 1904. — *RB* XIII 622–623. o

536 Bugge (C. A.), Die Haupt-Parabeln Jesu. Gießen 1903. — *RB* XIII 108–117.

537 Cheyne (T. K.), The Book of Psalms. London 1904. — *RB* XIII 460–461.

538 Chiappelli (A.), Nuove pagine sul christianesimo antico. Firenze 1902. — *RB* XIII 153. o

539 Clermont-Ganneau (Ch.), Deux statues palmyréniennes à inscriptions. — *RB* XIII 316.

540 Cook (S. A.), The laws of Moses and the Code of Hammurabi. London 1903. — *RB* XIII 312–313. o

541 Denifle (R. P.), Luther and Luthertum, Bd I. Mainz 1904. — *RB* XIII 298–300. o

542 Driver (S. R.), The Book of Genesis. Oxford. — *RB* XIII 459–460.

543 Féret (P.), La Faculté de théologie de Paris et ses docteurs. Vol. XII : XVIIe siècle. Paris 1904. — *RB* XIII 300. o

544 Fillion (L. Cl.), Les Psaumes. 1893. — *RB* XIII 251–259.

545 Geffcken (G.), Komposition und Entstehungszeit der Oracula Sibyllina (*TU*). — *RB* XIII 627–629. o

546 Gunkel (H.), Zum religionsgeschichtlichen Verständnis des Neuen Testaments. Göttingen 1903. — *RB* XIII 271–273.

547 Hauck (A.), Herzog's Realencyclopädie für protestantische Theologie und Kirche³. Bd I bis XII. Leipzig 1896–1903. — *RB* XIII 451–453.

548 Headlam (A. C.), The sources and authority of dogmatic theology. London 1903. — *RB* XIII 296. o

549 Hehn (J.), Sünde und Erlösung, nach biblischer und babylonischer Anschauung. Leipzig 1903. — *RB* XIII 314–315. o

550 Herford (R. T.), Christianity in Talmud and Midrash. London 1903. — *RB* XIII 307. o

551 Holzinger (H.), Numeri. Tübingen 1903. — *RB* XIII 308–309. o

552 Jastrow (M.), The study of religion. London 1901. — *RB* XIII 295. o

553 Kennedy (H. A. A.), Saint Paul's conceptions of the last things. London 1904. — *RB* XIII 615–617. o

554 Kley (J.), Die Pentateuchfrage, ihre Geschichte und ihre Systeme. Münster 1903. — *RB* XIII 625–626. o

555 Labanca (B.), Gesù Cristo nella letteratura contemporanea straniera e italiana. Turino 1903. — *RB* XIII 153–154. o

556 Lepin (M.), Jésus, Messie et Fils de Dieu d'après les Évangiles synoptiques. Paris 1904. — *RB* XIII 457–458.

557 Loisy (A.), Études évangéliques. Paris 1902. — *RB* XIII 108–117.

558 Mariano (R.), Papa, clero e Chiesa in Italia. Polemiche e dibattiti. Firenze 1903. — *RB* XIII 152–153. o

559 Mercati (G.), Varia sacra. Roma 1903. — *RB* XIII 155. o

560 Müller (D. H.), Die Gesetze Hammurabis. Wien 1903. — *RB* XIII 313–314. o

561 Muss-Arnolt (W.), A concise dictionary of the Assyrian language, Part XIII. Berlin. — *RB* XIII 145. o

562 Pègues (Th. M.), Autour des fondements de la foi. Critique et tradition. Lettres à l'abbé Loisy (*RTh* 1904). — RB XIII 454.

563 Pesch (C.), Theologische Zeitfragen. Freiburg i. Br. 1902. — *RB* XIII 293–295. o

564 Preuschen (E.), Mönchtum und Sarapiskult. Giessen 1903. — *RB* XIII 306. o

565 — — Origenes' Johannes-Kommentar (*GCS*). Leipzig 1903. — *RB* XIII 297–298. o

566 Rahmani (J. E.), Studia syriaca [fragments anonymes d'apocryphes, pièces de S. Éphrem, de S. Jacques d'Édesse, de S. Isaac, des vies. . .]. Charfé 1904. — *RB* XIII 454–457.

567 Rose (V.), Évangile selon S. Matthieu. Paris 1904. — *RB* XIII 612–615. o

568 — — Évangile selon S. Marc. Paris 1904. — *RB* XIII 612–614. o

569 Rose (V.), Évangile selon S. Luc. Paris 1904. — *RB* XIII 612–614. o

570 Saleilles (R.), La méthode historique et la Bible — étude à propos d'un livre récent. Genève 1903. — *RB* XIII 296–297. o

571 Scerbo (F.), Il Vecchio Testamento e la critica odierna. Firenze 1902. — *RB* XIII 154–155. o

572 Scheil (V.), Textes élamites-anzanites, 2ᵉ série (Mémoires Morgan, Vol. V). Paris 1904. — *RB* XIII 464–465.

573 Schmidt (C.), Die alten Petrusacten in Zusammenhang der apocryphen Apostelliteratur nebst einem neuentdeckten Fragment. Leipzig 1903. — *RB* XIII 305–306. o

574 Semeria (G.), Il pensiero di S. Paolo nella lettera ai Romani. Roma 1903. — *RB* XIII 152. o

575 — — Domma, Gerarchia e culto nella Chiesa primitiva. Roma 1902. — *RB* XIII 152. o

576 Smidtke (A.), Die Evangelien eines alten Unzialcodex, nach einer Abschrift des dreizehnten Jahrhunderts. Leipzig 1903. — *RB* XIII 136–137. o

577 Volz (P.), Jüdische Eschatologie von Daniel bis Akiba. Tübingen und Leipzig 1903. — *RB* XIII 600–604.

578 Weiss (B.), Das Neue Testament, nach D. Martin Luthers Übersetzung. Leipzig 1904. — *RB* XIII 614–615. o

579 Weiss (J.), Die Predigt Jesu vom Reiche Gottes, 2ᵗᵉ völlig neubearbeitete Ausg., Göttingen 1900. — *RB* XIII 106–108.

580 Wellhausen (J.), Das Evangelium Marci. Berlin 1903. — *RB* XIII 300–302. o

581 Wernle (P.), Die Anfänge unserer Religion. Tübingen 1901. — *RB* XIII 302–303. o

582 Zapletal (V.), Alttestamentliches. Fribourg en Suisse 1903. — *RB* XIII 309–310. o

1905

583 Éclaircissement sur la Méthode historique, à propos d'un livre du R. P. Delattre, S.J. In-16 de XII–106 pp. (Pro manuscripto). Paris, Lecoffre.

584 **Le Messianisme dans les psaumes.** *RB* XIV 39–57; 188–202.

585   Deux bustes palmyréniens. *RB* XIV 266–268.
586   Notes sur le Messianisme au temps de Jésus. *RB* XIV
      481–514.

BOOK REVIEWS

587   ABBOTT (E. A.), Paradosis or « in the night in which he was
      betrayed ». London 1904. — *RB* XIV 293–295.
588   AYLES (H.), A critical commentary on Genesis II 4–III 25.
      — *RB* XIV 299. o
589   BONACCORSI (G.), Questioni bibliche. Bologna 1904. — *RB* XIV
      287–289. o
590   CONDAMIN (A.), Le livre d'Isaïe. Paris 1905. — *RB* XIV 276–
      282.
591   DELATTRE (A. J.), Autour de la Question Biblique. Liége 1904.
      — *RB* XIV 284–287. o
592   DOUAIS (Mgr), Lettre sur l'étude de la Sainte Écriture. Paris
      1905. — *RB* XIV 453. o
593   FRIEDLÄNDER (M.), Griechische Philosophie im Alten Testa-
      ment. Berlin 1904. — *RB* XIV 632–634. o
594   GUTJAHR, Die Glaubwürdigkeit des irenäischen Zeugnisses
      über die Abfassung des vierten kanonischen Evangeliums. Gratz
      1904. — *RB* XIV 295–296. o
595   HEYES (J.), Bibel und Aegypten, Abraham und seine Nach-
      kommen in Aegypten. Münster 1904. — *RB* XIV 639–641. o
596   HOMMEL (F.), Grundriss der Geographie und Geschichte des
      alten Orients. — *RB* XIV 303–304. o
597   HÖPFL (H.), Das Buch der Bücher. Freiburg i. Br. — *RB* XIV
      448–450. o
598   LEMONNYER (A.), Épîtres de saint Paul. Vol. I : Lettres aux
      Thess., Gal., Cor., Rom. Paris 1905. — *RB* XIV 295. o
599   MASPERO (G.), Sur la XVIIIe et la XIXe dynastie de Manéthon
      (Recueil de travaux 1905). — *RB* XIV 642–645. o
600   MEINERTZ (M.), Der Jakobusbrief und sein Verfasser in Schrift
      und Überlieferung. Freiburg i. Br. 1905. — *RB* XIV 628–
      629. o
601   MIKETTA (K.), Der Pharao des Auszuges; eine exegetische
      Studie zu Exodus I–XV. Freiburg i. Br. 1903. — *RB* XIV 641–
      642. o
602   NIKEL (J.), Genesis und Keilschriftforschung. Freiburg i. Br.
      1903. — *RB* XIV 300–302.
603   Oxford Society of Historical Theology. The New Testament in
      the Apostolic Fathers. Oxford 1905. — *RB* XIV 615–617.
604   PELT (J. B.), Histoire de l'Ancien Testament. Paris 1904. —
      RB XIV 298–299. o
605   POELS (H. A.), La loi de l'histoire et l'encyclique Providentis-
      simus (*The Cath. University Bull.*, 1905). — *RB* XIV 452–
      453. o

606 SEEBERG (A.), Das Evangelium Christi. Leipzig 1905. — *RB* XIV 459–460. o

607 SPIEGELBERG (W.), Aegyptologische Randglossen zum Alten Testament. Strasburg 1904. — *RB* XIV 637–639. o

608 ZANECCHIA (D.), Scriptor sacer sub divina Inspiratione juxta sententiam Card. Franzelin. Romae 1903. — *RB* XIV 450–452. o

1906

609 La Genèse (ch. I–VI). In-8⁰ (Pro manuscripto). Paris, Lecoffre.

610 Nouveau fragment du grand rescrit impérial byzantin de Bersabée. *CrAcInscrBl* 154–155.

611 Exploration de l'École des Dominicains de Jérusalem au nord de la péninsule du Sinaï. *CrAcInscrBl* 211–212.

612 Notes sur les prophéties messianiques des derniers prophètes. *RB* XV 67–83.

613 L'avènement du Fils de l'homme. *RB* XV 382–411; 561–574.

614 Pascal et les prophéties messianiques. *RB* XV 533–561.

BOOK REVIEWS

615 ABBOTT (E. A.), A comparison of the words of the Fourth Gospel with those of the three. London 1905. — *RB* XV 332–333. o

616 BARRY (W.), The tradition of Scripture, its origin, authority and interpretation. London 1906. — *RB* XV 491.

617 BATIFFOL (P.), L'enseignement de Jésus. Paris 1905. — *RB* XV 647–650. o

618 BELSER (J. E.), Das Evangelium des heiligen Johannes übersetzt und erklärt. Freiburg i. Br. 1905. — *RB* XV 493–494.

619 BREEN (A. E.), A harmonized exposition of the four Gospels. Rochester. — *RB* XV 164–165. o

620 BROOKE (A. E.) and MC LEAN (N.), The Old Testament in Greek. Cambridge 1906. — *RB* XV 496. o

621 BRUSTON (C.), Vraie et fausse critique biblique. Dôle 1905. — *RB* XV 163. o

622 CALMES (Th.), Évangile selon S. Jean. Paris 1906. — *RB* XV 494–495.

623 CARR (A.), St John. The Revised Version. Cambridge. — *RB* XV 165. o

624 Congrès des orientalistes à Alger 1905 (section sémitique). — *RB* XV 163–164. o

625 CORMIER (H.), Lettre à un étudiant en Écriture Sainte. Fribourg en Suisse 1905. — *RB* XV 324–326.

626 DELAPORTE (L.) : cfr MARTIN (F.).

627 DELEHAYE (H.), Les légendes hagiographiques. Bruxelles 1905.
       — *RB* 334. o

628 DUJARDIN (E.), La source du fleuve chrétien : le Judaïsme.
       Paris 1906. — *RB* XV 497. o

629 DUPIN (A.-J.) [= TURMEL (J.)], Origines des controverses
       trinitaires (*RHLR* 1906). — *RB* XV 643–644. o

630 FONCK (L.), Der Kampf um die Wahrheit der Heiligen Schrift
       seit 25 Jahren. Innsbruck 1905. — *RB* XV 148–160.

631 FRANÇOIS (R. P.), Liber psalmorum hebraicae veritati restitutus.
       Liége 1903. — *RB* XV 172. o

632 FRANÇON (J.) : cfr MARTIN (F.).

633 FRIEDRICH (Th.), Anciens contrats babyloniens de Sippar
       (*BzAss* V 4). — *RB* XV 498. o

634 GAUTIER (L.), Introduction à l'Ancien Testament. Lausanne
       1906. — *RB* XV 616–621.

635 HARNACK (A.), Lukas der Arzt. Leipzig 1906. — *RB* XV 644–
       645. o

636 HAUSHEER (Dr), Die Mu allaka des Zuhair mit dem Kommentar
       des Abu Ga far Aḥmad Ibn Muḥammad an-Naḥḥâs. Berlin
       1906. — *RB* XV 340–341. o

637 HEHN (J.), [Prières en l'honneur de Mardouk] (*BzAss* V 3).
       — *RB* XV 498. o

638 HEITMÜLLER (W.), Im Namen Jesu. Göttingen. — *RB* XV 641–
       642. o

639 HERMANN (J.), Die Idee der Sühne im Alten Testament. Leipzig
       1905. — *RB* XV 174. o

640 HOBERG (G.), Moses und der Pentateuch. Freiburg i. Br. 1905.
       — *RB* XV 135–139.

641 HOUTIN (A.), La question biblique au XXe siècle. Paris 1906.
       — *RB* XV 502–506.

642 JACOB (B.), Im Namen Gottes. Berlin. — *RB* XV 643. o

643 KITTEL (R.), Biblia hebraïca. Leipzig. — *RB* XV 167–168. o

644 KLOSTERMANN (E.), Eusebius Werke, Bd IV (*GCS*). Leipzig
       1906. — *RB* XV 652–653. o

645 KÖNIG (E.), Altorientalische Weltanschauung und Altes Testa-
       ment. Berlin 1905. — *RB* XV 173. o

646 — — Die babylonische Gefangenschaft der Bibel als beendet
       erwiesen. Stuttgart 1905. — *RB* XV 174. o

647 KREYENBÜHL (J.), Das Evangelium der Wahrheit. Bd II. Berlin
       1905. — *RB* XV 495–496. o

648 LAKE (K.), Facsimiles of the Athos fragments of codex H of
       the Pauline epistles. Oxford 1905. — *RB* XV 165–166. o

649 LE CAMUS (Mgr), L'œuvre des Apôtres. Tours 1905. — *RB*
       XV 492.

650 LEGRIS (B.) : cfr MARTIN (F.).

651 LEPIN (M.), Jésus Messie et Fils de Dieu². Paris 1905. — *RB* XV 166–167. o

652 LESÊTRE (H.), Chronologie biblique et âge des patriarches (*RApo* 1906). — *RB* XV 492. o

653 LITTMANN (E.), Semitic inscriptions. New York 1904. — *RB* XV 175–177.

654 LOISY (A.), Morceaux d'exégèse. Paris 1906. — *RB* XV 474–479.

655 MAC RORY (J.), [Articles de « The Irish Theological Quarterly », avril 1906]. — *RB* XV 491–492. o

656 MARTIN (F.), DELAPORTE (L.), FRANÇON (J.), LEGRIS (B.), PRESSOIR (J.), Le livre d'Hénoch. Paris 1906. — *RB* XV 621–624.

657 MAZZELLA (H.), Praelectiones scholasticae dogmaticae. Romae 1904. — *RB* XV 490–491. o

658 MC LEAN (N.) : cfr BROOKE (A. E.).

659 MINOCCHI (S.), I Salmi. Roma. — *RB* XV 168–171. o

660 MOZLEY (F. W.), The psalter of the Church. Cambridge 1905. — *RB* XV 172–173. o

661 MUSS-ARNOLT (W.), A concise dictionary of the Assyrian language. Parts XVII–XIX. Berlin. — *RB* XV 344–345. o

662 PADOVANI (Ch.), I Salmi secondo l'Ebraico e la Vulgata. — *RB* XV 171–172. o

663 PESCH (C.), De Inspiratione Sacrae Scripturae. Freiburg i. Br. 1906. — *RB* XV 303–314.

664 PRESSOIR (J.) : cfr MARTIN (F.).

665 RAMPOLLA DEL TINDARO (Card.), Santa Melania Giuniore senatrice romana. Roma 1905. — *RB* XV 300–303.

666 ROCHAT (E.), La Revue de Strasbourg et son influence sur la théologie moderne. Genève 1904. — *RB* XV 161–163. o

667 SANDAY (W.), The criticism of the Fourth Gospel. Oxford 1905. — *RB* XV 495.

668 SCHIFFINI (R. P.), Divinitas Scripturarum adversus hodiernas novitates asserta et vindicata, Augustae Taurinorum 1905. — *RB* XV 323–324.

669 SMITH (S. F.), The nature of Inspiration (*The Month*, 1905). — *RB* XV 492–493.

670 SMITH (W. B.), Der vorchristliche Jesus. Gießen 1906. — *RB* XV 645–647. o

671 SOBERNHEIM (M.), Mitteilungen der vorderasiastischen Gesellschaft 1905. — *RB* XV 177–179.

672 SOUTER (A.), A study of Ambrosiaster. Cambridge 1905. — *RB* XV 651–652.

673 TURMEL (J.) : cfr DUPIN (A. J.).

674 VEBER (M.), [Études sur le livre de Tobie et la légende d'Achikar] (*ThQ* 1905). — *RB* XV 175. o

675 Weiss (J.), [Contribution à l'histoire religieuse et littéraire.]
     Göttingen. — RB XV 642. o
676 Winckler (H.), Der alte Orient und die Geschichtsforschung
     (Mitteilungen der Vorderas, Gesellschaft 1906). — RB XV
     498–499. o
677 Zapletal (V.), Das Deboralied. Fribourg en Suisse 1905. —
     RB XV 497. o
678 —— Der biblische Samson. Fribourg et Suisse 1906. — RB
     XV 497. o

1907

679 Le livre de la Sagesse : Sa doctrine des fins dernières.
     RB XXVI 85–104.
680 La Crète ancienne. RB XXVI 163–206; 325–348; 489–514.
681 Les papyrus araméens d'Éléphantine. RB XXVI 258–271.
682 Encore le nom de Jahvé. RB XXVI 383–386.
683 Le décret « Lamentabili sane exitu » et la critique his-
     torique. RB XXVI 542–554.
684 Où en est la question de l'alphabet? RSsPhilTh I 281–294.

BOOK REVIEWS

685 Abbott (E. A.), Johannine Grammar. London 1906. — RB XVI
     149–150. o
686 Alès (A. d'), La théologie de Tertullien. Paris 1905. — RB
     XVI 151. o
687 Bainvel (R. P.), De magisterio vivo et traditione. Paris 1905.
     — RB XVI 289.
688 Bonaccorsi (G.), Letture scelte dal Nuovo Testamento. Firenze
     1906. — RB XVI 148–149. o
689 Bousset (W.), Die Religion des Judentums im neutestament-
     lichen Zeitalter². Berlin 1906. — RB XVI 146. o
690 Brandscheid (F.), Novum Testamentum graece et latine³. Vol.
     I, Evang. Freiburg i. Br. 1906. — RB XVI 149. o
691 —— Novum Testamentum graece et latine³. Vol. II, Aposto-
     licum. Freiburg i. Br. 1907. — RB XVI 450. o
692 Cellini (A.), Critica e fede nella esegesi biblica. Firenze 1906.
     — RB XVI 143–145. o
693 —— Gli ultimi capi del tetramorfo e la critica razionalistica.
     Roma 1906. — RB XVI 452. o
694 Charles (R. H.), The Ethiopic version of the Book of Enoch.
     Oxford 1906. — RB XVI 459–460. o
695 Cheyne (T. K.), Traditions and beliefs of ancient Israël. Lon-
     don 1907. — RB XVI 626–627. o
696 Diettrich (G.), Ein Apparatus criticus zur Pešitto zum
     Propheten Jesaia. Gießen 1905. — RB XVI 457–458. o

697 ERBT (W. von), Die Hebräer. Kanaan im Zeitalter der hebra-
ischen Wanderung und hebraïscher Staaten gründungen. Leipzig
1906. — RB XVI 151–153. o
698 FALOCI (Mgr), La S. Casa di Loreto secondo un affresco di
Gubbio. Roma 1907. — RB XVI 467–471. o
699 FEDER (L.), Justins des Märtyrers Lehre von Jesus Christus.
Freiburg i. Br. 1906. — RB XVI 452–454. o
700 FEI (R.), De evangeliorum inspiratione, de dogmatis evolutione,
de arcani disciplina. Paris 1906. — RB XVI 145. o
701 GAYRAUD (Abbé), La foi devant la raison. Paris 1906. — RB
XVI 289–298.
702 GIBSON (M. D.) : cfr LEWIS (A.).
703 GLATIGNY (J. B. de), Les commencements du canon de l'Ancien
Testament. Roma 1906. — RB XVI 306–312.
704 GROOT (De), Summa apologetica de Ecclesia catholica. Regensburg 1906. — RB XVI 292.
705 GUNKEL (H.), Ausgewählte Psalmen. Göttingen 1905. — RB
XVI 455–456. o
706 HARNACK (A.), Sprüche und Reden Jesu. Leipzig 1907. — RB
XVI 624–626. o
707 HEIGL (B.), Verfasser und Adresse des Briefes an die Hebräer.
Freiburg i. Br. 1905. — RB XVI 146–148.
708 HERZOG (G.-J.) = TURMEL (J.), La conception virginale du
Christ (Bull. d'hist. et de litt. rel. 1907). — RB XVI 446–
449. o
709 HÖLSCHER (G.), Der Sadduzäismus. Leipzig 1906. — RB XVI
461–462. o
710 HUMMELAUER (F. de), Commentarius in Paralipomenon. Vol. I.
Paris 1905. — RB XVI 303–306.
711 KNABENBAUER (J.), Commentarius in duos libros Macha-
baeorum. Paris 1907. — RB XVI 630–632. o
712 KÖNIG (E.), Prophetenideal, Judentum, Christentum. Leipzig
1906. — RB XVI 444–446. o
713 — — Ahasver « der ewige Jude » nach seiner ursprüngl. Idee
und seiner liter. Verwertung betrachtet. Gütersloh 1907. — RB
XVI 462–463. o
714 LEGENDRE (Mgr), Nazareth (DB). — RB XVI 145. o
715 LEIPOLDT (Jo.), Geschichte des neutestamentlichen Kanons. Bd.
I. Leipzig 1907. — RB XVI 450–452. o
716 LE MORIN (J.), Vérités d'hier? La théologie traditionnelle et
les critiques catholiques. Paris 1906. — RB XVI 293–296.
717 LEWIS (Mrs. A. SMITH) and GIBSON (Mrs. M. D.), Forty-one
facsimiles of dated christian arabic mss. Cambridge 1907. —
RB XVI 634–635. o
718 LODS (A.), La croyance à la vie future et le culte des morts dans
l'antiquité israélite. Paris 1906. — RB XVI 422–433.

719 Löhr (M.), Sozialismus und Individualismus im A. T. Gießen 1906. — *RB* VII 461. o

720 Martin (R. M.), De necessitate credendi et credendorum. Louvain 1906. — *RB* XVI 289–290.

721 Martinelli (P.), I primi tre capitoli della sacra Bibbia annotati secondo il sistema delle apparenze. Turbanti 1906. — *RB* XVI 454–455. o

722 Meyer (E.), Die Israeliten und ihre Nachbarstämme. Halle 1906. — *RB* XVI 627–630. o

723 Minocchi (S.), Tre mesi in Palestina; impressioni e giudizi (*StRel*). — *RB* XVI 637. o

724 Monceaux (P.), Histoire littéraire de l'Afrique chrétienne. Vol. III. Le IVe siècle, d'Arnobe à Victorin. Paris 1905. — *RB* XVI 150–151. o

725 Monnier (H.), La mission historique de Jésus. Paris 1906. — *RB* XVI 298–300.

726 Nägeli (Th.), Der Wortschatz des Apostels Paulus. Göttingen 1905. — *RB* XVI 626. o

727 Nau (F.), Histoires d'Ahoudemmeh et de Marouta (*PO*). — *RB* XVI 150. o

728 Nestle (E.), Novum Testamentum latine. Novum Testamentum graece et latine6. Stuttgart 1906. — *RB* XVI 302–303.

729 Noort (G. Van), Tractatus de fontibus Revelationis necnon de Fide divina. Amsterdam 1906. — *RB* XVI 291–292.

730 Nösgen (K. F.), Der Heilige Geist, sein Wesen und die Art seines Wirkens. Berlin 1905. — *RB* XVI 290–291.

731 Ollivier (M. J.), La vie cachée de Jésus. Paris. — *RB* XVI 301–302.

732 Pasteris (E.), Il messianismo secondo la Bibbia. Roma 1907. — *RB* XVI 444. o

733 Procksch (O.), Das Nordhebräische Sagenbuch, die Elohimquelle, übersetzt und untersucht. Leipzig 1906. — *RB* XVI 153–155. o

734 Rahlfs (A.), Septuaginta Studien. Heft II : Der Text des Septuaginta-Psalters. Göttingen 1906. — *RB* XVI 456–457. o

735 Rothstein (G.), Unterricht im Alten Testament. Halle 1907. — *RB* XVI 460–461. o

736 Schmidt (N.), The prophet of Nazareth. New-York 1905. — *RB* XVI 296–300.

737 Thieme (G.), Die Inschriften von Magnesia aus Mäander und das Neue Testament. Göttingen 1906. — *RB* XVI 626. o

738 Turmel (J.) : cfr Herzog (G. J.).

739 Weiss (J.), Die Schriften des Neuen Testaments, neu übersetzt und für die Gegenwart erklärt, Göttingen 1907. — *RB* XVI 622–623. o

740 WREDE (W.), Das literarische Rätsel des Hebräerbriefes. — RB XVI 148. o

741 WRIGHT (A. H.), Daniel and its critics. London 1906. — RB XVI 458–459. o

742 ZELLINGER (J. B.), Die Dauer der öffentlichen Wirksamkeit Jesu. Münster 1907. — RB XVI 449–450. o

1908

743 La Crète ancienne. Extrait de la *RB*, avec un ch. complémentaire. In-8° de 155 pp. Paris, Gabalda.

744 **Mésa.** *DB* Vol. IV 1013–1021.

745 **Palmyre** (Histoire, monuments, inscriptions, religion), *Cor* CCXXXII (Nouvelle série CXCVI) 932–952. [= n° 1108, pp. 32–68.]

746 **Le règne de Dieu dans l'Ancien Testament.** *RB* XVII 36–62.

747 **La revision de la Vulgate.** *RB* XVII 102–113.

748 **Les fouilles d'Éléphantine.** *RB* XVII 260–267.

749 **Les nouveaux papyrus d'Éléphantine.** *RB* XVII 325–350.

750 **Le règne de Dieu dans le judaïsme.** *RB* XVII 350–367.

751 **La Paternité de Dieu dans l'Ancien Testament.** *RB* XVII 481–500.

752 **Nouveau fragment non canonique relatif à l'Évangile.** *RB* XVII 538–553.

BOOK REVIEWS

753 ABBOTT (E. A.), Notes on New Testament criticism. London 1907. — *RB* XVII 299. o

754 ALÈS (A. d'), La théologie de saint Hippolyte. Paris. — *RB* XVII 142–143. o

755 BAENTSCH (B.), Altorientalischer und israelitischer Monotheismus. — *RB* XVII 143.

756 BLUDAU (A.), Juden und Judenverfolgung im alten Alexandria. Münster 1906. — *RB* XVII 149.

757 BRASSAC (A.), Manuel biblique : Nouveau Testament. Paris 1908. — *RB* XVII 297. o

758 BRÜCKER (R. P.), L'Église et la critique biblique. Paris 1908. — *RB* XVII 601–603.

759 BUCHANAN (S.), The four Gospels from the Codex Corbeiensis (*ff* or *ff*²) . . . with fragments of the catholic Epistles, of the Acts and of the Apocalypse from the Fleury palimpsest (*h*). Oxford 1907. — *RB* XVII 608. o

760 BUONAJUTI (M.), Lo Gnosticismo. Storia di antiche lotte religiose. Roma 1907. — *RB* XVII 295–296. o

761 CHARLES (R. H.), The Greek versions of the Testaments of the
twelve Patriarchs. Oxford 1908. — *RB* XVII 442–445.

762 — — The Testaments of the twelve Patriarchs. London 1908.
— *RB* XVII 442–445.

763 CUMONT (F.), Les religions orientales dans le paganisme romain.
Paris 1907. — *RB* XVII 309–311. o

764 DEISSMANN (A.), New Light on the New Testament. Edinburgh
1907. — *RB* XVII 297–298. o

765 FÉRET (P.), La Faculté de théologie de Paris et ses docteurs les
plus célèbres. Vol. V : XVIIIe siècle. Paris 1907. — *RB* XVII
603–604. o

766 GARDNER (P.), The growth of christianity. London 1907. — *RB*
XVII 294. o

767 GLATIGNY (J. B. de), Les commencements du canon de l'Ancien
Testament. Rome 1906. — *RB* XVII 154–159.

768 GREGORY (C. R.), Das Freer-Logion. Leipzig 1908. — *RB* XVII
608. o

769 GUTHE (H.) : cfr SIEVERS (E.).

770 HARNACK (A.), Die Apostelgeschichte. Leipzig 1908. — *RB* 620–
622. o

771 HAUPT (P.), Biblische Liebeslieder. Leipzig 1907. — *RB* XVII
308–309. o

772 — — Purim. Leipzig 1906. — *RB* XVII 306–307. o

773 HEJCL (J.), Das alttestamentliche Zinsverbot, im Lichte der
ethnologischen Jurisprudenz sowie des altorientalischen Zins-
wesens. Freiburg i. Br. — *RB* XVII 302–303. o

774 HETZENAUER (M.), Theologia biblica, sive scientia historiae
et religionis utriusque Testamenti catholica. Vol. I, Vetus Testamentum. Freiburg i. Br. 1908. — *RB* XVII 604–607.

775 HOBERG (G.), Die Genesis. Freiburg i. Br. 1908. — *RB* XVII
623–625. o

776 HOLTZMANN (H. J.), Das messianische Bewußtsein Jesu.
Tübingen 1907. — *RB* XVII 280–293.

777 LAKE (K.), Facsimiles of the Athos fragments of the Shepherd
of Hermas. Oxford 1907. — *RB* XVII 296. o

778 LOISY (A.), Les Évangiles synoptiques. Ceffonds 1907–1908. —
RB XVII 608–620.

779 — — Quelques lettres sur des questions actuelles et sur des
événements récents. Ceffonds 1908. — *RB* XVII 608–620.

780 MÖLLER (W.), Die messianische Erwartung der vorexilischen
Propheten. Gütersloh 1906. — *RB* XVII 143–144.

781 MORGAN (J. de), Les travaux de la délégation scientifique en
Perse au cours de la campagne de 1906–1907 (*CrAcInscrBl*
1907). — *RB* XVII 147–149.

782 Müller (D. H.), Komposition und Strophenbau. Wien 1907. — *RB* XVII 144–145.

783 Pannier (E.), Psalterium juxta hebraicam veritatem. Lille 1908. — *RB* XVII 625–627. o

784 Rosadi (G.), Le procès de Jésus. Paris 1908. — *RB* XVII 299–300. o

785 Sanday (W.), The Life of Christ in recent research. Oxford 1907. — *RB* XVII 280–293.

786 Schürer (E.), Geschichte des Jüdischen Volkes im Zeitalter Jesu Christi. Bd II⁴. Leipzig 1907. — *RB* XVII 296–297. o

787 Sievers (E.) und Guthe (H.), Amos, metrisch bearbeitet. Leipzig 1907. — *RB* XVII 145–147.

788 Soden (H. von), Die Schriften des N. Test. in ihrer ältesten erreichbaren Textgestalt. Bd I, 3. Berlin 1907. — *RB* XVII 299. o

789 Steinmetzer (F.), Neue Untersuchung über die Geschichtlichkeit der Juditherzählung. Leipzig. — *RB* XVII 304–306. o

790 Streane (A. W.), The Book of Esther. Cambridge 1907. — *RB* XVII 307–308. o

791 Swete (H. B.), The Apocalypse of St. John. London 1906. — *RB* XVII 140–141. o

792 Tillmann (F.), Der Menschensohn. Freiburg i. Br. 1907. — *RB* XVII 280–293.

793 Wessely (C.), Les plus anciens monuments du christianisme écrits sur papyrus (*PO*. Vol. IV, 2). — *RB* XVII 298. o

794 Zapletal (V.), Das Hohelied, Fribourg en Suisse. 1907. — *RB* XVII 308.

794a — — Hermeneutica Biblica². Fribourg en Suisse 1908. — *RB* XVII 607–608. o

1909

795 **Le Messianisme chez les Juifs** 150 av. J.-C. à 200 ap. J.-C. (*ÉB*). In-8⁰ de VIII–349 pp. Paris, Gabalda.

796 **Un sanctuaire lihyanite.** *CrAcInscrBl* 457–461.

797 **La parabole en dehors de l'Évangile.** *RB* XVIII 198–212; 342–367.

BOOK REVIEWS

798 Abbot (E. A.), Indices to Diatessarica. London 1907. — *RB* XVIII 308. o

799 Batiffol (P.), L'Église naissante et le catholicisme. — *RB* XVIII 128–129.

800 Belser (J. E.), Der Epheserbrief des Apostels Paulus. Freiburg i. Br. 1908. — *RB* XVIII 313–314. o

801 BRESKY (B.), Das Verhältnis des zweiten Johannesbriefes zum dritten. Münster 1906. — *RB* XVIII 315. o

802 BROOKE (A. E.) and McLEAN (N.), The Old Testament in Greek. Cambridge 1909. — *RB* XVIII 641–642.

803 BROS (A.), La religion des peuples non civilisés. Paris 1907. — *RB* XVIII 483–486. o

804 CAMERLYNCK (A.) et COPPIETERS (H.), Evangeliorum secundum Matthaeum, Marcum et Lucam Synopsis juxta vulgatam editionem. Brugis. — *RB* XVIII 308–309. o

805 CAUSSE (A.), L'évolution de l'espérance messianique dans le christianisme primitif. Paris 1908. — *RB* XVIII 481–482. o

806 CELLINI (A.), Il valore del titolo « Filio di Dio » nella sua attribuzione a Gesù presso gli Evangeli Sinottici. Roma 1907. — *RB* XVIII 310–312. o

807 CLEMEN (C.), Religionsgeschichtliche Erklärung des Neuen Testaments. Gießen 1909. — *RB* XVIII 280–284.

808 CLERMONT-GANNEAU (Ch.), Inscription minéenne (*CrAcInscrBl* 1908 546–560). — *RB* XVIII 486–487. o

809 Congress. Transaction of the third international congress for the history of religions. Oxford 1908. — *RB* XVIII 295–296. o

810 COPPIETERS (H.) : cfr CAMERLYNCK (A.).

811 DEISSMANN (A.), Licht vom Osten. Tübingen 1908. — *RB* XVIII 626–628.

812 DILLENSEGER (R. P.), L'authenticité de la II^a Petri, étude critique et historique (*MelUnSJos*). — *RB* XVIII 314–315. o

813 DURAND (A.), L'enfance de Jésus-Christ. — *RB* XVIII 479–480. o

814 ENGELKEMPER (W.), Heiligtum und Opferstätten. Paderborn 1908. — *RB* XVIII 642–645.

815 GREGORY (C. R.), Die griechischen Handschriften des Neuen Testaments. Leipzig 1908. — *RB* XVIII 303–306. o

816 —— Einleitung in das Neue Testament. Leipzig 1909. — *RB ibid.*

817 GRENFELL (B. P.) and HUNT (A. S.), The Oxyrhynchus Papyri Vol. VI. London 1908. — *RB* XVIII 294–295. o

818 HEER (J. M.), Die versio latina des Barnabasbriefes. Freiburg i. Br. 1908. — *RB* XVIII 316–317. o

819 HOLZAMMER (J. B.) : cfr SCHUSTER (J.).

820 HOLZMEISTER (U.), II Cor. III 17; Dominus autem Spiritus est. Innsbruck 1908. — *RB* XVIII 312–313. o

821 HOMANNER (M. W.), Die Dauer der öffentlichen Wirksamkeit Jesu. Freiburg i. Br. 1908. — *RB* XVIII 309–310. o

822 HÖNNICKE (G.), Das Judenchristentum im ersten und zweiten Jahrhundert. Berlin 1908. — *RB* XVIII 315–317. o

823 HUNT (A. S.) : cfr GRENFELL (B. P.).

824 JACQUIER (E.), Histoire des livres du Nouveau Testament. Vol. III. Paris 1908. — *RB* XVIII 146–147. o

825 JORDAN (W. G.), Biblical criticism and modern thought. Edinburgh 1909. — *RB* XVIII 465–466. o

826 JUGIE (M.), Histoire du canon de l'Ancien Testament dans l'Église grecque et l'Église russe. Paris 1909. — *RB* XVIII 466–467. o

827 LADEUZE (P.), La résurrection du Christ devant la critique contemporaine. Louvain 1907. — *RB* XVIII 148–149. o

828 LAKE (K.), The historical evidence for the resurrection of Jesus Christ. London 1907. — *RB* XVIII 147–148. o

829 LEIPOLDT (J.), Geschichte des neutestamentlichen Kanons. Bd II. Leipzig 1908. — *RB* XVIII 306–307. o

830 LEPIN (M.), Les théories de M. Loisy; exposé et critique. Paris 1908. — *RB* XVIII 317–318. o

831 LEWIS (F. G.), Testimonium S. Irenaei in S. Joannem. Chicago. — *RB* XVIII 146. o

832 LEWIS (Mrs. A. Smith), Codex Climaci rescriptus (*Horae semiticae*. Vol. VIII). Cambridge 1909. — *RB* XVIII 640–641.

833 MACKENSIE, Cretan palaces and the Aegean civilization (*The annual of the British school at Athens*. Vol. XI). — *RB* XVIII 325–326.

834 MADER (J.), Allgemeine Einleitung in das Alte und Neue Testament. Münster 1908. — *RB* XVIII 302. o

835 MC LEAN (N.) : cfr BROOKE (A. E.).

836 MEINERTZ (M.), Jesu und die Heidenmission. Münster 1908. — *RB* XVIII 310. o

837 MÜLLER (G. H.), Zur Synopse. Göttingen 1908. — *RB* XVIII 309. o

838 NAU (F.), Histoire et sagesse d'Ahikar l'Assyrien. Paris 1909. — *RB* XVIII 476–478. o

839 ORR (J.), The resurrection of Jesus (*Exp* 1908). — *RB* XVIII 148. o

840 PARIBENI (R.), Monumenti antichi pubblicati per cura della Reale Accademia dei Lincei. Vol. XIX. (Hagia Triada). Milano. — *RB* XVIII 326–327. o

841 POSSELT (W.), Der Verfasser der Eliu-Reden. Freiburg i. Br. 1909. — *RB* XVIII 645–646.

842 SCHUMANN (A.), Paulus an Philemon. Leipzig 1908. — *RB* XVIII 314. o

843 SCHUSTER (J.) und HOLZAMMER (J. B.), Handbuch zur biblischen Geschichte[6]. Bd I : Das Alte Testament. Freiburg i. Br. 1906. — *RB* XVIII 144–145. o

844 SIRET (L.), L'Espagne préhistorique (mémoires divers extraits de la *Rev. des Qu. Sc.*). — *RB* XVIII 488–489. o

845 SPIEGELBERG (W.), Catalogue général des antiquités égyptiennes
du Musée du Caire. Die demotischen papyrus. Strasbourg 1908.
— *RB* XVIII 628–629. o

846 STEINMANN (A.), Der Leserkreis des Galaterbriefes. Münster
1908. — *RB* XVIII 313. o

847 SWETE (H. B.), The appearances of our Lord after the Passion.
London 1907. — *RB* XVIII 149–150. o

848 THOMPSON (E. F.), [Étude sur les mots μετανοέω et μεταμέλει]
(*Historical and Linguistic Studies*). Chicago. — *RB* XVIII
146. o

849 TILLMANN (F.), Die Wiederkunft Christi nach den paulinischen
Briefen. Freiburg i. Br. 1909. — *RB* XVIII 646–650.

850 TISSERANT (E.), Ascension d'Isaïe (trad. de la version éthio-
pienne avec les principales variantes des versions grecque, latine
et slave). Paris 1909. — *RB* XVIII 478–479. o

851 TOBAC (E.), Le problème de la justification dans saint Paul.
Louvain. — *RB* XVIII 150. o

852 VOGELS (H. J.), St Augustins Schrift *De consensu evangelis-*
tarum. Freiburg i. Br. — *RB* XVIII 301–302. o

853 WEISS (J.), Die Schriften des Neuen Testaments. Göttingen.
— *RB* XVIII 307–308. o

1910

854 Quelques remarques sur l' « Orpheus » de M. S. Reinach.
In-12 de 78 pp. Paris, Gabalda.
— English translation: Notes on the Orpheus of M. Solo-
mon Reinach. By C. C. Martindale, S.J. Oxford, 1910.

855 **A travers les papyrus grecs,** dans Conférences de Saint-
Étienne (*ÉPO*). Paris, Gabalda, 53–88.

856 **Les religions orientales et les origines du christianisme** à
propos de livres récents : CUMONT F., *Les religions orientales*
dans le paganisme romain. Paris; LAFAYE G., *Histoire du culte*
des divinités d'Alexandrie. Paris 1884; DREXLER, *Isis,* dans le
Lexikon, de Roscher; GUIMET E., *L'Isis romaine;* CUMONT F.,
Textes et documents figurés relatifs aux mystères de Mithra;
REINACH S., *Orpheus;* WINCKLER H., *Mitteilungen der*
Deutschen Orient. Gesellschaft, 1907; BOISSIER G., *La Religion*
romaine; TOUTAIN J., *Les Cultes païens dans l'empire romain.*
Cor CCXL (Nouvelle série CCIV), 209–241. [= n° 1108, pp.
69–130.]

857 **Le but des paraboles d'après l'Évangile selon saint Marc.**
RB XIX 5–35.

BOOK REVIEWS

858 ABBOT (E. A.), The message of the Son of Man. London 1909.
— *RB* XIX 144. o

859 ALLO (B.), L'Évangile en face du syncrétisme païen. Paris 1910. *RB* XIX 609–610. o

860 AMANN (E.), Protévangile de Jacques. Paris 1910. — *RB* XIX 616–618. o

861 ARCHAMBAULT (G.), Le dialogue de saint Justin avec Tryphon (*Textes et documents*). Paris. — *RB* XIX 149. o

862 BELSER (J. E.), Die Epistel des heiligen Jakobus. Freiburg i. Br. 1909. — *RB* XIX 147–148. o

863 BOISSIER (G.), La religion romaine. Paris. *Cor.* CCXL (nouvelle série CCIV) 209–241. [= n° 1108, pp. 69–130.]

864 BRANDT (W.), Die jüdischen Baptismen. Gießen 1910. — *RB* XIX 612–614. o

865 CAMERLYNCK (A.), Commentarius in Epistolas Catholicas. Brugis 1909. — *RB* XIX 146–147. o

866 —— Commentarius in Actus Apostolorum. Brugis 1910. — *RB* XIX 607–608. o

867 CHARLES (B.) : cfr SCHMIDT (N.).

868 CONYBEARE (F. C.), The ring of Pope Xystus together with the prologue of Rufinus. London 1910. — *RB* XIX 610. o

869 DENNEFELD (L.), Der alttestamentliche Kanon der antiochenischen Schule. Freiburg i. Br. 1909. — *RB* XIX 610–611. o

870 DESSAU, Der Name des Apostels Paulus (*Herm* XLV). — *RB* XIX 605. o

871 DUFOURCQ (A.), Études sur les Gesta martyrum romains. Vol. IV. Le néo-manichéisme et la légende chrétienne. Paris 1910. — *RB* XIX 611–612. o

872 EGGER (F.), Absolute oder relative Wahrheit der heiligen Schrift? Brixen 1909. — *RB* XIX 298. o

873 EVANS (A. J.), Scripta Minoa. Vol. I. Oxford 1909. — *RB* XIX 445–450.

874 FEINE (P.), Theologie des Neuen Testaments. Leipzig 1910. — *RB* XIX 583–585.

875 FÉRET (P.), La Faculté de théologie de Paris et ses docteurs les plus célèbres. Vol. VI et VII. Paris 1910. — *RB* XIX 301–302. o

876 GLANE und HELM, Das gotisch-latinische Bibelfragment der Großherzoglichen Universitätsbibliothek. Giessen (*ZNW* 1910). — *RB* XIX 460.

877 GRANBERY (J. C.), Outline of New Testament Christology. Chicago 1909. — *RB* XIX 609. o

878 GREGORY (C. R.), Textkritik des Neuen Testaments. Leipzig 1909. — *RB* XIX 303. o

879 —— Wellhausen und Johannes. Leipzig 1910. — *RB* XIX 607.

880 GRY (L.), Les paraboles d'Hénoch et leur messianisme. Paris 1910. — *RB* XIX 615–616. o

881 HARNACK (A.), Ein jüdisch-christliches Psalmbuch aus dem ersten Jahrhundert: *The odes of Salomon, now first published from the Syriac version by J. Rendel Harris,* 1909. Leipzig 1910. — *RB* XIX 593–596.

882 HAWKINS (J. C.), Horae synopticae. Oxford 1909. — *RB* XIX 269.

883 HEER (J. M.), Evangelium Gatianum. Freiburg i. Br. 1910. — *RB* XIX 604–605. o

884 HELM : cfr GLANE.

885 HOLZHEY (C.), Fünfundsiebzig Punkte zur Beantwortung der Frage : Absolute oder relative Wahrheit der Heiligen Schrift? München 1909. — *RB* XIX 299–300. o

886 HUNT (A. S.), The Oxyrhynchus Papyri. Vol. VII. London 1907. — *RB* XIX 458–459. o

887 JORDAN (L. H.), The study of religion in the Italian universities. Oxford 1909. — *RB* XIX 461–462. o

888 JOYCE (M. C.), The inspiration of prophecy. Oxford 1910. — *RB* XIX 603–604. o

889 KENYON (F. G.), The codex Alexandrinus in reduced photographic facsimile. London 1909. — *RB* XIX 462. o

890 LEBRETON (J.), Les origines du dogme de la Trinité. Paris 1910. — *RB* XIX 585–593.

891 LEPIN (M.), La valeur historique du quatrième Évangile. Paris 1910. — *RB* XIX 269–276.

892 MADER (E.), Die Menschenopfer der alten Hebräer und der benachbaren Völker. Freiburg i. Br. 1909. — *RB* XIX 306–309. o

893 MANGENOT (E.), La résurrection de Jésus. Paris 1910. — *RB* XIX 608–609. o

894 MARGOLIS (M. L.), Lehrbuch der aramaïschen Sprache des babylonischen Talmuds. München 1910. — *RB* XIX 614–615. o

895 MARUCCHI (O.), Epigrafia cristiana. Milano 1910. — *RB* XIX 612. o

896 MERTENS (L.), Discours aux prêtres incrédules de l'Église romaine. Paris 1909. — *RB* XIX 302–303. o

897 MIGNOT (Mgr), L'Église et la critique. Paris 1910. — *RB* XIX 298. o

898 — — Lettres sur les études ecclésiastiques. Paris 1908. — *RB* XIX 298. o

899 MONTEFIORE (C. G.), The Synoptic Gospels. London 1909. — *RB* XIX 464–465. o

900 MÜLLER (D. H.), Die Bergpredigt in Lichte der Strophentheorie. Wien 1908. — *RB* XIX 463. o

901 PEAKE (S.), A critical introduction to the New Testament. London 1909. — *RB* XIX 604. o

902 RAUSCHEN, L'Eucharistie et la Pénitence durant les six premiers siècles de l'Église. Trad. fr. Decker et Richard; trad. ital. Bonaccorsi. — *RB* XIX 612. o

903 REGNAULT (H.), Une province procuratorienne au début de l'empire romain; le procès de J. C. Paris 1909. — *RB* XIX 465–467. o

904 REINACH (S.), Orpheus. Histoire générale des religions. *RB* XIX 129–141.

905 SANDAY (W.), Christologies ancient and modern. Oxford 1910. — *RB* XIX 579–583.

906 SARDI (M.), Le Fils de l'homme (*Rivista storico-critica delle scienze teologiche* 1909). — *RB* XIX 145. o

907 SCHÄFER : cfr SELBST.

908 SCHMIDT (N.) and CHARLES (B.), Greek inscriptions from the Negeb (*AmJArch* 1910). — *RB* XIX 633–634.

909 SCHÜRER (E.), Geschichte des Jüdischen Volkes im Zeitalter Jesu Christi. Bd III. Leipzig 1910. — *RD* XIX 465.

910 SCHWARTZ (E.), Eusebius Kirchengeschichte (GCS). Leipzig 1909. — *RB* XIX 148–149. o

911 SELBST und SCHÄFER, Handbuch zur biblischen Geschichte. Freiburg i. Br. 1910. — *RB* XIX 603. o

912 SKIBNIEWSKI (L. de), De בר נשא, Filio hominis. Wien. — *RB* XIX 144–145. o

913 SODEN (H. von), Die Schriften des Neuen Testaments in ihrer ältesten erreichbaren Textgestalt. Bd II. — *RB* XIX 605–607. o

914 SPITTA (F.), Jesus und Heidenmission. Gießen 1909. — *RB* XIX 145. o

915 STANTON (V. H.), The Gospels as historical documents. Vol. II. The Synoptic Gospels. Cambridge 1909. — *RB* XIX 266–269.

916 STAUDT (C. K.), The idea of resurrection in the ante-nicene period. Chicago 1909. — *RB* XIX 148. o

917 STRACK (H. L.), Michna : Sanhedrin; Makkoth. Leipzig 1910. — *RB* XIX 614. o

918 SWETE (H. B.), Essays on some biblical questions of the day. London 1909. — *RB* XIX 300–301. o

919 —— The Holy Spirit in the New Testament. London 1909. — *RB* XIX 304–305. o

920 TOUSSAINT (C.), Épîtres de saint Paul. Vol. I. Paris 1910. — *RB* XIX 303–304. o

921 TOUTAIN (J.), Les cultes païens dans l'empire romain. Paris. — *Cor. CCXL* (nouvelle série CCIV) 209–241. [= n° 1108, pp. 69–130.]

922 VALBUENA (R. F.), La arqueologia greco-latina ilustrando el evangelio. Vol. I. Toledo 1909. — *RB* XIX 143–144. o

923 VIOLET (B.), Die Esdra-Apokalypse. Bd. I. Leipzig 1910. — *RB* XIX 616. o

1911

924 **L'Évangile selon saint Marc** (*ÉB*). In-8º de CLI–456 pp.
Paris, Lecoffre.
— 4ᵉ éd. corrigée et augmentée. In-8º de CXCII–481 pp.
5th edition, 1929.

925 A la recherche des sites bibliques dans *Conférences de
Saint-Étienne* (*ÉPO*). Paris, Gabalda, 13–56.

926 Où en est la question du recensement de Quirinius? *RB*
XX 60–84.

927 La prétendue violation de la mosquée d'Omar. *RB* XX
440–442.

928 Le catalogue des vices dans l'Épître aux Romains (I,
28–31). *RB* XX 534–549.

BOOK REVIEWS

929 ALLGEIER (A.), Über Doppelberichte in der Genesis. Freiburg
i. Br. 1911. — *RB* XX 467–468. o

930 ALMA (J. d'), Philon d'Alexandrie et le quatrième évangile. Paris
1910. — *RB* XX 305. o

931 ANCEL, Connaissances élémentaires et genèse de la matière.
Nancy 1910. — *RB* XX 151–152. o

932 ARNAUDET (Dʳ), Genèse et science. Paris 1910. — *RB* XX
151. o

933 BATIFFOL (P.), Orpheus et l'Évangile. Paris 1910. — *RB* XX
149. o

934 BOURCHANY, Les miracles évangéliques. Paris 1911. — *RB* XX
304–305. o

935 BRANDT (W.), Jüdische Reinheitslehre und ihre Beschreibung in
den Evangelien. Gießen. — *RB* XX 461–463.

936 BRASSAC (A.), Manuel biblique : Nouveau Testament². Paris.
— *RB* XX 149–150. o

937 BULTMANN (R.), Der Stil der Paulinischen Predigt und die
kynischstoïsche Diatrilie. Göttingen 1910. — *RB* XX 463–
465. o

938 CAMERLYNCK (A.) et COPPIETERS (H.), Evangeliorum syn-
opsis². Brugis 1910. — *RB* XX 305. o

939 CHAPMAN (A. T.), An Introduction to the Pentateuch. Cambridge 1911. — *RB* XX 622–623. o

940 CHAPMAN (J.), John the presbyter and the fourth Gospel. Oxford 1911. — *RB* XX 459–461. o

941 COPPIETERS (H.) : cfr CAMERLYNCK (A.).

942 CORNELY (R.), Historicae et criticae Introductionis in U. T.
libros sacros compendium. Paris 1909. — *RB* XX 145–146. o

943 — — Commentarius in librum Sapientiae. Paris 1910. — *RB*
XX 308–309. o

944 CRAMPON (A.), Bible abrégée. Paris 1910. — *RB* XX 302–303. o

945 FELTEN (J.), Neutestamentliche Zeitgeschichte oder Judentum und Heidentum zur Zeit Christi und der Apostel. Regensburg 1910. — *RB* XX 136–138.

946 GIOVANNOZZI (R. P.), I problemi dell'Esistenza. Firenze 1911. *RB* XX 453. o

947 GLAZEBROOK (M. G.), Studies in the Book of Isaiah. Oxford 1910. — *RB* XX 152–153.

948 GOGUEL (M.), L'Évangile de Marc et ses rapports avec ceux de Matthieu et de Luc. Paris 1909. — *RB* XX 132–135.

949 GREGORY (C. R.), Vorschläge für eine kritische Ausgabe des gr. Neuen Testaments. Leipzig 1911. — *RB* XXI 613–614. o

950 GWYNN (J.), Remnants of the later Syriac versions of the Bible. London 1909. — *RB* XX 300–301. o

951 HARNACK (A.), Neue Untersuchungen zur Apostelgeschichte und zur Abfassungszeit der synoptischen Evangelien. Leipzig 1911. — *RB* XX 615–618. o

952 HAUTSCH, Der Lukiantext des Oktateuch. Berlin 1910. — *RB* XX 627–630. o

953 HEER (J. M.), Die Stammbäume Jesu nach Matthäus und Lukas. Freiburg i. Br. 1910. — *RB* XX 447–451. o

954 HUMBERT (A.), Renaissance de l'antiquité chrétienne. Paris 1911. *RB* XX 307. o

955 HUNT (A. S.), The Oxyrhynchus Papyri. Vol. VIII. London 1911. — *RB* XX 611–612. o

956 HUTTON (E. A.), An atlas of textual criticism. Cambridge 1911. — *RB* XX 453–454. o

957 JACQUIER (E.), La résurrection de Jésus-Christ. Paris 1911. — *RB* XX 304. o

958 — — Le Nouveau Testament dans l'Église chrétienne : Préparation, formation et définition du canon du N. T. Paris 1911. — *RB* XX 620–621. o

959 KNABENBAUER (J.), Commentarius in Proverbia. Paris 1910. — *RB* XX 309–310. o

960 KÖNIG (E.), Hebraïsches und aramaïsches Wörterbuch zum Alten Testament. Leipzig 1910. — *RB* XX 156–157. o

961 LEPIN (M.), Évangiles canoniques (*DA*). — *RB* XX 618–620. o

962 LEWIS (Mrs A. Smith), The old Syriac Gospels. London 1910. — *RB* XX 146–147. o

963 LIPPL (J.), Das Buch des Propheten Sophonias. Freiburg i. Br. 1910. — *RB* XX 307–308. o

964 LOISY (A.), Jésus et la tradition évangélique. Paris 1910. — *RB* XX 294–299.

965 MANGENOT (E.), Les Évangiles synoptiques. Paris 1911. — *RB*
     XX 303–304. o
966 MARGARET (Lady), Studies in the Synoptic problem. Oxford
     1911. — *RB* XX 454–459. o
967 MEFFERT (F.), Die geschichtliche Existenz Christi. M. Glad-
     bach 1910. — *RB* XX 306. o
968 MESSMER (Mgr), Outlines of Bible Knowledge. Freiburg i. Br.
     1910. — *RB* XX 146. o
969 MICHEL (C.), Évangiles apocryphes. Vol. I. Protévangile de
     Jacques, Pseudo-Matthieu, Évangile de Thomas. Paris 1911. —
     RB XX 465–466. o
970 NAU (F.), Nestorius : Le livre d'Héraclite de Damas. Paris 1910.
     — *RB* XX 466–467. o
971 PEETERS (P.), Histoire de Joseph le charpentier. Paris 1911. —
     RB XX 466. o
972 SANDERS (H. A.), The Washington manuscript of Deuteronomy
     and Joshua. New York 1910. — *RB* XX 301–302. o
973 SCHADE (T. L.), Die Inspirationslehre des heiligen Hieronymus.
     Freiburg i. Br. 1910. — *RB* XX 602–607. o
974 SCHULZ, Geschichte und Erbauung im Alten Testament. Brauns-
     berg 1911. — *RB* XX 468–469. o
975 SEELIGMÜLLER (A.), War Paulus Epileptiker? Leipzig 1910. —
     RB XX 465. o
976 SICARD (M. M.), Sainte Marie-Madeleine. La tradition et la
     critique. Paris 1910. — *RB* XX 306. o
977 SKINNER (J.), A critical and exegetical commentary on Genesis.
     Cambridge 1910. — *RB* XX 138–140.
978 SOUTER (A.), Novum Testamentum graece. Oxonii 1910. — *RB*
     XX 614–615. o
979 THOMPSON (J. M.), Jesus according to S. Mark. Oxford 1909.
     — *RB* XX 135–136.
980 VOGELS (H. J.), Die Harmonistik im Evangelientext des Codex
     Cantabrigiensis. Leipzig 1910. — *RB* XX 148–149. o
981 VOGT (P.), Der Stammbaum Christi bei den heiligen Evan-
     gelisten Matthäus und Lukas. Freiburg i. Br. 1907. — *RB* XX
     443–447.

1912

982 **La colonie juive de l'île d'Éléphantine.** *Cor* CCXLVII
     (Nouvelle série CCXI) 466–482. [= n° 1108, pp. 1–31.]
983 **La philosophie religieuse d'Épictète et le christianisme.**
     RB XXI 5–21; 192–212.
984 **La secte juive de la Nouvelle Alliance au pays de Damas.**
     RB XXI 213–240; 321–360.

985 La nouvelle inscription de Sendjirli. *RB* XXI 253–259.
986 Jésus a-t-il été oint plusieurs fois et par plusieurs femmes? *RB* XXI 504–532.
987 A propos d'une critique par le R. P. Rinieri du Commentaire de saint Marc. *RB* XXI 633–637.
988 Ouvrages divers sur Éléphantine : UNGNAD A., *Aramaïsche Papyrus aus Elephantine*. Leipzig 1911; LIDZBARSKI M., dans la *Deutsche Literaturzeitung* du 25 nov. 1911; MEYER E., *Der Papyrusfund von Elephantine*. Leipzig 1912; STAERK W., *Alte und neue aramäische Papyri*. Bonn 1912; ARNOLD W. R., *The Passover papyrus from Elephantine* (*JBiblLit* 1912); STEUERNAGEL C., *Die jüdisch-aramäischen Papyri und Ostraka aus Elephantine* (*ZDPV* 1912); GRIMME H., *Die Jahotriade von Elephantine* (*OLZ* 1912); LÉVI J., *Nouveaux papyrus araméens d'Éléphantine* (*RÉtJuiv* 1912); EPSTEIN J. N., *Jahu, ASMbēthēl und ANTbēthēl* (*ZAW* 1912). — *RB* XXI 575–587.

BOOK REVIEWS

989 BAUDISSIN (W. W.), Adonis und Esmun. Leipzig 1911. — *RB* XXI 117–127.
990 BODIN, Nouveau Testament gréco-latin. Paris 1912. — *RB* XXI 607–608. o
991 BOYER (P.), La vie de Jésus-Christ d'après ses contemporains. Paris 1910. — *RB* XXI 145. o
992 BOYSSON (A. de), La Loi et la Foi. Paris 1912. — *RB* XXI 619. o
993 BRICOUT (J.), Où en est l'histoire des religions? Paris 1912. — *RB* XXI 455–460.
994 CELLINI (A.), Considerazioni esegetico-dommatiche sul Prologo dell'evangelo secondo Giovanni. Firenze 1911. — *RB* XXI 144–145. o
995 CREUSEN (J.), Tabulae fontium traditionis christianae. Freiburg i. Br. 1911. — *RB* XXI 614. o
996 DEWICK (E. C.), Primitive Christian eschatology. Cambridge 1912. — *RB* XXI 619–620. o
997 DUCHESNE (L.), Gnose (*DA*). — *RB* XXI 613. o
998 DURAND (A.), Frères du Seigneur (*DA*). — *RB* XXI 613. o
999 FURNEAUX (W. M.), The Acts of the Apostles. Oxford 1912. — *RB* XXI 616–617. o
1000 GAMBER (S.), Le discours de Jésus sur la montagne. Paris. — *RB* XXI 614. o
1001 GIBSON (Mrs D.), The Commentaries of Isho 'dad of Merv, bishop of Hadatha. *Horae semiticae*. Vol. V–VII). Cambridge 1911. — *RB* XXI 143–144.
1002 GOBLET D'ALVIELLA (Cte), Croyances, rites, institutions. Paris 1911. — *RB* XXI 300–303. o

1003 GRAMATICA (L.), Delle edizioni della « Clementina » 1912. — *RB* XXI 607. o

1004 GRAY (G. B.) and PEAKE (A. S.), The Book of Isaiah. Edinburgh 1912. — *RB* XXI 623–626.

1005 HOSKIER (H. C.), Concerning the genesis of the versions of the New Testament (Gospels). London. — *RB* XXI 608–609.

1006 —— Concerning the date of the Bohairic version. London 1911. — *RB* XXI 609. o

1007 HOZAKOWSKI (W.), Klemens z Aleksandryi o 70 tygodniach Daniela proroka. Poznán 1912. — *RB* XXI 620. o

1008 HUBY (J.), Christus : Manuel d'histoire des religions. Paris 1912. — *RB* XXI 460–462.

1009 KÖNIG (E.), Geschichte der Alttestamentlichen Religion. Gütersloh 1912. — *RB* XXI 621–623.

1010 LABAUCHE (L.), Leçons de théologie dogmatique. Paris 1911. — *RB* XXI 138–139. o

1011 LEBON (J.), A propos de la « version philoxénienne de la Bible » (*RHE* 1911). — *RB* XXI 141–143. o

1012 NAU (F.), La Didascalie des douze Apôtres (traduite du syriaque). Paris. — *RB* XXI 620–621. o

1013 —— Compte rendu du ms. syriaque du Sinaï (*JAs* 1911). — *RB* XXI 144. o

1014 PASQUIER (H.), La solution du problème synoptique. Tours 1911. — *RB* XXI 280–284.

1015 PEAKE (A. S.) : cfr Gray (G. B.).

1016 PFÄTTISCH (J. M.), Die Dauer der Lehrtätigkeit Jesu. Freiburg i. Br. — *RB* XXI 139–140. o

1017 PLUMMER (A.) : cfr ROBERTSON (A.).

1018 PRAT (F.), La théologie de saint Paul. Vol. II. Paris 1912. *RB* XXI 617–619. o

1019 ROBERTSON (A.) and PLUMMER (A.), The first Epistle of St Paul to the Corinthians. Edinburgh 1911. — *RB* XXI 140–141. o

1020 SACHAU (E.), Aramaïsche Papyrus und Ostraka aus einer jüdischen Militärkolonie zu Elephantine. Leipzig 1911. — *RB* XXI 127–137.

1021 SANDAY (W.), Personality of Christ and in ourselves. Oxford 1911. — *RB* XXI 146. o

1022 SCHMIDTKE (A.), Neue Fragmente und Untersuchungen zu den Judenchristlichen Evangelien. Leipzig 1911. — *RB* XXI 587–596.

1023 SCHUMACHER (H.), Die Selbstoffenbarung Jesu bei Mat. XI 27 = Luc X 22. Freiburg i. Br. 1912. — *RB* XXI 614–616. o

1024 VALENSIN (A.), Jésus-Christ et l'étude comparée des religions. Paris 1912. — *RB* XXI 612–613. o

1025 VOGELS (H. J.), Die Altsyrischen Evangelien in ihrem Verhältnis zu Tatians Diatessaron. Freiburg i. Br. 1911. — *RB* XXI 284–294.

1026 VRÉGILLE (P. de), Galilée (*DA*). — *RB* XXI 613. o

1027 ZAPLETAL (V.), Der Schöpfungsbericht der Genesis. Regensburg 1911. — *RB* XXI 149. o

1028 — — Über einige Aufgaben der katholischen alttestamentlichen Exegese. Fribourg en Suisse 1910. — *RB* XXI 148.

1029 ZARANTONELLO (L.), I Vangeli delle Dominiche. Vicenza 1911. — *RB* XXI 145.

1913

1030 **Les fouilles de Suse** d'après les travaux de la délégation en Perse : J. DE MORGAN, *Histoire et travaux de la délégation en Perse du ministère de l'instruction publique.* Paris 1891–1905. *Cor* CCL (Nouvelle série CCXIV) 126–150. [= n° 1108, pp. 280–332.]

1031 **Le miracle grec et les rythmes de l'art,** à propos d'un livre récent : W. DEONNA, *L'Archéologie, sa valeur, ses méthodes.* Paris 1912. *Cor CCLI* (Nouvelle série CCXV) 440–468. [= n° 1108, pp. 227–279.]

1032 **Marc-Aurèle : le jeune homme, le philosophe, l'empereur.** *RB* XXII 243–259; 394–420; 568–587.

1033 **Une nouvelle édition du Nouveau Testament** (von Soden). *RB* XXII 481–524.

BOOK REVIEWS

1034 BEERMANN (G.) und GREGORY (C. R.), Die Koridethi Evangelien ⊙ 038. Leipzig 1913. — *RB* XXII 463. o

1035 BÖHLIG (H.), Die Geisteskultur von Tarsos im augusteischen Zeitalter mit Berücksichtigung der paulinischen Schriften. Göttingen 1913. — *RB* XXII 621–622.

1036 BROOKE (A. E.), A critical and exegetical commentary on the Johannine epistles. Edinburgh 1912. — *RB* XXII 464–465. o

1037 DURAND (A.), Inerrance biblique (*DA*). — *RB* XXII 459–461.

1038 FRAME (J. E.), A critical and exegetical commentary on the Epistles to the Thessalonians. New York 1912. — *RB* XXII 465–466. o

1039 GREGORY (C. R.) : cfr BEERMANN (G.).

1040 HARNACK (A.), Über den privaten Gebrauch der Heiligen Schriften in der alten Kirche. Leipzig 1912. — *RB* XXII 461–463. o

1041 HARTMANN (R. P.), Mk V 20 (*BibZ* 1913). — *RB* XXII 615–616.

1042 KNABENBAUER (J.), Commentarii in S. Pauli epistolas ad Ephesios, Philippenses et Colossenses. Paris 1912. — *RB* XXII 305–306. o

1043 MERKELBACH (H.), L'inspiration des divines Écritures. Principes et applications. Liége 1913. — *RB* XXII 613.

1044 RAMSAY (W. M.), Luke's narrative of the birth of Christ (*Exp* 1912). — *RB* XXII 617–618.

1045 SODEN (H. von), Die Schriften des Neuen Testaments. Bd II : Text mit Apparat. Göttingen 1913. — *RB* XXII 481–524.

1046 SZÉKELY (S.), Introductio historico-critica in libros apocryphos utriusque Testamenti. — *RB* XXII 613–614.

1047 VOLLMER (H.), Materialien zur Bibelgeschichte und religiösen Volkskunde des Mittelalters, Bd I. Berlin 1912. — *RB* XXII 614–615.

1048 VOUAUX (L.), Les actes de Paul et ses lettres apocryphes. Paris 1913. — *RB* XXII 466–468. o

1914

1049 **Saint Justin** (Coll. « Les Saints »). In-12 de XII–204 pp. Paris, Gabalda.

1050 **Daphné** (par Alfred de Vigny). *Cor* CCLIV (Nouvelle série CCXVIII) 911–929. [= n° 1108, pp. 130–166.]

1051 **La conception surnaturelle du Christ d'après saint Luc.** *RB* XXIII 60–71; 188–208.

1052 **La justification d'après saint Paul.** *RB* XXIII 321–343; 481–503. [= partiellement n° 1124, pp. 123–141.]

BOOK REVIEWS

1053 AMANN (F.), Die Vulgata Sixtina von 1590. Freiburg i. Br. 1912. — *RB* XXIII 146–147. o

1054 BATIFFOL (P.), L'Eucharistie, la présence réelle et la transsubstantiation. Paris 1913. — *RB* XXIII 140. o

1055 BENZ (K.), Die Ethik des Apostels Paulus. Freiburg i. Br. — *RB* XXIII 292.

1056 BOUILLON (L.), L'Église apostolique et les Juifs philosophes jusqu'à Philon. Orthez 1913. — *RB* XXIII 293–294.

1057 BRIGGS (C. A.), Theological symbolics. Edinburgh 1914. — *RB* XXIII 616. o

1058 BUDGE (W.), Coptic biblical texts in the dialect of Upper Egypt. London 1912. — *RB* XXIII 139. o

1059 BURRAGE (C.), Nazareth and the beginnings of Christianity. Oxford 1914. — *RB* XXIII 608. o

1060 CHARLES (R. H.), The apocrypha and pseudepigrapha of the Old Testament. Oxford 1913. — *RB* XXIII 131–136.

1061 CLEMEN (C.), Der Einfluß der Mysterienreligionen auf das älteste Christentum. Gießen 1913. — *RB* XXIII 142–144. o

1062 DARD (A.), La dernière année. Lectures évangéliques. Paris 1913. — *RB* XXIII 287.

1063 DARLEY (E.), Les Acta Salvatoris (= Acta Pilati). Paris 1913. — *RB* XXIII 144–145. o

1064 DUSSAUD (R.), Introduction à l'histoire des religions. Paris 1914. — *RB* XXIII 616–618. o

1065 EURINGER (S.), Überlieferung der arabischen Übersetzung des Diatessarons. Freiburg i. Br. 1912. — *RB* XXIII 139–140. o

1066 FERGUSON (W. D.), The legal terms common to the Macedonian inscriptions and the New Testament. Cambridge 1913. — *RB* XXIII 293.

1067 FIEBIG (P.), Michna : Roch ha-chanah. Gießen. 1914. — *RB* XXIII 615. o

1068 FOUCART (P.), Les mystères d'Éleusis. Paris 1914. — *RB* XXIII 619–621. o

1069 GALLOWAY (G.), The philosophy of religion. Edinburgh 1914. — *RB* XXIII 615–616. o

1070 GHIO (G.), La parabola del buon Samaritano. Genève 1913. — *RB* XXIII 140. o

1071 GLAZEBROOK (M. G.), The layman's Old Testament. — *RB* XXIII 286.

1072 GRAMATICA (L.), Bibliorum sacrorum juxta Vulgatam clementinam nova editio 1914. — *RB* XXIII 136. o

1073 HAMMER (H.), Traktat vom Samaritaner Messias. Studien zur Frage der Existenz und Abstammung Jesu. Bonn 1913. — *RB* XXIII 293.

1074 HEIKEL (I. A.), Eusebius Werke. Bd VI. Die Demonstratio Evangelica. (*GCS*) Leipzig 1913. — *RB* XXIII 145–146. o

1075 HEINRICI (G.), Divers travaux en son honneur : de BAUDISSIN, Adonis dans les enfers; CLEMEN, Isis et le N. T.; HEITMÜLLER, σφαγίς; FIEBIG, Tradition orale antérieure aux Synoptiques; B. WEISS, A propos des sources de Spitta; von DOBSCHÜTZ, Abus de la théorie des sources; FEINE, Contre les excès de l'eschatologisme; SCHMIDT, Deux anciennes prières chrétiennes. Leipzig 1914. — *RB* XXIII 604–605. o

1076 HELM (R.), Eusebius Werke, Bd VII : Die Chronik des Hieronymus (*GCS*). Leipzig 1913. — *RB* XXIII 146. o

1077 HITCHCOCK (G. S.), The Epistle to the Ephesians, an encyclical of St Paul. London 1913. — *RB* XXIII 288.

1078 HOLLEAUX (M.), Mélanges Holleaux. Paris 1913. — *RB* XXIII 621. o

1079 HÖPFL (H.), Beiträge zur Geschichte der Sixto-Klementinischen Vulgata. Freiburg i. Br. 1913. — *RB* XXIII 147–149. o

1080 HUDAL (A.), Die religiösen und sittlichen Ideen des Spruchbuches, Rom 1914. — *RB* XXIII 612–614. o

1081 KNABENBAUER (J.), Commentarii in S. Pauli epistolas ad Thessalonicenses, ad Timotheum, ad Titum et ad Philemonem. Paris 1913. — *RB* XXIII 292–293.

218 BIBLIOGRAPHICAL TABLES

1082 LEMONNYER (A.) : cfr SCHMIDT (G.).

1083 LINCK (K.), De antiquissimis veterum quae ad Jesum Nazarenum spectant testimoniis. Gießen 1913. — *RB* XXIII 144. o

1084 MAICHLE (A.), Das Dekret « de editione et usu sacrorum Librorum », seine Entstehung und Erklärung. Freiburg i. Br. — *RB* XXIII 602. o

1085 MARTI (K), [Divers travaux en hommage à Wellhausen, édités per Marti.] Gießen 1914. — *RB* XXIII 608–610. o

1086 MEZZACASA (G.), Il libro dei Proverbi di Salomone. Roma 1913. — *RB* XXIII 300–302.

1087 MOORE (G. F.), History of religions. Vol. I. Edinburgh 1914. — *RB* XXIII 618–619.

1088 MORIN (G.), Anecdota Maredsolana : Études, textes, Découvertes. Maredsous 1913. — *RB* XXIII 145. o

1089 MUNTZ (W. S.), Roma, St Paul and the early Church. London 1913. — *RB* XXIII 293.

1090 MURILLO (L.), El Génesis. Roma 1914. — *RB* XXIII 294–298.

1091 NAVILLE (E.), Archaeology of the Old Testament. London 1913. *RB* XXIII 298.

1092 — — Archéologie de l'Ancien Testament. L'Ancien Testament a-t-il été écrit en Hébreu? (trad. de l'Anglais). Paris. — *RB* XXIII 610–612. o

1093 PADOVANI (Ch.), Nouvelle édition de Cornelius a Lapide pour les Évangiles. Turin 1913. — *RB* XXIII. o

1094 PEETERS (P.), Évangiles apocryphes. Paris 1914. — *RB* XXIII 607–608. o

1095 PIROT (L.), L'œuvre exégétique de Théodore de Mopsueste. Rome 1913. — *RB* XXIII 271–275.

1096 POPE (H.), The catholic student's « Aids » to the Bible. London 1913. — *RB* XXIII 153. o

1097 RÜCKER (A.), Über das Gleichnis vom ungerechten Verwalter (*Lc.* XVI 1–13). Freiburg i. Br. 1912. — *RB* XXIII 287.

1098 SCHMIDT (G.), La Révélation primitive et les donnés actuelles de la science (trad. du R. P. Lemonnyer). Paris 1914. — *RB* XXIII 298–300.

1099 SCHUMACHER (H.), Christus in seiner Präexistenz und Kenose nach Phil. II 5–8. Roma 1914. — *RB* XXIII 605–607. o

1100 SCHWEITZER (A.), Geschichte der paulinische Forschung von der Reformation bis auf die Gegenwart. — *RB* XXIII 288–292.

1101 Societas Goerresiana, Concilium Tridentinum (Diariorum, actorum, epistularum, tractatuum nova collectio). Societas Goerresiana. Vol. I–V. Fribourg en Brisgau 1901–1911. — *RB* XXIII 591–597.

1102 SPITTA (F.), Die synoptische Grundschrift in ihrer Überlieferung durch Lukasevangelium. Leipzig 1912. — *RB* XXIII 602–604. o

1103 Toussaint (C.), Épîtres de S. Paul. Vol. II : l'Épître aux Romains. Paris 1913. — *RB* XXIII 140–142. o

1104 Vernes (M.), Les emprunts de la Bible hébraïque au grec et au latin. Paris 1914. — *RB* XXIII 613–615. o

1105 Vogels (H. J.), Collectanea biblica latina. Vol. II : Codex Rehdigeranus. Rome 1913. — *RB* XXIII 138. o

1106 Walde (B.), Die Esdrasbücher der Septuaginta. Freiburg i. Br.
*   — *RB* XXIII 302–304.

1107 Windfur (W.), Michna : Horayot. Gießen 1914. — *RB* XXIII 615. o

1915

1108 Mélanges d'histoire religieuse (*ÉPO*). Extr. de *RB* et du *Cor*. In-16 de VI–333 pp. Paris, Gabalda.

   I. La colonie juive de l'île d'Éléphantine . . .   1–31
   II. Palmyre   32–68
   III. Les religions orientales et les origines du Christianisme, à propos de livres récents   69–130
   IV. Daphné, par Alfred de Vigny   131–166
   V. Saint Jérôme et saint Augustin, à propos des origines de la Vulgate   167–184
   VI. Un évêque syrien du Ve siècle, Rabulas, évêque d'Edesse, † 435   185–226
   VII. Le miracle grec et les rythmes de l'art, à propos d'un livre récent   227–279
   VIII. Les fouilles de Suse d'après les travaux de la délégation de Perse   280–232

1109 **A Jérusalem pendant la guerre.** *Cor* CCLVIII (Nouvelle série CCXXII) 640–658.

1110 **Et la Palestine?** *Cor* CCLIX (Nouvelle série CCXXIII) 723–734.

1111 **La religion de l'Iran.** *DA* II 1103–1135.

1112 **Langue, style, argumentation dans l'Épître aux Romains.** *RB* XXIV 216–235. [= n° 1124, pp. XLII–LX.]

1113 **Après vingt-cinq ans.** *RB* XXIV 248–261.

1114 **Le commentaire de Luther sur l'Épître aux Romains.** *RB* XXIV 456–484.

BOOK REVIEWS

1115 Batiffol (P.), La Paix constantinienne et le catholicisme, Paris 1914. — *RB* XXIV 1915, 274–275. o

1116 GRANDMAISON (L. de), Jésus-Christ (*DA*), Paris 1915. — *RB* XXIV 576–581.

1117 HEADLAM (A. C.), The miracle of the New Testament, London 1914. — *RB* XXIV 1915, 275–276. o

1118 HOONACKER (A. Van), Une communauté judéo-araméenne à Éléphantine, en Égypte, aux VIᵉ et Vᵉ siècles av. J.-C., Londres. — *RB* XXIV 595–598.

1119 KENYON (F. G.), The codex Alexandrinus : Old Testament, Part. I. Genesis-Ruth, London 1915. — *RB* XXIV 1915, 274. o

1120 MERCATI (S. G.), S. Ephrem Syri opera, Romae. *RB* — XXIV 276–277. o

1121 PARIS, L'agape mithriaque (*RArch* XXIV). *RB* XXIV 277–278.

1122 RIVIÈRE (J.), Le dogme de la Rédemption, Paris 1914. — *RB* XXIV 275. o

1123 VACCARI (A.), Un commento a Giobbe di Giuliano di Eclana, Roma. — *RB* XXIV 595.

1916

1124 Saint Paul : Épître aux Romains (*ÉB*). In-8º de LXXXIV–395 pp. Paris, Gabalda.
— éd. augum. de LXXII–21 *., 404 pp., 4ᵉ mille. Paris 1930.

1125 **Luther avant la révolte. *RApo* XXI 387–408.**

1126 **La Vulgate latine de l'Épître aux Romains et le texte grec. *RB* XXV 225–239.**

1127 **L'homicide d'après le code de Hammourabi et d'après la Bible. *RB* XXV 440–471.**

1128 **Le commentaire de Luther sur l'Épître aux Romains (suite). *RB* XXV 90–120.**

BOOK REVIEWS

1129 ALÈS (A. d'), Lumen vitae : l'espérance du salut au début de l'ère chrétienne, Paris 1916. — *RB* XXV 613–614.

1130 BONACCORSI (G.), Psalterium latinum cum graeco et hebraeo comparatum. Florentiae 1915. — *RB* XXV 282–284. o

1131 BOVER (J. M.), La ascética de san Pablo. Barcelona 1915. — *RB* XXV 1916 277–278. o

1132 CART (L.), Au Sinaï et dans l'Arabie Pétrée (*Bulletin de la Société neuchâteloise de Géographie* 1914–1915). — *RB* XXV 600–608.

1133 CHAUVIN (Abbé), Job (*DA*). — *RB* XXVI 273. o

1134 CONDAMIN (A.), Jonas (*DA*). — *RB* XXV 273–274. o

1135 — — Judith (*DA*). — *RB* XXV 274. o

1136 DYNELEY PRINCE (J.), The so-called Epic of Paradise (*JAMOr-Soc* 1916). — *RB* XXV 615–616.
1137 GAUCKLER (P.), Nécropoles puniques de Carthage. Paris 1915. — *RB* XXV 292–293.
1138 GRENFELL (B. P.) and HUNT (A. S.), The Oxyrhynchus Papyri. Vol. XI. London 1915. — *RB* XXV 276–277; 290–292.
1139 HUBY (J.), Christus. Manuel d'histoire des religions. Paris 1916. — *RB* XXV 619–620. o
1140 HUMBERT (P.), Qohéleth (*RThPh* 1915). — *RB* XXV 279–282.
1141 HUNT (A. S.) : cfr GRENFELL (B. P.).
1142 JASTROW (M. junior), Hebrew and Babylonian traditions. University of Pennsylvania 1914. — *RB* XXV 593–600.
1143 — — The Sumerian view of Beginnings (*JAMOrSoc* 1914). — *RB* XXV 616–618.
1144 LANGDON (S.), Sumerian epic, the flood and the fall of Man, Philadelphia 1915. — *RB* XXV 262–268.
1145 LAWRENCE (T. E.) : cfr WOOLLEY (C. L.).
1146 LIBERTY (S.), The political relations of Christ's ministry. Oxford 1916. — *RB* XXV 612–613. o
1147 LOISY (A.), L'Épître aux Galates. Paris 1916. — *RB* XXV 250–259.
1148 POEBEL (A.), A new creation and deluge text. Philadelphia 1914. — *RB* XXV 259–262.
1149 REILLY (W. S.), Sieges of Jerusalem. The first two (*The ecclesiastical Review*, 1915). — *RB* XXV 284–286. o
1150 SALVATORELLI (L.), La Bibbia. Roma. — *RB* XXV 274–276. o
1151 SÉMACH (Y), Mission de l'Alliance israélite au Yémen. Paris. — *RB* XXV 294–295. o
1152 SOUTER (A.), A pocket lexicon to the Greek New Testament. Oxford 1916. — *RB* XXV 278–279. o
1153 THUREAU-DANGIN (F.), Mode de notation chronologique assyrienne (*RAss* 1914). — *RB* XXV 618–619. o
1154 UNGNAD (A.), Babylonian letters of the Hammurapi period. Philadelphia 1915. — *RB* XXV 290. o
1155 VANDERVORST (J.), Israël et l'ancien Orient, Bruxelles 1915. — *RB* XXV 286–289. o
1156 VERNES (M.), Sinaï contre Kadès : les grands sanctuaires de l'exode israélite et les routes du désert (étude archéologique et géographique). Paris 1915. — *RB* XXV 289–290. o
1157 WATSON (C. M.), Fifty years' work in the Holy Land. London 1915. — *RB* XXV 295–297. o
1158 WOOLLEY (C. L.), and LAWRENCE (T. E.) The wilderness of Zin. London. — *RB* XXV 268–272.
1159 WORREL (W.), The coptic Psalter in the Freer collection. New York 1916. — *RB* XXV 614. o

1917

1160   Religion of Palmyrenes (*Enc. of Rel. and Eth* 1917). 592–
       596.
1161   Les Français et les Allemands en Palestine. *RA* XXIV
       385–404.
1162   Le Marquis de Vogüé. *RB* XXVI 5–8.
1163   Les Judaïsants de l'Épître aux Galates. *RB* XXVI 138–
       167. [= nº 1184, pp. XXIX–LVIII.]
1164   La Vulgate latine de l'Épître aux Galates et le texte
       grec. *RB* XXVI 424–450.
1165   La mosaïque de Chellâl en Palestine. *RB* XXVI 569–572.
       Cfr XXVII 595–596.
1166   Inscription au Khân Younès. *RB* XXVI 572–573.

BOOK REVIEWS

1167   ARNOLD (W. R.), Ephod and Ark. Cambridge 1917. — *RB*
         XXVI 578–584.
1168   BARTON (G. A.), Récit épique de la création d'après des
         tablettes de Nippour (*JAMOrSoc* 1917). — *RB* XXVI 603–
         604. o
1169   CONTENEAU (G.), Umma sous la dynastie d'Ur. Paris 1916.
         — *RB* XXVI 605–606. o
1170   COOK (S. A.), A Lydian-Aramaic Bilingual (*JHellSt* 1917). —
         RB XXVI 601–602. o
1171   CUMONT (Fr.), Deux milliaires de Septime Sévère (*CrAcInscrBl*
         1916). — *RB* XXVI 603. o
1172   — — Un fragment de sarcophage judéo-chrétien (*RArch* 1916).
         — *RB* XXVI 318–319. o
1173   HAUPT (P.), [Genesis III 14 s.] (*JBibLit* 1916). — *RB* XXVI
         307–308. o
1174   — — [Études sur Amos] (*JBibLit* 1916). — *RB* XXVI 600–
         601. o
1175   JASTROW (M. junior), Sumerian myths of Beginnings (*JSemLL*
         1917). — *RB* XXVI 604–605. o
1176   LANDRIEUX (Mgr), Au pays du Christ. Paris 1917. — *RB* XXVI
         592. o
1177   NAVILLE (E.), L'Ancien Testament a-t-il été écrit en hébreu?
         (*RThPh* 1916). — *RB* XXVI 309–310. o
1178   PEPE (G.), La filosofia religiosa di Epitteto : Epitteto e il
         cristianesimo (*Rivista di Filosofia Neoscolastica* 1916). — *RB*
         XXVI 593.
1179   REIDER (J.), Prolegomena to a Greek-Hebrew index to Aquila.
         Philadelphia 1916. — *RB* XXVI 598–600. o
1180   TOUZARD (J.), Le peuple juif dans l'Ancien Testament (*DA*).
         — *RB* XXVI 593–598.

1181 VOSTÉ (J. M.), Commentarius in Epistolas ad Thessalonicences. Romae. — *RB* XXVI 574–577.

1182 WIENER (H. M.), The date of Exodus (*Bibliotheca sacra* 1916). — *RB* XXVI 1917 308–309.

1183 WOOD (W. C.), [La religion de Canaan] (*JBibLit* 1916). — *RB* XXVI 602–603.

1918

1184 **Saint Paul : Épître aux Galates** (*ÉB*). Paris, Gabalda. 3ᵉ éd. In-8⁰ de LXXXIV–176 pp.

1185 **Le sens du christianisme d'après l'exégèse allemande** (*ÉB*) : Conf. données à l'Institut Cath. de Paris. In-16 de XX–337 pp. Paris, Gabalda.

I. L'exégèse de l'Église catholique 1–30
II. Le pseudo-mysticisme de Luther 31–66
III. L'accusation d'imposture par les déistes . . . 67–96
IV. Les explications naturalistes du rationalisme éclairé 97–127
V. L'interprétation mystique de Strauss 128–162
VI. La critique des origines chrétiennes par l'école de Tubingue 163–229
VII. Le compromis des libéraux 230–268
VIII. L'école du syncrétisme judéo-païen 269–305
IX. Conclusions 306–335
— English translation : The meaning of Christianity according to Luther and his followers in Germany. By W. S. Reilly, S.S. New York: Longmans, 1920.

1186 **Luther on the Eve of his Revolt.** Translated by W. S. Reilly, S.S. (an adaptation of articles in, the *RB* and *RApo,* etc.). In-16 de 135 pp. Baltimore and New York, 1918.

1187 **Le nationalisme juif et la Palestine autrefois et aujourd'hui.** *Cor* CCLXXI (Nouvelle série CCXXXV) 3–30.

1188 **La revision de la Vulgate par saint Jérôme.** *RB* XXVII 254–257.

1189 **La vie de Jésus d'après Renan.** *RB* XXVII 432–506. [= n⁰ 1384.]

BOOK REVIEWS

1190 ALÈS (A. d'), Lorette (*DA*). — *RB* XXVII 582.

1191 ASSOUAD (N.), Polysema sunt sacra Biblia. Vol. I. St-Maurice 1917. — *RB* XXVII 583. o

1192 BOISSIER (A.), La situation du paradis terrestre. Genève 1916. — *RB* XXVII 594–595. o

1193 BRUSTON (C.), Les trois épîtres de l'apôtre Paul aux Corinthiens. Paris 1917. — *RB* XXVII 588. o

1194 — — Les plus anciens cantiques chrétiens (Odes de Salomon).
Paris 1912. — *RB* XXVII 588–589. o

1195 CAGNAT (R.), Notice sur la vie et les travaux de M. Gaston
Maspero (*CrAcInscrBl* 1917). — *RB* XXVII 596–597. o

1196 CHARLES (R. H.), The Book of Jubilees. London 1917. — *RB*
XXVII 274–275. o

1197 — — The Apocalypse of Baruch. London 1917. — *RB* XXVII
275–276. o

1198 CORDOVANI (R. P.), Il regno di Dio. Roma 1918. — *RB* XXVII
588. o

1199 COWLEY, The Samaritan Liturgy (*CrAcInscrBl* 1917). — *RB*
XXVII 598. o

1200 CUMONT (F.), Études syriennes. Paris 1917. — *RB* XXVII
288–290. o

1201 — — Repas sacrés (*CrAcInscrBl* 1917). — *RB* XXVII 290–
291. o

1202 CUQ (E.), Les nouveaux fragments du Code de Hammourabi sur
le prêt à intérêt et les sociétés. Paris 1918. — *RB* XXVII 593–
594. o

1203 GAMPERT (A.), Les « 480 ans » de I Rois VI 1 (*RThPh* 1913).
— *RB* XXVII 281.

1204 GOGUEL (M.), La Sainte Bible : Les Évangiles synoptiques.
Paris 1918. — *RB* XXVII 581–582. o

1205 GRENFELL (B. P.) and HUNT (A. S.), The Oxyrhynchus Papyri.
Vol. XII. London 1916. — *RB* XXVII 285.

1206 HUNT (A. S.) : cfr GRENFELL (B. P.).

1207 JAMES (M. R.), The biblical Antiquities of Philo. — *RB* XXVII
276. o

1208 JASTROW (M. junior), Constructive elements in the critical study
of the Old Testament (*JBibLit* 1917). — *RB* XXVII 589. o

1209 JUSTER (J.), Les Juifs dans l'empire romain. — *RB* XXVII
258–267.

1210 KYLE, A new solution of the Pentateuchal problem (*JBibLit*
1917). — *RB* XXVII 589–590. o

1211 LABORDE (A. de), Deux ouvrages mystiques inédits du XIVe
s. (*CrAcInscrBl* 1917). — *RB* XXVII 597. o

1212 MC NEILE (A. H.), The Gospel according to S. Matthew. London 1915. — *RB* XXVII 584–587. o

1213 MARGOLIS (M. L.), The story of Bible translations. Philadelphia. — *RB* XXVII 268–270.

1214 MARMORSTEIN (A.), Eine unbekannte jüdische Sekte (*ThT*
1918). — *RB* XXVII 591–592. o

1215 NAVILLE (E.), The text of the Old Testament. London 1916.
— *RB* XXVII 590–591. o

1216 OESTERLEY (W. O. E.), The Wisdom of Salomon. London 1917.
— *RB* XXVII 273. o

1217 PETERS (J. P.), The worship of Tammuz (*JBibLit* 1917).—
      RB XXVII 590. o
1218 PLUMMER (A.), The Gospel according to S. Mark. Cambridge
      1914.— *RB* XXVII 583–584. o
1219 RAMSY (W. M.), The teaching of Paul in terms of the present
      Day² 1913.— *RB* XXVII 587–588. o
1220 RICO (M. R.), La Poliglota de Alcala. Madrid 1917.— *RB*
      XXVII 276–277. o
1221 Saint Office. Décret du 5 juin 1918 sur la science du Christ.—
      RB XXVII 580–581. o
1222 SCHEIL (V.), Travaux divers (*RAss* 1914–1917).— *RB* XXVII
      286–288. o
1223 THACKERAY (H. St. J.), The Letter of Aristeas. London 1917.
      — *RB* XXVII 274.
1224 THUREAU-DANGIN (F.), Tablettes d'El-Amarna (*CrAcInscrBl*
      1917).— *RB* XXVII 597–598. o
1225 TRUYOLS (A. Fernandez), Breve introducción a la critica textual
      del A. T. Roma 1917.— *RB* XXVII 281–284.
1226 UBACH (B.), Legisne Toram ? Montserrati 1918.— *RB* XXVII
      1918 592–593. o
1227 The holy Scripture according to the Masoretic text; a new
      translation. Philadelphia 1917.— *RB* XXVII 270–272.
1228 The codex Alexandrinus in reduced photographic facsimile.
      Part. I. Genesis-Ruth. London 1915.— *RB* XXVII 268.

1919

1229 **Les mystères d'Éleusis et le Christianisme.** *RB* XXVIII
     157–217.
1230 **Attis et le Christianisme.** *RB* XXVIII 419–480.
1231 **Critique biblique. Réponse à l'article de la « Civiltà cat-
     tolica » : Venticinque anni dopo l'enciclica « Provi-
     dentissimus ».** *RB* XXVIII 593–600.

BOOK REVIEWS

1232 BALL (C. J.), Epistle of Jeremy. Giessen 1913.— *RB* XXVIII
      286–288. o
1233 BÉDIER (J.), Les légendes épiques. Paris 1912.— *RB* XXVIII
      272–275.
1234 BURKITT (F. C.), Jewish and Christian apocalypses. Oxford
      1914.— *RB* XXVIII 290–293. o
1235 BURNEY (C. F.), The Book of Judges. London 1918.— *RB*
      XXVIII 569–573.
1236 BUZY (D.), Enseignements paraboliques (*RB* XXVI 1917,
      pp. 168–207) — *RB* XXVIII 281–283.
1237 CAVALLERA (F.), [Note à propos de la revision du N. T. par
      saint Jérôme] *BLitE* 1918).— *RB* XXVIII 283. o

1238 DAKSE (J.), Die gegenwärtige Krisis in der alttestamentlichen Kritik. Gießen 1914. — *RB* XXVIII 283–285. o

1239 EJARQUE (R.), La « Fraccion del pan ». Barcelona 1916. — *RB* XXVIII 588. o

1240 FOCKE (F.), Die Entstehung der Weisheit Salomos. Göttingen 1913. — *RB* XXVIII 1919 267–272.

1241 HARNACK (A. von), Die Entstehung des neuen Testaments und die wichtigsten Folgen der neuen Schöpfung. Leipzig 1914. — *RB* XXVIII 255–261.

1242 HOLLEAUX (M.), La mort d'Antiochos IV Epiphanès (*REtA* 1916). — *RB* XXVIII 589–590. o

1243 JACKSON (L. H.), The problem of the Fourth Gospel. Cambridge 1918. — *RB* XXVIII 279–280. o

1244 LIETZMANN (H.), H. von Soden, Ausgabe des Neuen Testaments. Die drei Rezensionen (*ZNW* 1914). — *RB* XXVIII 276. o

1245 LINDEMANN (H.), Florilegii hebraici lexicon. Freiburg i. Br. 1914. — *RB* XXVIII 592–593. o

1246 MacNEILL (H. L.), The christology of the Epistle to the Hebrews. Chicago 1914. — *RB* XXVIII 266–267.

1247 MANY (V.), Études évangéliques. Montréal 1918. — *RB* XXVIII 587–588. o

1248 MAYER (H. H.), Über die Pastoralbriefe (II Tim. Tit.). Göttingen 1913. — *RB* XXVIII 280–281. o

1249 NAUMANN (W.), Untersuchungen über den apocryphen Jeremiasbrief. Gießen 1913. — *RB* XXVIII 286–288. o

1250 ORFALI (G.), De Arca Fœderis. Paris 1918. — *RB* XXVIII 588–589. o

1251 POPE (H.), The catholic student's « Aids » to the study of the Bible. Vol. II, The New Testament. London 1918. — *RB* XXVIII 585–587. o

1252 RYLE (H. E.), The Book of Genesis. — *RB* XXVIII 285–286. o

1253 SANDERS (H. A.), The Old Testament manuscripts in the Freer collection. New York 1917. — *RB* XXVIII 585–586. o

1254 SCHWAB (J.), Der Begriff der nefeš in den Heiligen Schriften des Alten Testaments. Leipzig 1913. — *RB* XXVIII 288–289. o

1255 SMITH (G. A.), The Book of Deuteronomy. Cambridge 1918. — *RB* XXVIII 564–568.

1256 UBACH (B.), Legisne Thoram? Montserrat 1919. — *RB* XXVIII 592.

1257 VACCARI (A.), Hesychius de Jérusalem et son « Commentarius in Leviticum ». Bessarione 1918. — *RB* XXVIII 289–290. o

1258 VALBUENA (R. F.), La religion a través de los siglos. Vol. I. Madrid 1918. — *RB* XXVIII 591–592. o

1259 WEISS (J.), Das Urchristentum. Göttingen 1914. — *RB* XXVIII 276–279. o

1260 WINDISCH (H.), Der Hebräerbrief. Tübingen 1913. — *RB* XXVIII 261–266.

1920

1261 The reunion of the Churches. *Blackfriars* I 390–403.

1262 A propos des destinataires de l'épître aux Galates. *RApo* XXX 393–398.

1263 L'exégèse biblique en Allemagne durant la guerre. *RB* XXIX 285–300.

1264 L'ancienne version syriaque des Évangiles. *RB* XXIX 321–352.

BOOK REVIEWS

1265 ALFARIC (P.), Les Écritures manichéennes. Paris 1918. — *RB* XXIX 148–149.

1266 AYTOUN (A.), The ten Lucan hymns of the Nativity in their original language (*JThSt* 1917). — *RB* XXIX 459–460.

1267 BACON (B. W.), The Fourth Gospel in research and debate. — *RB* XXIX 138–144.

1268 — — Is Mark a roman Gospel? Cambridge 1919. — *RB* XXIX 458–459.

1269 BILLOT (C^al), La Parousie. Paris 1920. — *RB* XXIX 596. o

1270 CADBURY (H. J.), The diction of Luke and Acts. Cambridge 1919. — *RB* XXIX 145–147. o

1271 COLSON (F. H.), Myths and genealogies (*JThSt* 1918). — *RB* XXIX 460.

1272 CRONIN, Abilene, the Jewish Herods and S. Luke (*JThSt* 1917). — *RB* XXIX 460.

1273 DANBY (H.), Tractate Sanhedrin : Mishnah and Tosefta. London 1919. — *RB* XXIX 601–602. o

1274 DAUSCH (P.), Die Heilige Schrift des Neuen Testaments. Bonn. — *RB* XXIX 456–457.

1275 — — Die drei älteren Evangelien. Bonn. — *RB* XXIX 456–457. o

1276 HARNACK (A. von), Zur Revision der Prinzipien der neutestamentlichen Textkritik. Leipzig 1916. — *RB* XXIX 450–452.

1277 HOSKIER (H. C.), Codex B and its allies. London 1914. — *RB* XXIX 448–450. —

1278 HUBER (K.), Untersuchungen über den Sprachcharakter des griechischen Leviticus. Gießen 1916. — *RB* XXIX 599–600. o

1279 HYVERNAT (H.), A check list of Coptic manuscripts. New York 1919. — *RB* XXIX 1920 447–448.

1280 KURZE (G.), Der Engels- und Teufelsglaube des Apostels Paulus. Freiburg i. Br. 1915. — *RB* XXIX 597. o

1281 LEBRETON (J.), Les origines du dogme de la Trinité. Paris 1919. — *RB* XXIX 597–598.

1282 LOISY (A.), Les mystères païens et le mystère chrétien. Paris 1919. — *RB* XXIX 420–446.

1283 MACLER (F.), Le texte arménien de l'Évangile d'après Matthieu et Marc. Paris 1919. — *RB* XXIX 452–456.

1284 MAGER (H.), Die Peschittho zum Buche Josua. Freiburg i. Br. 1915. — *RB* XXIX 600–601.

1285 MEINERTZ (M.), Der Jakobusbrief. Bonn 1916. — *RB* XXIX 458.

1286 MERCIER (C^al), La vie intérieure. Bruxelles 1919. — *RB* XXIX 447.

1287 MERCIER (Ch.), HUMBERT (P.), RANDON (L.), HENRY (A.-B.), LODS (A.), Les psaumes (extrait de la Bible du Centenaire). Paris 1920. — *RB* XXIX 1920 599. o

1288 PESERICO (L.), Cronologia egiziana. Vicenza 1920. — *RB* XXIX 459.

1289 PIROT (L.), Les Actes des Apôtres et la Commission biblique. Paris 1919. — *RB* XXIX 147–148.

1290 ROPES (J. H.), A critical and exegetical commentary on the Epistle of S. James. New York 1916. — *RB* XXIX 457–458.

1291 SICKENBERGER (J.), Geschichte des Neuen Testaments. Bonn. — *RB* XXIX 456. o

1292 STEINMANN (A.), Die Briefe an die Galater. Bonn 1918. — *RB* XXIX 457. o

1293 VALBUENA (R. F.), La religion a través de los siglos. Vol. II. Madrid. — *RB* XXIX 446.

1294 WEBER (S.), Sancti Irenaei episcopi Lugdunensis demonstratio apostolicate predicationis. Freiburg i. Br. 1917. — *RB* XXIX 598–599.

1295 WRZOL (J.), Die Echtheit des zweiten Thessalonicherbriefes. Freiburg i. Br. 1916. — *RB* XXIX 596–597.

1921

1296 **Évangile selon saint Luc** (*ÉB*). In-8⁰ de CLVIII–630 pp. Paris, Gabalda.
— 4ᵉ éd. de CLXVII–635 pp.

1297 **Compte rendu sommaire des fouilles d'"Aïn Doûq.** *CrAc-InscrBl* 141–200.

1298 **L'ancienne version syriaque des Évangiles** (suite). *RB* XXX 11–44.

1299 **Une des paroles attribuées à Jésus.** *RB* XXX 233–237.

BOOK REVIEWS

1300 ALÈS (A. d'), Origénisme (*DA*). — *RB* XXX 470. o

1301 Batiffol (P.), Le catholicisme de saint Augustin. Paris 1920.
— RB XXX 296. o

1302 Brassac (A.), Manuel biblique : Les Saints Évangiles[15]. Paris.
— RB XXX 290–291. o

1303 Brillant (M.), Mystères d'Eleusis. Paris 1920. — RB XXX
157–158.

1304 Browne (L. E.), Early Judaism. Cambridge 1920. — RB XXX
297. o

1305 Burkitt (F. C.), The old Latin and the Itala (TS 1896);
Saint Augustine's Bible and the Itala (JThSt 1910, 258 ss.).
— RB XXX 464–466. o

1306 Causse (A.), Essai sur le conflit du christianisme primitif et de
la civilisation. Paris 1920. — RB XXX 145–147. o

1307 Cavallera (F.), Saint Jérôme et la Vulgate des Actes, des
Épîtres et de l'Apocalypse (BLitE 1920). — RB XXX 292–
293. o

1308 Chapman (J.), [Harmonisations dues à Marcion] (RBen
1912). — RB XXX 141–142. o

1309 Dessau, Inscr. Latin-select. III 162 (Quirinius). — RB XXX
143. o

1310 Frazer (J. G.), The magical origin of Kings (trad. fr. de P. H.
Loyson). Paris 1920. — RB XXX 151–156.

1311 Gwilliam (G. H.), The New Testament in Syriac. London
1905–1920. — RB XXX 289. o

1312 Harnack (A. von), Marcion : Das Evangelium vom fremden
Gott. Leipzig 1921. — RB XXX 602–611.

1313 Harris (J. R.), Testimonies. Cambridge 1916–1920. — RB
XXX 612–614.

1314 Herbigny (M. d'), De Deo universos vocante ad sui regni
vitam, seu de institutione Ecclesiae primaeva[2]. Vol. I. Paris
1920. — RB XXX 295–296. o

1315 Hetzenauer (M.), De recognitione principiorum criticae textus
Novi Testamenti secundum Adolfum de Harnack. Romae 1920.
— RB XXX 139. o

1316 Hollard (A.), L'apothéose de Jésus. Paris 1921. — RB XXX
470. o

1317 Houde (G.), L'Évangile selon S. Mat., S. Mc., S. Lc., S. Jean.
Nice 1920. — RB XXX 289–290. o

1318 Jacquier (E.), Études de critique et de philologie du Nouveau
Testament. Paris 1915. — RB XXX 290. o

1319 —— Les mystères païens et saint Paul (DA). — RB XXX
470. o

1320 Loyson (P. H.) : cfr Frazer (J. G.).

1321 Mathis (M. A.), The Pauline πίστις-ὑπόστασις 1920. — RB
XXX 292. o

1322 NASCIMBENE (R.), Il problema escatalogico in S. Paolo (*Scuol-Catt* 1919). — *RB* XXX 292 o

1323 PALLIS (A.), To the Romans. Liverpool 1920. — *RB* XXX 469. o

1324 PINARD DE LA BOULLAYE (H.), Les infiltrations païennes dans l'ancienne Loi d'après les Pères de l'Église (*RScRel* 1919). — *RB* XXX 156. o

1325 REYNÈS-MONLAUR (Mlle), Les appels du Christ. Paris 1920. — *RB* XXX 148. o

1326 ROSLANIEC (Fr.), Sensus genuinus et plenus locutionis « Filius hominis ». Romae 1920. — *RB* XXX 143–144. o

1327 RUFFINI (E.), La Gerarchia della Chiesa negli Atti degli Apostoli e nelle lettere di S. Paolo. Roma 1921. — *RB* XXX 621–622. o

1328 SCHLÖGL (N.), Die Heiligen Schriften des neuen Bundes. Wien 1920. — *RB* XXX 466–469. o

1329 SCHÜTZ (R.), Der parallele Bau der Satzglieder im Neuen Testament und seine Verwertung für die Textkritik und Exegese. Göttingen 1920. — *RB* XXX 142–143. o

1330 SICKENBERGER (J.), Kurzgefaßte Einleitung in das Neue Testament². Freiburg i. Br. 1920. — *RB* XXX 138–139.

1331 STEGMANN (A.), Silvanus als Missionar und Hagiograph. Rottenburg 1917. — *RB* XXX 620–621. o

1332 TATON (R.), The Gospel according to S. Mark with introduction, text and notes. London 1920. — *RB* XXX 291. o

1333 TIXERONT (J.), Mélanges de patrologie et d'histoire des dogmes. Paris 1921. — *RB* XXX 296–297. o

1334 TURNER (C. H.), The study of the New Testament. Oxford 1920. — *RB* XXX 469. o

1335 VALBUENA (R. F.), La religion a través de los siglos. Vol. III. Madrid 1920. — *RB* XXX 466. o

1336 VOGELS (H. J.), Novum Testamentum graece. Düsseldorf 1920. — *RB* XXX 139–141. o

1337 — — Untersuchungen zur Geschichte der lateinischen Apocalypse-Übersetzung. Düsseldorf 1920. — *RB* XXX 293–294. o

1338 WEBER (V.), Des Paulus Reiserouten bei der zweimaligen Durchquerung Kleinasiens. Würzburg 1920. — *RB* XXX 291–292. o

1339 WEISS (J.), Das Urchristentum. Bd II : Schluß. Nach dem Tode des Verfassers herausgegeben von D. R. Knopf. Göttingen 1917. — *RB* XXX 144–145. o

1340 WHITE (E.), The Sayings of Jesus from Oxyrhynchus. Cambridge 1920. — *RB* XXX 294–295. o

1341 ZSCHOKKE (Mgr), Historia Sacra Veteris Testamenti. Vienne 1920. — *RB* XXX 148. o

1922

1342 L'Évangile selon saint Marc : édition abrégée (*ÉB*). In-12 de XIV–177. Paris, Gabalda. 4ᵉ éd.
— English translation : The Gospel according to St. Mark. New York: Benziger Bros., 1930.

1343 Découverte à Beit-Djibrin d'une salle pavée en mosaïques. *CrAcInscrBl* 41.

1344 L'Évangile selon les Hébreux. *RB* XXXI 161–181; 321–349.

1345 La seconde parole d'Oxyrhynque. *RB* XXXI 427–433.

1346 Le prétendu messianisme de Virgile. *RB* XXXI 552–572.

BOOK REVIEWS

1347 Albrecht (K.), Michna : Bikkurim. Gießen 1922. — *RB* XXXI 626. o

1348 Amann (E.), Le dogme catholique dans les Pères de l'Église. Paris 1922. — *RB* XXXI 627. o

1349 Assouad (N.), Polysema sunt Sacra Biblia. Vol. II. — *RB* XXXI 141–142. o

1350 Baumstark (A.), Nichtevangelische syrische Perikopenordnungen des ersten Jahrtausends. Münster 1921. — *RB* XXXI 306. o

1351 — — Geschichte der syrischen Literatur. Bonn 1922. — *RB* XXXI 627–628. o

1352 Besson (É.), La Didachè ou enseignement des Douze Apôtres. Sotteville-lez-Rouen 1921. — *RB* XXXI 455. o

1353 Brun (L.) und Fridrichsen (A.), Paulus und die Urgemeinde. Gießen 1921. — *RB* XXXI 148–149. o

1354 Bruyne (De), Les fragments de Freising (épîtres de saint Paul et épîtres catholiques). Rome 1921. — *RB* XXXI 145–147.

1355 Bultmann (R.), Die Geschichte der synoptischen Tradition. Göttingen 1921. — *RB* XXXI 286–292.

1356 Bundy (E.), The psychic Health of Jesus. New-York 1922. — *RB* XXXI 625–627. o

1357 Burkitt (F. C.), Itala problems (*Miscellanea Amelli*). — *RB* XXXI 140. o

1358 Burney (C. F.), The Aramaic origin of the Fourth Gospel. Oxford 1922. — *RB* XXI 614–616.

1359 Buzy (D.), Saint Jean-Baptiste. *Paris* 1922. — *RB* XXXI 616–621.

1360 Cadbury (H. J.), The style and literary method of Luc. Vol. II. The treatment of sources in the Gospel. Cambridge 1920. — *RB* XXXI 147–148.

1361 Camerlynck (A.), Evangelorium secundum Matthaeum, Marcum et Lucam Synopsis. Brugis 1921. — *RB* XXXI 303–304. o

1362 CARNOY (A.), L'idée du « royaume de Dieu » dans l'Iran (*Mus.* XXXIV). — *RB* XXXI 631–632.

1363 CAUSSE (A.), Les « pauvres » d'Israël. Strasbourg 1922. — *RB* XXXI 622–624.

1364 CONDAMIN (A.), Le livre de Jérémie. Traduction et commentaire. Paris 1920. — *RB* XXXI 130–135.

1365 DUPERRAY (J.), Le Christ dans la vie chrétienne d'après S. Paul. Lyon 1920. — *RB* XXXI 149–150. o

1366 FILLION (L.-Cl.), L'Étude de la Bible. Paris 1922. — *RB* XXXI 452. o

1367 FRIDRICHSEN (A.) : cfr BRUN (L.).

1368 GLOTZ (G.), Les fêtes d'Adonis sous Ptolémée II (*Revue des études grecques* 1920). — *RB* XXXI 309–312. o

1369 HARRIS (J. R.), Enoch and 2. Corinthians (*ExpTim* 1922). — *RB* XXXI 625.

1370 HERBIGNY (M. d'), De Deo universos evocante ad sui regni vitam. Vol. II. Paris 1921. — *RB* XXXI 306–307.

1371 MALLON (A.), Les Hébreux en Égypte. Roma 1921. — *RB* XXXI 628–631.

1372 MESSEL (N.), Der Menschensohn in den Bilderreden des Henoch. Gießen 1922. — *RB* XXXI 624–625. o

1373 MEYER (E.), Ursprung und Anfänge des Christentums. Bd I. Die Evangelien. Bd II, Die Entwicklung des Judentums und Jesus von Nazareth. Berlin 1921. — *RB* XXXI 453–455.

1374 REITZENSTEIN (R.), Das iranische Erlösungsmysterium. Bonn 1921. — *RB* XXXI 282–286.

1375 SCHÜTZ (R.), Apostle und Jünger. Gießen 1921. — *RB* XXXI 304–306. o

1376 SOIRON (Th.), Die Logia Jesu. Münster. — *RB* XXXI 307–308. o

1377 STANTON (V. H.), The Gospels as historical documents. Vol. III. The Fourth Gospel. Cambridge 1920. — *RB* XXXI 142–144. o

1378 STODERL (W.), Zur Echtheitsfrage von Baruch, I–III 8. Prag 1922. — *RB* XXXI 626. o

1379 TISSET (P.), Contribution à l'histoire de la présomption de paternité. Paris 1921. — *RB* XXXI 309. o

1380 VOSTÉ (J.), Commentarius in Epistolam ad Ephesios. Paris 1921. — *RB* XXXI 144–145.

1381 WHITE (H. J.), Novum Testamentum Domini Nostri Jesu Christi latine secundum editionem sancti Hieronymi. Vol. II² : Epistula ad Corinthios prima. Oxford 1922. — *RB* XXXI 452–453. o

1382 WILL (R.), La liberté chrétienne. Étude sur le principe de la piété chez Luther. Strasbourg. — *RB* XXXI 632–633.

1923

1383 L'Évangile selon saint Matthieu (*ÉB*). In-8º de CLXXXVIII–560 pp. Paris, Gabalda.
— 4ᵉ éd. augmentée de CLXXXVIII–571 pp.
1384 La vie de Jésus d'après Renan. In-16 de 145 pp. Paris, Gabalda.
— English translation : Christ and Renan — A commentary on Ernest Renan's « Life of Jesus. » Translated by Maisie Ward. New York: Benziger Bros., 1928.
1385 Le Logos dHéraclite. *RB* XXXII 96–107.
1386 Vers le Logos de saint Jean. *RB* XXXII 161–184; 321–371.

BOOK REVIEWS

1387 ABBOT-SMITH (G.), A manual Greek Lexicon of the New Testament. Edinburgh 1922. — *RB* XXXII 148–149. o
1388 BERTRAM (G.), Die Leidensgeschichte Jesu und der Christuskult. — *RB* XXXII 442–445.
1389 CALLAN (C. J.), The Epistles of saint Paul. New York 1922. — *RB* XXXII 308–309. o
1390 CARCOPINO (J.), Le tombeau de Lambiridi et l'hermétisme africain (*RArch* 1922). — *RB* XXXII 311–312. o
1391 GELDNER, Zoroastrianism (*Enc. Biblica*). — *RB* XXXII 152–155. o
1392 GUIDI (J.), L'Arabie antéislamique. Paris 1921. — *RB* XXXII 312–313. o
1393 HOLZMEISTER (U.), Die Magdalenenfrage in der kirchlichen Überlieferung (*ZKTh* 1922). — *RB* XXXII 309. o
1394 MOULTON (J. H.), A grammar of New Testament Greek. Vol. II, 2. Edinburgh 1920. — *RB* XXXII 146–148.
1395 PIEPENBRING (C.), Jésus historique². Strasbourg 1922. — *RB* XXXII 309–311. o
1396 SCHEFTELOWITZ (J.), Die altpersische Religion und das Judentum. Gießen 1920. — *RB* XXXII 151–152. o
1397 VOGELS (H. J.), Novum Testamentum graece et latine. Düsseldorf 1922. — *RB* XXXII 149–150. o
1398 WAGNER (E.), Die Erklärung des 118 Psalmes durch Origenes. Linz 1916–1921. — *RB* XXXII 150–151. o

1924

1399 Où en est la dissection littéraire du Quatrième Évangile? *RB* XXXIII 321–342.
1400 L'hermétisme. *RB* XXXIII 481–497.

BOOK REVIEWS

1401 BESSON (*E.*), Les Logia agrapha. — *RB* XXXIII 287–288.

1402 CADMAN (W. H.), The last journey of Jesus to Jerusalem. Oxford 1923. — *RB* XXXIII 630–631.

1403 DALMAN (G.), Jesus-Jeschua. Leipzig 1922. — *RB* XXXIII 271–273.

1404 DURAND (A.), Évangile selon saint Matthieu. Paris 1924. — *RB* XXXIII 628–630.

1405 FONCK (L.), Le parabole del Signore nel Vangelo[3]. Roma 1924. — *RB* XXXIII 630.

1406 GOGUEL (M.), Introduction au Nouveau Testament. Vol. II. Le quatrième Évangile. Paris 1924. — *RB* XXXIII 605–611.

1407 GRANDMAISON (L. de), Une nouvelle crise moderniste est-elle possible? (*Et* 1923). — *RB* XXXIII 159–160.

1408 HARNACK (A. von), Neue Studien zu Marcion. Leipzig 1923. — *RB* XXXIII 267–268.

1409 —— Erforschtes und Erlebtes. Bd IV. Gießen 1923. — *RB* XXXIII 283–285.

1410 JÜLICHER (A.), Der echte Tatiantext (*JBibLit* 1924). — *RB* XXXIII 626–628.

1411 McNEILE (A. H.), New Testament teaching in the Light of St Paul's. Cambridge 1923. — *RB* XXXIII 286–287.

1412 MALDEN (R. H.), Problem of the New Testament to-day. — *RB* XXXIII 285–286.

1413 MONTGOMERY (J. A.), The origin of the Gospel according to St John. Philadelphia 1923. — *RB* XXXIII 285.

1414 POPE (H.), The Catholic student's « Aids » to the study of the Bible. Vol. III. London 1923. — *RB* XXXIII 130. o

1415 QUENTIN (H.), Mémoire sur l'établissement du texte de la Vulgate. Paris 1922. — *RB* XXXIII 114–123.

1416 SANDAY (W.), Novum Testamentum sancti Irenaei episcopi Lugdunensis. Oxford 1923. — *RB* XXXIII 260–263.

1417 SCHMIDT (H.), ΕΥΧΑΡΙΣΤΗΡΙΟΝ. *Studien z. Religion u. Literatur des A. und N. Test. Hermann Gunkel zum 60. Geburtstag dargebracht* : R. BULTMANN, Der religionsgeschichtliche Hintergrund des Prologs zum Johannes Evangelium; M. DIBELIUS, Stilkritisches zur Apostelgeschichte; K. L. SCHMIDT, Die Stellung der Evangelien in der allgemeinen Literaturgeschichte; B. VIOLET, Die « Verfluchung » des Feigenbaums; H. WINDISCH, Der Johanneische Erzählungsstil; J. HEMPEL, Hermann Gunkels Bücher, Schriften und Aufsätze. Göttingen. — *RB* XXXIII 278–283.

1418 TISCHLEDER (P.), Wesen und Stellung der Frau nach der Lehre des heiligen Paulus. Münster 1923. — *RB* XXXIII 631.

1419 VANNUTELLI (P.), De evangeliorum origine. — *RB* XXXIII 288.

1420 —— Il figlio dell' Uomo. — *RB* XXXIII 289.

1421 VOGELS (H. J.), Beiträge zur Geschichte des Diatessaron im Abendland. Münster 1919. — *RB* XXXIII 624–626.

1422 —— Handbuch der neutestamentlichen Textkritik. Münster 1923. — *RB* XXXIII 263–267.

1423 ZAPLETAL (V.), Das Buch der Richter. Münster 1923. — *RB* XXXIII 136. o

1925

1424 **L'Évangile selon saint Jean** (*ÉB*). In-8° de CXCIX–551 pp. Paris, Gabalda.
— 5ᵉ éd. augmentée de CXCIX–560 pp.

1425 **Ce que fut, d'après M. Lasserre, le prétendu drame de la métaphysique chrétienne** (P. Lasserre, La jeunesse d'Ernest Renan. Histoire de la crise religieuse au XIXᵉ siècle. Vol. I. De Tréguier à Saint-Sulpice. Vol. II. Le Drame de la métaphysique chrétienne. Paris 1925). *Cor* CCCI (Nouvelle série CCLXV) 182–199.

1426 **L'hermétisme** (suite). *RB* XXXIV 82–104; 368–396; 547–574.

1427 **L'origine de la version syro-palestinienne des Évangiles.** *RB* XXXIV 481–504.

BOOK REVIEWS

1428 BANDAS (G.), The Master-Idea of Saint Paul's Epistles, or the Redemption. Bruges 1925. — *RB* XXXIV 615–616.

1429 BAUER (W.), Griechisch-Deutsches Wörterbuch zu den Schriften des Neuen Testaments. Gießen 1925. — *RB* XXXIV 458–459.

1430 BAUMANN (É.), Saint Paul. Paris 1925. — *RB* XXXIV 614–615.

1431 BELL (H. I.), Jews and Christians in Egypt. London 1924. — *RB* XXXIV 621–623.

1432 BUYSSE (P.), L'Église de Jésus devant la raison et le cœur de l'homme. Bruges 1925. — *RB* XXXIV 620.

1433 CERFAUX (L.), Influence des mystères sur le judaïsme alexandrin avant Philon (*Mus* 1924). — *RB* XXXIV 150–152.

1434 DONAVAN (J.), The logia in ancient and recent literature. — *RB* XXXIV 445–446.

1435 GOGUEL (M.), Introduction au Nouveau Testament. Vol. IV. Épîtres pauliniennes. Paris 1925. — *RB* XXXIV 446–448.

1436 GRANDMAISON (L. de), Jésus dans l'histoire et dans le mystère. Paris 1925. — *RB* XXXIV 443–444.

1437 HETZENAUER (M.), De genealogia Jesu Christi. Romae 1922. — *RB* XXXIV 444–445.

1438 HUBY (J.), Évangile selon saint Marc. Paris 1924. — *RB* XXXIV 442–443.

1439 KNOX (W. L.), Saint Paul and the Church of Jerusalem. Cambridge 1925. — *RB* XXXIV 616–619.

1440 KRAFT (B.), Die Evangelienzitate des heiligen Irenäus. Freiburg i. Br. 1924. — *RB* XXXIV 449–454.

1441 MUNDLE (W.), Die Herkunft der « marcionitischen » Prologe zu den paulinischen Briefen (*ZNW* 1925). — *RB* XXXIV 619–620.

1442 SCOTT (W.), Hermetica : the ancient Greek and Latin writings which contain religious or philosophic teachings ascribed to Hermes Trismegistus. Vol. I et II. Oxford 1924. — *RB* XXXIV 432–436; 593–597.

1443 SIMON (H.), Praelectiones biblicae ad usum scholarum. Vol. I. Introductio et Evangelia. Augustae Taurinorum 1924. — *RB* XXXIV 132–139.

1444 STREETER (B. H.), The four Gospels. London 1924. — *RB* XXXIV 454–458.

1445 VOGELS (H. J.), Grundriß der Einleitung in das Neue Testament. Münster 1925. — *RB* XXXIV 613–614.

1446 WERNER (M.), Der Einfluß paulinischer Theologie im Markusevangelium. Gießen 1923. — *RB* XXXIV 448–449.

1926

1447 **Synopsis evangelica graece** [en collaboration avec le Père C. Lavergne]. In-4° de XXVII–178 pp. Barcelona, éditions « Alpha ».

— Synopse des quatre Évangiles en français d'après la Synopse grecque du R. P. Lagrange par le R. P. C. Lavergne, O.P. Paris, Gabalda, 1927.

— Sinopsi Evangelica, text grec de M. J. Lagrange O.P., versio catalana i notes de LL Carreras i J. M. LLovera. Barcelona, éd. « Alpha », 1927.

— Sinossi dei quattro Vangeli secondo la Sinossi Greca del P. M. J. Lagrange. Brescia, Morcelliana, 1931.

— A Catholic Harmony of the Four Gospels, being an adaptation of the « Synopsis Evangelica » of P. Lagrange . . . by the Rev. John Barton with a preface of his Grace the Archbishop of Liverpool, Mgr R. Downey. London, Burns Oates and Washbourne, 1930.

1448 L'auteur du canon de Muratori. *RB* XXXV 83–88.

1449 Le manuscrit sinaïtique. *RB* XXXV 89–93.

1450 Les prologues prétendus Marcionites. *RB* XXXV 161–173.

1451 L'hermétisme (fin). *RB* XXXV 240–264.

1452 La conception qui domine le IVe Évangile (échanges de vues avec le R. P. Olivieri). *RB* XXXV 382–397.

1453 Platon théologien. *RTh* XXXIe année 188–218.
1454 La discorde au camp d'Agramant (Turmel-Loisy). *Vit* XL 34–39.

BOOK REVIEWS

1455 BACON (B. W.), The Gospel of Mark : its composition and date. Oxford 1925. — *RB* XXXV 312–314.
1456 BALDI (D.), L'infanzia del Salvatore. Roma 1925. — *RB* XXXV 442–444.
1457 BAUER (W.), Griechisch-Deutsches Wörterbuch zu den Schriften des Neuen Testaments (Heft 2). Gießen. — *RB* XXXV 453.
1458 BLUDAU (A.), Die Schriftfälschungen der Häretiker. Münster 1925. — *RB* XXXV 444–445.
1459 BLUNT (W. F.), The epistle of Paul to the Galatians. Oxford. — *RB* XXXV 452–453.
1460 BOULANGER (A.), Orphée : rapports de l'orphisme et du christianisme. Paris 1925. — *RB* XXXV 453–455.
1461 BOUVIER (H.), et HEMMER (H.), L'abbé Claude Bouvier (1866–1914), professeur à l'école Saint-Maurice de Vienne. Paris 1926. — *VS* XV 774–776.
1462 BOVER (J. M.), [Articles dans les « Estudios ecclesiasticos »]. — *RB* XXXV 314–316.
1463 DELAFOSSE (H.) = TURMEL (J.), L'Épître aux Romains. Paris 1926. — *RB* XXXV 450–452.
1464 HEMMER (H.) : cfr BOUVIER (H.).
1465 HOLTZMANN (O.), Das Neue Testament nach dem Stuttgarter griechischen Text. Gießen 1925. — *RB* XXXV 445–447.
1466 LAGRANGE (M. J.), et LAVERGNE (C.), Synopsis evangelica. Paris 1926. — *RB* XXXV 613–615.
1467 MEINERTZ (M.), Jesus und die Heidenmission². Münster 1925. — *RB* XXXV 314.
1468 MORTIER (R. P.), L'Évangile : simples commentaires pour la vie chrétienne. Paris 1925. — *RB* XXXV 445.
1469 PERNOT (H.), Pages choisies des Évangiles traduites de l'original et commentées à l'usage du public lettré. Paris 1925. — *RB* XXXV 296–300.
1470 POMMIER (J.), La pensée religieuse de Renan. Paris 1920. — *RB* XXXV 447–450.
1471 TONDELLI, Gesù nella storia al centro della critica biblica. Milano 1926. — *RB* XXXV 439–442.
1472 TURMEL (J.), Comment j'ai donné congé aux dogmes. — *Vit* XL 34–38.
1472a — — cfr DELAFOSSE (H.).

1927

1473 L'hermétisme. *Cor* CCCVI (Nouvelle série CCLX) 648–665.

1474　La gnose mandéenne et la tradition évangélique. *RB* XXXVI 321–349; 481–515.

1475　Un nouveau papyrus contenant un fragment des Actes. *RB* XXXVI 549–560.

1476　Attis ressuscité. *RB* XXXVI 561–566.

1477　Les péripatéticiens jusqu'à l'ère chrétienne. *RTh* XXXIIe année 196–213.

1478　Sur le sentiment religieux dans la religion grecque. *Vit* XLV 657–661.

BOOK REVIEWS

1479　CARCOPINO (J.), La basilique pythagoricienne de la Porte Majeure. Paris 1926. — *RB* XXXVI 599–607.

1480　— — Études romaines. La basilique pythagoricienne de la Porte Majeure. Paris 1926. — *RTh* XXXIIe année 250–251.

1481　DIÈS (A.), Autour de Platon (*Bibl. des Arch. de Philo.*). Paris 1927. — *RTh* XXXIIe année 252–253.

1482　EASTON (B. S.), The Gospel according to S. Luke. New York 1926. — *RB* XXXVI 123–124. o

1483　HEADLAM (A. C.), Jesus-Christ in history and faith. London 1925. — *RB* XXXVI 129–130. o

1484　LAGRANGE (M. J.) et LAVERGNE (C.), Synopsis Evangelica. Textum graecum. Barcinone 1926. — *RB* XXXVI 477–478.

1485　LAVERGNE (C.) : cfr LAGRANGE (M. J.).

1486　LÉVY (J.), Recherches sur les sources de la légende de Pythagore. Paris 1926. — *RB* XXXVI 607.

1487　NOCK (A. D.) [Traité de Sallustius], Concerning the gods and the universe. Cambridge 1926. — *RB* XXXVI 608.

1488　PESCH (C.), De inspiratione Sacrae Scripturae (supplementum). Freiburg i. Br. 1926. — *RB* XXXVI 140.

1489　SCOTT (R.), The expectation of Elijah (*The Canadian Journal of religious thought* 1926). — *RB* XXXVI 447.

1490　TAYLOR (V.), Behind the third Gospel. Oxford 1926. — *RB* XXXVI 120–123. o

1491　VERDUNOY (Ch.), Manuel d'Écriture Sainte. Vol. III. Nouveau Testament. Dijon 1925. — *RB* XXXVI 118–119. o

1492　WINDISCH (H.), Johannes und die Synoptiker. Leipzig 1926. — *RB* XXXVI 124–129. o

1928

1493　L'Évangile de Jésus-Christ (*ÉB*). Pages XXI–656 with illustrations, maps, and plan of Jerusalem at the time of Christ. (Translated into German, Spanish, Dutch, Italian. English translation: **The Gospel of Jesus Christ.** By Luke Walker, O.P., and Reginald Ginns, O.P. London: B.O. & W., 1938. Two volumes.)

1494 La religion de Cicéron d'après le « De natura deorum ».
EphThLov V 413–425.
1495 La gnose mandéenne et la tradition évangélique (suite
et fin). RB XXXVII 5–36.
1496 L'évangile de saint Marc n'a pas été écrit en latin. RB
XXXVII 106–116.
1497 Un nouvel évangile de l'enfance édité par M. R. James.
RB XXXVII 544–557.
1498 Réponse à une lettre de M. Couchoud. RB XXXVII 637–
638.
1499 La religion des Stoïciens avant Jésus-Christ. RTh
XXXIIIᵉ année 46–68.
1500 La religion de Sénèque. RTh XXXIIIᵉ année 324–346.
1501 La divinité de Jésus. Vit I 10–28.
1502 Julien l'Apostat prédicateur de retraites sacerdotales.
VSS XVII 242–248.

BOOK REVIEWS

1503 BIDEZ (J.), Lettres de Julien. Paris 1924. — VSS XVII 242–
248.
1504 COUCHOUD (P. L.), Jubilé Alfred Loisy. Paris 1928. — RB
XXXVII 604–611.
1505 COULANGE (L.) = TURMEL (J.), La messe. Paris. — RB
XXXVII 149.
1506 DELAFOSSE (H.) [= TURMEL (J.)], Lettres de S. Ignace
d'Antioche. Paris 1927. — RB XXXVII 149.
1507 DUFOURCQ (A.), l'avenir du christianisme. Première partie.
Histoire ancienne de l'Église. Vol. II. La révolution religieuse.
Jésus⁶. — RB XXXVII 294–297.
1508 DUJARDIN (E.), Le Dieu Jésus. Essai sur les origines et la
formation de la légende évangélique. Paris. — RB XXXVII
289–294.
1509 FERGUSON, cfr SCOTT (E. F.).
1510 HARNACK (A. von), Ecclesia Petri propinqua (SbAkPreuss
1927). — RB XXXVII 150–152.
1511 KLAUSER (Th.), Die Cathedra im Totenkult der heidnischen
und christlichen Antike. Münster i. W. 1927. — RB XXXVII
150.
1512 OWEN (E. C.), Some authentic acts of the early martyrs.
Oxford 1927. — RB XXXVII 149.
1513 REITZENSTEIN (R.), Die hellenistischen Mysterienreligionen.
Leipzig 1927. — RB XXXVII 153.
1514 SCOTT (W.) and FERGUSON (W. D.) Hermetica. Vol. III.
Oxford. — RB XXXVII 156–157.
1515 TURMEL (J.) : cfr COULANGE (L.) et DELAFOSSE (H.).

1929

1516 La régénération et la filiation divine dans les mystères d'Éleusis. *RB* XXXVIII 63–81; 201–214.

1517 Un nouveau papyrus évangélique (Pap. Michigan). *RB* XXXVIII 161–177.

1518 Le groupe dit Césaréen des manuscrits des Évangiles. *RB* XXXVIII 481–512.

1519 Une morale indépendante dans l'antiquité : les Cyniques. *RTh* XXXIVᵉ année 35–52.

1520 Les doctrines religieuses successives de l'Académie fondée par Platon. *RTh* XXXIVᵉ année 320–334.

1521 Monseigneur Pierre Battiffol. *Vit* II 398–423.

BOOK REVIEWS

1522 Bruyne (D. De), Les plus anciens prologues des Évangiles (*RBen* 1928). — *RB* XXXVIII 115–121.

1523 Groag (E.), A propos de P. Sulpicius Quirinius (Jahreshefte des österreichischen archaeologischen Institutes in Wien 1924, col. 446–478). — *RB* XXXVIII 448–449.

1524 Lebreton (J.), Histoire du Dogme de la Trinité. Vol. II. De S. Clément à S. Irénée. Paris 1928. — *RB* XXXVIII 135.

1525 Lévy (J.), La légende de Pythagore, de Grèce en Palestine. Paris. — *RB* XXXVIII 135–138.

1526 Nestle (E.), Novum Testamentum graece et latine⁹. Stuttgart 1928. — *RB* XXXVIII 298–300.

1527 Schmid (J.), Der Epheserbrief des Apostels Paulus. Seine Adresse, Sprache und literarischen Beziehungen. Freiburg i. Br. 1928. — *RB* XXXVIII 290–293.

1528 Silver (A. H.), A history of messianic speculation in Israël. New York 1927. — *RB* XXXVIII 138–140.

1529 Stummer (F.), Einführung in die lateinische Bibel. Paderborn 1928. — *RB* XXXVIII 300–301.

1530 Vogels (H. J.), Die Evangelien der Vulgata untersucht auf ihre lateinische und griechische Vorlage. Münster 1928. — *RB* XXXVIII 261–264.

1930

1531 Jean-Baptiste et Jésus d'après le texte slave de la Guerre des Juifs de Josèphe. *RB* XXXIX 29–46.

1532 La prophétie des soixante-dix semaines de Daniel. *RB* XXXIX 179–198.

1533 L'Évangile et la guerre. *Vit* IX 356–367.

1534 Les cultes helléniques en Égypte et le Judaïsme. *RTh* XXXVᵉ année 309–328.

BOOK REVIEWS

1535 ALFARIC (P.), Les Évangiles. — Saint Marc. — Pour comprendre la vie de Jésus. Paris 1929. — *RB* XXXIX 612–613.

1536 CARCOPINO (J.), Virgile et le mystère de la IVᵉ Églogue. Paris 1930. — *RB* XXXIX 452.

1537 CHARLES (R. H.), A critical and exegetical commentary on the Book of Daniel. Oxford 1929. — *RB* XXXIX 276–283.

1538 FASCHER (E.), Vom Verstehen des Neuen Testamentes. Gießen 1930. — *RB* XXXIX 625–626.

1539 GODARD (A.), Les règnes de Dieu. Le messianisme. Paris 1930. — *RB* XXXIX 612.

1540 GRAAFEN (J.), Die Echtheit des zweiten Briefes an die Thessalonicher. Münster 1930. — *RB* XXXIX 619.

1541 GREIFF (A.), Johanneische Studien. Vol. I. Das älteste Pascharituale der Kirche : Did. 1–10 und das Johannes Evangelium. Paderborn 1929. — *RB* XXXIX 615–617.

1542 GRESHAM MACHEN (J.), The virgin birth of Christ. New York and London 1930. — *RB* XXXIX 614–615.

1543 HARNACK (A. von), Die ältesten Evangelien-Prologe und die Bildung des neuen Testaments (*ZbAkPreuss* 1928). — *RB* XXXIX 619–621.

1544 JOÜON (P.), L'Évangile de Notre-Seigneur Jésus-Christ (traduction et commentaire du texte original grec, compte tenu du substrat sémitique). Paris 1930. — *RB* XXXIX 463–466.

1545 KÜMMEL (W. G.), Römer 7 und die Bekehrung des Paulus. Leipzig 1929. — *RB* XXXIX 618–619.

1546 KUNDSIN (K.), Das Urchristentum im Lichte der Evangelienforschung. Gießen 1929. — *RB* XXXIX 623–625.

1547 MALDEN (R. H.), Religion and the New Testament. London 1928. — *RB* XXXIX 622–623.

1548 MICHEL (O.), Paulus und seine Bibel. Gütersloh 1929. — *RB* XXXIX 617–618.

1549 ODEBERG (H.), 3 Enoch or the Hebrew Book of Enoch, edited and translated for the first time with introduction, commentary and critical notes. Cambridge. — *RB* XXXIX 452–455.

1550 — — The Fourth Gospel. Upsala 1929. — *RB* XXXIX 455–458.

1551 RIGGENBACH (E.), Das Comma Johanneum. Gütersloh 1928. — *RB* XXXIX 617.

1552 RIVIÈRE (J.), Le Modernisme dans l'Église. Paris 1929. — *RB* XXXIX 298.

1553 ROPES (J. H.), The singular problem of the espistle to the Galatians. Cambridge 1929. — *RB* XXXIX 619.

1554 SICKENBERGER (J.) [A propos de Mt. XXII 1–14] (*ByzZ* XXX). — *RB* XXXIX 614.

1555 STREETER (B. H.), The primitive Church. London 1929. — *RB*
XXXIX 621–622.

1556 VOGELS (H. J.), Codicum Novi Testamenti specimina. Bonn
1929. — *RB* XXXIX 462.

1557 VOSTÉ (J.), Studia Joannea. Romae 1930. — *RB* XXXIX
287–288.

1931

1558 **Le Judaïsme avant Jésus-Christ** (*ÉB*). In-8⁰ de XXVII–
624 pp. Paris, Gabalda.

1559 **La morale de l'Évangile.** Réflexions sur « Les morales de
l'Évangile » de M. A. Bayet (dans la coll. « Vie Chrétienne »). In-12 de 250 pp. Paris, Grasset.

1560 La lettre de Claude aux Alexandrins. *RB* XL 270–276.

1561 Théocrite et le mystère de la IVᵉ églogue de Virgile. *RB*
XL 613–614.

1562 La Présentation de Jésus au Temple. *VS* XXVI 129–135.

1563 L'amour de Dieu, loi suprême de la morale de l'Évangile.
VSS XXVI 1–16.

1564 Les préliminaires historiques de la mystique catholique.
VSS XXVII 76–93.

BOOK REVIEWS

1565 BAUER (W.), Flavius Josèphe slave (*ThLZg* 1930). — *RB* XL
463–464.

1566 BLUM (L.), Flavius Josèphe contre Apion. Paris 1930. — *RB*
XL 462.

1567 DONAVAN (J.), The Papias presbyteri puzzle (*Irish ecclesiastical
Record,* February 1931). — *RB* XL 611.

1568 DRAGUET (R.), Le juif Josèphe, témoin du Christ (*RHE*
1930). — *RB* XL 462–463.

1569 ENSLIN (M. S.), The ethics of Paul. New York 1930. — *RB*
XL 309–310.

1570 FESTUGIÈRE (A. J.), La trichotomie de I Thess. V 23 et la
philosophie grecque (*RScRel* 1930). — *RB* XL 310.

1571 GALLEGOS ROCAFULL (J. M.), El Misterio de Jesus. Madrid
1930. — *RB* XL 459–460.

1572 HAUGG (D.), Judas Iskarioth in den neutestamentlichen Be-
richten. Freiburg i. Br. 1930. — *RB* XL 611–612.

1573 HERMANN (L.) : cfr MATHIEU (G.).

1574 HÖRNLE (E. S.), The record of the loved disciple. Oxford 1931.
— *RB* XL 1931 610–611.

1575 JEREMIAS (J.), Zur Hypothese einer schriftlichen Logienquelle
Q (*ZNW* 1930). — *RB* XL 456–457.

1576 MATHIEU (G.), et HERMANN (L.), Josèphe : Antiquités
judaïques (traduction). Paris 1929. — *RB* XL 461–462.

1577 MEINERTZ (M.) und TILLMANN (F.), Die Gefangenschaftsbriefe des heiligen Paulus. Bonn 1931. — RB XL 613.
1578 MICHAELIS (W.), Pastoralbriefe und Gefangenschaftsbriefe.
Zur Echtheitsfrage der Pastoralbriefe. Gütersloh 1930. — RB
XL 308–309.
1579 — — Die Gefangenschaft des Paulus in Ephesus. Gütersloh
1925. — RB XL 309.
1580 NAU (F.), L'araméen chrétien. Les traductions faites du grec en
syriaque au Vii⁣e siècle (RHR 1929). — RB XL 120–129.
1581 — — Versions syriennes. Saint Rabboula d'Édesse (RHR 1929).
— RB XL 120–121.
1582 OBIOLS (S.), La Biblia. Epistoles de Sant Paul. Montserrat
1930. — RB XL 612–613.
1583 ÖMMELEN (H. J.), Zur dogmatischen Auswertung von Röm V
12–14. Münster 1930. — RB XL 305–308.
1584 PEETERS (P.), La vie de Rabboula, évêque d'Édesse (RScRel
1928). — RB XL 121–129.
1585 PINARD DE LE BOULLAYE (H.), Jésus Messie. Paris 1930. —
RB XL 457–459.
1586 REINACH (Th.), Flavius Josèphe : Contre Apion. Paris 1930.
— RB XL 462.
1587 SANGRAN Y GONZALEZ (J. de), La profecia del Apocalipsis y
los tempos actuales. Madrid 1929. — RB XL 460.
1588 SCHÄFER (K. T.), Untersuchungen zur Geschichte der lateinischen Übersetzung des Hebräerbriefes. Freiburg i. Br. 1929. —
RB XL 452–454.
1589 SCHLIER (H.), Christus und die Kirche im Epheserbriefe.
Tübingen 1930. — RB XL 612–613.
1590 SCHMID (J.), Matthäus und Lukas. Freiburg i. Br. 1930. — RB
XL 608–609.
1591 STAHL (R.), Les Mandéens et les origines chrétiennes. Paris
1930. — RB XL 147–151.
1592 TAYLOR (V.), The Gospels. London 1930. — RB XL 305.
1593 THACKERAY (H. St. J.), Josephus, The man and the historian.
New York 1929. — RB XL 460–462.
1594 TILLMANN (F.), Das Johannesevangelium übersetzt und erklärt.
Bonn 1931. — RB XL 609–610.
1595 — — : cfr aussi MEINERTZ (M.).
1596 VANNUTELLI (Primo), Iterum de presbytero Joanne apud
Papiam (ScuolCatt 1931). — RB XL 1931 611.
1597 WESENDONK (O. G.), Flavius Josèphe slave (OLZ 1930). —
RB XL 464.
1598 ZEITLIN (S.), Flavius Josephus on Jesus called the Christ.
Philadelphia 1930. — RB XL 464.

1932

1599 Monsieur Loisy et le modernisme. A propos des « Mémoires » d'A. Loisy. Petit in-8⁰ de 251 pp. Paris, Éditions du Cerf.

1600 Un sanctuaire d'Allat à Iram. *CrAcInscrBl* 225–226.

1601 Saint Paul ou Marcion. *RB* XLI 5–30.

1602 De quelques opinions sur l'ancien psautier latin. *RB* XLI 161–186.

1603 Le site de Sodome d'après les textes. *RB* XLI 489–514.

1604 La religion de Goethe. *Vit* XV 290–311.

BOOK REVIEWS

1605 BARDY (G.) et TRICOT (A.), Le Christ. Paris 1932. — *RB* XLI 630–631.

1606 BOX (G. H.), Helps to the study of the Bible. London 1931. — *RB* XLI 115.

1607 CASAMASSA (A.), Miscellanea Agostiniana. Vol. II. Romae 1931. — *RB* XLI 115.

1608 DAUSCH (P.), Die drei älteren Evangelien. Bonn 1932. — *RB* XLI 299.

1609 DUESBERG (H.), Le roi Hérode et autres essais. Maredsous 1932.

1610 DUJARCIN (E.), Grandeur et décadence de la critique, sa rénovation. Le cas de l'abbé Turmel. Paris 1931. — *RB* XLI 459–460.

1611 FILSON (F. V.), S. Paul's conception of recompense. Leipzig 1931. — *RB* XLI 628–630.

1612 GÄCHTER (P.), Maria in Kana (extrait de *ZKTh* 1931). — *RB* XLI 121–122.

1613 GOETHALS (A.), Anti-Eisler. Un peu de polémique. Paris 1932. — *RB* XLI 456–457.

1614 GOGUEL (M.), Jésus et les origines du christianisme. La vie de Jésus. Paris 1932. — *RB* XLI 598–614.

1615 GOOSSENS (W.), Les origines de l'Eucharistie, Sacrement et Sacrifice. Gembloux 1931. — *RB* XLI 120–121.

1616 HARNACK (A. von), Studien zur Geschichte des neuen Testaments und der alten Kirche. Bd I. Zur Neutestamentlichen Textkritik. Berlin 1931. — *RB* XLI 297–298.

1617 HOROVITZ (H. S.) und RABIN (I. A.), Mechilta D'Rabbi Ismael. Frankfort 1931. — *RB* XLI 468–469.

1618 JUNKER (H.), Untersuchungen über literarische und exegetische Probleme des Buches Daniel. Bonn 1932. — *RB* XLI 466–467.

1619 —— Die biblische Urgeschichte in ihrer Bedeutung als Grundlage der alttestamentlichen Offenbarung. Bonn 1932. — *RB* XLI 460–462.

1620 KALT (E.), Das Buch Baruch. Bonn 1931. — *RB* XLI 465–466.

1621 KENYON (F. G.), [Les papyrus Chester Beatty, d'après le *Times* du 19 nov. 1931.] — *RB* XLI 453–454.

1622 KITTEL (G.), Theologisches Wörterbuch zum Neuen Testament. Stuttgart. — *RB* XLI 626.

1623 LEBRETON (J.), La vie et l'enseignement de Jésus-Christ Notre-Seigneur. Paris 1931. — *RB* XLI 299–300.

1624 LIETZMANN (H.), An die Galater³. Tübingen 1932. — *RB* XLI 630.

1625 MANSON (T. W.), The teaching of Jesus. Cambridge 1931. — *RB* XLI 457–459.

1626 MARTY (J.) : cfr ROBILLOT (J.).

1627 MEINERTZ (M.), Die Pastoralbriefe des heiligen Paulus⁴. Bonn 1931. — *RB* XLI 124.

1628 —— und VREDE (W.), Die Katholischen Briefe. Bonn 1932. — *RB* XLI 460.

1629 MEINHOLD (J.), Das alte Testament und evangelisches Christentum. Gießen 1931. — *RB* XLI 116–118.

1630 MESSENGER (E. C.), Evolution and theology. London 1931. — *RB* XLI 462–464.

1631 MICHAELIS (W.), Reich Gottes und Geist Gottes nach dem Neuen Testament. Basel 1930. — *RB* XLI 118.

1632 PAFFRATH (Th.), Die Klagelieder. Bonn 1931. — *RB* XLI 465–466.

1633 PAQUIER (J.), La création et l'évolution. La révélation et la science. Paris 1932. — *RB* XLI 464.

1634 RABIN (J. A.) : cfr HOROVITZ (H. S.).

1635 RAHLFS (A.), Septuaginta Studien. Bd X. Psalmi cum Odis. Göttingen 1931. — *RB* XLI 289–292.

1636 ROBILLOT (J.) et MARTY (J.), Le legs d'Israël (trad. de l'anglais). Paris 1931. — *RB* XLI 445–451.

1637 SCHLATTER (A.), Das Neue Testament. Stuttgart 1931. — *RB* XLI 116.

1638 SCHMID (J.), Zeit und Ort der paulinischen Gefangenschaftsbriefe. Freiburg i. Br. 1931. — *RB* XLI 122–124.

1639 SICKENBERGER (J.), Leben Jesu nach den vier Evangelien. Münster 1931. — *RB* XLI 300–301.

1640 SILVERSTONE (A. E.), Aquila and Onkelos. Manchester 1931. — *RB* XLI 467–468.

1641 SPICQ (C.), La révélation de l'espérance dans le Nouveau Testament. Avignon 1932. — *RB* XLI 455–456.

1642 STEIGER (R.), Die Dialektik der paulinischen Existenz. Leipzig 1931. — *RB* XLI 626–628.

1643 SZCZYGIEL (P.), Das Buch Job. Bonn 1931. — *RB* XLI 464–465.

1644 TRICOT (A.) : cfr BARDY (G.).

1645 TURNER (C. H.), The oldest manuscripts of the Vulgate Gospels. Oxford 1931. — *RB* XLI 296–297.

1646 VANNUTELLI (P.), Gli evangeli in sinossi. Roma 1931. — *RB* XLI 285–289.

1647 VREDE (W.) : cfr MEINERTZ (M.).

1648 WENDLAND (H. D.), Die Eschatologie des Reiches Gottes bei Jesu. Gütersloh 1931. — *RB* XLI 118–120.

1649 WIKENHAUSER (A.), Zur synoptischen Frage (*Röm* Q 1931). — *RB* XLI 298–299.

1650 ZANCAN (L.), Sull'iscrizione di Nazareth. Venezia 1932. — *RB* XLI 457.

1651 ZEITLIN (S.), Josephus on Jesus, with particular reference to the slavonic Josephus and the hebrew Josippon. Philadelphia 1931. — *RB* XLI 301–302.

1933

1652 Introduction à l'étude du Nouveau Testament : I. Histoire ancienne du canon du Nouveau Testament (*ÉB*). In-8⁰ de IX–188 pp. Paris, Gabalda.

1653 Le Messianisme de Virgile. *Cor* CCCII (Nouvelle série CCXCVI) 837–854.

1654 Le canon d'Hippolyte et le fragment de Muratori. *RB* XLII 161–186.

1655 Un nouveau papyrus évangélique. *RB* XLII 402–404.

1656 Projet de critique textuelle rationnelle du Nouveau Testament. *RB* XLII 481–498.

1657 Le développement du dogme selon Newman. *Vit* XXIV 194–199.

BOOK REVIEWS

1658 ADAM (K.), Le Christ notre frère. Paris 1932. — *RB* XLII 127–130.

1659 BALDENSPERGER (G.), Le tombeau vide (*RHPR* 1933). — *RB* XLII 583–584.

1660 BARTHAS (C.), Évangile et nationalisme. Paris 1933. — *RB* XLII 445.

1661 BAUER (W.), Das Johannes-evangelium³. Tübingen 1933. — *RB* XLII 446–447.

1662 BRAUN (F. M.), Où en est le problème de Jésus? Bruxelles 1932. — *RB* XLII 288–289.

1663 BUZY (D.), Les Paraboles. Paris 1932. — *RB* XLII 441–445.

1664 CADBURY (H. J.) : cfr JACKSON (F. J. F.).

1665 CLARK (A. C.), The Acts of the Apostles. Oxford 1933. — *RB* XLII 425–427.

1666 DABROWSKI (E.), Przemienienie Chrystusa [Transfiguration de Jésus]. Warsawa 1931. — *RB* XLII 293.

1667 DIRKSEN (A. H.), The New Testament concept of Metanoia. Washington 1932. — *RB* XLII 445–446.

1668 ERDMANN (G.), Die Vorgeschichten des Lukas- und Matthäus-Evangeliums und Vergils vierte Eglogue. Göttingen 1932. — *RB* XLII 289–291.

1669 FUCHS (M. E.), Christus und der Geist bei Paulus. Leipzig 1932. — *RB* XLII 295–296.

1670 GOGUEL (M.), La foi en la résurrection de Jésus dans le christianisme primitif. Paris 1933. — *RB* XLII 569–583.

1671 GUIGNEBERT (Ch.), Questions évangélique. Jésus. Paris 1933. — *RB* XLII 435–440.

1672 GUITTON (J.), La philosophie de Newman. Essai sur l'idée de développement. Paris 1933. — *Vit* XXIV 194–199.

1673 GUNTERMANN (F.), Die Eschatologie des heiligen Paulus. Münster 1932. — *RB* XLII 293–295.

1674 « HEGESIPPUS », The speech that moved the world. London 1932. — *RB* XLII 446.

1675 JACKSON (F. J. F.), LAKE (K.), CADBURY (H. J.), The beginnings of christianity : The Acts of the Apostles. London 1933. — *RB* XLII 423–425.

1676 JEANMAIRE (H.), Le messianisme de Virgile. Paris 1930. — *RB* XLII 291–293.

1677 KITTEL (G.), Die Religionsgeschichte und das Urchristentum. Gütersloh. — *RB* XLII 130–132.

1678 —— Theologisches Wörterbuch zum Neuen Testament (Hefte 7 bis 10). — *RB* XLII 132 606–608.

1679 LAKE (K.) : cfr JACKSON (F. J. F.).

1680 LÉVY (A. J.), Rashi's Commentary on Ezechiel XL–XLVIII edited on the basis of eleven Mss. Philadelphia 1931. — *RB* XLII 1933 296–297.

1681 LIETZMANN (H.), Geschichte der alten Kirche. Vol. I. Berlin 1932. — *RB* XLII 440–441.

1682 LLAMAS (J.), Un manuscrito desconocido, ejemplar directo del texto hebreo Complutense. Escorial 1933. — *RB* XLII 605.

1683 LUCE (H. K.), The Gospel according to S. Luke. Cambridge 1933. — *RB* XLII 608–609.

1684 MOLITOR (H.), Die Auferstehung der Christen und Nichtchristen nach dem Apostel Paulus. Münster 1933. — *RB* XLII 609–610.

1685 PALLIS (A.), Notes on S. Mark and S. Matthew. Oxford 1932. — *RB* XLII 124–125.

1686 PELLEGRINO (C.), La Bibbia e il pensiero greco. Roma 1933. — *RB* XLII 611.

1687 PFEIFFER (E.), Praeparation zum Neuen Testament. Evangelium nach Markus. Leipzig 1932. — *RB* XLII 125.

1688 RASCHI sur Ézechiel XL–XLVIII. — *RB* XLII 296–297.

1689 RIERA (J. M.), La Biblia de Montserrat. Vol. XIX. Evangeli segons sant Joan. Actes dels Apostols. Montserrat 1933. — *RB* XLII 609.

1690 ROHR (I.), Der Hebräerbrief und die geheime Offenbarung des heiligen Johannes. Tübingen. 1932 — *RB* XLII 126.

1691 SCHWEITZER (A.), Die Mystik des Apostels Paulus. Tübingen 1932. — *RB* XLII 114–123.

1692 SICKENBERGER (J.), Die Briefe des heiligen Paulus an die Korinther und Römer. Bonn 1932. — *RB* XLII 125–126.

1693 SOUBIGOU (L.), Sous le charme de l'Évangile selon saint Luc. Paris 1933. — *RB* XLII 608.

1694 SOUTER (A.), Pelagius's expositions of thirteen epistles of Saint Paul : Pseudo-Jerome interpolations. Cambridge 1931. — *RB* XLII 296.

1695 TONDELLI (L.), Il mandeismo e le origini cristiane. — *RB* XLII 610–611.

1696 VACCARI (A.), S. Alberto Magno e l'esegesi medievale (*Bi* 1932). — *RB* XLII 282–286.

1697 VOSTÉ (J.), S. Albertus Magnus, sacrae paginae Magister. Romae 1932. — *RB* XLII 282–286.

1698 WILLAM (F. M.), Das Leben Jesu im Lande und Volke Israel. Freiburg i. Br. 1933. — *RB* XLII 288.

1699 WOBBE (J.), Der Charis-Gedanke bei Paulus. Münster 1932. — *RB* XLII 126–127.

1700 WOOD (H.), Amicitiae Corolla. A volume of essays presented to James Rendel Harris, D. Litt. on the occasion of his eightieth birthday. Cfr FINDLAY, J. A. The first Gospel and the Book of Testimonies; HOWARD, W. F. John the Baptist and Jesus; K. and S. LAKE, The text of Mark in some dated lectionaries. Birmingham 1933. — *RB* XLII 605–606.

1934

1701 **Origines de la théologie.** *Cahiers du cercle thomiste du Caire,* janvier 1934 4–11.

1702 **Les papyrus Chester Beatty pour les Évangiles.** *RB* XLIII 5–41.

1703 **Le papyrus Beatty des Actes des Apôtres.** *RB* XLIII 161–171.

1704 **Le papyrus Chester Beatty pour les Épîtres de saint Paul et l'Apocalypse.** *RB* XLIII 481–493.

BOOK REVIEWS

1705 BACON (B. W.), The Gospel of the Hellenists. New York. — *RB* XLIII 305–306.

1706 BERNARDIN (J. B.), The intercession of our Lord. New York 1933. — RB XLIII 138.

1707 BLUMENTHAL (M.), Formen und Motive in den apocryphen Apostelgeschichten. Leipzig 1933. — RB XLIII 285–288.

1708 BONACCORSI (G.), Primi saggi di filologia neotestamentaria. Lettere scelte dal Nuovo Testamento greco. Torino 1933. — RB XLIII 444.

1709 BONNER (C.), A papyrus codex of the Shepherd of Hermas. Michigan 1934. — RB XLIII 453–454.

1710 BORNKAMM (G.), Mythos und Legende in den Apocryphen Thomas-Acten. Göttingen 1933. — RB XLIII 288–290.

1711 CONDAMIN (A.) Poèmes de la Bible. Paris 1933. — RB XLIII 128–132.

1712 CRISTIANI (L.), Vie de Jésus-Christ, Fils de Dieu, Sauveur. Lyon 1933. — RB XLIII 136.

1713 GLUNG (H. H.), Britannien und Bibeltext. Leipzig 1930. — RB XLIII 141–143.

1714 GUÉNIN (P.), Y a-t-il eu conflit entre Jean-Baptiste et Jésus? Genève 1933. — RB XLIII 138–139.

1715 HOLZMEISTER (U.), Chronologia vitae Christi. Romae 1933. — RB XLIII 301–302.

1716 JACK (J. W.), The historic Christ. An examination of Dr Robert Eisler's theory. London 1933. — RB XLIII 445–446.

1717 KLAUSNER (J.), Jésus de Nazareth. Paris 1933. — RB XLIII 136–138.

1718 KLEIN (F.), La vie humaine et divine de Jésus-Christ Notre-Seigneur. Paris 1933. — RB XLIII 136.

1719 KLOSTERMANN (E.), Origenes'Werke, Bd. XI : Matthäus-Erklärung. Leipzig 1933. — RB XLIII 151–153.

1720 LAKE (K. and Silva), Six collations of New Testament Manuscripts. Cambridge 1932. — RB XLIII 141.

1721 LUMINI (L.), O Sobrenatural nos Evangelhos Sinoticos. Sao Paulo 1933. — RB XLIII 444–445.

1722 MARIÈS (L.), Études préliminaires à l'édition de Diodore de Tarse sur les Psaumes. Paris 1933. — RB XLIII 150–151.

1723 MATZKOW (W.), De vocabulis quibusdam Italae et Vulgatae christianis. Berlin 1933. — RB XLIII 298–299.

1724 MERK (A.), Novum Testamentum graece et latine. Rome 1933. — RB XLIII 139–141.

1725 — — Codex Evangeliorum et Actuum in collectione papyrorum Chester Beatty (Miscellanea biblica II, 375–406). Romae 1934. — RB XLIII 612–613.

1726 MICHAELIS (W.), Die Datierung des Philipperbriefes. Gütersloh 1933. — RB XLIII 447–448.

1727 PRAT (F.), Jésus-Christ, sa vie, sa doctrine, son œuvre. Paris 1933. — *RB* XLIII 299–301.

1728 SICKENBERGER (J.), Die Geschichte des Neuen Testamentes. Bonn 1934. — *RB* XLIII 613–614.

1729 STAURIDÈS (C. J.), La chronologie de la Passion. Paris 1934. — *RB* XLIII 445.

1730 TAYLOR (V.), The formation of the Gospel Tradition. London 1933. — *RB* XLIII 302–303.

1731 TORREY (C. C.), The four Gospels. A new translation. New York and London 1933. — *RB* XLIII 303–305.

1732 VAGANAY (L.), Initiation à la critique textuelle néotestamentaire. Paris 1934. — *RB* XLIII 612.

1733 VANNUTELLI (Primo), Quaestiones de synopticis evangeliis. Romae 1933. — *RB* XLIII, 305.

1734 VILAR (J.), Les citations bibliques de Sant Pacià. Barcelone 1932. — *RB* XLIII 298–299.

1935

1735 Introduction à l'étude du Nouveau Testament : II. Critique textuelle. La critique rationnelle (en collaboration avec le R. P. Lyonnet, S.J.), (*ÉB*). In-8º de XVI–685 pp. Paris, Gabalda.

1736 Socrate et Notre-Seigneur Jésus-Christ, d'après un livre récent. *RB* XLIV 5–21.

1737 L'histoire ancienne du canon du Nouveau Testament. *RB* XLIV 212–219.

1738 Deux nouveaux textes relatifs à l'Évangile. *RB* XLIV 321–343.

1739 La critique textuelle avant le Concile de Trente. *RTh* XXXIXᵉ année 400–409.

BOOK REVIEWS

1740 DABROWSKI (E.), Proces Chrystusa. Warsawa 1934. — *RB* XLIV 296.

1741 GÄCHTER (P.), Der formale Aufbau der Abschiedsrede Jesu (*ZKTh* 1934). — *RB* XLIV 105–108.

1742 HATCH (W. H. P.), The Greek manuscripts of the New Testament at Mount Sinai. Paris 1932. — *RB* XLIV 297–298.

1743 HEADLAM (A. C.), Christian faith. The doctrine of God. Oxford 1934. — *RB* XLIV 296–297.

1744 HOLLARD (A.), Saint Paul. Paris 1934. — *RB* XLIV 301.

1745 HOPKIN-JAMES (J.), The Celtic Gospels. Oxford 1934. — *RB* XLIV 119–120.

1746 LABRIOLLE (P. de), La réaction païenne. Étude sur la polémique antichrétienne du Iᵉʳ au VIᵉ siècle. Paris 1931. — *RB* XLIV 606–609.

1747 LAKE (K. and S.), Dated Greek minuscule manuscripts to the year 1200. Boston. — *RB* XLIV 1935 119.

1748 — — Manuscripts in Venice. Boston 1934. — *RB* XLIV 624–625.

1749 LANWER (B.), Die Grundgedanken der Berpredigt auf dem Hintergrunde des Alten Testamentes und Spätjudentums. Hiltrup 1934. — *RB* XLIV 300–301.

1750 LEGG (S. C. E.), Novum Testamentum graece secundum textum Westcotto-Hortianum. Evangelium secundum Marcum. Oxonii 1935. — *RB* XLIV 623–624.

1751 LIETZMANN (H.), Zur Würdigung des Chester-Beatty Papyrus der Paulusbriefe (*SbAkPreuss* 1934). — *RB* XLIV 627–629.

1752 MACRORY (Cᵃˡ). The New Testament and Divorce. Dublin 1934. — *RB* XLIV 296.

1753 MOLLAND (E.), Das Paulinische Evangelion. Das Wort und die Sache. Oslo 1934. — *RB* XLIV 301–302.

1754 PONTIFICIUM INSTITUTUM BIBLICUM, Miscellanea biblica. — *RB* XLIV 115–117.

1755 — — La Redenzione. Conferenze bibliche, tenute nell' anno Giubilare 1933 all'Istituto biblico. Roma 1934. — *RB* XLIV 117.

1756 RIDEAU (É.), En marge de la question synoptique (*Bi* XV 1934 484–504). — *RB* XLIV 279–283.

1757 ROPES (J. H.), The Synoptic Gospels. Harvard University 1934. — *RB* XLIV 121–122.

1758 RUSSEL (W. H.), The function of the New Testament in the formation of the catholic high school teacher. Washington 1934. — *RB* XLIV 120–121.

1759 SANDERS (H. A.), A third-century papyrus codex of the Epistles of Paul. Michigan 1935. — *RB* XLIV 625–627.

1760 SCHMIDT (H.), Die Psalmen. Tübingen. — *RB* XLIV 125.

1761 STEINMANN (A.), Die Apostelgeschichte, übersetzt und erklärt. Bonn 1934. — *RB* XLIV 122.

1762 SUNDWALL (J.), Die Zusammensetzung des Markusevangeliums. Abo 1934. — *RB* XLIV 299–300.

1763 VALENTINE RICHARDS (A. V.), The text of Acts in codex 614 and its allies. Cambridge 1914. — *RB* XLIV 298–299.

1764 VOSTÉ (J.), De Baptismo, Tentatione et Transfiguratione Jesu. Romae 1934. — *RB* XLIV 295–296.

1765 WINDISCH (H.), Paulus und Christus. Leipzig 1934. — *RB* XLIV 5–21.

1766 ZARBS (S. M.), De historia Canonis utriusque Testamenti. Romae 1934. — *RB* XLIV 117–119.

1936

1767 Les origines du dogme paulinien de la divinité du Christ. *RB* XLV 5–33.

1768 La Vie de Jésus par M. François Mauriac. *RB* XLV 321–345.

1769 Les légendes pythagoriennes et l'Évangile. *RB* XLV 481–511.

1770 La lecture de la Bible et l'âme dominicaine. V Dom 160–165; 201–206; 233–338; 265–272; 309–314; 333–337; 367–372.

BOOK REVIEWS

1771 Bonsirven (J.), Le Judaïsme palestinien au temps de Jésus-Christ. Paris 1935. — *RB* XLV 263–265.

1772 Dujardin (E.), Histoire ancienne du Dieu Jésus. La première génération chrétienne. Son destin révolutionnaire. — *RB* XLV 575–581.

1773 Florit (E.), Il metodo della « Storia delle Forme ». Roma 1935. — *RB* XLV 131–132.

1774 Giardino (J.), Il messaggio sociale di Gesù. Milano 1935. — *RB* XLV 132–133.

1775 Goodenough (E. R.), By Light, Light. Yale University 1935. — *RB* XLV 265–269.

1776 Steinmann (A.), Die Briefe an die Thessalonicher und Galater[4]. Bonn 1935. — *RB* XLV 133.

1777 Vannutelli (P.), Matteo e Marco in Papia — L'originalità dell' evangelo di Marco (*ScuolCatt* 1935). — *RB* XLV 132.

1778 Zeiller (J.), Les origines chrétiennes dans les provinces danubiennes. Saint Jérôme et les Goths (*Miscellanea Geronimiana* 1920). — *RB* XLV 133–134.

1937

1779 Introduction à l'étude du Nouveau Testament : IV. Critique historique. Les mystères : l'Orphisme (*ÉB*). In-8º de VIII–243 pp. avec illustr. Paris, Gabalda.

1780 Les légendes pythagorienne et l'Évangile. *RB* XLVI 5–28.

1781 Le réalisme historique de l'Évangile selon S. Jean. *RB* XLVI 321–341.

1782 Le réalisme et le symbolisme de Dante. *RB* XLVI 481–505.

1783 Souvenirs de Salamanque. *VDom* 179–183; 221–225; 244–248.

BOOK REVIEWS

1784 SCHMIDTKE (A.), Zum Hebräerevangelium (*NTZ* 1936. —
RB XLVI 282–284.
1785 STEINMÜLLER (J. E.), Some problems of the Old Testament.
Milwaukee 1936. — *RB* XLVI 122–124.

1938

1786 L'authenticité mosaïque de la Genèse et la théorie des
documents. *RB* XLVII 163–183.

INDEX OF AUTHORS REVIEWED

ABBOTT (E. A.), 525, 587, 615, 685, 753, 798, 858.
ABBOTT (L.), 451.
ABBOTT (T. K.), 184.
ABBOT-SMITH (G.), 1387.
ADAM (K.), 1658.
ALBRECHT (K.), 1347.
ALÈS (A. d'), 686, 754, 1129, 1190, 1300.
ALFARIC (P.), 1265, 1535.
ALLGEIER (A.), 929.
ALLO (B.), 859.
ALMA (J. d'), 930.
AMANN (E.), 860, 1348.
AMANN (F.), 1053.
AMÉLINEAU (E.), 101.
AMELLI (A.), 452.
ANCEL, 931.
ARCHAMBAULT (G.), 861.
ARINTERO (J. G.), 12, 312, 153.
ARNAUDET (D^r), 932.
ARNOLD (W. R.), 988, 1167.
ASSOUAD (N.), 1191, 1349.
AYLES (H.), 588.
AYTOUN (A.), 1266.
AZIBERT (J.), 74, 185.

BACHER (W.), 313.
BACON (B. W.), 1267, 1268, 1455, 1705.
BAEDEKER (K.), 29.
BAENTSCH (B.), 755.
BAETHGEN, 186.
BAILLET (J.), 526, 527.
BAINVEL (R. P.), 687.
BALDENSPERGER (G.), 528, 1659.
BALDI (D.), 1456.
BALL (C. J.), 154, 1232.
BANDAS (G.), 1428.
BARDENHEWER (O.), 529.
BARDY (G.), 1605.
BARNABÉ d'Alsace (R. P.), 453, 454, 455, 530.
BARNES (E.), 456.
BARRY (W.), 616.
BARTHAS (C.), 1660.

BARTON (G. A.), 1168.
BARTON (J.), 1447.
BATIFFOL (P.), 155, 259, 617, 799, 933, 1054, 1115, 1301.
BAUDISSIN (W. W.), 376, 989, 1075.
BAUER (W.), 531, 1429, 1457, 1565, 1661.
BAUMANN (É.), 1430.
BAUMSTARK (A.), 1350, 1351.
BAYET (M. A.), 1559.
BEDIER (J.), 1233.
BEERMANN (G.), 1034.
BELL (H. I.), 1431.
BELSER (J. E.), 103, 618, 800, 862.
BENSON (E. W.), 260.
BENZ (K.), 1055.
BENZINGER (J.), 314.
BÉRARD (V.), 315, 532.
BERNARDIN (J. B.), 1706.
BERTHOLET (A.), 261, 316.
BERTRAM (G.), 1388.
BESSON (É.), 1352, 1401.
BIDEZ (J.), 1503.
BILLOT (C^{al}), 1269.
BLASS (Fr.), 220.
BLISS (F. J.), 13, 51, 71.
BLOCH, 14.
BLUDAU (A.), 756, 1458.
BLUM (L.), 1566.
BLUMENTHAL (M.), 1707.
BLUNT (W. F.), 1459.
BODIN, 990.
BÖHLIG (H.), 1035.
BÖHMER (J.), 457.
BOISSIER (A.), 1192.
BOISSIER (G.), 856, 863.
BONACCORSI (G.), 458, 533, 589, 688, 1130, 1708
BONNER (C.), 1709.
BONSIRVEN (J.), 1771.
BONUS (A.), 156.
BORNKAMM (G.), 1710.
BOUILLON (L.), 1056.
BOULANGER (A.), 1460.

BOUR (R. S.), 187.
BOURCHANY, 934.
BOUSSET (W.), 459, 534, 689, 1263.
BOUVIER (H.), 1461.
BOVER (J. M.), 1131, 1462.
BOYER (P.), 991.
BOX (G. H.), 1606.
BOYSSON (A. de), 992.
BRANDSCHEID (F.), 317, 690, 691.
BRANDT (W.), 864, 935.
BRASSAC (A.), 757, 936, 1302.
BRAUN (F. M.), 1662.
BREEN (A. E.), 262, 619.
BRESKY (B.), 801.
BRICOUT (J.), 993.
BRIGGS (C. A.), 1057.
BRIGGS (E. G.), 263.
BRILLANT (M.), 1303.
BROGLIE (de), 157.
BROOKE (A. E.), 620, 802, 1036.
BROS (A.), 803.
BROSSE (E.), 158.
BROWNE (L. E.), 1304.
BRÜCKER (R. P.), 758.
BRUDERS (H.), 535.
BRUN (L.), 1353.
BRUSTON (C.), 621, 1193, 1194.
BRUYNE (De), 1354, 1522.
BUCHANAN (S.), 759.
BUDDE (K.), 188, 264, 460.
BUDGE (W.), 1058.
BUGGE (C. A.), 536.
BUHL (F. R.), 112.
BULTMANN (R.), 937, 1355, 1417.
BUNDY (E.), 1356.
BUONAJUTI (M.), 760.
BURKITT (F. C.), 75, 377, 1234, 1305,
   1357.
BURNEY (C. F.), 461, 1235, 1358.
BURRAGE (C.), 1059.
BUYSSE (P.), 1432.
BUZY (D.), 1236, 1359, 1663.

CADBURY (H. J.), 1270, 1360, 1675.
CADMAN (W. H.), 1402.
CAGNAT (R.), 1195.
CALLAN (C. J.), 1389.
CALMES (Th.), 622.
CALMET (Dom), 523.
CAMERLYNCK (A.), 804, 865, 866, 938,
   1361.
CARA (R. P. de), 55.

CARCOPINO (J.), 1390, 1479, 1480, 1536.
CARLETON (G.), 462.
CARNOY (A.), 1362.
CARPENTER (B.), 463.
CARR (A.), 464, 623.
CARRERAS (LL.), 1447.
CART (L.), 1132.
CARUCCI (Y.), 159.
CASAMASSA (A.), 1607.
CAUSSE (A.), 805, 1306, 1363.
CAVALLERA (F.), 1237, 1307.
CELLINI (A.), 692, 693, 806, 994.
CERESETO, 465.
CERFAUX (L.), 1433.
CHABOT (J. B.), 76, 105.
CHAMARD (Fr.), 466.
CHAPMAN (A. T.), 939.
CHAPMAN (J.), 940, 1308.
CHARLES (B.), 908.
CHARLES (R. H.), 189, 467, 694, 761,
   762, 1060, 1196, 1197, 1537.
CHAUVIN (Abbé), 1133.
CHEVALIER (U.), 468.
CHEYNE (T. K.), 77, 265, 266, 267, 268,
   318, 378, 469, 537, 695.
CHIAPPELLI (A.), 538.
Civiltà Cattolica, 1231.
CLARK (A. C.), 1665.
CLEMEN (C.), 807, 1061, 1075.
CLERMONT-GANNEAU (Ch.), 269, 379,
   380, 539, 808.
COLSON (F. H.), 1271.
CONDAMIN (A.), 590, 1134, 1135, 1364,
   1711.
CONTENEAU (G.), 1169.
CONYPEARE (F. C.), 78, 106, 868.
COOK (S. A.), 540, 1170.
COPPIETERS (H.), 804, 938.
CORDOVANI (R. P.), 1198.
CORMIER (H.), 625.
CORNELY (R.), 270, 942, 943.
CORNILL (H.), 320.
Corpus Inscriptionum sem., 107, 321,
   381.
CORSSEN (P.), 162.
COUCHOUD (P. L.), 1498, 1504.
COULANGE (L.), 1505.
COWLEY, 1199.
CRAMPON (A.), 944.
CREUSEN (J.), 995.
CRISTIANI (L.), 1712.
CRONIN, 1272.

CUMONT (F.), 382, 763, 856, 1171, 1172, 1200, 1201.
CUQ (E.), 1202.

DABROWSKI (E.), 1666, 1740.
DAKSE (J.), 1238.
DALMAN (G.), 221, 1403.
DANBY (H.), 1273.
DARD (D.), 1062.
DARLEY (E.), 1063.
DAUBNEY (Rev.), 322.
DAUSCH (P.), 79, 1274, 1275, 1608.
DEISSMANN (A.), 190, 764, 811.
DELAFOSSE (H.), 1463, 1506.
DELAPORTE (L.), 656.
DELATTRE (A. J.), 583, 591.
DELEHAYE (H.), 627.
DELITZSCH (F.), 383.
DENIFLE (R. P.), 541.
DENNEFELD (L.), 869.
DEONNA (W.), 1031.
DESJARDINS (G.), 323.
DESPRÉS (J.), 222.
DESSAILLY (Abbé), 271.
DESSAU, 870, 1309.
DEWICK (E. C.), 996.
DIÈS (A.), 1481.
DIETTRICH (G.), 696.
DILLENSEGER (R. P.), 812.
DIBELIUS (M.), 1417.
DIRKSEN (A. H.), 1667.
DITTMAR (W.), 272.
DOBSCHÜTZ (E. von), 384, 1075.
DÖLLER (J.), 471.
DONAVAN (J.), 1434, 1567.
DORNSTETTER (P.), 385.
DOUAIS (Mgr), 592.
DRAGUET (R.), 1568.
DREXLER, 856.
DRIVER (S. R.), 30, 108, 542.
DUCHESNE (L.), 997.
DUESBERG (H.), 1609.
DUFOURCQ (A.), 871, 1507.
DUHM (B.), 223, 324.
DUJARDIN (E.), 628, 1508, 1610, 1772.
DUPERRAY (J.), 1365.
DUPIN (A.-J.), 629.
DURAND (A.), 813, 998, 1037, 1404.
DUSSAUD (R.), 325, 1064.
DYNELEY PRINCE (J.), 224, 1136.

EASTON (B. S.), 1482.

ECK (Abbé), 225.
ECKER (J.), 472.
EGGER (F.), 872.
EISLER (R.), 1531.
EJARQUE (R.), 1239.
ENGELKEMPER (W.), 386, 814.
ENSLIN (M. S.), 1569.
EPSTEIN (J. N.), 988.
ERBT (W. von), 697.
ERDMANN (G.), 1668.
ERMANN (A.), 80.
EURINGER (S.), 16, 1065.
EUTING (J.), 17, 109.
EVANS (A. J.), 873.

FALOCI (Mgr), 698.
FASCHER (E.), 1538.
FAULHABER (M.), 273.
FEDER (L.), 699.
FEI (R.), 700.
FEINE (P.), 326, 874, 1075.
FELTEN (J.), 945.
FÉRET (P.), 274, 543, 765, 875.
FERGUSON (W. D.), 1066, 1514.
FÉROTIN (M.), 327.
FESTUGIÈRE (A. J.), 1570.
FIEBIG (P.), 1067.
FILLION (L. Cl.), 31, 523, 544, 1366.
FILSON (F. V.), 1611.
FINDLAY (J. A.), 1700.
FIOROVICH (R. P.), 81.
FLORIT (E.), 1773.
FOCKE (J.), 1240.
FONCK (L.), 275, 630, 1405.
FONTAINE (R. P.), 328.
FOSSEY (C.), 362, 473.
FOUCART (P.), 1068.
FRACASSINI (Abbé), 474.
FRAME (J. E.), 1038.
FRANÇOIS (R. P.), 631.
FRANÇON (J.), 656.
FRANKENBERG, 226.
FRAZER (J. G.), 1310.
FRIDRICHSEN (A.), 1353.
FRIEDLÄNDER (M.), 593.
FRIEDRICH (Th.), 633.
FUCHS (M. E.), 1669.
FURNEAUX (W. M.), 999.

GÄCHTER (P.), 1612, 1741.
GALL (A. von), 227.
GALLEGOS ROCAFULL (J. M.), 1571.

GALLOWAY (G.), 1069.
GAMBER (S.), 1000.
GAMPERT (A.), 1203.
GARDNER (P.), 330, 766.
GAUCKLER (P.), 1137.
GAUTIER (L.), 110, 111, 331, 634.
GAYRAUD (Abbé), 387, 701.
GEBHARDT (O. von), 32, 388.
GEFFCKEN (G.), 545.
GELDNER, 1391.
GESENIUS (W.), 112.
GHIO (G.), 1070.
GIARDINO (J.), 1774.
GIBSON (Mrs D.), 113, 717, 1001.
GIESEBRECHT (F.), 332.
GIGOT (F. E.), 191, 333.
GIOVANNOZZI (R. P.), 946.
GLANE, 876.
GLATIGNY (J. B. de), 703, 767.
GLAZEBROOK (M. G.), 947, 1071.
GLOTZ (G.), 1368.
GLUNG (H. H.), 1713.
GOBLET D'ALVIELLA (Cᵗᵉ), 1002.
GODARD (A.), 1539.
GOETHALS (A.), 1613.
GOGUEL (M.), 948, 1204, 1406, 1435, 1614, 1670.
GOODENOUGH (E. R.), 1775.
GOOSSENS (W.), 1615.
GORE (C.), 114.
GRAAFEN (J.), 1540.
GRAMATICA (L.), 1003, 1072.
GRANBERY (J. C.), 877.
GRANDMAISON (L. de), 1116, 1407, 1436.
GRANELLI (E.), 475.
GRAY (G. B.), 1004.
GREGORY (C. R.), 334, 389, 768, 815, 816, 878, 879, 949, 1034.
GRIEFF (A.), 1541.
GRENFELL (B. P.), 817, 1138, 1205.
GRESHAM MACHEN (J.), 1542.
GRIMM (K. J.), 476.
GRIMME (H.), 163, 390, 477, 988.
GROAG (E.), 1523.
GROOT (De), 704.
GRY (L.), 880.
GUÉNIN (P.), 1714.
GUIDI (J.), 1392.
GUIGNEBERT (Ch.), 1671.
GUILLAUME II, 478.
GUIMET (E.), 856.
GUITTON (J.), 1672.

GUNKEL (H.), 335, 479, 546, 705, 853.
GUNTERMANN (F.), 1673.
GUTHE (H.), 276, 787.
GUTJAHR, 594.
GWILLIAM (G. H.), 1311.
GWYNN (J.), 950.

HACKSPILL (L.), 164, 391.
HAHN (L.), 33.
HALÉVY (J.), 34, 56, 165.
HAMMER (H.), 1073.
HARNACK (A. von), 336, 635, 706, 770, 881, 951, 1040, 1241, 1276, 1312, 1408, 1409, 1510, 1543, 1616.
HARRIS (J. R.), 115, 277, 1313, 1369.
HARTMANN (R. P.), 1041.
HASTINGS (J.), 278.
HATCH (E.), 35, 82, 166.
HATCH (W. H. P.), 1742.
HAUCK (A.), 192, 547.
HAUGG (D.), 1572.
HAULER (E.), 279.
HAUPT (E.), 116.
HAUPT (P.), 280, 771, 772, 1173, 1174.
HAUSHEER (Dʳ), 636.
HAUTSCH, 952.
HAWKINS (J. C.), 882.
HEADLAM (A. C.), 548, 1117, 1483, 1743.
« HEGESIPPUS », 1674.
HEER (J. M.), 818, 883, 953.
HEHN (J.), 549, 637.
HEIGL (B.), 707.
HEIKEL (I. A.), 1074.
HEINEKE (R.), 228.
HEINRICI (G.), 1075.
HEITMÜLLER (W.), 638, 1075.
HEJCL (J.), 773.
HELM (R.), 876, 1076.
HEMMER (H.), 1461.
HEMPEL (J.), 1417.
HENRY (A.-B.), 1287.
HERBIGNY (M. d'), 1314, 1370.
HERFORD (R. T.), 550.
HERMANN (J.), 639.
HERMANN (L.), 1576.
HERZOG (G. J.), 708.
HETZENAUER (M.), 167, 337, 480, 774, 1315, 1437.
HEYES (J.), 595.
HILPRECHT (H. V.), 481.
HITCHCOCK (G. S.), 1077.
HJELT (A.), 392.

HOBERG (G.), 482, 640, 775.
HOGAN, 393.
HOLBORN, 483.
HOLLARD (A.), 1316, 1744.
HOLLEAUX (M.), 1078, 1242.
HOLLMANN, 853.
HÖLSCHER (G.), 709.
HOLTZMANN (H. J.), 168, 281, 776.
HOLTZMANN (O.), 1465.
HOLZAMMER (J. B.), 843.
HOLZHEY (C.), 885.
HOLZINGER (H.), 193, 338, 551.
HOLZMEISTER (U.), 820, 1393, 1715.
HOMANNER (M. W.), 821.
HOMMEL (F.), 117, 118, 119, 169, 394, 596.
HÖNNICKE (G.), 822.
HOONACKER (A. VAN), 57, 83, 120, 229, 1118.
HÖPFL (H.), 395, 597, 1079.
HOPKIN-JAMES (J.), 1745.
HÖRNLE (E. S.), 1574.
HOROVITZ (H. S.), 1617.
HOSKIER (H. C.), 1005, 1006, 1277.
HOUDE (G.), 1317.
HOUTIN (A.), 396, 641.
HOWARD (W. F.), 1700.
HOZAKOWSKI (W.), 1007.
HUBER (K.), 1278.
HUBY (J.), 1008, 1139, 1438.
HUDAL (A.), 1080.
HÜGEL (B^on von), 194.
HÜHN (E.), 282, 283.
HUMBERT (A.), 954.
HUMBERT (P.), 1140, 1287.
HUMMELAUER (F. de), 195, 196, 230, 231, 232, 339, 484, 710.
HUNT (A. S.), 817, 886, 955, 1138, 1205.
HUTTON (E. A.), 956.
HYVERNAT (H.), 1279.

JACK (J. W.), 1716.
JACKSON (F. J. F.), 1675.
JACKSON (L. H.), 1243.
JACOB (B.), 642.
JACQUIER (E.), 824, 957, 958, 1318, 1319.
JAMES (M. R.), 42, 121, 197, 1207, 1497.
JASTROW (M.), 233, 552.
JASTROW (M. jr), 1142, 1143, 1175, 1208.
JEAMMAIRE (H.), 1676.

JENSEN (P.), 397.
JÉQUIER (G.), 349.
JEREMIAS (A.), 485.
JEREMIAS (J.), 1575.
JONES, 486.
JORDAN (L. H.), 887.
JORDAN (W. G.), 825.
JOÜON (P.), 1544.
JOYCE (M. C.), 888.
JUGIE (M.), 826.
JÜLICHER (A.), 1410.
JULIUS (C.), 398.
JÜNGST (J.), 84.
JUNKER (H.), 1618, 1619.
JUSTER (J.), 1209.

KALT (E.), 1620.
KAUTZSCH (E.), 399.
KAUTZSCH (K.), 284.
KENNEDY (H. A. A.), 553.
KENYON (F. G.), 341, 889, 1119, 1621.
KEPPLER (P. W.), 58, 122.
KIRWAN (de), 123.
KITTEL (G.), 1622, 1677, 1678.
KITTEL (R.), 285, 643.
KLAUSER (Th.), 1511.
KLAUSNER (J.), 1717.
KLEIN (F.), 1718.
KLEY (J.), 554.
KLOSTERMANN (E.), 644, 1719.
KNABENBAUER (J.), 198, 400, 711, 959, 1042, 1081.
KNOX (W. L.), 1439.
KNUDTZON (J. A.), 401.
KÖBERLE (J.), 402.
KÖHLER, 853.
KÖNIG (E.), 170, 403, 404, 405, 406, 645, 646, 712, 713, 960, 1009.
KRAFT (B.), 1440.
KREYENBÜHL (J.), 647.
KRÜGER (G.), 286.
KÜMMEL (W. G.), 1545.
KUNDSIN (K.), 1546.
KURZE (G.), 1280.
KYLE, 1210.

LABANCA (B.), 555.
LABAUCHE (L.), 1010.
LABORDE (A. de), 1211.
LABRIOLLE (P. de), 1746.
LADEUZE (P.), 827.
LAFAYE (G.), 856.

LAGRANGE (M. J.), 487, 1466, 1484.
LAKE (K.), 648, 777, 828, 1675, 1700, 1720, 1747, 1748.
LAKE (S.), 1700, 1720, 1747, 1748.
LAMMENS (H.), 407.
LAMPRE (G.), 349.
LANDRIEUX (Mgr), 1176.
LANGDON (S.), 1144.
LANWER (B.), 1749.
LASSERRE (P.), 1425.
LAVERGNE (C.), 1466, 1484.
LAWRENCE (T. E.), 1158.
LEBON (J.), 1011.
LEBRETON (J.), 890, 1281, 1524, 1623.
LE CAMUS (Mgr), 649.
LEGENDRE (Mgr), 714.
LEGG (S. C. E.), 1750.
LEGRIS (B.), 656.
LEIPOLDT (Jo.), 715, 829.
LEMONNYER (A.), 598, 1098.
LE MORIN (J.), 716.
LEPIN (M.), 556, 651, 830, 891, 961.
LESÊTRE (H.), 18, 652.
LÉVI (J.), 408, 988.
LÉVY (J.), 1486, 1525.
LÉVY (A. J.), 1680.
LEWIS (MRS A. SMITH), 124, 199, 488, 717, 832, 962.
LEWIS (F. G.), 831.
LIBERTY (S.), 1146.
LIDZBARSKI (M.), 287, 489, 988.
LIETZMANN (H.), 1244, 1624, 1681, 1751.
LINCK (K.), 1083.
LINDEMANN (H.), 1245.
LINDL (E.), 409.
LIPPL (J.), 963.
LITTMANN (E.), 653.
LLAMAS (J.), 1682.
LLOVERA (J. M.), 1447.
LODS (A.), 718, 1287.
LÖHR (M.), 234, 719.
LOISY (A.), 37, 235, 236, 237, 343, 410, 490, 557, 654, 778, 779, 964, 1147, 1282, 1454, 1599.
LOYSON (P. H.), 1310.
LUCE (H. K.), 1683.
LUMINI (L.), 1721.
LUTHER (B.), 411.

MAC FAYDEN, 491.
MACKENSIE, 833.
MACLER (F.), 1283.

MAC NEILL (H. L.), 1246.
MACRIDY-BEY, 375.
MAC RORY (J.), 655, 1752.
MADAN (F.), 85.
MADER (E.), 38, 892.
MADER (J.), 835.
MAGER (H.), 1284.
MAGNIER, 412.
MAICHLE (A.), 1084.
MALDEN (R. H.), 1412, 1547.
MALLON (A.), 1371.
MANDELKERN (S.), 126, 238.
MANGENOT (E.), 893, 965.
MANSON (T. W.), 1625.
MANY (V.), 1247.
MARGARET (Lady), 966.
MARGIVAL (Abbé), 200.
MARGOLIS (M. L.), 894, 1213.
MARIANO (R.), 558.
MARIÈS (L.), 1722.
MARMORSTEIN (A.), 1214.
MARTI (K.), 125, 344, 1085.
MARTIMPREY, 407.
MARTIN (F.), 345, 492, 656.
MARTIN (R. M.), 720.
MARTINELLI (P.), 721.
MARTY (J.), 1636.
MARUCCHI (O.), 895.
MASPERO (G.), 239, 288, 599.
MATHIEU (G.), 1576.
MATHIS (M. A.), 1321.
MATZKOW (W.), 1723.
MAURIAC (F.), 1768.
MAYER (H. H.), 1248.
MAZOYER (P.), 127.
MAZZELLA (H.), 657.
MC LEAN (N.), 620, 802.
MC NEILE (A. H), 1212, 1411.
MÉCHINEAU (R. P.), 240.
MEFFERT (F.), 967.
MEINERTZ (M.), 600, 836, 1285, 1467, 1577, 1627, 1628.
MEINHOLD (J.), 1629.
MEISSNER (B.), 414, 415.
MEISTERMANN (B.), v. Barnabé d'Alsace.
MENUGE (Abbé), 171.
MERCATI (G.), 346, 559.
MERCIER (C^{a1}), 1286.
MERCIER (Ch.), 1287.
MERK (A.), 1724, 1725.
MERKELBACH (H.), 1043.
MERTENS (L.), 896.

MERX (A.), 59.
MESSEL (N.), 1372.
MESSENGER (E. C.), 1630.
MESSMER (Mgr.), 968.
MEYER (A.), 128.
MEYER (E.), 722, 988, 1373.
MEZZACASA (G.), 1086.
MICHAELIS (W.), 1578, 1579, 1631, 1726.
MICHEL (C.), 969.
MICHEL (O.), 1548.
MIGNOT (Mgr), 347, 897, 898.
MIKETTA (K.), 601.
MINOCCHI (S.), 493, 494, 495, 659, 723.
MOLITOR (H.), 1684.
MOLLAND (E.), 1753.
MÖLLER (W.), 780.
MONCEAUX (P.), 416, 724.
MONNIER (H.), 725.
MONTEFIORE (C. G.), 899.
MONTGOMERY (J. A.), 1413.
MOORE (G. F.), 348, 1087.
MORGAN (J. de), 349, 781, 1030.
MORIN (G.), 172, 1088.
MORTIER (R. P.), 1468.
MOULTON (J. H.), 1394.
MOZLEY (F. W.), 660.
MÜLLER (D. H.), 129, 241, 350, 560, 782, 900.
MÜLLER (G. H.), 837.
MÜLLER (M.), 351, 352, 496, 497.
MUNDLE (W.), 1441.
MUNTZ (W. S.), 1089.
MURILLO (L.), 1090.
MUSS-ARNOLT (W.), 86, 130, 417, 561, 661.

NAGEL (G.), 498.
NÄGELI (Th.), 726.
NASCIMBENE (R.), 1322.
NAU (F.), 727, 838, 970, 1012, 1013, 1580, 1581.
NAUMANN (W.), 1249.
NAVILLE (E.), 1091, 1092, 1177, 1215.
NESTLE (E.), 131, 289, 418, 499, 728, 1526.
NIKEL (J.), 602.
NISIUS (J. B.), 290.
NOCK (A. D.), 1487.
NOORT (G. Van), 729.
NÖSGEN (K. F.), 730.
NOURRY, 201.

OBIOLS (S.), 1582.
ODEBERG (H.), 1549, 1550.
OESTERLEY (W. O. E.), 1216.
ÖMMELEN (H. J.), 1583.
OLIVIERI (R. P.), 1452.
OLLIVIER (M. J.), 87, 731.
OMONT (H.), 420.
ORFALI (G.), 1250.
ORR (J.), 839.
OWEN (E. C.), 1512.

PADOVANI (Ch.), 662, 1093.
PAFFRATH (Th.), 1632.
PALLIS (A.), 1323, 1685.
PALMER, 500.
PANNIER (E.), 783.
PAQUIER (J.), 1633.
PARIBENI (R.), 840.
PARIS, 1121.
PARISOT (J.), 291.
PASQUIER (H.), 1014.
PASTERIS (E.), 732.
PATERSON (J. A.), 353.
PEAKE (S.), 901, 1004.
PEETERS (P.), 971, 1094, 1584.
PÈQUES (Th. M.), 562.
PEISER, 501.
PELLEGRINO (C.), 1686.
PELT (J. B.), 421, 604.
PEPE (G.), 1178.
PERLES (F.), 502.
PERNOT (H.), 1469.
PESCH (C.), 563, 663, 1488.
PESERICO (L.), 1288.
PETAVEL-OLLIFF (E.), 503.
PETERS (J. P.), 422, 1217.
PETERS (N.), 504.
PFÄTTISCH (J. M.), 1016.
PFEIFFER (E.), 1687.
PIEPENBRING (C.), 292, 1395.
PINARD DE LA BOULLAYE (H.), 1324, 1585.
PIROT (L.), 1095, 1289.
PLUMMER (A.), 242, 1019, 1218.
POEBEL (A.), 1148.
POELS (H. A.), 173, 605.
POMMIER (J.), 1470.
POPE (H.), 1096, 1251, 1414.
PORTMANS (M.), 39.
PÖRTNER (B.), 40.
POSSELT (W.), 841.
PRAT (F.), 354, 1018, 1727.

PRESSOIR (J.), 656.
PREUSCHEN (E.), 355, 564, 565.
PROCKSCH (O.), 505, 733.

QUENTIN (H.), 1415.

RAABE (R.), 132.
RABIN (I. A.), 1617.
RAHLFS (A.), 734, 1635.
RAHMANI (J. E.), 566.
RAHMER (M.), 243.
RAMPOLLA DEL TINDARO (Cardinal), 665.
RAMSAY (W. M.), 1044, 1219.
RANDON (L.), 1287.
RASCHI, 1688.
RAUSCHEN, 902.
REDPATH (H. A.), 35, 82, 166, 356.
REGNAULT (H.), 903.
REIDER (J.), 1179.
REILLY (W. S.), 1149.
REINACH (S.), 357, 358, 423, 424, 854, 856, 904.
REINACH (Th.), 202, 1586.
REITZENSTEIN (R.), 1374, 1513.
RENAN (E.), 1189, 1384.
RESCH (A.), 133, 203.
RÉVILLE (A.), 204.
REYNÈS-MONLAUR (Mlle), 1325.
RICO (M. R.), 1220.
RIDEAU (É.), 1756.
RIEDEL (W.), 506.
RIERA (J. M.), 1689.
RIGGENBACH (E.), 1551.
RIVIÈRE (J.), 1122, 1552.
ROBERT (V.), 293.
ROBERTSON (A.), 1019.
ROBILLOT (J.), 1636.
ROBINSON (M. A.), 134.
ROBINSON (M. F.), 135.
ROCHAT (E.), 666.
ROHART (Abbé), 60.
ROHR (I.), 1690.
ROLFFS, 425.
RONZEVALLE (S.), 426.
ROPES (J. H.), 1290, 1553, 1757.
ROSADI (G.), 784.
ROSE (V.), 567, 568, 569.
ROSLANIEC (Fr.), 1326.
ROTHSTEIN (G.), 244, 735.
ROUVIER (D^r), 427.
ROYER (J.), 428.
RÜCKER (A.), 1097.

RUCKERT, 205.
RUFFINI (E.), 1327.
RUSSEL (W. H.), 1758 .
RYLE (H. E.), 42, 1252.

S. (A.), 19.
SABATIER (A.), 206.
SACHAU (E.), 1020.
SALEILLES (R.), 570.
SALMON (G.), 207.
SALVATORELLI (L.), 1150.
SANDAY (W.), 208, 667, 785, 905, 1021, 1416.
SANDERS (H. A.), 972, 1253, 1759.
SANDERS (L.), 507.
SANGRAN Y GONZALEZ (J. de), 1587.
SARDI (M.), 906.
SCERBO (F.), 571.
SCHADE (T. L.), 973.
SCHÄFER (K. T.), 911, 1588.
SCHANZ (P.), 136.
SCHEFTELOWITZ (J.), 1396.
SCHEIL (V.), 43, 308, 359, 360, 361, 362, 429, 430, 572, 1222.
SCHICK (C.), 89.
SCHIFFERS (M.), 61.
SCHIFFINI (R. P.), 668.
SCHLATTER (A.), 1637.
SCHLIER (H.), 1589.
SCHLÖGL (N.), 431, 1328.
SCHMID (J.), 1527, 1590, 1638.
SCHMIDT (C.), 573.
SCHMIDT (G.), 1098.
SCHMIDT (H.), 1417, 1760.
SCHMIDT (K. L.), 1417.
SCHMIDT (N.), 736, 908.
SCHMIDTKE (A.), 1022, 1784.
SCHOLZ (A. von), 432.
SCHÖPFER (D^r), 175.
SCHRADER (E.), 433, 508.
SCHULTEN (A.), 363.
SCHULZ, 974.
SCHUMACHER (H.), 1023, 1099.
SCHUMANN (A.), 842.
SCHÜRER (E.), 245, 786, 909.
SCHUSTER (J.), 843.
SCHÜTZ (R.), 1329, 1375.
SCHWAB (J.), 1254.
SCHWARTZ (E.), 910.
SCHWEITZER (A.), 1100, 1691.
SCOTT (R.), 1489.
SCOTT (W.), 1442, 1514.

SEEBERG (A.), 606.
SEELIGMÜLLER (A.), 975.
SELBST, 911.
SELLIN (E.), 246.
SÉMACH (Y.), 1151.
SEMERIA (G.), 574, 575.
SENSE (P. C.), 434.
SICARD (M. M.), 976.
SICKENBERGER (J.), 1291, 1330, 1554, 1639, 1692, 1728.
SIEGFRIED (C.), 137.
SIEVERS (E.), 787.
SILVER (A. H.), 1528.
SILVERSTONE (A. E.), 1640.
SIMON (H.), 1443.
SINGER (W.), 247.
SIRET (L.), 844.
SKIBNIEWSKI (L. de), 912.
SKINNER (J.), 977.
SMIDTKE (A.), 576.
SMITH (D.), 509.
SMITH (G. A.), 1255.
SMITH (H. P.), 294.
SMITH (S. F.), 669.
SMITH (W. B.), 670.
SOBERNHEIM (M.), 671.
SODEN (H. von), 788, 913, 1033, 1045.
SÖDERBLOM (N.), 435.
SOIRON (Th.), 1376.
SOUBIGOU (L.), 1693.
SOULLIER (Chan.), 138.
SOUTER (A.), 672, 978, 1152, 1694.
SPICQ (C.), 1641.
SPIEGELBERG (W.), 607, 845.
SPITTA (F.), 914, 1102.
STADE (B.), 137.
STAERK (W.), 988.
STAHL (R.), 1591.
STANTON (V. H.), 915, 1377.
STAUDT (C. K.), 916.
STAURIDÉS (C. J.), 1729.
STEGMANN (A.), 1331.
STEIGER (R.), 1642.
STEINDORFF (G.), 90.
STEINMANN (A.), 846, 1292, 1761, 1776.
STEINMETZER (F.), 789.
STEINMÜLLER (J. E.), 1785.
STEUERNAGEL (C.), 295, 436, 988.
STODERL (W.), 1378.
STRACK (H. L.), 917.
STREANE (A. W.), 790.
STREETER (B. H.), 1444, 1555.

STUMMER (F.), 1529.
SUCONA Y VALLÈS (T.), 438.
SUNDWALL (J.), 1761.
SWETE (H. B.), 44, 364, 511, 791, 847, 918, 919.
SZCZYGIEL (P.), 1643.
SZÉKELY (S.), 1046.

TATON (R.), 1332.
TAYLOR (C.), 248.
TAYLOR (V.), 1490, 1592, 1730.
THACKERAY (H. St. J.), 1223, 1593.
THIEME (G.), 737.
THOMPSON (E. F.), 848, 979.
THUREAU-DANGIN (F.), 1153, 1224.
TILLMANN (F.), 792, 849, 1577, 1594, 1595.
TISCHLEDER (P.), 1418.
TISSERANT (E.), 850.
TISSET (P.), 1379.
TIXERONT (J.), 1333.
TOBAC (E.), 851.
TONDELLI (L.), 1471, 1695.
TORGE (P.), 439.
TORREY (C. C.), 249, 250, 1731.
TOSTIVINT (Abbé), 140.
TOUSSAINT (C.), 920, 1103.
TOUTAIN (J.), 856, 921.
TOUZARD (J.), 1180.
TOY (C. H.), 296.
TRENKLE (F. S.), 209.
TRICOT (A.), 1605.
TRUYOLS (A. Fernandez), 1225.
TURMEL (J.), v. COULANGE, DELAFOSSE, DUPIN, HERZOG, 1454, 1472.
TURNER (C. H.), 1334, 1645.

UBACH (B.), 1226, 1256.
UNGNAD (A.), 988, 1154.

VACCARI (A.), 1123, 1257, 1696.
VAGANAY (L.), 1732.
VALBUENA (R. F.), 297, 298, 440, 922, 1258, 1293, 1335.
VALENSIN (A.), 1024.
VALENTINE RICHARDS (A. V.), 1763.
VANDERVORST (J.), 1155.
VANNUTELLI (P.), 1419, 1420, 1596, 1646, 1733, 1777.
VEBER (M.), 674.
VERDUNOY (Ch.), 1491.
VERNES (M.), 20, 1104, 1156.

VIÇWA-MITRA, 21.
VIGIL (B. M.), 46.
VIGNY (A. de), 1050.
VIGOUROUX (F.), 46ᵃ, 51, 441.
VILAR (J.), 1734.
VINCENT (M.), 210.
VIOLET (B.), 923, 1417.
VITEAU (J.), 91.
VOGELS (H. J.), 852, 980, 1025, 1105,
  1336, 1337, 1397, 1421, 1422, 1445,
  1530, 1556.
VOGT (P.), 981.
VOGÜÉ (Mˡˢ de), 1162.
VOLLMER (H.), 1047.
VOLZ (P.), 577.
VOSTÉ (J. M.), 1181, 1380, 1557, 1697,
  1764.
VOUVAUX (L.), 1048.
VREDE (W.), 1628.
VRÉGILLE (P. de), 1026.

WAGNER (E.), 1398.
WALDE (B.), 1106.
WATSON (C. M.), 1157.
WEATHERALL, 512.
WEBER (O.), 442.
WEBER (S.), 1294.
WEBER (V.), 365, 1338.
WEISS (B.), 251, 578, 1075.
WEISS (J.), 579, 675, 739, 853, 1259,
  1339.
WELLHAUSEN (J.), 580.
WENDLAND (H. D.), 1648.
WESSELY (C.), 793.
WERNER (M.), 1446.
WERNLE (P.), 581.
WESENDONK (O. G.), 1597.

WHITE (E.), 1340.
WHITE (H. J.), 302, 1381.
WIEDEMANN (A.), 299.
WIENER (H. M.), 1182.
WIKENHAUSER (A.), 1649.
WILL (R.), 1382.
WILLAM (F. M.), 1698.
WINCKLER (H.), 301, 366, 433, 513, 514,
  515, 676, 856.
WINDFUR (W.), 1107.
WINDISCH (H.), 1260, 1417, 1492, 1736,
  1765.
WINER (B.), 92.
WOBBE (J.), 1699.
WOOD (H.), 1700.
WOOD (W. C.), 1183.
WOOLLEY (C. L.), 1158.
WORDSWORTH (J.), 302.
WORREL (W.), 1159.
WREDE (W.), 516, 740.
WRIGHT (A.), 303.
WRIGHT (A. H.), 741.
WRZOL (J.), 1295.

ZAHN (Th.), 304, 517.
ZANCAN (L.), 1650.
ZANECCHIA (D.), 252, 608.
ZAPLETAL (V.), 367, 518, 582, 677, 678,
  794, 794ᵃ, 1027, 1028, 1423.
ZARANTONELLO (L.), 1029.
ZARB (S. M.), 1766.
ZEILLER (J.), 1778.
ZEITLIN (S.), 1598, 1651.
ZELLINGER (J. B.), 742.
ZIMMERN (H.), 310, 368, 508.
ZSCHOKKE (Mgr), 1341.

ANALYTICAL INDEX
TO THE BIBLIOGRAPHY

Abgarus
Apocryphal letter of Jesus to King A.
CLERMONT-GANNEAU *269*

Abilene
CRONIN *1272*

Abraham
Origins of the Hebrew People
DORNSTETTER *385*
In Egypt
HEYES *595*
See: Genesis, Israel

Acts of the Apostles
Introductions, Commentaries
CAMERLYNCK *866*
FURNEAUX *999*
JACKSON and LAKE *1675*
STEINMANN *1761*
Sources
JUNGST *84*
Literary criticism
HARNACK *770, 951*
CADBURY *1270*
11:27–28 Prophecy of Abgarus
HARNACK *1616*
17:23 Altar to the Unknown God
HARNACK *499*
18:1–27 Prisca and Aquila
HARNACK *1616*
18:27–19:16 Paul's Third Journey:
cf. Michigan Papyrus. 1475
19:2 "Semicinctia" of Paul
NESTLE *418*
See: Papyrus, P⁴⁵
Textual Criticism
MORIN *1088*
CLARK *1665*

Acts of the Holy See
See: Biblical Commission, Councils, Encyclicals, Holy Office

Adonis-Tammuz
and Eshmun: BAUDISSIN *989*
in Hades: BAUDISSIN *1075*
Cult: PETERS *1217*
Feasts under Ptolemy II: GLOTZ *1368*
See: Mysteries (pagan), Religions

Ahasver
The Wandering Jew
KÖNIG *713*

Ahudemmeh and Maruta
Histories of (Syriac text)
NAU *727*

Ahikar
History and Wisdom of
NAU *838*
See: Tobias

'Ain Duq
Excavations of the Ecole biblique at:
1297

'Ain Kades 98

Alexandria
Divinities: LAFAYE *856*
Sibyl and infancy accounts: ERDMANN
1668
Jews and persecutions: BLUDAU *756*
Letter of Claudius: BELL *1431*
See: Diaspora, Mysteries (pagan),
Philo

Alexandrinus
See: Manuscripts (biblical)

Allat
Sanctuary at Iram: 1600

Alphabet
State of the question: 684
Pentateuch in cuneiform
NAVILLE *1177 1215*
See: Inscriptions, Mesa

Amarna (Tell el-)
Tablets
KNUDTZON *401*
THUREAU-DANGIN *1224*

Ambrosiaster
SOUTER *672*
MORIN *1088*

Amos
Meter
SIEVERS *787*
See: Israel, Prophets, Prophecies

Amwas
Church
BARNABAS of Alsace *454*
See: Emmaus, Inscriptions,
Kubaibeh

Angel of Yahweh 448

Antilegomena
PREUSCHEN *355*

265

Antioch
See: Canon of the OT
Antiochus IV Epiphanes
His death
  HOLLEAUX 1242
Apocalypse (of St. John)
Commentaries
  BENSON 260
  ROHR 1690
  SWETE 791
  WEISS, J. 853
Latin translations
  VOGELS 1337
Literary study
  WEISS, J. 675
And the present times
  SANGRAN Y GONZALEZ 1587
See: Apringius de Beja
Apocalypses, apocryphal
Jewish and Christian
  BURKITT 1234
of the OT
  See: Judaism
of the NT
  of Peter
  GEBHART 32
  of the Twelve Apostles
  HARRIS 277
Apocrypha
Collections
  Antilegomena
  PREUSCHEN 355
  Versions, Syriac and Arabian
  GIBSON 113
Introduction to Apocr. of both Testaments
  SZEKELY 1046
In the early Church
  DAUBNEY 322
of the NT
  See: Acts, Apocalypses, Gospels, Judaism, Manicheism, Odes of Solomon, Transitus Mariae
Apocryphal Acts
of John: JAMES 197
of Paul and Thecla: GEBHARDT 388
of Peter: SCHMIDT 573
of Thomas: BORNKAMM 1710
of Pilate: DARLEY 1063
Forms and themes of apocryphal Acts: BLUMENTHAL 1707
See: Apocrypha
Apologetics
  BUYSSE 1432
  GAYRAUD 387 701
  GROOT (de) 704

  MIGNOT 347
  NOORT (VAN) 729
  VIGIL 46
  See: Church, Faith, Historical Method, Inerrancy, Problem of Jesus
Apostles
And disciples
  LE CAMUS 649
Mission
  LOISY 654
Work
  SCHUTZ 1375
Apringius of Beja
Comm. on the Apocalypse
  FÉROTIN 327
Aqueduct
To Jerusalem 309
Aquila
And Onkelos
  SILVERSTONE 1640
Prolegomena to a Lexicon
  REIDER 1179
Arabia
Pre-Islamic
  GUIDI 1392
  See: Islam
Aramaic
Grammar
  MARTI 125
Christian (translations, 7th c.)
  NAU 1580 1581
Talmudic
  MARGOLIS 894
Substratum of Gospels
  DALMAN 1403
  JOUON 1544
  See: NT: translations: Rabbula of Edessa, Sendjirli, Syriac
Arcana
Discipline of
  FEI 700
Archaeology
Of the OT:
  NAVILLE 1091 1092
Judaeo-Christian sarcophagus
  CUMONT 1172
  See: 'Ain Duq, Amwas, B. Djibrin, Chellal, Crete, Greece, Homs, Inscriptions, Islam, Jerusalem, Koushiva, Lihyanite, Madaba, Negeb, Palmyra, Rome, Syria
Aristeas (Letter of)
  See: Judaism: apocryphal texts

Aristotle (pseudo-) (*presumed author*)
De mundo 1477
Ark of the Covenant
POELS 173
ORFALI 1250
ARNOLD 1167
Armenian
Translation of Matthew and Mark
MACLER 1283
Ashera and Astarte 307
TORGE 439
See: Semites (religion of the)
Assyria
Grammar:
SCHEIL and FOSSEY 362
Dictionary:
MUSS-ARNOLT 86 130 561 661
Texts:
El-Amarna Tablets
KNUDTZON 401
Religious
MARTIN 345 492
Religion and magic
JASTROW 233
FOSSEY 473
Myths and epics
JENSEN 397
Archaeology and history
Chronology
THUREAU-DANGIN 1153
Political evolution
WINCKLER 301
Varia
SCHEIL 361
And the Bible
Sennacherib at Jerusalem
NAGEL 498
See: Ancient Peoples, Babylon
Astarte
See: Ashera
Astronomy
And the Bible
WINCKLER 366
Attis 1476
See: Mysteries (pagan), Religions
Augustine, St.
De Consensu Evangelistarum
VOGELS 852
Catholicism of
BATIFFOL 1301
Jerome and Augustine 219
Varia
CASAMASSA 1607
See: Itala, Vulgate

Babylon
Collection of texts
MARTIN 345 492
NIKEL 602
SCHRADER 433 508
WINCKLER 515
Particular texts
Babylonian letters
UNGNAD 1154
Contracts
FRIEDRICH 633
Creation and the Deluge
POEBEL 1148
BARTON 1168
El-Amarna tablets
THUREAU-DANGIN 1224
Gilgamesh (fragment)
MEISSNER 415
Hunting with falcons
MEISSNER 414
Myths and epics (epopees)
JENSEN 397
Prayers to Marduk
HEHN 637
Various works
SCHEIL 359 1222
Babylon and the Bible
DELITZCH 383
DÖLLER 471
GUNKEL 479
HEHN 549
HOMMEL 394
JASTROW 1142
JEREMIAS 485
KÖNIG 645 646
LOISY 410
NIKEL 602
SCHRADER 433 508
WINCKLER 676
ZIMMERN 368
Religion
JASTROW 233
ZIMMERN 310
History and archaeology (Babylon.)
Date of first dynasties
LINDL 409
Political evolution
WINCKLER 310
Temple of Bel
HILPRECHT 481
Babylonian Culture
WINCKLER 513
See: Ancient Peoples, Assyria, Hammurabi, Nippur, Religions, Umma
Balsamen (God of heaven)
LIDZBARSKI 489
See: Semites (religion of the)

Baptism
Jewish
   BRANDT *864*
Christian
   HEITMULLER *638*
   See: Jesus
Barnabas, Letter of
   HEER *818*
Baruch
Commentary
   PAFFRATH *1632*
1–3:8 authenticity of
   STODERL *1378*
Ancient Latin version
   HOBERG *482*
   See: Israel, Judaism: apocryphal
   texts, Prophets, Prophecies
Basilica
Of Porta Maggiore
   CARPOCINO *1479 1480*
   See: Pythagoras
Batiffol, P. 1521
Beatty, Chester
   See: Papyrus
Beelzeboul
   LOISY *654*
Behnessa
   See: Logia
Beit-Djibrin
Hypogea 370
Mosaics 1343
Berossus
Cosmogony 180
Bersabee
   See: Inscriptions
Bethabara
   See: Bethany
Bethany beyond the Jordan
Tradition of Origen 69
Bethlehem
Tombs 71
Beza
   See: Manuscripts
Bible
Introduction to the whole
   BOX *1606*
   BRASSAC *757 936 1302*
   CARPENTER *463*
   CORNELY *270 942*
   GIGOT *333*
   HOPFL *597*
   MADER *835*
   MESSMER *968*
   POPE *1096 1251 1414*

General commentary
   FILLION *31*
   See: Biblical Question, Canon,
   Hermeneutics, Historical Method,
   Inspiration, Inerrancy, Manu-
   scripts, NT, OT, Study and Read-
   ing, Versions
Biblical Chronology
   LESÊTRE *652*
   See: Jesus: Public Ministry
Biblical Question
   ANONYMOUS *19 152*
   ARINTERO *312*
   BRÜCKER *758*
   BRUSTON *621*
   CERESETO *465*
   CIVILTÀ CATTOLICA *470 1231*
   DELATTRE *591*
   DESSAILLY *271*
   FONCK *630*
   HOUTIN *396 641*
   JORDAN *825*
   LOISY *779*
   MAGNIN *412*
   MARGIVAL *200*
   MAZOYER *127*
   MERTENS *896*
   MIGNOT *347 897 898*
   NISIUS *290*
   SCERBO *571*
   SCHIFFINI *668*
   See: Historical Method, Holy
   Office, Inspiration, Inerrancy,
   Loisy, Pentateuch, Providentis-
   simus
Bostan-esh-Sheikh
   See: Saida
Bouvier, Abbé Claude
Biography:
   BOUVIER and HEMMER *1461*
Brothers of Jesus
   DURAND *998*
   ZAHN *304*

Caesarean (text) 1518
   See: Biblical Manuscripts: Kori-
   dethi, Ferrar
Calmet, Dom
   See: Exegesis
Canaan
At the time of the Israelite migra-
tion
   ERBT *697*
Religion
   WOOD *1183*
   See: Israel

Canon (of OT and NT)
History
  ZARB *1766*

Canon of the OT
Beginnings
  GLATIGNY *703 767*
At Antioch
  DENNEFELD *869*
In the Greek Church
  JUGIE *826*
Authority of the deuterocanonical books
  PÖRTNER *40*
  See: Judaism: apocryphal texts

Canon of the NT
Early history of 1654 1737 **1652**
  BAUER *531*
  DAUSCH *79*
  DUFOURCQ *871*
  JACQUIER *958*
  HARNACK *1241*
  LEIPOLDT *715 829*
  ZAHN *304*
  See: Apocrypha of the NT, Clement of Alexandria, Muratori

Canticle of Canticles
Commentaries
  HAUPT *771*
  SCHLÖGL *431*
  ZAPLETAL *794*

Canticles
  See: Exodus, Isaias, Judges, Magnificat, Numbers, OT, Psalms

Captivity of the Jews
  TOSTIVINT *140*

Captivity of St. Paul
At Ephesus?
  MICHAELIS *1579*

Captivity, Letters of the
Commentaries
  KNABENBAUER *1042*
  MEINERTZ and TILLMANN *1577*
Place and date
  MICHAELIS *1578*
  SCHMID *1638*
  See: Captivity of Paul, Colossians, Ephesians, Paul, Pauline Epistles, Philippians, Philemon

Carthage
Punic Necropolis
  GAUCKLER *1137*

Catholicism
Early Church
  BATIFFOL *799*

Peace of Constantine
  BATIFFOL *1115*
St. Augustine
  BATIFFOL *1301*

Chellal
Mosaic 1165

Christianity
Origin and growth
  DOBSCHÜTZ *384*
  GARDNER *766*
  HÖNNICKE *822*
  MEIER *1373*
  KUNDSIN *1546*
  WEISS, J. *1259 1339*
And history of religions
  CLEMEN *807*
  GUNKEL *546*
  KITTEL, G. *1677*
And civilization
  CAUSSE *1306*
According to German Exegesis 1185
  GARDNER *330*
  HARNACK *336*
  ROLFFS *425*
  See: Catholicism, Church, Jesus, Mysteries (pagan), Paul, Problem of Jesus, Religions

Christology
Of the NT
  GRANBERRY *877*
Of Hebrews
  MAC NEILL *1246*
Of St. Justin
  FEDER *699*
Ancient and Modern
  SANDAY *905*
Incarnation
  GORE *114*
Knowledge of Christ
  Holy Office *1221*
Personality of Jesus
  SANDAY *1021*
Prayer of Jesus
  BERNARDIN *1706*
Preexistence and Kenosis
  SCHUMACHER *1099*
Redemption
  MÉLANGES *1754*
  See: Dogmas, Jesus, Problem of Jesus, Theology

Chronicles (book of)
Commentaries
  BENZINGER *314*
  HUMMELAUER *710*

City of David
  See: Sion

Church
History
    DUFOURCQ *1507*
    LIETZMANN *1681*
Organization and dogma
    BATIFFOL *799 1115*
    BRUDERS *535*
    LOISY *490*
    RUFFINI *1327*
    SEMERIA *575*
    STREETER *1555*
Treatises "De Ecclesia"
    BAINVEL *687*
    GROOT (DE) *704*
    HERBIGNY (D') *1314*
    See: Biblical Question, Didache, Ephesians (epistle to), Primacy

Churches
American Church
    HEADLAM *1743*
Reunion of Churches 1261

Cicero
Religion of, acc. to "De Natura Deorum" 1494

Claudius
Letter to the Jews of Alexandria
    BELL *1431*

Clement of Alexandria
The 70 Weeks of Daniel
    HOZAKOWSKI *1007*
Canon of the NT
    DAUSCH *79*

Climaci rescriptus
    See: Syriac: versions and manuscripts

Colossians (epistle to the)
Commentary
    ABBOTT *184*
    See: Captivity (letters of the), Pauline epistles

Comma Joanneum
    RIGGENBACH *1551*
    See: John (letters)

Commission, Biblical
Reply concerning the Acts
    PIROT *1289*

Concordances
Hebrew
    MANDELKERN *126 238*
Greek (LXX)
    HATCH and REDPATH *35 82 166 356*

Concordism
    See: Creation, Historical Method, Inerrancy

Congress
Catholics
    Paris (1891) *15*
    Fribourg (1897) *160*
    Munich (1901) *319*
History of religions
    Oxford (1908) *809*
Orientalists
    London (1892) *26*
    Geneva (1893) *54*
    Paris (1897) *161*
    Algiers (1905) *624*

Consciousness, Messianic
    See: Messias, Jesus as

Coptic
Grammar
    STEINDORFF *90*
Bohairic version
    HOSKIER *1006*
Sahidic texts
    BUDGE *1058*
Mss.: Morgan Collection
    HYVERNAT *1279*
Mss.: bilingual, NT
    AMELINEAU *101*
Apocryphal gospels
    ROBINSON *135*
Psalter: Freer Collection
    WORREL *1159*

Corinthians, Epistles to
Three epistles
    BRUSTON *1193*
Commentaries
    1–2 Corinthians
        SICKENBERGER *1692*
    1 Corinthians
        ROBERTSON and PLUMMER *1019*
    2 Cor 3:17 "Dominus autem Spiritus est"
        HOLZMEISTER *820*
    See: Henoch, Pauline Epistles

Corpus Inscriptionum Semiticarum
    See: Inscriptions

Couchoud, P. L.
Reply to a letter: 1498
    See: Problem of Jesus

Creation
Age of the world
    KOPPEL *1754*
According to Genesis
    HUMMELAUER *195 230*
    JUNKER *1619*
    MARTINELLI *721*
    ZAPLETAL *1027*
    Gen 2:4–3:25
        AYLES *588*

See: Babylon, Berossus, Earthly
Paradise, Evolution, Genesis, Historical Method, Pentateuch,
Sumer
Crete, ancient 680 743
Aegean palace and civilization
MACKENSIE *833*
Scripta Minoa
EVANS *873*
See: Hagia Triada
Criticism, textual, of the NT
Introduction and general studies 1656
1735
GREGORY *334 389 815 816 949*
HARNACK *1276 1616*
HETZENAUER *337*
HUTTON *956*
NESTLE *131 289*
SALMON *207*
SCHÜTZ *1329*
SICKENBERGER *1728*
SODEN (VON) *788, 913, 1045*
TRUYOLS *1225*
TURNER *1334*
VAGANAY *1732*
VOGELS *1422*
WEISS, B. *251*
Particular studies
Before the Council of Trent 1739
Caesarean Text 1518
Harmonizations due to Marcion
CHAPMAN *1308*
NT Revision by Jerome
CAVALLERA *1237*
Origen (topographical tradition)
69 95
Parallelism
SCHÜTZ *1329*
Western Text
BOVER *1462*
See: Exegesis, Harnack, Hermeneutics, Manuscripts, Papyrus, Versions
Cross
See: Stauros (Grk)
Cuneiform
See: Alphabet, Amarna, Assyria,
Babylon, Elan
Cynics 1519

Daniel
And the Critics
WRIGHT *741*
Commentaries
CHARLES *1537*
DYNELEY PRINCE *224*
MARTI *344*

Greek additions
JULIUS *398*
Literary and exegetical studies
JUNKER *1618*
Messianic Prophecies 524
See: Clement of Alexandria, Israel, Prophecies, Prophets
Dante
Realism and Symbolism 1782
Daphné, Vigne 1108
Dead (the) and the Future Life
According to Mazdeism
SODERBLOM *435*
Among the Semites 373
In ancient Israel
LODS *718*
In Egypt
WIEDEMAN *299*
Cult of the dead
KLAUSNER *1511*
Dead Sea
GAUTIER *331*
Debora
See: Judges
Deluge
Universality
ARINTERO *12 153*
VALBUENA *298*
See: Babylon, Genesis, Sumer
Deuterocanonical books, authority
Of the OT
PÖRTNER *40*
Deuteronomy
Commentaries
BERTHOLET *261*
DRIVER *108*
HUMMELAUER *399*
SMITH *1255*
STEUERNAGEL *295*
See: Israel, Manuscripts
Djedeideh (Tell ed-)
Bliss excavations 258
Diaspora, Jewish
*Judaism of the Diaspora, and the
Mysteries*
GOODENOUGH *1775*
At Alexandria
CERFAUX 1560 *1433*
At Damascus 984
In Egypt 1534
BELL *1431*
BLUDAU *756*
In the Roman Empire
JUSTER *1209*

Jewish Philosophers
  BOUILLON *1056*
  See: Judaism, Philo
Diatessaron
  Text and History
    JULICHER *1410*
    VOGELS *1421*
  Arab translation
    EURINGER *1065*
  Greek Fragment 1738
  Relations with ancient Syriac versions 1264
    HJELT *392*
  See: Ephrem, Syriac
Diatribe, Stoic
  In St. Paul
    BULTMANN *937*
Dictionaries
  See: Assyrian, Encyclopedia, Greek,
    Hebrew, Theology
Didache
  Paschal ritual and St. John's Gospel
    GREIFF *1541*
  See: Literature: Ancient Christian
Didascalia
  Translation of the Syriac
    NAU *1012*
  Latin fragments of Verona
    HAULER *279*
Diodorus of Tarsus
  Commentary on the psalms
    MARIES *1722*
Dionysos
  See: Orphism
Disciples
  See: Apostles
Divinity of Jesus 1501 1736
  CELLINI *806*
  HOLLARD *1316*
  GRANDMAISON *1436*
  LEPIN *556 651*
  See: Jesus, Problem of Jesus
Divorce
  In the Bible
    MINOCCHI *493*
  In the NT
    MAC RORY *1752*
Dogma
  Among the Fathers
    AMANN *1348*
  Development of
    FEI *700*
  In the OT 444

According to Newman 1657
  GUITTON *1672*
  See: Christology, Eucharist, Modernism, Justification, Redemption, Resurrection of the Body, Trinity
Dormition of the Blessed Virgin
  And the house of John Mark 217
'Ebed Yahweh
  See: Isaias
Ecclesiastes
  See: Qohelet
Ecclesiasticus
  Commentaries
    KNABENBAUER *400*
    LEVI *408*
  Hebrew Text
    PETERS *504*
Ecole Biblique
  Foundation 47
  After 25 years 1113
  Impressions of the Holy Land
    MINOCCHI *723*
Edessa
  See: Rabbula
Editions, critical
  See: OT, NT Versions
Egerton
  See: Apocryphal gospels, Papyrus
Egypt
  History and archaeology
    Antiquities of the Cairo museum
      SPIEGELBERG *845*
    Chronology
      PESERICO *1288*
    Royal lists
      MÜLLER *351*
    XVIII and XIX Dynasties
      MÜLLER *599*
    The Sons of Misraim
      MÜLLER *497*
    Treaty of Ramses II with Hethites
      MASPERO *496*
    Voyage of Unu-Amon in Phoenicia
    nicia
      MÜLLER *352*
  Varia
    SCHEIL *361*
  And the Bible
    HEYES *595*
    MALLON *1371*
    MIKETTA *601*
    VALBUENA *297 440*

Religion and morals 1534
  BAILLET *526 527*
  WIEDEMAN *299*
  See: Alexandria, Amarna, Ancient
  Peoples, Diaspora, Elephantine,
  Exodus, Hermetism, Isis and
  Osiris, Pagan Mysteries, Papyrus,
  Religions, Seraphis
Egyptian
  Grammar
  ERMANN *80*
  STEINDORFF *90*
  Marginal glosses in the OT
  SPEIGELBERG 607
  See: Coptic
El and Yahweh
  See: Yahweh
Elam 308
  Texts
  SCHEIL *360 429 572*
  See: Susa
Elephantine
  Excavations 748
  Jewish Colony 982
  HOONACKER (VAN) *1118*
  Papyrus and ostraca 681 749
  SACHAU *1020*
  Various works 988
Eleusis
  Mysteries of 1229 1516
  BRILLANT *1303*
  FOUCART *1068*
Elias
  Expectation of his return
  SCOTT *1489*
Emesene
  See: Inscriptions
Emmanuel
  See: Isaias
Emmaus
  Question of Emmaus in Luke
  SCHIFFERS 61
  See: Amwas, Kubaibeh
Encyclical
  Providentissimus Deus 63 1599
  POELS *605*
Encyclopedia
  CHEYNE *318 378 469*
  HASTINGS *278*
  VIGOUROUX *46ᵃ 250ᵃ 441*
  HAUCK (Realencyclopedia) *192
  547*
Enoch
  See: Henoch

Ephesians, epistle to
  Addressees and vocabulary
  SCHMID *1527*
  Christ and the Church
  SCHLIER *1589*
  Commentaries
  ABBOTT *184*
  BELSER *800*
  HITCHCOCK *1077*
  VOSTÉ *1380*
  See: Captivity (Letters of), Epis-
  tles, Pauline, Paul
Ephod
  ARNOLD *1167*
Ephrem, St.
  Commentary on the Diatessaron
  HARRIS *115*
  Citations of Scripture
  BURKITT *377*
Epictetus
  *Religious Philosophy of, and Chris-
  tianity* 983
  PEPE *1178*
Epigraphy
  Christian (manual)
  MARUCCHI *895*
  Semitic
  Ephemerides
  LIDZBARSKI *287*
  See: Inscriptions
Epistles, Catholic
  Commentaries and critique
  CAMERLYNCK *865*
  MEINERTZ and VREDE *1628*
  MICHAELIS *1578*
  See: Freising, James, John, Peter
Epistles, Pauline
  Text
  Codex H
  LAKE *648*
  Fragment of Freising
  BRUYNE *1354*
  Papyrus Chester Beatty (P⁴⁶)
  1704
  SANDERS *1759*
  LIETZMANN *1751*
  General Commentaries
  CALLAN *1389*
  LEMONNYER *598*
  TOUSSAINT *1103*
  Vocabulary and style
  NÄGELI *726*
  BULTMANN *937*

See: Ambrosiaster, Captivity (ep. of), Cor., Gal., Pagan Mysteries, Pastorals, Paul, Pelagius, Prologues, Thessalonians

Eschatology
Jewish
    VOLZ *577*
In Job
    ROYER *428*
In Wisdom 679
In the Gospel 613 **1185**
    HAUPT *116*
    WEISS, J. *579*
    LOISY *490 654*
    MICHAELIS *1631*
    WENDLAND *1648*
In Primitive Christianity
    DEWICK *996*
Excesses in interpretation
    FEINE *1075*
See: Apocalypses, Judaism, Son of Man, Paul, Parousia, Problem of Jesus, Kingdom of God

Esdras
Composition and historical value
    TORREY *249*
According to the LXX
    WALDE *1106*
See: Israel, Judaism: apocryphal texts, Nehemias

Eshmun
Adonis and Eshmun
    BAUDISSIN *989*
See: Inscriptions: Saïda

Esther
Commentary
    STREANE *790*

Etudes bibliques
Projet d'un commentaire complet 257

Eucharist
During the first six centuries
    RAUSCHEN *902*
Fractio panis
    EJARQUE *1239*
Real Presence and Transubstantiation
    BATIFFOL *1054*
Sacrament and sacrifice
    GOOSSENS *1615*
See: Arcana, Didache

Eusebius
Adversus Marcellum (GCS)
    KLOSTERMANN *644*
Historia ecclesiastica (GCS)
    SCHWARTZ *910*
Demonstratio evangelica (GCS)
    HEIKEL *1074*

Hieronymi Chronicon (GCS)
    HELM *1076*

Euthalius
Colometry
    ROBINSON *134*

Evolution
Divine Plan
    PETAVEL-OLLIFF *503*
And Creation
    PAQUIER *1633*
And Theology
    MESSENGER *1630*

Excavations 211 215
Fifty years work in the Holy Land
    WATSON *1157*
See: 'Ain Duq, Beit-Djibrin, Crete, Djedeideh, Elephantine, Gezer, Hesy, Jerusalem, Palmyra, Saïda, Sippar, Susa
See: Inscriptions

Exegesis, Catholic
Principles 4 63 254 257 683 **1185**
    BONACCORSI *589*
    CELLINI *692*
    HÖPFL *395*
    LE MORIN *716*
    NISIUS *290*
    PEGUES *562*
    SCHIFFINI *668*
    ZAPLETAL *1028*
See: Biblical Commission, Biblical Question, Encyclical, Hermeneutics, Historical Method, Holy Office, Inspiration, Modernism, Study and Reading of the Bible
Albert the Great
    VACCARI *1696*
    VOSTÉ *1697*
Calmet
    NOURRY *201*
Theodore of Mopsuestia
    PIROT *1095*
Tyconius
    BURKITT *75*

Exegesis, Protestant
In Germany 1263 **1185**
Toward Understanding the NT
    FASCHER *1538*

Exegesis, Rabbinic
See: Rabbinism

Exodus
Commentaries
    HOLZINGER *338*
    HUMMELAUER *196*
Pharao of the Exodus
    MIKETTA *601*

Itinerary of the Israelites 253
   VERNES *1156*
Canticle of Moses (15:1–18) 216
   See: 'Aïn Kades, Gessen, Israel,
   Mekilta, Moses, Pentateuch, Sinai

Ezechiel
Allegory of the bride
   HALÉVY *34*
   See: Israel, Prophets, Prophecies,
   Raschi

Faith
Christian: God
   HEADLAM *1743*
And the Law
   BOYSSON (DE) *992*
And reason
   GAYRAUD *701*
Crisis
   GAYRAUD *387*
Pistis-hypostasis
   MATHIS *1321*
   See: Apologetics, Paul: justifica-
   tion

Fathers, apostolic
Use of the NT
   OXFORD *603*

Ferrar (group)
   See: Greek manuscripts

Flora, Palestinian
   FONCK *275*

Form Criticism
   BERTRAM *1388*
   BLUMENTHAL *1707*
   BULTMANN *1355 1417*
   DIBELIUS *1417*
   FLORIT *1773*
   FIEBIG *1075*
   SCHMIDT *1417*
   TAYLOR *1730*

Freer
Logion of Mark:
   GREGORY *768*
   See: Greek manuscripts

Freising
Fragments of letters
   BRUYNE (DE) *1354*

Gadarenians
Topographical tradition (Origen) 69
   ZAHN *517*

Galatians (letters to)
Text 1164
Commentaries **1184**
   BLUNT *1459*
   LIETZMANN *1624*

   LOISY *1147*
   SICKENBERGER *1291*
   STEINMANN *1292 1776*
Date and addresses 1262
   WEBER *365*
   STEINMANN *846*
Judaisers 1163
   ROPES *1553*
Apologia of Paul
   BELSER *103*
   See: Epistles, Pauline; Paul.

Galilee
   VRÉGILLE *1026*
   See: Geography, Biblical, Palestine

Genesis
Commentaries **609**
   BALL *154*
   DRIVER *542*
   GUNKEL *335*
   HOLZINGER *193*
   MURILLO *1090*
   RYLE *1252*
   SKINNER *977*
Gen 1–3
   MARTINELLI *721*
Gen 2:4–3:25
   AYLES *588*
Gen 3:14
   HAUPT *1173*
Gen 10 (Sons of Misraim)
   MÜLLER *497*
Gen 49 (Prophecy of Jacob) 181
Authenticity and theory of documents
   1786
Doublets
   ALLGEIER *929*
Indian origin
   BROSSE *158*
Jewish Tradition 182
   See: Abraham, Babylon, Deluge, In-
   nocence and sin, Israel Origins
   of the World, OT, Paradise, Patri-
   archs, Pentateuch, Prophecies,
   Semites

Geography, biblical
Ancient East
   HOMMEL *596*
Palestine and Syria
   Anonymous 73
   BAEDEKER *29*
Itinerarium curiense
   MADER *38*
Searching for biblical sites 925
   See: Abilene, 'Ain Duq, 'Ain Kades
   Crete, Dead Sea, Gadarenians,
   Gessen, Gezer, Hesy (Tell-el),
   Jordan, Masada, Mizzeh, Moab,

Nazareth, Negeb, Palestine, Petra, Philistia, Phounon, Sinai, Syria, Zin

Gerasenians
See: Gadarenians

Gergesenians
See: Gadarenians

Gessen
Itinerary of the Israelites 253

Gezer
Excavations 211 215

Gnosticism
DUCHESNE *997*
BUONAJUTI *760*

Goethe
His religion 1604

Golenischeff
See: Egypt — voyage of Unu-Amon

Gospels
Meaning of word
SEEBURG *606*
Commentaries — general 1493
BREEN *262 619*
CORNELIUS A LAPIDE *1093*
MORTIER *1468*
ZARANTONELLO *1029*
Criticism, literary and philological
ABBOT *753*
BATIFFOL *617 933*
HARNACK *951*
LEPIN *961*
MÜLLER *837*
TAYLOR *1592*
NESTLE *131*
Historical documents
BATIFFOL *933*
STANTON *915 1377*
Moral questions
Love of God 1563
Morale and morals
BAYET **1559**
Sources
SCHÜTZ *1375*
SOIRON *1376*
STREETER *1444*
TAYLOR *1730*
Nationalism
BARTHAS *1660*
Social message
GIARDINO *1774*
War 1533
See: Apocryphal gospels, Form Criticism, Isho'dad, Jesus, NT, Prologues, Synopses, Synoptics

Gospels, apocryphal
Collections
MICHEL *969*
PEETERS *1094*
PREUSCHEN *355*
Protoevangelium of James
AMANN *860*
LEWIS *488*
Story of Joseph the Carpenter
PEETERS *971*
Infancy Gospel
RESCH *203*
New Infancy gospel
JAMES *1497*
Gospel of Peter
GEBHARDT *32*
Gospel of the Hebrews 1344 1784
Gospel of the 12 Apostles
HARRIS *277*
Judeo-Christian gospels
SCHMIDTKE *1022*
Unknown Gospel (Egerton)
BELL *1738*
Transitus Mariae
LEWIS *488*
Parallels
RESCH *133*
Coptic fragments
ROBINSON *135*
Logia and Agrapha
TAYLOR *248*
See: Canon of the NT, NT Apocrypha, Papyrus

Greek
Grammars of biblical Greek
MOULTON *1394*
VITEAU *91*
WINER *92*
Dictionaries and lexicons
ABBOTT-SMITH *1387*
BAUER-PREUSCHEN *1429 1457*
SOUTER *1152*
Special readings
BONACCORSI *688 1708*
DEISSMANN *190*
PERNOT *1469*
See: Papyrus

Greeks
Archaeology, Greco-Latin, and the Gospels
VALBUENA *922*
Goddesses, nude
REINACH *423*
Greek miracle and the rhythm of art 1031 1108
Religious feeling 1478
See: Pagan mysteries, Philosophy

Gunkel
See: Mélanges

Habacuc
The Prophet
PEISER 501
See: Israel, Prophets, Prophecies

Habiri 213

Hagia Triada
Sarcophagus
PARIBENI 840
See: Crete

Hagiography
Hagiographical legends
DELAHAYE 627
Saint Nino
Studia biblica 437
Saint Justin 1049
FEDER 699
Melania the Younger
RAMPOLLA 665

Hamites
Vicwa-Mitra 21

Hammurabi
Code of
GRIMME 477
JONES 486
MÜLLER 560
WINCKLER 514
Price of interest
CUQ 1202
Hammurabi and Moses
COOK 540
GRIMME 477
Homicide 1127
See: Babylon

Harnack
Textual Criticism of the NT
HETZENAUER 1315

Harris
See: Mélanges

Hebrew tongue
History
KÖNIG 405
MINOCCHI 495
Dictionaries
GESENIUS 112
LINDEMANN 1245
KÖNIG 960
SIEGFRIED and STADE 137
Grammars
CHABOT 105
UBACH 1226 1256

Writing
NAVILLE 1092
See: Inscriptions: Mesa
Philological notes
Accents and vocalization
GRIMME 163
Meter
CORNILL 320
GRIMME 390
SIEVERS 787
Selah-Diapsalma
BRIGGS 263
PARISOT 291
Strophes and Responses
MÜLLER 241 900
Style, theory of
KÖNIG 404

Hebrews
See: Israel, Judaism

Hebrews, epistle to
Commentaries
HOLLMANN 853
ROHR 1690
WINDISCH 1260
Christology
MACNEILL 1246
Literary Criticism
HEIGL 707
WREDE 740
11:1 pistis-hypostasis
MATHIS 1321

Hebrews, gospel of
SCHMIDTKE 1784
See: NT apocrypha, apocryphal
gospels

Henoch
Book of
CHARLES 694
MARTIN, DELAPORTE, etc. 656
Influence on Paul
HARRIS 1369
Parables and messianism
GRY 880
Son of Man
MESSEL 1372
3rd Henoch (Hebrew)
ODEBERG 1549
See: Judaism: apocryphal texts,
Son of Man

Heraclitus
See: Logos

Heretics
Falsification of the Scriptures
BLUDAU 1458
See: Manicheans, Marcion

Hermas
Fragments from Mt. Athos
    LAKE 777
Papyrus Codex
    BONNER 1709

Hermeneutics
Manuals
    HETZENAUER 480
    LE MORIN 716
    HÖPFL 597
    ZAPLETAL 794a
Senses of Scripture
    ASSOUAD 1349
    See: Biblical Question, Exegesis,
    Historical Method, Inspiration,
    Tyconius

Hermetism 1400 1426 1451 1473
African Hermetism
    CARCOPINO 1390
Corpus Hermeticum
    SCOTT 1442 1514

Herod
King Herod
    DUESBERG 1609
And St. Luke
    CRONIN 1272

Hesy (Tell-el)
English excavations 1351

Hesychius
Commentary on Leviticus
    VACCARI 1257
Interpretatio Isaiae
    FAULHABER 273

Hetheans
    See: Hittites

Hexameron
    See: Origin of the world

Hexateuch
    See: Pentateuch

Hippolytus
Canon of & Muratorian Fragment
    1654
Theology
    ALÈS (d') 754

History
And the "Providentissimus"
    POELS 605
    See: (Ancient) Peoples, Antiochus,
    Babylon, Capitivity, Church,
    Egypt, Inerrancy, Israel, Juda-
    ism, Nehemias, Origin of the
    world, Osee, Pentateuch, Proph-
    ets, Religions, Wellhausen

Hittites
Migration
    CARA (DE) 55
Treaty with Ramses II
    MÜLLER 496

Holleaux
    See: Mélanges

Holy Office
Decree "Lamentabili" 683 **1599**
Knowledge of Christ 1221

Holy Sepulcher
    See: Inscriptions: Kufic

Holy Spirit
In the NT
    SWETE 919
In St. Paul
    MICHAELIS 1631
    FUCHS 1669
Nature and operation
    NOSGEN 730

Homs
Bas-relief
    RONZEVALLE 426

Hope
In the NT
    ALÈS (D') 1129
    SPICQ 1641
In Primitive Christianity
    CAUSSE 805
    See: Messianism

Ignatius of Antioch
Letters
    DELAFOSSE-TURMEL 1506

Inerrancy, biblical
    DURAND 1037
Truth, absolute or relative
    HOLZHEY 885
    EGGER 872
    FONCK 630
    See: Exegesis, Historical method,
    Inspiration

Innocence and sin
In Genesis 147

Inscriptions
Amwas (Samaritan) 23 143
Anterior Asia
    SODERHEIM 671
Bersabee (imperial rescript) 520 610
Emesene (epigraphical notes)
    LAMMENS and MARTIMPREY 407
Eshmun
    See: Saïda
Hebrew 372
Jerusalem (Kufic, Holy Sepulchre)
    150

Khan Younes (Greek: dedication to St. George) 1166
Lambiridi
   CARCOPINO *1390*
Macedonian (Legal terms appearing in NT)
   FERGUSON *1066*
Madaba 141
Magnesia (relations with NT)
   THIEME 737
Mesa (King of Moab; Phoenician) 311 744
Minean
   See: South Arab
Nabateans
   Sabbatical year of 3 142 179
   CLERMONT-GANNEAU *379*
   Rights of the poor
   CLERMONT-GANNEAU *380*
Nazareth (Tomb violations)
   ZANCAN 1650
Negeb (Greek)
   SCHMIDT and CHARLES 908
Palmyrian (funerary) 8 372 745
   Two inscribed statues
   CLERMONT-GANNEAU *539*
Petra
   See: Nabatean
Phoenician 7
Quirinius (of Antioch)
   BOUR *187*
   DESSAU *1309*
Sabean
   See: South Arab
Saïda (Temple of Eshmun at Bostan esh-Sheikh)
   MACRIDI-BEY 375 450
Sepulcher (the Holy)
   See: Jerusalem
Samaritan
   See: Amwas
Sardis (bilingual: Lydian and Aramean)
   COOK *1170*
Semitic 27
   Corpus Inscriptionum Semit. 107 321 381
   Collection
   LITTMANN 653
Sendjirli
   Aramaic, land of Jodi 985, **446**
Sinaitic (from the Church of the Burning Bush) 28
   EUTING *17 109*
South Arab
   (Controversy Mineo-Sabeo-biblical) 374
   CLERMONT-GANNEAU *808*

Inspiration
  Treatises
   FRANZELIN *608* 96
   JOYCE *888*
   MAZELLA *657*
   MERKELBACH *1043*
   PESCH *663 1488*
   SCHIFFINI *668*
   SMITH *669*
   ZANECCHIA *252*
  Nature of 96
  Of the Gospels
   FEI *700*
  Thought of St. Thomas 70
  Thought of St. Jerome
   SCHADE *973*
  Verbal
   GRANNELLI *475*
  Sacred Writers and their Sources
   PRAT *354*
  Exigencies of criticism 99
   See: Bible, Exegesis, Catholic, Hermeneutics, Historical method, Inerrancy

Introductions
  See: Bible, NT, OT

Irenaeus, Saint
  Demonstratio apostol. praedic.
   WEBER *1294*
  Gospel citations
   KRAFT *1440*
  New Testament
   SANDAY *1416*
  Concerning the 4th Gospel
   GUTJAHR *594*
   LEWIS *831*

Isaias
  Introductions and commentaries
   CHEYNE *265–8*
   CONDAMIN *590*
   GRAY and PEAKE *1004*
  Literary Criticism
   CHEYNE *77*
   GLAZEBROOK *947*
  7:13–16 The Virgin and Emmanuel, 10
  9:1–6 The Messianic King
   BARNES *456*
  24–27 Apocalypse 49
  Servant Songs
   BUDDE *264*
   See: Hesychius, Israel, Prophets, Prophecies

Isaias
  Ascension of
   See: Judaism: apocryphal texts

Isho'dad of Merv
Commentary on the four Gospels
GIBSON *1001*
Isis
CLEMEN *1075*
DREXLER 856
GUIMET 856
Islam
Dynasty of the Lahmides
ROTHSTEIN 244
Manuscripts: Arab-Christian
LEWIS 717
Mu'allaka des Zuhair
HAUSHEER 636
South Arabic Antiquities
HOMMEL 118
MÜLLER 350
WEBER 442
Works on
HOMMEL 117
See: Inscriptions, Minean, Mosque of Omar, Sabean
Israel
General History
GIGOT *191*
GUTHE 276
MENUGE *171*
PELT *421 604*
PIEPENBRING 292
SCHUSTER and HOLZAMMER *843*
SELBST and SCHÄFER *911*
TOUZARD *1180*
VANDERVORST *1155*
WINCKLER *366*
ZSCHOKKE *1341*
Religion and Belief
Religion of the OT (History of)
KÖNIG *1009*
Places of cult
GALL (VON) 227
Traditions and beliefs
CHEYNE 695
Future life
LODS 718
Heritage of Israel
ROBILLOT and MARTY *1636*
The "Anawim" (poor) of Israel
CAUSSE *1363*
See: Abraham, Ancient Peoples, Judaism, Prophets, Prophecies, Religions, Semites
Special Questions
Ancient tradition
HOMMEL *169*
Abraham and the beginnings of the Hebrew People
DORNSTETTER 385

Entry into Canaan
STEUERNAGEL *436*
History of Israelites at the time of Moses 218
Israelite tribes
LUTHER *411*
Captivity
TOSTIVINT *140*
History of Israel and Osee 6
Neighboring peoples
MEYER 722
Critical Studies
WINCKLER *366*
Itala 1735
Augustine, St.
BURKITT *1305*
DEBRUYNE *1354*
Old Latin and the Itala
BURKITT *1305*
Word study
MATZKOW *1723*
See: Versions of the Bible, *Latin, Vulgate*

Jacob
Prophecy 181
James, Epistle of
Commentaries
HOLLMANN *853*
BELSER *862*
MEINERTZ *1285*
ROPES *1290*
Authenticity
MEINERTZ 600
See: Epistles, Catholic
Jeremias
Epistle of
NAUMANN *1249*
BALL *1232*
Lamentations, Letter
PAFFRATH *1632*
Prophecies
DUHM 324
CONDAMIN *1364*
CORNILL 320
Vocation
HACKSPILL 391
See: Baruch, Israel, Judaism, Prophets, Prophecies
Jerome, Saint
And St. Augustine 219
And the Goths
ZEILLER *1778*
Biblical Inspiration
SCHADE 973
Genesis 182
Psalms
MORIN *1088*

Revision of the NT
   CAVALLERA *1237 1307*
Unedited homilies
   MORIN *1088*
Various studies
   SANDERS *507*
Vision of Isaias
   AMELLI *452*
   See: Vulgate

Jerusalem
  Aqueduct, Roman 309
  Eucharistic Lamp 28
  History of Buildings
   SCHICK *89*
  Mt. of Olives, Church 64
  Orphic mosaic 305 306
  Site of Cenacle
   BLISS 64 71
  Temple area 22
  Topography of the city 5
  War years at (1914–18) 1109
   See: Dormition, Gethsemani, In-
    scriptions, Madaba (mosaic),
    Orpheus (mosaic), Pretorium,
    Sion, Stephen

Jesus
  Chronology
   HOLZMEISTER *1715*
  Lives and general studies **1493**
   BARDY and TRICOT *1605*
   BOYER *991*
   CRISTIANI *1712*
   DUFOURCQ *1507*
   GALLEGOS ROCAFULL *1571*
   GRANDMAISON (DE) *1116*
   GOGUEL *1614*
   GUIGNEBERT *1671*
   KLAUSNER *1717*
   KLEIN *1718*
   LEBRETON *1623*
   LESÊTRE *18*
   MAURIAC *1768*
   PRAT *1727*
   RENAN *1189* **1384**
   WILLAM *1698*
   SICKENBERGER *1639*
  Infancy 65
   DURAND *813*
   BALDI *1456*
   OLLIVIER *731*
   MANY *1247*
   ERDMANN *1668*
   Genealogies
    HEER *953*
    VOGT *981*
   Conception and birth 1051
    GORE *114*

GRESHAM MACHEN *1542*
GOGUEL *1204*
HERZOG *708*
RAMSAY *1044*
Census
  See: Quirinius
Presentation in the Temple 1562
Public Ministry
  Baptism
   VOSTÉ *1764*
  Temptation
   LIBERTY *1146*
   VOSTÉ *1764*
  Duration of Public Ministry
   HOMANNER *821*
   PFATTISCH *1016*
   ZELLINGER *742*
  Miracles
   BOURCHANY *934*
   LUMINI *1721*
  Anointing *986*
  Testimony, Personal
   SCHUMACHER *1023*
   VOSTÉ *1764*
  Transfiguration
   DABROWSKI *1666*
  Apostolate among the pagans
   MEINERTZ *836 1467*
   SPITTA *914*
  Relations with political powers
   LIBERTY *1146*
  Last Trip to Jerusalem
   CADMAN *1402*
Teaching and doctrine
  Languages spoken
   DALMAN *1403*
   MEYER *128*
  Sayings and discourses
   HARNACK *706 1409*
  Teaching
   BATIFFOL *617*
   MANSON *1625*
  Sermon on the Mount
   GAMBER *1000*
   LANWER *1749*
   MÜLLER *900*
  Moral teaching
   ABBOTT *451*
   BAYET **1559**
   GIARDINO *1774*
  Use of Proverbs
   SMITH *509*
Passion
  BERTRAM *1388*
  CADMAN *1402*
  DALMAN *1403*
  DABROWSKI *1740*

DARD *1062*
DUESBERG *1609*
HARNACK *1616*
ROSADI *784*
STAURIDES *1729*
Resurrection and Appearances to Others
ADAM *1658*
BALDENSPERGER *1659*
CELLINI *693*
GOGUEL *1670*
JACQUIER *957*
LADEUZE *827*
LAKE *828*
MANGENOT *893*
ORR *839*
SWETE *847*
See: Apostles, Brothers of Jesus, Christology, Divinity of Christ, Eschatology, John the Baptist, Messianism, Myth of Jesus, Problem of Jesus, Quirinius, Son of Man, Tomb (empty)

Jesus, Non-canonical References
In Ancient Times
LINCK *1083*
LABRIOLLE *1746*
Josephus, Flavius
See: Josephus
See: Myth of Jesus

John, Epistles of
BAUMGARTEN *853*
BRESKY *801*
1 Jn 5:7–8 (Johannine Comma)
RIGGENBACH *1551*

John, Gospel of
Commentaries **1424**
BAUER *1661*
BELSER *618*
BROOKE *1036*
CALMES *622*
CARR *623*
KNABENBAUER *198*
KREYENBÜKL *647*
TILLMANN *1594*
VOSTÉ *1557*
Historicity **1781**
Main Idea **1452**
Relations with the Synoptics
LEPIN *891*
WINDISCH *1492*
Textual and literary criticism
ABBOTT *525*
BACON *1267 1705*
BURNEY *1358*
GREGORY *879*
HARNACK *1409 1616*

HÖRNLE *1574*
JACKSON *1243*
MONTGOMERY *1413*
WINDISCH *1417*
Vocabulary and style
ABBOTT *615 685*
GACHTER *1741*
WINDISCH *1417*
1:1–18 (Prologue)
BULTMANN *1417*
CELLINI *994*
2:1–12 (Cana)
GACHTER *1612*
LOISY *237*
13:1–17:26 (Farewell discourse)
GACHTER *1741*
See: Gospels, Irenaeus, John the Presbyter, Judaism, Mandeism, Mystique, Pagan Mysteries, Papias, Philo

John the Baptist
History of
BUZY *1359*
LOISY *654*
Relationship to Jesus
HOWARD *1700*
GUENIN *1714*
See: Josephus (Slavic), Mandeism

John the Presbyter
Author of the 4th Gospel?
CHAPMAN *940*
See: Papias

Job
CHAUVIN *1133*
Commentary
SZCYGIEL *1643*
Discourse of Elihu
LOISY *37*
POSSELT *841*
Eschatology
ROYER *428*
See: Julian of Eclane

Jonas
CONDAMIN *1134*
See: Israel, Prophets, Prophecies

Jordan 9 64 253

Josephus (Flavius)
The Man and the Historian
THACKERAY *1593*
Antiquities (transl.)
MATHIEU and HERMANN *1576*
Against Apion
BLUM *1566*
Concerning Jesus
REINACH *202*
War of the Jews (transl. Slavic) *1531*

Theory of R. Eisler
BAUER *1565*
DRAGUET *1568*
GOETHALS *1613*
JACK *1716*
WESENDONCK *1597*
ZEITLIN *1598 1651*

Josue
Commentary
HUMMELAUER *485*
See: Israel, Syriac

Jubilees, book of
See: Judaism: apocryphal texts

Judaism (from the 2nd Temple on)
586 795 **1558**
Apocryphal Texts
Apocalypse of Baruch
CHARLES *1197*
Apocalypse of Esdras
JAMES *121*
VIOLET *923*
Apocalyptic (Jewish)
BOUSSET *534*
Apocalypses (Jewish)
BURKITT *1234*
Apocrypha of the OT
CHARLES *1060*
KAUTZCH *284*
Aristeas, Letter of
THACKERAY *1223*
Ascension of Isaias
TISSERANT *850*
Assumption of Moses
CHARLES *189*
Henoch (*See:* Henoch)
CHARLES *694*
MARTIN *656*
Jubilees
SINGER *247*
Psalms of Solomon
FRANKENBERG *226*
RYLE and JAMES *42*
TORREY *249*
Sibylline Oracles
GEFFCKEN *545*
Testament of the 12 Patriarchs
CHARLES *761 762*
History
BROWNE *1304*
DUJARDIN *628*
KÖNIG *712*
MEYER *1373*
REGNAULT *903*
SCHÜRER *245 786 909*
SELLIN *246*
Religion
BONSIRVEN *1771*

BOUSSET *459*
PERLES *502*
REINACH *357*
Sects
Pharisees
LOISY *654*
Sadducees
HOLSCHER *709*
Sadokites
MARMORSTEIN *1214*
Of the New Alliance (Damascus)
984
See: Diaspora, Kingdom of God,
Mazdeism, Mekilta, Messianism,
Mishna, Philo, Purifications,
Rabbinism, Talmud

Judas Iscariot
In the NT
HAUGG *1572*

Judeo-Christianity
See: Christianity

Judith
History and literary genre
SCHULZ *974*
STEINMETZER *789*
CONDAMIN *1135*

Judges 445
Commentaries
BUDDE *188*
BURNEY *1235*
MOORE *348*
ZAPLETAL *1423*
5: (*Canticle of Debora*) 256
VERNES *45*
ZAPLETAL *677*
11:30–39 (*Jephthe's Vow*)
HOONACKER (VAN) *57*

Julian the Apostate
Letters
BIDEZ *1503*
Retreat-Master 1502

Julian of Eclane
Commentary on Job
VACCARI *1123*

Justification
See: Paul

Justin, St., 1049
Dialogue with Trypho
ARCHAMBAULT *861*
Life 1049
Doctrine concerning Jesus Christ
FEDER *699*

Kenosis
SCHUMACHER *1099*
See: Philippians (epistle to)

Khabiri 213

Kingdom of God 746
In the OT
    BÖHMER *457*
In Judaism 750
In the Gospel
    CORDOVANI *1198*
    WEISS, J. *579*
In Mazdeism
    CARNOY *1362*
And the Church
    LOISY *490*
And the Spirit
    MICHAELIS *1631*

Kings, books of
Commentary
    KITTEL *285*
Note on Hebrew text
    BURNEY *461*
1 Kgs. 6:1 (480 years)
    GAMPERT *1203*
1 Kgs 17:17–24 (Widow of Sarephta)
    MACFAYEN *491*

Koridethi
See: Manuscripts (biblical)

Koushiva
Arab milestone 93

Kubaibeh
    BARNABAS D'ALSACE, *434*

Lambiridi
Tomb and mosaic
    CARCOPINO *1390*

Law (Rights)
Principle of Origin and its applications in Roman Law 1
Possession = title 1
Law of the poor (Nabateans)
    CLERMONT-GANNEAU *380*
Presumption of paternity (Hebrew)
    TISSET *1379*
See: Hammurabi, *Price of Interest*

Lazare, St.
Connections with St. Maximin
    MORIN *172*

Le Camus, Msgr.
On the Parousia 649

Legends
Epic
    BEDIER *1233*
Hagiographical
    DELAHAYE *627*

Letters, Christian
    WESSELY *793*

Leviticus
Commentaries
    HUMMELAUER *196*
    BERTHOLET *316*
Peculiarities of the Greek version
    HUBER *1278*
See: Hesychius, Israel, Pentateuch

Lihyanite
Sanctuary 796

Literature (Ancient Christian)
General history
    BARDENHEWER *529*
    BATIFFOL *155*
Literary History of Christian Africa (4th c.)
    MONCEAUX *724*
See: Ambrosiaster, Apringius of Beja, Augustine, Barnabas, Clement of Alexandria, Diodorus of Tarsus, Ephrem, Eusebius, Euthalius, Hesychius, Hippolytus, Ireneus, Isho'dad, Jerome, Justin, Letters (Christian), Nestorius, Pacian, Papyrus, Pelagius, Peter the Iberian, Rabbula, Rufinus, Syriac, Tatian

Logia
Freer Logion
    GREGORY *768*
See: Papias, Pre-evangelical Tradition, Synoptic Problem
Logia of Oxyrhynchus 1299, 1345
    THE TIMES *176*
    TAYLOR *248*
    WESSELY *793*
    WHITE *1340*
Logia agrapha
    BESSON *1401*
Logion joanneum (Mt 10:22 = Lk 11:27)
Source Q
    JEREMIAS *1575*
    SCHUMACHER *1023*

Logos
Of Heraclitus 1385
Of the Stoics 1386
Of Philo 1386
Of St. John 1386
Of St. Justin **1049**

Loisy
Exposition and Criticism
    LEPIN *830*
Jubilee
    COUCHOUD *1504*
Modernism 779 **1599**

Loretto
Shrine
  ALÈS (D') *1190*
And the Fresco of Gubbio
  FALOCI *698*

Luke
Commentaries **1296**
  BLASS *220*
  EASTON *1482*
  HAHN *33*
  LUCE *1683*
  PLUMMER *242*
  ROSE *569*
  SOUBIGOU *1693*
  WRIGHT *303*
Sources 62 94
  CADBURY *1360*
  SENSE *434*
Literary criticism
  CADBURY *1270*
  CRONIN *1272*
  HARNACK *635*
  TAYLOR *1490*
See: Testimonia
Lk 1–2 (Infancy Gospel) 65
Supernatural conception 1051
Birth of Jesus
  RAMSAY *1044*
  GRESHAM MACHEN *1542*
Christmas hymns
  AYTOUN *1266*
Presentation 1562
7:47 (Remittuntur ei peccata multa)
  BUZY *1236*
10:22 (Logion joanneum)
  SCHUMACHER *1023*
15:11–32 (Good Samaritan)
  GHIO *1070*
16:1–13 (Parable of the Unjust Steward)
  RUCKER *1097*
22:44–63 (Gethsemani)
  BOVER *1462*
See: Abilene, Amwas, Emmaus, Gospels, Kubaibeh, Lysanias, Magnificat, Parables, Quirinius, Synoptic Problem, Synoptics

Lucian
Recension of the Octateuch
  HAUTSCH *952*
See: Versions of the Bible

Lucian (priest)
Finding of relics of St. Stephen 255

Luther
Translation of the NT
  WEISS, B. *578*

Commentary on Romans 1114 1128
Pseudo-mysticism of 1185
Before the revolt 1125
The revolt **1186**
Christian Liberty
  WILL *1382*
Father of Lutheranism
  DENIFLE *541*

Maccabees
Commentary
  KNABENBAUER *711*
Wars
  DUESBERG *1609*
See: Israel

Madaba
Mission 306
Mosaic: geographical map 141
Jerusalem according to the mosaic 148
  SCHULTER *363*
Journies of Mr. Bliss 71

Magdalen
See: Mary Magdalen

Magic
Assyrian
  FOSSEY *473*
Origin (magical) of kings
  FRAZER *1310*

Magnesia
See: Inscriptions

Magnificat
Attributed to Elizabeth
  HARNACK *1616*
  LOISY *343*

Mandeism
And the gospel tradition 1474 1497
  STAHL *1591*
  TONDELLI *1695*

Manicheism
Neo-manicheism and the Christian legend
  DUFOURCQ *871*
Manichean writings
  ALFARIC *1265*

Manuscripts (biblical)
Greek
Collections
Bodleian
  MADAN *85*
British Museum
  KENYON *241*
Freer
  SANDERS *1253*
Venice
  LAKE *1748*

Mt. Sinai
  HATCH *1742*
Publications of
  GREGORY *815*
  LAKE *1747*
  SODEN (VON) *913*
  VOGELS *1556*
Descriptions
  A (Alexandrinus)
    KENYON *889 1119 1228*
  B (Vaticanus and allied mss)
    HOSKIER *1277*
  D (Beza)
    VOGELS *980*
  Hᴾ (Fragments from Mt. Athos)
    LAKE *648*
  N (Purple, Matthew)
    OMONT *420*
  W (Washington)
    SANDERS *972*
  Θ (Koridethi)
    BEERMANN 1518 *1034*
  Ψ (Athos) *437*
  Ω (Athos)
    LAKE *1720*
  543 (Ferrar Group)
    LAKE *1720*
  597 (Paris)
    SCHMIDTKE *576*
  614 (Milan)
    VALENTINE RICHARDS *1762*
  1071 (Ferrar Group) *437*
  1175 (Patmos)
    LAKE *1720*
  1342 (Jerusalem)
    LAKE *1720*
  1739 (Athos)
    LAKE *1720*
Latin
  ff and ff² (Corbiensis)
    BUCHANAN *759*
  h (Fleury)
    BUCHANAN *759*
  Rehdigeranus
    VOGELS *1105*
  Fragment: Atinoë
    GLANE & HELM *876*
Hebrew
  G–I–5 (Escorial)
    LLAMAS *1682*
  See: Polyglot
  See: Coptic, Papyrus, Syriac, Textual Criticism of NT, Vulgate

Marcion
  HARNACK *1312 1408*
Marcionism of Luke
  SENSE *434*

Marcionite Harmonisations
  CHAPMAN *1308*
Paul or Marcion 1601
  See: Ignatius of Antioch, Mass, Prologues
Marcus Aurelius
The Young Man, the Philosopher, the Emperor 1032
Marduk
  See: Babylon
Mark
  Commentaries 924 1342
    ALFARIC *1535*
    HUBY *1438*
    PLUMMER *1218*
    ROSE *568*
    TATON *1332*
    WELLHAUSEN *580*
  Literary criticism
    BACON *1455*
    SUNDWALL *1762*
    ROPES *1757*
  Textual criticism
    HYVERNAT *1279*
    LAKE *1700*
    MACLER *1283*
  Historicity
    BACON *1268*
  Latin Origin?
    COUCHOUD 1496 1498
  Paulinism
    WERNER *1446*
  Philological Notes
    PFEIFFER *1687*
  Jesus, acc. to Mark
    THOMPSON *979*
  5:20
  3:20–21 (Thought mad)
    HARTMANN *1041*
  11:12–14 (Cursing of Fig Tree)
    VIOLET *1417*
  16:9–20 (Final verses of)
    CONYBEARE *106*
    GREGORY *768*
  See: Gospels, Papias, Synoptic Problem, Synoptics (gospels)
Mary (Bl. Virgin)
  At Cana
    GÄCHTER *1612*
  See: Jesus, Virgin
Mary Magdalen (St.)
  Life
    SICARD *976*
  Question of the 3 Marys 986
  In ecclesiastical tradition
    HOLZMEISTER *1393*
    MORIN *172*

Maruta
See: Ahudemmeh

Maspero
His life and works
CAGNAT 1195

Mass
COULANGE (= TURMEL) 1505

Matthew (Gospel of)
Commentaries 1383
ROSE 567
MC NEILE 1212
DURAND 1404
ORIGEN (GCS) 1719
Text
OMONT 420
MACLER 1283
2.3 (Nazarenus vocabitur)
BURRAGE 1059
11:27 (Logion joanneum)
SCHUMACHER 1023
16:16–19 (Tu es Petrus)
HARNACK 1510
HERBIGNY 1314
STREETER 1555
WEISS, J. 739
22:1–14 (The Invited Guests)
SICKENBERGER 1554
25:41–26:39 (Eschatological Discourse. Cf. Papyrus of Vienne).
1655
26:19–52 (Last Supper Papyrus Michigan). 1517
28:16–20 (Last Appearances)
SWETE 511
See: Gospels, Logia, Origen, Synoptic Problem, Syntopics

Maximin, St.
MORIN 172

Mazdeism
Religion of Iran 1111
Reform of Zoroaster 522
GELDNER 1391
Salvation mysteries
REITZENSTEIN 1374
Kingdom of God
CARNOY 1362
Future Life
SÖDERBLOM 435
Persian religion and Judaism
SCHEFTELOWITZ 1396
See: Pagan Mysteries, Religions, Suza

Mekilta
Of Rabbi Ismael
HOROVITZ 1617

Mélanges
GUNKEL 1417
HARRIS 1700
HOLLEAUX 1078
LOISY 1504
SWETE 918
TIXERONT 1333
WELLHAUSEN 1085

Melania the Younger
RAMPOLLA 665

Mesha
Inscription 311 744

Messianism
In the Bible
PASTERIS 732
In the Psalms 584
Before the Exile
MÖLLER 780
After the Exile
SELLIN 246
In Later Judaism 795 1558
BALDENSPERGER 528
Time of Christ 586
In Primitive Christianity
CAUSSE 805
Among the Samaritans
MERX 59
HAMMER 1073
Among Jews of the Middle Ages
SILVER 1528
Development of Messianic hope
LOISY 235
See: Apocalyptic, Eschatology, Judaism, Prophets, Prophecies, Virgil

Messias, Jesus as
GRANDMAISON 1116
HOLTZMANN 776
LEPIN 556 651
PINARD DE LA BOULLAYE 1585
TONDELLI 1471
WREDE 516
See: Jesus, Josephus (Slavic), Problem of Jesus, Son of Man, Messianic Secret

Metanoia
In the NT
THOMPSON 848
DIRKSEN 1667

Method, Historical 444 583
Applied to the OT
HÜGEL 194
STEINMÜLLER 1785
SCERBO 571
In Theology
SANDAY 208

Solutions of P. Lagrange
  SALEILLES *570*
Concordism
  ARINTERO *312*
  KIRWAN (DE) *123*
Bible and Science
  SCHÖPFER *175*
  See: Biblical Question, Creation, Evolution, Exegesis, Genesis, Hermeneutics, Inspiration, Inerrancy, Origin of World, Pentateuch, Wellhausen
Mineans
Controversy Mineo-Sabeo-Biblical 374
Antiquity of Kingdom
  WEBER *442*
Minean Inscription
  CLERMONT-GANNEAU *808*
Miracles
In the NT
  HEADLAM *1117*
  See: Jesus
Mishna
Bikkurim
  ALBRECHT *1347*
Horayot
  WINDFUR *1107*
Makkoth
  STRACK *917*
Rosh Ha-Shanah
  FIEBIG *1067*
Sanhedrin (Engl. transl.)
  STRACK *917*
  DANBY *1273*
Misraim
  See: Egypt, Genesis
Mithra
Texts and documents
  CUMONT 856 *1108*
Mithraic agape
  PARIS *1121*
  See: Pagan mysteries, Religions
Mizzeh 48
Moab
Voyage of Mr. Bliss 71
  See: Madaba
Modernism
In the Church
  RIVIÈRE *1552*
  LOISY *1599*
Rejection of dogma
  TURMEL *1472*
Still possible?
  GRANDMAISON (DE) *1407*

  See: Biblical Question, Church, Dogma, Holy Office, Loisy, Problem of Jesus, Turmel
Monachism
And Serapism
  PREUSCHEN *564*
Monotheism
In the ancient East and in Israel
  BAENTSCH *755*
Morals
  See: Egypt, Gospel, Paul
Mosaic Law
Historicity
  GIESEBRECHT *332*
  See: Pentateuch
Mosaics
  See: 'Ain Duq Beit-Djibrin, Madaba, Jerusalem
Moses
  See: Judaism: apocryphal texts, Pentateuch, Exodus
Mosque of Omar
Alleged violation of 927
Muratori
Canon of Hippolytus 1448
Mysteries, pagan
  LOISY *1282*
Iranian
  REITZENSTEIN *1374*
Hellenistic
  REITZENSTEIN *1513*
In Alexandrian Judaism
  CERFAUX *1433*
  GOODENOUGH *1775*
In Roman Paganism
  CUMONT *856*
Influence on Christianity
  CLEMEN *1061*
Influence on St. Paul
  JACQUIER *1319*
Syncretism and the Gospel
  ALLO *859*
  See: Adonis, Eleusis, Eshmun, Isis and Osiris, Loisy, Mandeism, Mazdeism, Mithra, Orphism, Paganism
Mysticism
Historical preliminaries 1564
Jewish, and St. John
  ODEBERG *1550*
  See: John, Paul
Myth of Jesus
The hypothesis
  ALFARIC *1535*
  COUCHOUD *1504*

DUJARDIN *1508 1772*
SMITH *670*
PIEPENBRING *1395*
Judgment of
  GRANDMAISON *1436*
  MEFFERT *967*
  See: Jesus, Noncanonical testimony
  concerning Jesus
Mythology
  See: Pagan mysteries, Origins of
  the world

Nabateans 183
Rights of the Poor
  CLERMONT-GANNEAU *380*
Epigraphical survey, Petra 179
Sabbatical year
  CLERMONT-GANNEAU *379*
  See: Inscriptions, Orotalt, Petra

Nazareth
  LEGENDRE 714
Birthplace of Jesus
  BURRAGE 1059
  See: Inscriptions

Negeb
Archaeological survey 521
  See: Inscriptions

Nehemias, book of
Composition and historicity
  TORREY 249
Jewish restoration
  HOONACKER (VAN) *120*
Before Esdras 53 66
  See: Zorobabel

Nestorius
Book of Heraclitus of Damascus
  NAU *970*

Newman
Development of dogma 1657
Essay on the Idea of Development
  GUITTON *1672*

New Testament
Greek or Greek-Latin text
  BODIN *990*
  BRANDSCHEID *317 690 691*
  GREGORY *878*
  HETZENAUER *337*
  LEGG *1750*
  MERX *1724*
  NESTLE *728 1526*
  VOGELS *1336 1397*
  SODEN (VON) *1033 1244*
  WEISS, B. *251*
Introductions
  DESJARDINS *323*

GOGUEL *1406 1435*
JACQUIER *824*
PEAKE *901*
SICKENBERGER *1330*
SIMON *1443*
TRENKLE *209*
VERDUNOY *1491*
General Commentaries
  Die Heilige Schrift des NT
  DAUSCH *1274*
  Die Schriften des NT
  WEISS, J. *739 853*
  Das Neue Testament
  HOLTZMANN, O. *1465*
Old, in the New
  DITTMAR *272*
  HUHN *283*
Literary Criticism, Philology
  BONACCORSI *1708*
  GUNKEL *546*
  DUJARDIN *1610*
  FASCHER *1538*
  JACQUIER *1318*
  MALDEN *622 623 1412*
  SCHMIDT *1417*
  SCHÜTZ *1329*
  TURNER *1334*
Translations
  Origin of versions
  HOSKIER *1005*
  Armenian
  MACLER *1283*
  Coptic
  See: Coptic
  English
  CARR *464*
  TORREY *1731*
  Ethiopian (Gospels)
  HACKSPILL *164*
  French
  HOUDE *1317*
  JOUON *1544*
  German
  LUTHER *578*
  SCHLATTER *1637*
  SCHLÖGEL *1328*
  Latin (Gatianum)
  HEER *883*
  BRUYNE (DE) *1354* (Freising)
  Syriac
  See: Syriac
  See: Acts, Apocalypse, Apocrypha,
  Bible, Canon, Encyclopedia, Gos-
  pels, Greek, Itala, Jesus, Juda-
  ism, Letters (Pauline), Mysteries
  (pagan), Paul, Religions, Syriac,
  Textual Criticism, Theology, Ver-
  sions, Vulgate

Nippur
Creation story
  BARTON *1168*
Temple of Bel
  HILPRECHT *481*
Nosairis
History and religion
  DUSSAUD *325*
Numbers, book of
Commentaries
  HUMMELAUER *232*
  PATERSON *353*
  HOLZINGER *551*
  21:27–30 (Song of Hesebon) 216
  33:42 (Phonoun) 178
  See: Pentateuch
Numismatics
  See: Phoenicia

Octateuch
  See: Pentateuch, Lucian
Odes of Solomon
  HARNACK *881*
  BRUSTON *1194*
Odyssey
  Phoenician
  BERARD *315*
Old Testament
Hebrew Text
  Hebrew Bible:
  KITTEL *643*
  Polychrome (Rainbow) Bible
  HAUPT *280*
  Polyglot of Alcala
  RICO *1220*
  Liturgical appendices
  GRIMM *476*
  Borrowings from Greek and Latin
  VERNES *1104*
  Marginal notes (Egyptian)
  SPIEGELBERG *607*
Introductions
  BAUDISSIN *376*
  GAUTIER *634*
  ROTHSTEIN *735*
  WEATHERALL *512*
  See: Bible (Introduction to)
Religion of
  History of Jewish religion
  KÖNIG *1009*
  Paternity of God 751
  Prayer
  KOBERLE *402*
Poems and canticles
  Poems of the Bible
  CONDAMIN *1711*

Canticle of Debora
  ZAPLETAL *677*
Love songs
  HAUPT *711*
War songs 216
Servant songs
  BUDDE *264*
Old in the New Testament
  DITTMAR *272*
  HÜHN *283*
Problems (various)
  STEINMÜLLER *1785*
  ZAPLETAL *582*
OT and Christianity
  MEINHOLD *1629*
Laity, the
  GLAZEBROOK *1071*
OT and St. Paul
  MICHEL *1548*
Permanent value
  KAUTZCH *399*
New scholarship
  PETERS *422*
See: Babylon, Bible, Biblical Question, Canon, Canticles, Deuterocanonical, Egypt, Hermeneutics, Historical Method, Inspiration, Inerrancy, Israel, Judaism, Manuscripts, Marcion. Cf. also each book of the OT.

Olivieri
Exchange of views on the 4th Gospel, 1452
Onkelos
Aquila and
  SILVERSTONE *1640*
  See: Versions
Oracles
  See: Prophecies, Sibylline
Orientalism
  See: Congress
Origen
Topographical tradition 69 95
De Libris S. Scr.
  BATIFFOL *259*
Comm. on St. John (GCS)
  PREUSCHEN *565*
Comm. on St. Matthew (GCS)
  KLOSTERMANN *1719*
Comm. on Ps. 118
  WAGNER *1398*
Origins of the World
Primitive History
  JUNKER *1619*
  See: Creation, Pre-history

Orotalt
  CUMONT *382*
Orpheus
  Manual of History of Religions
    REINACH *904* 854 856
    BATIFFOL *933*
Orphism 1779
  BOULANGER *1460*
  See: Pagan Mysteries, Religions
Osee
  New History of Israel and, 6
  9:10–13
    LOISY *236*
Ostraca
  See: Elephantine
Oxyrhynchus
  See: Logia, Papyrus

Pacian, St.
  Biblical citations
    VILAR *1734*
Paganism
  Roman
    BOISSIER 856
    TOUTAIN *921* 856
  Oriental religions in
    CUMONT 763 856
  Infiltrations into the Law
    PINARD DE LA BOULLAYE *1324*
  Time of Christ
    FELTEN *945*
  Pagan reaction
    LABRIOLLE *1746*
    See: Pagan mysteries, Religions,
    Sallust
Palestine
  Geography and voyages
    BAEDEKER *29*
    KEPPLER *122*
    LANDRIEUX *1176*
  Lexicon of Palestinian geography
    ANONYMOUS *73*
  Map of Madaba 145
    SCHULTEN *363*
  Modern
    French and Germans in Palestine
    1161
    Jewish Nationalism 1187
    Political status 1110
    See: Biblical Geography, Excava-
    tions
Palmyra 745 1108
  Religion 1160
  Funerary busts 24 585
  See: Inscriptions

Panbabylonianism
  See: Babylon and the Bible
Pantheism
  In sacred history 11
Papias
  On Matthew and Mark
    VANNUTELLI *1777*
  Logia
    HARRIS *1313*
  Presbyters
    DONAVAN *1567*
    VANNUTELLI *1596*
Papyrus, Greek
  General notions 855
    DEISSMANN *764* 811
  Noncanonical texts
    Egerton
      BELL *1737*
    Golenischeff
      MÜLLER *352*
    Oxyrhynchus
      GRENFELL & HUNT 752 *1205* 1299
    Ancient Christian texts
      WESSELY *793*
  Canonical texts
    Chester Beatty
      KENYON *1621*
    (Gospels) = P⁴⁵ 1702
    (Acts) = P⁴⁵ 1703
    (Pauline Epistles) = P⁴⁶ 1704
      LIETZMANN *1751*
      SANDERS *1759*
    Michigan *1570* (Mt 27: 19–52) =
    P³⁷ 1517
    Michigan *1571* (Acts 18:27–19:16)
    = P³⁸ 1475
    Oxyrhynchus
      GRENFELL and HUNT *817 886 955
      1138* 1205
    Vindob. 31974 (Mt 25:41–26:39)
    = P⁴⁵ (fragment) 1655
    Pap. Greek & Latin I, n. 2, and II,
    n. 124 of Lk 22:44–63 = 0171
      BOVER *1462*
      WESSELY *793*
    See: Diatessaron, Eléphantine, Her-
    mas, Letters (Christian), Logia
Parables
  In the Gospels
    FONCK *1405*
  Outside the Gospel 797
  Purpose 857
    HOLZMEISTER *1754*
  Chief parables
    BUGGE *536*

Mt 22:1–14 (The Discourteous Invited Guests)
SICKENBERGER *1554*
Lk 15:11–32 (Good Samaritan)
GHIO *1070*
16:1–13 (Dishonest Steward)
RÜCKER *1097*

Paradise, earthly
BOISSIER *1192*
ENGELKEMPER *386*
HOMMEL *394*
KÖNIG *403*

Paradosis
ABBOTT *587*

Paralipomena
See: Chronicles

Parousia
BILLOT *1269*
In the Gospel
TONDELLI *1471 1695*
Saint Paul
TILLMANN *849*
Msgr. Le Camus 649

Pascal
Messianic Prophecies 614

Passion
See: Jesus

Pastoral (epistles)
Commentaries
KNABENBAUER *1081*
KÖHLER *853*
MAYER *1248*
MEINERTZ *1627*
Authenticity
MICHAELIS *1578*
Myths and genealogies
COLSON *1271*

Patriarchs
Longevity
LESÊTRE *652*
See: Genesis, Israel

Patrology
Catholic Dogma and the Fathers
AMANN *1348*
Mélanges Tixeront 1333
See: Literature, Christian

Paul
His person, life
BAUMANN *1430*
DESSAU *870*
HOLLARD *1744*
MICHAELIS *1579*
SEELIGMÜLLER *975*
WEBER *1338*

Conversion
KÜMMEL *1545*
WINDISCH *1765*
Relations with the Church
BRUN and FRIDRICHSEN *1353*
KNOX *1439*
MUNTZ *1089*
Use of the Bible
MICHEL *1548*
Teaching
Influence of Roman Law
MUNTZ *1089*
Modern terms
RAMSAY *1219*
Doctrine
His Gospel
MOLLAND *1753*
His theology
PRAT *1018*
STEIGER *1642*
Christ *1767*
SCHUMACHER *1099*
WINDISCH *1765*
Christ and the Spirit
FUCHS *1669*
Redemption
BANDAS *1428*
Justification 1052
TOBAC *851*
Law and faith
BOYSSON (DE) *992*
Grace and Law
WOBBE *1699*
Charisms
WOBBE *1699*
Eschatology
GUNTERMANN *1673*
KENNEDY *553*
NASCIMBENE *1322*
Resurrection of the body
MOLITOR *1684*
Angelology
KURZE *1280*
Moral teaching (= ethics)
BOVER *1131*
BENZ *1055*
ENSLIM *1569*
TILSCHLEDER *1418*
Mysticism
DUPERRAY *1365*
SCHWEITZER *1691*
Critical Research
SCHWEITZER *1100*
NT and St. Paul
MC NEILE *1411*
See: Acts, Apocryphal Acts, Diatribe, Eschatology, Henoch, Mark, Marcion, Pagan Mys-

teries, Parousia, Pauline Letters, Pelagius, Tarsus

Pelagius
Comm. on St. Paul
  SOUTER *1694*

Penance
First six centuries
  RAUSCHEN *902*
  See: Metanoia

Pentateuch
Mosaic authenticity and sources 177 218 1786
  BONACCORSI *589*
  DAKSE *1238*
  DESPRES *222*
  HOBERG *640*
  KYLE *1210*
  HOLBORN *483*
  HÜGEL (VON) *194*
  JASTROW *1208*
  KLEY *554*
  MECHINEAU *240*
  PROCKSCH *733*
  SALVATORELLI *1150*
Historical value
  Studies *510*
  BONACCORSI *589*
Original Language and Writing
  NAVILLE *1092 1177*
Sanctuary and Priesthood
  HOONACKER (VAN) *83 229*
  HUMMELAUER *231*
Mosaic Law
  GIESEBRECHT *332*
  See: Biblical Question, Deuteronomy, Exodus, Genesis, Historical Method, Inerrancy, Israel, Numbers, Wellhausen

Peoples, ancient
Précis of history
  HOMMEL *596*
Classical Orient
  MASPERO *239 288*
  VANDERVORST *1155*
  See: Assyria, Babylon, Egypt, Elam, Gadarenians, Habiri, Hamites, Hittites, Phoenicians

Peripatetics
Up to the Christian era 1477

Persians
  See: Mazdeism

Peshitta
  See: Syriac

Peter
  See: Apocryphal Acts, Primacy

Peter the Iberian
  RAABE *132*

Peter, epistles of
1 Peter
  GUNKEL *853*
2 Peter
  DILLENSEGER *812*
  HOLLMANN *853*
  See: Catholic epistles

Petra
Exploration 142 146
  CART *1132*
Epigraphical surveys of 179
  See: Inscriptions, Nabateans

Pharisees
  See: Judaism

Philemon, epistle to
Commentaries
  VINCENT *210*
  SCHUMANN *842*

Philippians, epistle to
Commentary
  VINCENT *210*
Date
  MICHAELIS *1726*
  See: Captivity, Pauline Epistles, Paul

Philistia and the Philistines
Philistia
  GAUTIER *111*
Philistines
  MÜLLER *351*
  See: Crete, Israel

Philo
Biblical Antiquities
  JAMES *1207*
Two treatises (Papyrus)
  SCHEIL *43*
Contemplative life
  CONYBEARE *78*
Fourth Gospel
  ALMA (D') *930*
  See: Alexandria, John, Logos, Pagan mysteries

Philosophy
Of Religion
  GALLOWAY *1069*
Greek, and 1 Thes 5:23
  FESTUGIÈRE *1570*
In the OT
  FRIEDLANDER *593*
Jewish philosophers to Philo
  BOUILLON *1056*
Problem of existence
  GIOVANNOZZI *946*

See: Academy, Cicero, Cynics,
Epictetus, Marcus Aurelius,
Heraclitus, Peripatetics, Philo,
Plato, Stoics

Phoenicians
Glossary
BLOCH *14*
Numismatics
ROUVIER *427*
In the Odyssey
BERARD *315 532*
See: Inscriptions

Phounon
See: Numbers

Pilate
See: Apocryphal Acts, Jesus: Passion

Plato
The Theologian 1453
On Plato
DIES *1481*

Poems and Canticles
See: Canticles

Polyglott of Alcala
RICO *1220*
LLAMAS *1682*

Polytheism
Among the Hebrews
VERNES *20*

Poor
Of Israel
CAUSSE *1363*
Rights of, Nabateans 380

Prayer
In the OT
KÖBERLE *402*
See: Marduk

Preaching
According to the Bible
HÖPFL *597*
Christian, and Jewish propaganda
DUESBERG *1609*

Prehistory
Age of man
SCHANZ *136*

Pretorium
Fortress Antonia
BARNABAS d'Alsace *455*

Price of Interest
Forbidden by Bible
HEJCL *773*

Priesthood, Israelite
Before Moses
HUMMELAUER (DE) *231*

Levitical
HOONACKER (VAN) *229*

Primacy
Of Peter
See: Matthew
Roman
HARNACK *1510*

Primitives
Religion
BROS *803*

Prisca
See: Apocryphal acts

Problem of Jesus
Exposé of the systems
BRAUN *1662*
FRACASSINI *474*
HEADLAM *1483*
LABANCA *555*
MALDEN *1412*
GARDNER *330*
SANDAY *785*
ROLFFS *425*
TONDELLI *1471*
Various essays
GOGUEL *1614*
GUIGNEBERT *1671*
HARNACK *336*
HOLLARD *1316*
KUNDSIN *1546*
LOISY *964*
RENAN 1189 *1384*
REVILLE *204*
SCHMIDT *736*
WEISS, J. *1259 1339*
WERNLE *581*
See: Divinity of Christ, Eschatology, Jesus, Messianic Consciousness, Myth of Jesus, Noncanonical testimony concerning Jesus, Son of Man

Prologues
Ancient gospels
BRUYNE (DE) *1522*
HARNACK *1543*
Marcionite, to Pauline epistles
MUNDLE *1441*
Monarchian
CORSSEN *162*

Prophecies
Original form
MÜLLER *129*
Against the Nations
ROHART *60*
Messianic
HÜHN *282*
See: Daniel, Eschatology, Isaias, Jacob, Pascal

Prophets
Prophetism
KÖNIG *712*
Minor Prophets
ANONYMOUS *102*
Before the Exile
MÖLLER *780*
PROCKSCH *505*
ROYER *428*
After the Exile 612
Protoevangelium
See: Apocryphal gospels
Proverbs
Commentaries
KNABENBAUER *959*
MEZZACASA *1086*
TOY *296*
Ethical and religious ideas
HUDAL *1080*
Psalms
Text
Coptic (Freer coll.)
WORREL *1159*
Hexaplaric ms.
MERCATI *346*
Latin Psalter 1602
Commentaries
BAETHGEN *186*
BONACCORSI *1130*
CALMET *523*
CHEYNE *537*
DUHM *223*
ECKER *472*
FILLION *523*
FRANCOIS *631*
GUNKEL *705*
MERCIER *1287*
MINOCCHI *659*
MOZLEY *660*
PADOVANI *662*
PANNIER *783*
SUCONA Y VALLES *438*
SCHMIDT *1760*
History of Ps.
MINOCCHI *494*
Ps 110 (109), and taking of Jerusalem
REILLY *1149*
See: Hebrew language, Messianism
Psalms of the Pharisees
See: Psalms of Solomon
Psalms of Solomon
See: Judaism: apocryphal texts
Purifications, Jewish
In the Gospel
BRANDT 935

Pythagoras
Legend — sources
LEVY *1486*
In Greece and Palestine
LEVY *1525*
Contacts with Gospel 1769 1780
See: Basilica of Porta Maggiore
Qoheleth
Masoretic text
EURINGER *16*
Commentary
SCHOLZ *432*
Literary criticism
HUMBERT *1140*
Quirinius
The Census 926
BONACCORSI *1708*
Once Governor of Syria
GROAG *1523*
See: Inscriptions
Rabbinism
Ancient exegetical terminology
BACHER *313*
See: Judaism, Mishna, Talmud
Rabbula
Life and work 2
NAU *1581*
PEETERS *1584*
See: Syriac
Raschi
Commentary on Ezechiel
LÉVI *1680*
Redemption
History of dogma
RIVIÈRE *1122*
Conference, Institut biblique 1755
See: Paul
Religions
Introduction, general history
BRICOUT *993*
DUSSAUD *1064*
GOBLET D'ALVIELLA *1002*
HUBY *1139*
REINACH *904*
History of, and the NT
CLEMEN *807*
GUNKEL *546*
KITTEL *1677*
VALENSIN *1024*
See: Academy, Adonis, Alexandria, Allat, Ashera, Astart, Assyria, Attis, Babylon, Canaan, Cicero, Congress, Death, Egypt, Eleusis, Eshmun, Future Life, Goethe, Greeks, Hermetism, Iran, Islam,

Israel, Jesus, Judaism, Julian the Apostate, Magic, Mandeism, Manicheism, Mazdeism, Mithras, Monotheism, Orphism, Paganism, Pagan Mysteries, Palmyra, Philosophy, Polytheism, Pythagoras, Sacred Meal, Sacrifices, Semites, Seneca, Stoics, Tammuz, Totemism.

Renaissance (1450–1521)
HUMBERT *954*

Renan
LASSERRE *1425*
POMMIER *1470*
Life of Jesus 1189 1384

Resurrection of the Body
MOLITOR *1684*
STAUDT *916*

Resurrection of Christ
See: Jesus

Revue Sémitique
HALÉVY *56*

Revue de Strasbourg
ROCHAT *666*

Ritual, Paschal
Didache 1–10 and John
GREIFF *1541*

Romans, epistle to
Text, Greek and Latin 1126
Commentaries 1124
LUTHER 1114 1128
PALLIS *1323*
SEMERIA *574*
SICKENBERGER *1692*
Translation
DELAFOSSE (= TURMEL) *1463*
Justification 1052
TOBAC *851*
1:28–31 (List of sins) 928
5:12–14 (Original sin)
OEMMELEN *1583*
7 (Paul's experience?)
KÜMMEL *1545*
See: Pauline Epistles, Paul

Rome
Religion
BOISSIER *863* *856* 1108
CUMONT *856*
Basilica, pythagorean
CARCOPINO *1479* *1480*
Church, ancient
MUNTZ *1089*
Jews in the Empire
JUSTER *1209*

Wine, price-fixing of
Mévente of wines
REINACH *424*

Rufinus
Seal of Pope Xystus
CONYBEARE *868*

Sabbatical year
See: Nabateans

Sabeans 374
See: South Arabic Inscriptions

Sacraments
See: Baptism, Eucharist, Penance

Sadducees
See: Sects: Jewish

Sadokites
See: Sects: Jewish

Sacred Meals
CUMONT *1200*

Sacrifice, human
Among the Hebrews and neighboring peoples
MADER *892*

Saïda
See: Inscriptions

Salamanca
Memories of Novitiate 1783

Sallust
On the Gods and the world
NOCK *1487*

Samaritans
Liturgy
CROWLEY 1199
See: Messianism, Inscriptions

Samson
ZAPLETAL *678*

Samuel, books of
Commentaries
BUDDE *460*
LÖHR *234*
SMITH *294*
Hebrew text
DRIVER *30*

Sanctuary
Places of sacrifice, in Pentateuch
ENGELKEMPER *814*
See: Temple

Sebbe (Masada) 50

Secret, messianic
See: Messianic consciousness of Jesus

Sects, Jewish
See: Judaism

Sela-Diapsalma
See: Hebrew tongue

Semicinctia of Paul
See: Acts 19:12 1475

Semites
Religion 487 **446**
See: Ashera, Assyria, Astarte, Babylon, Balsamen, Congress (Orientalists), El, Elam, Islam, Israel, Judaism, Nosairis, Yahweh

Sendjirli
See: Inscriptions

Seneca
Religion 1500

Sennacherib
Campaign against Jerusalem
NAGEL *498*

Senses of Scripture
See: Hermeneutics

Septimius Severus
Milestone of
CUMONT *1171*

Septuagint
Critical studies and editions
BROOKE and MC LEAN *620 802*
RAHLFS *734 1635*
Esdras, books of
SWETE *44 364*
WALDE *1106*
See: Concordances, Greek Versions

Serapis
And monachism
PREUSCHEN *564*

Sermon on the Mount
See: Jesus

Shroud of Turin (or of Lirey)
CHAMARD *466*

Sibylline Oracles
Composition and formation
GEFFCKEN *545*
See: Alexandria, Judaism: apocryphal texts

Silvanus
Missionary and hagiographer
STEGMANN *1331*

Sin
In the OT
HERMANN *639*
In Genesis 147
According to the Bible and the Babylonians
HEHN *549*

Sinai
Description of trips 100 144 149 214 253 611
CART *1132*
VERNES *1156*
See: Inscriptions

Sinaiticus
See: Manuscripts: biblical

Sion and City of David 5 148
SOULLIER *138*
RUCKERT *205*

Socialism
In the OT
LÖHR *719*

Socrates
And Jesus
WINDISCH *1765* 1736

Sodom
Situation, according to texts 1603

Solomon
See: Apocryphal texts, Israel, Judaism, Psalms of Solomon

Son of Man 613
In Henoch
MESSEL *1372*
In the Gospel
ABBOTT *753 858*
ROSLANIEC *1326*
SARDI *906*
SKIBNIEWSKI *912*
TILLMANN *792*
VANNUTELLI *1420*
See: Eschatology, Jesus, Judaism

Sophonias
Commentary
LIPPL *963*

Spain, prehistoric
SIRET *844*

Sphagis
HEITMÜLLER *1075*
See: Prophets, Prophecies

Stephen, St.
His sanctuary 47 52 212 255
FIOROVICH *81*
BARNABAS d'Alsace *530*

Strophs
Discourse after the Supper
GACHTER *1741*
Sermon on the Mount
MÜLLER *900*
See: Hebrew, language

Study and Reading of the Bible
1770
Clerical studies
HOGAN *393*

Constructive elements for OT study
  JASTROW *1208*
Letter on ecclesiastical studies
  MIGNOT *898*
Letter on the study of S. Scr.
  DOUAIS *592*
Letter to a student in Scripture
  CORMIER *625*
Private reading in early Church
  HARNACK *1040*
Reading the Bible 1770
State of biblical studies
  MARGIVAL *200*
Study of the Bible
  FILLION *1366*
  See: Exegesis, Hermeneutics, Historical method

Studies, biblical
Project for a complete commentary
  257

Sumer
Selections
  HOMMEL *119*
Texts concerning origins
  DYNELEY PRINCE *1136*
  JASTROW *1142 1175*
  LANGDON *1144*

Susa
Excavations: Persian Delegation
  MORGAN (DE) *349 781* 1030
  SCHEIL *308 42ᴵ ᴵ72 1222*

Swete
  See: Mélanges
Symbol
Of the Reform
  BRIGGS *1057*

Synagogue
'*Ain Duq* 1297

Syncretism, pagan
And the Gospel
  ALLO *859*
  See: Pagan mysteries

Synopses, gospel
Catalan
  CARRERAS and LLOVERA 1447
English
  BARTON 1447
French
  LAVERGNE 1447
Greek 1466 1484 1447
  HEINEKE *228*
Italian 1447
  VANNUTELLI *1646*
  AZIBERT *185*

Latin
  CAMERLYNCK and COPPIETERS 894
  938 1361
Synoptic Problem
  GOGUEL *948 1204*
  PASQUIER *1014*
  RIDEAU *1756*
  SCHMID *1590*
  SPITTA *1102 1075*
  STREETER *1444*
  VANNUTELLI *1419 1733*
  WIKENHAUSER *1649*
  See: Form Criticism, Introductions to NT, Logia, Papias
Synoptics (Gospels)
Commentaries
  DAUSCH *1275 1608*
  LOISY *778*
  MONTEFIORE *899*
In the Light of the Talmud
  HAWKINS *882*
Literary Criticism
  BONACCORSI *533*
  MANGENOT *965*
  MARGARET *966*
Relations with John
  WINDISCH *1492*
  See: Gospels, Mark, Matthew, Luke, Synopses, Synoptic Problem
Syria
Archaeology
  CUMONT *1200*
Geography and history
  BAEDEKER *29*
  ANONYMOUS *73*
Liturgy
  GREIFF *1541*
  BAUMSTARK *1350*
Syriac
Lexicon
  BROCKELMANN *76*
Literature
  BAUMSTARK *1351*
Versions of OT
  Peshitta
    NAU *1580*
  Josue
    MAGER *1284*
  Of the prophets
    DIETTRICH *696*
  Syro-hexaplaric (fragment)
    GWYNN *950*
Versions and Mss of the NT
  Sinaitic
    LEWIS *124 962 67 68*
    NAU *1013 1580*

Sin. and Cureton 1264 1298
  BONUS *156*
  HJELT *392*
  NAU *1580*
Peshitta
  GWILLIAM *1311*
Syro-palestinian
  LEWIS *832 1427*
Philoxenian
  LEBON *1011*
  NAU *1580*
Philoxenian and harklean
  GWYNN *950*
  NAU *1580*
Palestinian Lectionary
  LEWIS *199*
See: Diatessaron
Noncanonical texts
Ahudemmeh and Maruta
  NAU *727*
Protoevangelium of James
  LEWIS *488*
Varia
  GIBSON *113*
  RAHMANI *566*
See: Nestorius

Talmud
Christianity in the
  HERFORD *550*
See: Aramaic, Mishna

Tatian
See: Diatessaron

Temple of Jerusalem
Formation of the area 22
See: Sanctuary

Temptation
See: Jesus

Tertullian
Roman primacy
  HARNACK *1510*

Testament of the 12 Patriarchs
See: Judaism: apocryphal texts

Testimonia
  HARRIS *1313*
And the 3rd Gospel
  FINDLAY *1700*

Tetragrammaton
See: Yahweh

Theocritus
Mystery of the 4th Eclogue 1561

Theodore of Mopsuestia
Exegetical work
  PIROT *1095*

Theology
History
Origins 1701
Faculty of Paris
  FÉRET *274 543 765 875*
Influence of Revue de Strasbourg
  ROCHAT *666*
In the Anglican church
Normative sources
  HEADLAM *548*
Theology, Biblical
Old Testament
  HETZENAUER *774*
New Testament
  FEINE *874*
  HOLTZMANN *168*
  VOSTÉ *1764*
Dictionary
  KITTEL *1622 1678*
  HEADLAM *1743*
Theology, Biblical
Readings
  LABAUCHE *1010*
Theology, patristic
Hippolytus, St.
  ALÈS (D') *754*
Tertullian
  ALÈS (D') *686*
See: Baptism, Christology, Church, Dogma, Eucharist, Exegesis, Hermeneutics, Historical Method, Holy Spirit, Hope, Inerrancy, Inspiration, Tradition, Trinity, Symbol, Paul, Redemption

Thessalonians, epistles to
Commentaries
  FRAME *1038*
  KNABENBAUER *1081*
  VOSTÉ *1181*
  STEINMANN *1776*
1 Thes
Trichotomy of 5:23
  FESTUGIÈRE *1570*
2 Thes
Authenticity
  GRAFFEN *1540*
  WRZOL *1295*
See: Paul, Pauline Epistles

Tixeront
See: Mélanges

Tobias
Edifying story
  SCHULTZ *974*
Story of Ahikar
  VEBER *674*
See: Ahikar

Tomb, the empty
GOGUEL *1614*
BALDENSPERGER *1659*
See: Jesus, Resurrection

Totemism
Among the Celts
REINACH *358*
In Israel's religion
ZAPLETAL *367*

Tradition, ecclesiastical
BAINVEL *687*
PÉGUES *562*
Table of sources
CREUSEN *995*
See: Catholic exegesis, Historical method

Tradition, pre-evangelical
Logia
SOIRON *1376*
See: Form Criticism, Logia, Synoptic Problem

Translations
See: NT, Versions of the Bible

Transfiguration
See: Jesus

Transitus Mariae
See: Apocryphal gospels

Trent, Council of
Decree "De editione et usu Sacrarum Scripturarum"
MAICHLE *1084*
Diaria, acta, etc.
Soc. Goerresiana *1101*

Trinity
Controversies
DUPIN *629*
Origins of the dogma
LEBRETON *890 1281 1524*

Turmel
Critical system
DUJARDIN *1610*
And Loisy 1454
See: Modernism

Tyconius
Rules of exegesis
BURKITT *75*

Umma
Under the dynasty of Ur
CONTENAU *1169*

Vaticanus
See: Manuscripts, biblical

Versions of the Bible
Castillan
MONTSERRAT *1582 1689*
English
CARLETON *462*
French
CRAMPON *944*
Gothic
(Antinoë Fragment)
GLANE and HELM *876*
Greek
Introduction
SWETE *364*
Latin
Antinoë Fragment
GLANE and HELM *876*
Baruch
HOBERG *482*
Heptateuch
ROBERT *293*
In Africa
MONCEAUX *416*
Introduction
STUMMER *1529*
Itala
BURKITT *1305*
Psalter
VOGELS *1105 1602*
See: Aquila, Coptic, Itala, Lucian, NT, Onkelos, Septuagint, Vulgate

Virgil
Messianism of the 4th Eclogue 1346 1561 1653
CARCOPINO *1536*
ERDMANN *1668*
JEANMAIRE *1676*

Virgin, Blessed
See: Dormition, Jesus: Conception and birth, Mary, Isaias

Vogüe, Marquis de, 1162

Vulgate
Authenticity and errors 72
Critical Examination
(Galatians) 1164
(Gospels)
VOGELS *1530*
(Romans) 1126
Editions
New Testament
WORDSWORTH and WHITE *302* 1381
Sixtine, of 1590
AMANN *1053*
Sixto-Clementine of 1592
GRAMATICA *1003 1072*
HÖPFL *1079*

History
  At the Council of Trent
    BONACCORSI *458 589*
  In England
    GLUNG *1713*
Lexicon
  MATZKOW *1723*
Manuscripts
  HOPKIN-JAMES *1745*
  MERCATI *346*
  TURNER *1645*
Origin: Jerome and Augustine 219
Revision
  At Present 747
  By Jerome 1188
  Memoire of Dom Quentin *1415*
  See: Jerome, St.
Revision of the NT
  CAVALLERA *1237 1307*

Washington
  See: Manuscripts, biblical
Wellhausen
  DAKSE *1238*
  GREGORY *879*

  HALÉVY *165*
  RIEDEL *506*
  See: Mélanges
Wisdom
  Commentaries
    CORNELY *943*
    OESTERLEY *1216*
  Formation
    FOCKE *1240*
  The Last Things 679

Yahweh 25 449 682
  KÖNIG *170*
Yemenites
  Mission of Israelite Alliance
    SEMACH *1151*

Zin
  Desert
    WOOLLEY and LAWRENCE *1158*
Zoroaster
  See: Mazdeism
Zorobabel
  SELLIN *246*
  See: Esdras, Israel, Nehemias

APPENDIX

Sacra Congregatio Consistorialis

I

DECRETUM

De quibusdam rei biblicae commentariis in sacra seminaria
non admittendis.

Cum semper et ubique cavendum sit ne quis Scripturas Sanctas contra
eum sensum interpretetur, quem tenuit ac tenet sancta Mater Ecclesia
(S. Trid. Syn., Sessio IVa); id maxime necessarium est in Seminariis inter
alumnos qui in spem Ecclesiae adolescunt. Hoc enim prae ceteris oportet
sanis doctrinis imbui, quae venerandae Patrum traditioni sint conformes
et a legitima Ecclesiae auctoritate probatae; arceri autem a novitiatibus,
quae in dies audax quisque molitur, quaeque quaestiones praestant magis
quam edificationem Dei quae est in fide (Ia ad Tim. cap. IV); si vero inso-
litae legitimeque damnatae, in destructionem sunt et non in edificationem.

Iam vero evulgatum nuper est Paderbornae opus quod inscribitur:
Kurzgefasstes Lehrbuch der speziellen Einleitung in das Alte Testament
auctore D. Carolo doct. Holzhey in quo iuxta neotericas rationalismi et
hypercriticae theorias de libris Veteris Testamenti fere omnibus ac potissi-
mum de Pentateucho, de libris Paralipomenon, Tobiae, Iudith, Esther,
Ionae, Isaiae et Danielis, sententiae audacissimae propugnantur, quae anti-
quissimae traditioni Ecclesiae, venerabili Ss. Patrum doctrinae et recentibus
pontificiae Commissionis Biblicae responsis adversantur, et authentiam
atque historicum valorem sacrorum Librorum nedum in dubium revocant,
sed pene subvertunt.

Hunc itaque librum S. haec C. de mandato Ssmi. D.N. Papae prohibet
omnino, quominus in Seminaria introducatur, ne ad consultationem
quidem.

Cum vero alia habeantur similis spiritus commentaria in Scripturas
Sanctas tum Veteris tum Novi Testamenti, ceu scripta plura P. Lagrange
et recentissimum opus, cui titulus: *Die Heilige Schrift des Neuen Testaments,* editum Berolini an. 1912, auctore Dr. Fritz Tillmann, haec quoque
expungenda omnino esse ab institutione clericorum Ssmus D. mandat et
praescribit, salvo ampliore de iis iudicio ab illa auctoritate ferendo ad
quam de iure pertinet.

Datum Romae, ex aedibus sacrae Congregationis Consistorialis, die
29 iunii 1912.

C. Card. DE LAI, Episcopus Sabinen., Secretarius.

Analysis of the Consistorial Decree of 29 June 1912 on Certain Biblical
Commentaries Not to Be Used in Seminaries

Competency of Roman Congregations.

At the time of the Decree in question the competency of the various
dicasteries of the Roman Curia was determined by the Apostolic Constitution "Sapienti Consilio" of Pius X, which was effective from November
3, 1908. It is pertinent here to cite the determined competence of certain
dicasteries:

1. The *Holy Office* "doctrinam fidei et morum tutatur. *Eidem proinde
soli* manet iudicium de haeresi aliisque criminibus, quae suspicionem
haeresis inducunt" (Const. 'Sapienti Consilio', I, 1*, ##1 & 2).

2. The *Consistorial Congregation,* "modo Congregationi de Propaganda
Fide (dioeceses) subiectae non sint," . . . looks after "ea omnia quae ad
regimen, disciplinam, temporalem administrationem et studia Seminario-
rum pertinent" (*ibid.* I, 2*, #3).

3. The Congregation for *Religious* "iudicium sibi vindicat de iis tantum
quae ad Sodales religiosos utriusque sexus tum solemnibus, tum simplici-
bus votis adstrictos, et ad eos qui, quamvis sine votis, in communi tamen
vitam agunt more religiosorum. . ." (*ibid.* I, 5*, #1).

4. The Congregation *de Propaganda Fide* has its jurisdiction circum-
scribed by "regionibus, ubi sacra hierarchia nondum constituta, status
missionis perseverat.

"Unitam habet Congregationem pro negotiis *Rituum Orientalium"
(ibid.* I, 6*, ##1 & 6).

5. The Congregation of the *Index* was competent "non solum . . . libros
. . . prohibere; sed etiam inquirere . . . si quae in vulgus edantur scripta . . .
damnanda; et in memoriam Ordinariorum reducere, quam religiose te-
neantur in perniciosa scripta animadvertere. . ." (*ibid.* I, 7*, #1).

6. The Congregation of *Studies* is charged with the "moderatio stu-
diorum in quibus versari debeant maiora athenea, seu . . . Universitates"
(*ibid.* I, 11*). The other Roman dicasteries are not pertinent to the
present question.

7. Mention should be made of the *Biblical Commission,* established by
Leo XIII (Letter Apost. 'Vigilantiae', 30 Oct. 1902), "qui eam sibi habeant
provinciam omni ope curare et efficere ut divina eloquia et exquisitiorem
illam, quam tempora postulant, tractationem passim apud nostros in-
veniant, et incolumia sint non modo a quovis errore afflatu sed etiam
ab omni opinionum temeritate."

Limitations of the Consistorial Decree

Territorial. Unlike the Holy Office, which enjoyed universal jurisdiction both as to places and persons, the Consistorial Congregation was restricted to the countries subject to the *common law* of the Church.

Countries in which the hierarchy had been but imperfectly set up and which are called missionary countries, remained subject to the S. C. de Propaganda Fide and outside the competence of the Consistorial Congregation. Likewise the territories where the Oriental rites held sway were subject to the Congregation for the Affairs of the Oriental Rites — a section of the S. C. de Propaganda Fide. Among the missionary countries where the Consistorial decree had no effect were e.g. In Europe — Germany, Switzerland, Bosnia & Herzogovina, Denmark, Norway, Sweden, Gibraltar, Montenegro, Bulgaria, Rumania, Serbia, Albania, Candia, Greece, Constantinople; in Asia — Asia Minor, China, Korea, Japan, etc.; in S. America, Peru, Chile, Argentina, etc.; and elsewhere Australia, New Zealand, etc. Among the lands subject to the Oriental Congregation were Abyssinia. (Cf. Cappello, *De Curia Romana,* I, p. 238–240).

In a word, the Consistorial Decree touched only those dioceses which belonged to the Latin rite and which were subject to the common law of the Church. The works of Father Lagrange could then be used and studied in the seminaries subject to Propaganda either as missionary countries or as regions of an Oriental rite (if you could find a seminary in the latter).

Institutions. The decree was binding on seminaries in the territories mentioned in the foregoing paragraphs, as institutions subject to the Consistorial Congregation. It had no applications to ecclesiastical universities or to seminaries which the Holy See had empowered to grant degrees; for the latter in regard to studies and the former entirely were subject not to the Consistorial Congregation but to the Congregation of Studies (cf. Cappello, id. p. 349). Moreover, the decree did not touch the houses of studies of religious institutions, orders or congregations or societies of the common life, for the course of study in these was regulated by the Congregation for Religious.

Personal. While the professor in a faculty where academic degrees were conferred (and such seminaries were not rare then in Italy) could prescribe the reading of Fr. Lagrange's book by his students, the student in a simple seminary could not be taught from his books; it could not be a text-book in the seminary. For it was forbidden and excluded 'ab institutione clericorum.'

Doctrine. Questions of doctrine were and are reserved exclusively to